WC ES

The Neu ence Guide to Surviving and Thriving at Work

The Mind Press

Deborah R. Winograd, PhD
Beth A. Cohen, PhD

Workaches: The Neuroscience Guide to Surviving and Thriving at Work

Deborah R. Winograd
Beth A. Cohen

Published in the United States by The Mind Press, an imprint of the Organizational Mind Group, A Psychological Corporation

OrganizationalMindGroup.com
Workaches.com

International Standard Book Number
ISBN-13: 978-1-7325360-0-5
ISBN-10: 1-7325360-0-7
Printed in the United States of America
First Edition
7 6 5 3

The Mind Press

DISCLAIMERS

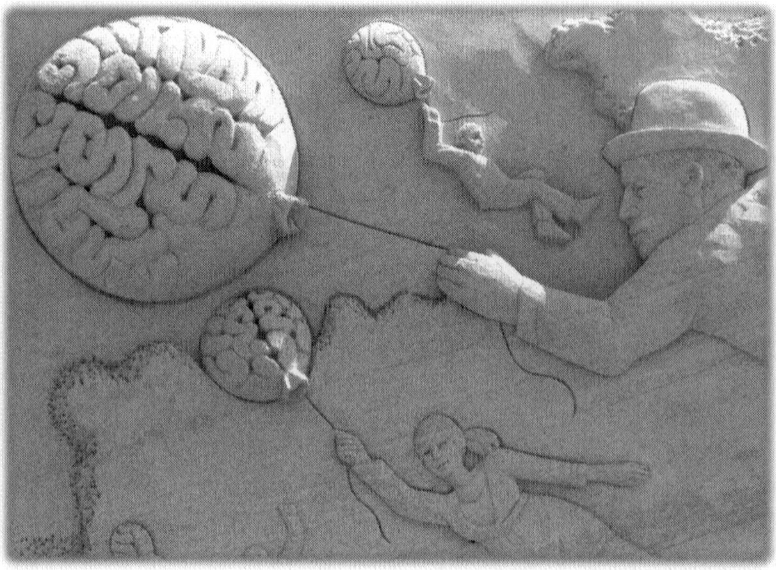

For our children, all children, and those
that once were children...

CONTENTS

FOREWORD

What keeps you up at night? I have asked that question—of senior executives, department directors, field managers, and frontline staff—countless times over the course of my career in human services. I have borne witness to these stories as a leader with my own share of sleepless nights while managing a workforce of over 10,000 employees and in representing top executives of human service organizations. While individual responses inevitably vary, concerns about the workforce—the very people we rely on to make work happen—are consistently top of mind across all organizational levels. In health and human services, senior leaders express this worry in terms of turnover rates and the struggle to recruit and retain the right talent. For field supervisors and staff, it manifests as stress and job dissatisfaction due to workload burdens, insufficient resources, and required tasks that detract from the reason he or she was drawn to the job in the first place. Inherent in both vantage points is the recognition that the workforce is critical to accomplishing the goals of any organization, and to excel, all employees from the front line to the board room must be healthy, well, and engaged with their work.

Workaches helps all of us dig deeper to understand what underlies these enduring challenges. Through clinical expertise, thousands of hours spent with staff at all levels, and a resolute focus on how our lived experiences—as well as our genetic inheritances—shape our interactions in the workplace, Drs. Winograd and Cohen shed light on why so many of us struggle to survive at work, rather than thrive. By connecting the incredible strides in what we now know about the functioning of the human brain (neuroscience) with an insightful look at the evolving and highly complex world of work today, *Workaches* illuminates a way forward for all of us.

I had the privilege of meeting Dr. Cohen a few years ago when she accepted an invitation to speak at an event sponsored by my organization, which represents public sector leaders in the health and human services field. As soon as I heard her speak, I was hooked. Through mastery of her field, the ability to translate science into actionable knowledge, and the willingness to share her own story with humor and vulnerability, Dr. Cohen helped spark a movement now underway in our field. Her remarks led busy executives, including myself, to push the pause button and self-reflect on how we "show up" to work each day. I quickly found myself asking: Am I walking my own talk, especially as to self-care? What is it that I need to be my best self at work and with others? Do I know enough about my own interactions at work to assess how the rest of the workforce is doing? I realized these were fundamental questions that I had too often overlooked. I became a willing student of Dr. Cohen and her long-time professional partner, Dr. Winograd.

Fast forward to today. *Workaches* provides powerful insights into what it takes to enhance organizational cultures and ignite the potential in others, starting with ourselves. In understanding how much of our interactions in the workplace are shaped by our own life journeys, we enhance our ability to see and respect the perspectives of our work colleagues. Each of us can recount stories from our own life experiences that stick with us wherever we go ... the boss with a critical eye who was always first to spot the flaw in our new idea, making us hesitant to be innovative at work ... or the team that didn't really work as one, shaping our perspective on group efforts.

Importantly, Drs. Cohen and Winograd help us put a label on those experiences—the "workaches"—that thrust us into survival mode. By illuminating the complicated interpersonal dynamics at play in workforce relations—both spoken and unspoken, conscious and unconscious—they help us gain insights about ourselves and others: why that person reacts that way to an offhand comment, why some people take feedback in stride and others do not. We learn how deeply embedded early experiences are for each of us and how our individual pasts continue to play out within our organizational cultures. We gain an appreciation of how some workaches (when understood) help shape us into better leaders while others, especially those that cut deep and are left unhealed, not only inhibit our professional growth, but impact our health and well-being.

Whether you lead a team or interact daily on the front line with customers and your community, *Workaches* will widen your lens on the world of work—unfolding the possibilities it holds to thrive when we truly appreciate the full landscape before us, roots and all. No matter our position or place of business, Drs. Winograd and Cohen are calling us to more fully understand how each of us "shows up" at work, and then do something about it so that we can all feel productive, engaged, and purposeful in what we do. In a time when all of us are increasingly called upon to innovate, problem solve, and adapt to an ever-changing world, I am convinced that collectively, and with a stronger understanding of how our minds work at work, we can help everyone achieve that sweet spot.

Tracy Wareing Evans, JD
President and CEO
American Public Human Services Association (APHSA)

PREFACE

Social heroes, unlike superheroes, require care and support but are heroes just the same.

A quiet, kind, and gentle man awoke every weekday morning at 5 a.m. to catch the bus to downtown Los Angeles to work in a sweat factory in the garment industry. The boss and foremen were condescending, and the factory conditions were deplorable. The man skillfully sewed women's coats together. The market for coats was seasonal. Sometimes there would be coats to sew and sometimes not. The factory doors would be locked shut if there was no work available. The man would return home, but always go back the next morning to check for work so he could support his family. He was never able to secure other work. His only skill was sewing, which he learned as a trade in adolescence and brought with him when he immigrated to America. Aggressive coworkers would grab the fabric away from him to gain the piecework or "per coat" wage. He was often humiliated and made to feel worthless about his social standing in the world. The man was incredibly generous though he walked with little in his pockets. He was poor financially yet wealthy in heart and soul. He worked in this unfortunate climate until he retired at age 65. He died of pancreatic cancer soon after. That man was my father. That man is behind this book. —D.W.

We have work to do at work. We are not referring to performing job duties here, but to improving the psychological and social—the *psychosocial*—conditions of the workplace. People work to serve and deliver for others. We give. This book is about receiving, with the understanding that the more we receive, the more we can offer. Individuals deserve to receive more than a paycheck. What most workers at all levels of the organizational hierarchy are giving is beyond what is listed as their job duties. Many in the workforce offer up their health, both physical and emotional, to work long hours and to dedicate decades of their lives to their organizations. Compromises and sacrifices are made in family, social, and personal lives. These costs are not a fair trade for just wages. The cultural institution of "work"—as we think of it in America—is well established and embedded in society and is therefore extremely resistant to change. Nonetheless, we must try. We are heartened and hopeful more so now than ever before, because we are increasingly interacting with innovative leaders who are open to blazing change in their organizations in service of the well-being of employees. We have come a long way in the evolution of work, but we need to evolve further. A critical update is to perceive work as a place to thrive, not just survive. In pursuit of this, we must first remove as many of the potential hazards and harm as possible. We have done better with protections for physical injuries. We have not done as well for psychological injuries.

We wish this book could offer the blueprints for exactly what it takes to get it right at work. Human behavior and creations are way too complex, and working conditions too varied, for there to be just one correct rulebook, but *Workaches* offers the wisdom we have gained over many years of working with individuals and organizations to promote well-being. We summarize the latest research that can assist leaders and employees in navigating the contemporary workplace. Few guides exist to assist us in adulthood as compared to childhood. We often do not fully know our personal goals and aspirations for work. When we serve others in our work, we often know our goals for them better than our own. But service to others does not have to result in disservice to self. Our consulting and clinical work has taught us that it is now imperative to make adaptations and changes to ourselves and our organizations. *Workaches* draws examples from and offers strategies for the health and human services (HHS) workforce, but the topics covered in the book apply to all workplaces, because most jobs ultimately involve working alongside other people.

Some of what falls on our paths in life or at work cannot be anticipated or controlled. Whether we are dealing with a critical boss, difficult employee, or negative outcome, most of our power comes from how we show up and navigate through. Consider the "wisdom" of Apple's *Siri* or Global Positioning Systems (GPS). *Siri* accepts what "is." She neither gets stressed by what is in front of her nor wastes her digital time struggling with traffic or other blockades. *Siri*, for example, mindfully assesses obstacles and calculates the most adaptive route to our desired destination. We sometimes go off the path by choice or because of obstacles, but we trust that *Siri* is always recalculating to get us back to our desired goals. Like *Siri,* we want to assist in getting you to your desired work goals in the most adaptive and healthiest ways possible. We must first identify what we are working with and then examine the obstacles—the "workaches"—those interpersonal struggles and resulting psychosocial stressors and traumas that are obstacles to our thriving at work. We encourage individuals to set "thriving" (meaning, fulfillment, purpose, enjoyment, authenticity) as their work-life destination rather than mere "surviving" (just getting by). Once we set the goal, we move forward to tackle the obstacles in our way. If we do not set the goal, we can get lost and forever circle around the obstacles. We have heard too many times about the "rat race." If both staff and leaders update their mindsets to make thriving the intended destination at work—then we are on our way.

We can attest to the psychosocial issues and injuries sustained in the workforce. Both of us have been on the ground and gone behind the scenes of countless organizations and have collected stories of struggle, vulnerability, helplessness, abuse, overwhelm, despair, resilience, and triumph. And strikingly, it has not mattered what position an individual held in an organization—everyone has workaches. Interpersonal struggles have been common core issues. Work is a complex social field. Assembling a full spectrum of individuals to relate to one another and perform joint functions creates issues. The bullies and the bullied from the playgrounds are here. The abused and the abusers are here. Those who experience themselves as inferior or superior to others are here. People with trauma histories are here. Individuals with all types of personal agendas and biases are here. We are all here, some disguised better than others with varying social masks that hide truer identities. Workgroups are complicated and vulnerable, and we must care for them as such. The workplace is far from being just a place to complete work tasks. The workgroup forms a unique world of its own.

Our passion as crusaders for healthier work environments comes from our professional experience with organizations as well as from our both being parents of working adult children and psychologists of adult clients. We have been up close and personal with the pain and the struggles of adults, particularly in work environments where they often must navigate on their own. We have attended to many different human systems over the years—from the individual to the large organizational system that includes many individuals. One of our goals here is to examine the fundamental unit of all health and human services organizations—the individual. Because whether customer, client, staff, leader, manager, board member or delivery driver, we all come with some basic operating blueprints passed down from long ago. With *Workaches*, we share what we have learned and where we believe organizations need to evolve. We are part of a movement to create a culture of work that fosters not just surviving—but thriving. We know this is possible because we have spent our careers assisting organizations and individuals to thrive. Now more than ever, due to breakthrough neuroscientific understanding of how our brains operate in all the different aspects of our workplaces, it is possible to learn to thrive at work.

Sadly, many have come to experience their work as stressful and unenjoyable. Work is a place to put in the time and leave as soon as possible. Doesn't this sound too similar to imprisonment? Many individuals wait for the end of the workday and the end of the work week. Days until vacation or retirement get counted down. Young people are searching for ways to disengage from the traditional workplace altogether. These are unfortunate perceptions and beliefs about work. Once beliefs have permeated the consciousness of a people, there is resistance to change. Cultural assumptions and beliefs are difficult to revise, and they get passed down through shared stories to next generations. People set their expectations based on these beliefs and then resign themselves, so it becomes a self-fulfilling prophecy to perceive work in this way. Individuals then selectively collect evidence to reaffirm their beliefs. This process is maladaptive given how much of their lives Americans devote to work. If we can motivate staff and leadership to work differently, we are on our way toward change. Work can be a place of deep interpersonal relations and safety, and a source of meaning, esteem, and connectedness. Work can even be a source of psychosocial healing.

In our work with public organizations, we have learned how deep the negative impacts can be on people who serve the needs of others; they often experience burnout, compassion fatigue, and secondary trauma.

Interpersonal office dynamics also influence people. Psychosocial realities and dynamics frequently bombard HHS professionals. Most do well at masking the pain and discomfort of office psychosocial politics. Nonverbal and judgmental communications, gossip, unfairness, exclusion, and shaming are a few of the deeply damaging events occurring behind the scenes. Imbalances of power and evaluations ignite fear. Human social behaviors have emotional costs. People are wired to feel these costs—to perceive when we are being judged and excluded from the group.

Redefining work as a place to thrive requires the belief that this is a worthy idea and possible. Building updated organizational and corporate structures will be facilitated by a change in mindset. We firmly believe the United States is ready for this shift, and changes are already happening in many organizations and industries. For example, the American Public Human Services Association (APHSA) has recently established a landmark initiative, "Igniting the Potential." One segment of this initiative is to study and promote the well-being of health and human service professionals. Data on health indicators will be collected to identify factors related to individual and organizational health and well-being. The HHS workforce matters.

The two of us met as doctoral interns at the Los Angeles County Sheriff's Department Employee Assistance Program (LASD-EAP). There, we had our first glimpses into the incredible stress encountered by the deputies on the streets and in the jails. We witnessed the added pressure they felt from their perceived lack of support and understanding from their superiors in the military-style hierarchy of the organization. There were stressors on the streets and inside the department. We counseled their families too, and thereby bore witness to how the stress the deputies endured in their roles impacted others close to them as well. Going "behind the scenes" and scrutinizing any organization reveals what few can know or understand. Back then in the mid-1980s, we did not have the benefits of recent scientific advances. We have witnessed a revolution in the field and a slow but steady evolution in the promotion of well-being in the individual and the organization. The EAP was the one resource the deputies and their families had to address some of their issues. However, our interventions were reactive, not proactive. The impacted individuals were already stressed and exhibiting symptoms.

The deputies had been well trained in how to use firearms and other tactical strategies for the field. They had not been taught how to manage personal triggers and reactions to incidents such as being spat upon or called names. They had not been trained in understanding and managing the military-style hierarchical organizational structure they found themselves within. This gap in training in emotional preparedness was dangerous to themselves and the citizens they served. The deputies got stationed in the jails and streets with little to no instruction in psychological self-defense and self-care. Those with trauma histories were quite vulnerable to acting out themselves and losing sight of their purpose and valued service to the community. We now advocate for, and increasingly see, inoculation training and other components of comprehensive EAPs that promote prevention, as well as after-incident interventions.

The two of us have had a long and winding professional path since the Sheriff's Department. Sadly, we continue to hear about similar issues. We have spoken to thousands of individuals who have entrusted us with their stories. We feel compelled to bring some of the significant issues to the forefront, in service of evolving the workplace. We aim to bring awareness of the psychosocial aspects, burnout, and traumas of those who work in HHS. We want to share:

- How the line staff eligibility worker feels informing the homeless family that the last county bed was already taken that frigid night
- How alone the behavioral health clinician feels when triggered about their own past trauma
- How intimidated the receptionist is when that frustrated customer expresses anger and disappointment
- How helpless the public health nurse feels while advocating for that patient in a community with limited resources
- How much despair the first responder experiences in being called to that catastrophic scene once again
- What the foster care specialist feels upon getting that call to find another placement
- And how tired most are with the office politics and bureaucracy on top of all the above

These workers are our social heroes. They are getting injured and wounded, and we must care for them. All of the above experiences trigger the human threat response. Nobody is immune, and the stress takes its toll. We must acknowledge the psychological wounds, which we now know turn into physical ones. HHS professionals are warriors, but they are human and vulnerable. They are you. Most fictional superheroes are invulnerable and spontaneously regenerate themselves. Social heroes must be taken care of, and practice self-care, but remain heroes nonetheless. As psychologists, we are finally witnessing some of our organizations paying attention to our needs and vulnerabilities. This recognition has been long in coming.

It seems that in serving others we have somehow forgotten about ourselves along the way. Some of us may need to "forget" and be distracted by the plights of others. We can avoid ourselves and thereby not have to attend to our own vulnerability and pain. The problem is that not paying attention also takes a toll. The agencies and organizations that we are part of, whose missions are to serve the vulnerable and underserved, have somehow forgotten about us. HHS professionals are not objects immune to suffering and invulnerable to the costs of adversity. We bleed too. Like our clients, some of us have been traumatized, abused, or harmed and have been subject to the toll of adverse strikes. There was no mention of self-care in our undergraduate, graduate, or doctoral internship experiences. Today we advocate for changes in undergraduate and graduate programs that produce those who will eventually serve others.

So, who cares for the "carers?" Specific individuals dedicated to the psychological protection and growth of adults do not exist as they do for children or dependent adults. As psychologists, we have borne witness to the effects of this lack of care in ourselves and colleagues. Self-care is crucial for this reason. There has long been an assumption of invulnerability in our service professionals. We must not maintain this myth and avoid the vulnerability of those who serve. We have witnessed an alarming and increasing rate of suicides in service professionals. We offer hazmat suits to those who enter a physically toxic work environment to clean up after chemical spills. We need to build and give psychological hazmat suits to those we send in to address psychosocially toxic environments and situations.

Our leaders in this endeavor are some of the foundational thinkers, researchers, writers, and pioneers in the social neurosciences, including Daniel Siegel, MD, Allan Schore, PhD, and Louis Cozolino, PhD. Dr. David Rock has extended this lens into organizational dynamics through the NeuroLeadership Institute, which is a global center researching and promoting the neurosciences in organizational leadership. We will explore his model for organizational management, called the SCARF. Additionally, we introduce the work of neuroscientist R. Douglas Fields, PhD, on what triggers our brain's threat system. We also share the scholarship of Yuval Harari on the history of humans and of Malcolm Gladwell on different human traits. We invite and welcome you into this world of evolving guesses, ideas, research, field stories, thoughts, and people all working toward the goal of improving human work conditions.

Workaches covers a variety of issues affecting individuals in the workplace. We hope that readers will be stimulated by the neuroscience and other research-based concepts and will find their ways to more in-depth and focused writings on topics of interest. Some may argue that delivering the newest findings in the neurosciences to the "field" is premature, but we believe that academic research and fresh ideas deserve to be translated, introduced, and operationalized as soon as possible into the workforce of those on the ground working with human dynamics and conditions. This is done with the knowledge that these findings are continually updating and evolving. We do our best to make them user-friendly for ourselves and others—our apologies in advance for some of the reductionism and over-statements involved in distilling and summarizing such complex concepts in neuroscience, anthropology, social psychology, and beyond.

Workaches focuses on the more negative aspects and adverse outcomes of human-to-human interactions in the workplace. However, let us acknowledge the incredible power and beauty of other human interactions. Let us recognize the noble heroes and the empathic souls that promote, care for, educate, lead, sacrifice, rescue, heal, and even die for one another. What has impressed us most in our work with individuals is the level of resilience we have witnessed. Some of the HHS professionals we have spoken with were once clients of the agencies for which they now work. They were assisted and thereafter motivated to serve others. Work is ideally an essential and meaningful part of our identities. Our goal, then, is to help leaders identify, manage, and reduce workaches in their organizations. We aim to provide a context for understanding the different dynamics that underlie most workaches in hopes that this assists in their address. We want to promote staff restoring work as a source of inspiration, meaning, and accomplishment—a source of thriving. We chose our target audience for the book to include both staff and leadership because we believe it is vital for both to be able to see through the lens of the other. This facilitates gaining understanding, appreciation, and empathy for the dilemmas and difficulties inherent in all roles at work.

The topics covered in *Workaches* are consolidated from those stories that many individuals over the years have shared with us about navigating the "wilds" of the workplace. Knowledge and understanding cannot always change circumstances; however, we strongly believe that the more we learn about ourselves and others, the better prepared we are as we face human nature in the workplace. Unfortunately, there are not many places in our culture where we are taught about ourselves and others or about relationship dynamics. Individuals and organizations historically contacted people like us once there were significant problems, crises, and diagnoses. Sometimes interventions after the fact are too late. Prevention requires updated knowledge, strategies, and implementations.

We have been following the recent discussions and debates about changing school curricula. Increasing emphasis is placed on learning about science, which is great. However, we are concerned that there has been no mention of applying science to learn about one's self or relationships. Students often emerge from school and enter the workplace knowing more about the inner workings of machines than they do about the inner workings of themselves. Is it not as important to learn how to build a thriving human being as it is to build a robot? Science can help students better understand why they might feel the impulse to bully another child or why they might have been targeted. Science can help students understand why they might react certain ways to differences. We aim to make up for this gap in information. It is not too late to learn about this in adulthood. We want you to know about what you are working with (complex human brains) and what you are working in (complex human organizations). The more we know, the better we can care for ourselves and each other.

Questioning, thinking about, and talking with others about work issues is valuable. Counseling appointments "after work hours" are popular spots. People come to discharge and process their feelings about the workday with the hope of working some of the issues out and making things better. We have long been concerned about those who do not deal with work triggers. Do some head to the local "happy hour" after work to self-medicate? Do others go home and take out their frustrations on their family? Do some hit the roads with aggressive driving and act out their feelings from the workday of being humiliated or feeling trapped? Working among and for so many different individuals in an organization inevitably triggers a multitude of feelings that deserve address.

We also felt compelled to write this book to call attention to aspects of work that most do not think about as being part of a daily work schedule. These aspects can sometimes take more energy than actual job tasks, yet minimal time and energy is often allotted for them.

"Incidental" Job Duties Not in Job Descriptions

- Manage your internal feelings with coworkers
- Manage your internal feelings with management
- Control reactions so you remain socially appropriate
- Fit in with your work group
- Compete for resources
- Worry about keeping your job
- Deal with feelings of loss of control
- Cover up what you do not know
- Find the energy and time to get to and from work
- Hide your fears and biases
- Juggle your personal life and work schedule
- Deal with disappointments and expectations of others
- Struggle with feelings of inadequacy and incompetence
- Cover your differences and vulnerabilities
- Fake energy you really don't have
- Hide true feelings and put on a game face
- Manage your stress

New graduates entering the workforce for the first time typically have little opportunity to stop and reflect about how they want to work. They have been primed to do well in school in order to get "that" job. Often, by the time they get to the workplace, they have student debt to be paid off and are looking at high lifestyle costs. There are the basic shelter needs in high-priced real estate markets and those "necessary unnecessary" objects to reflect status that they have learned is needed in the race. Time for reflection and contemplation is minimal when you are in a competition. So, they join what is in place and attempt to compete for that alluring lifestyle. If they have children, the race will be that much more competitive to "pass the baton" with as much advantage as possible to the next generation. So, whether you are just entering the job market or have been in it for years, we hope by reading *Workaches*, you pause a bit and reflect on how you are working and perhaps then make some adaptive changes to move toward thriving, rather than merely surviving. We want you to grapple with this question while you are reading: "Am I working wisely?" This question will make more sense as you read on. Perhaps, while reading, you offer yourself the opportunity to reflect on different aspects of your working life. We invite you to pay attention to what feelings and thoughts emerge as you read. What changes would you propose to improve working conditions?

America saw the rise of labor unions in the 1800s to protect workers from physical harm and exploitation. We have continued to keep this unbeaten movement alive and now are at the point in history to be able to continue to fine-tune and address the subtler psychological harm that occurs in the workplace. As we learn more about the vulnerabilities of the human brain and the potential for damage, we need updates in its care and protection. The next step in that evolution of human rights in the workforce is to protect our vulnerable minds and promote psychosocial safety. We have appreciated the growing awareness of the need for helmets to protect the brain from physical injuries, we advocate for similar awareness to protect the brain from psychological injuries. We welcome you to *Workaches* as part of this movement.

ACKNOWLEDGMENTS

Although our names are on the front of this book and the names of all the scientists, theorists, and writers who have contributed to our knowledge are referenced throughout, *Workaches* truly belongs to the thousands of individuals in the workforce who have shared their stories with us over the years. Collectively, we share over six decades of clinical and organizational knowledge and experience. But we are just the puzzle-makers who have assembled the data at an endpoint—the ones sitting at the computer, occasionally with a trusty pen—putting together all the pieces, from personal stories to scientific findings, in a coherent whole after spending many years in the field.

Our deepest gratitude goes to all the health and human service professionals who have bravely served others and borne witness to the struggles and traumas of existence. You are noble social warriors, far too often injured in the field and left with too few resources. We honor the purpose, meaning, and contributions of your work and hope you can too. We offer this book as one step toward recognition, understanding, and healing. We thank you for your dedicated service.

The following individuals made this work possible. First and foremost, we would like to thank our incredible editor, Amy Thomas. Amy earned her PhD in English Literature at UC Berkeley, has taught writing and literature at several universities, and now works as a freelance editor. We are honored to have *Workaches* takes its place among her other edited works. A special thank you goes to the staff at the UC Davis Human Services Programs for affording us the opportunity to serve so many health and human service professionals over the years. The following individuals are also named because they have collectively served as support, friends, colleagues, mentors, teachers, and guides in private corporations, academic institutions, health and human services organizations, and personal realms. Sincere appreciation and indebtedness go to Elizabeth Meyer, Susan Brooks, Jann Donnenwirth, Julie Gondry, Ginah Monroy, Tracy Wareing Evans, Donna Jarvis-Miller, Ana Pagan, Kate Kelley, Cynthia Señeriz, Roger Belcourt, Stacey Brezing, Leticia Anne Peplau, Cary Winograd, Joan Denson, Libbie Winograd, Sharon Ree, Rory Osborne, Nathan Nguyen, Maxwell Cohen, Rose Wolfe, Phyllis LaVay, June Troy,

Sean Winograd, Erica Winograd-Cohen, William Torricelli, Alice Miller, Jean Uelman, Judith Viorst, Dolores Cohen, Molly Egan, Lewis Thomas, and Jane Friedman. Although we do not list specific names, we thank all the leaders across the nation who have invited us into their organizations and shared openly about challenges and successes. Deep appreciation is extended to Drs. David Rock and R. Douglas Fields for their generous permission to share in *Workaches* some of their valuable contributions to the field.

A special thank you goes to our individual clients over the years who have bravely shared their journeys and taught us what it means to struggle toward being vulnerable and resilient. We have traveled together beyond the social facades and personas, through the tough terrain of the realities of life. We thank you for entrusting us with your precious reveals. Your truths are treasured. You have all greatly contributed to this book.

And finally, we extend our deepest gratitude to our respective families for providing the love, encouragement, opportunity, and support that facilitates our work.

1
INTRODUCTION

We are wired to survive, the thrive is on us.

Most of us go to work each day to do something positive. Make a difference. Create a smile. Make or sell a product. Offer a service. Our motivation to go is typically based on a mutual benefit to ourselves and others. We want to contribute, make a difference, and earn a living. This makes us feel good about ourselves. However, "other stuff" happens in the workplace. Sometimes when we go to work, we get emotionally wounded—by each other, our organizations, and even by those we seek to help. Sometimes these wounds are deep, and we call them traumas. Other times they are more superficial, and we call them annoyances. These different injuries cumulatively lead to adverse consequences for our organizations and ourselves. Relational and emotional vulnerabilities, resentments, entanglements, conflicts, and needs exist in our professional worlds as they do in our personal worlds. Our brains do not change just because we walk through the office door, though we put on our work attire and game face to cross this threshold.

Tremendous psychosocial labor gets exerted at work in addition to the physical and cognitive labor that goes into assigned work tasks themselves. Individuals become exhausted from this emotional labor that goes into dealing with others or workaches. We must not ignore or underestimate the toll all this takes on individuals at all levels of an organizational hierarchy. From the employee bullied by a coworker to the supervisor who fears repercussions from giving necessary feedback to a defensive employee, all are impacted by relational factors. Interpersonal dynamics can sometimes be the most distressing aspect of a person's workday.

We cannot escape the influences of other people—from the playground to the boardroom. The dynamics of the sandbox never end. Where there are humans, of whatever age, there are human dynamics and conflicts. There will be those competing for the shovel and those fighting for the bucket. Others will be there just to hang out in the sand or to engage in cooperative play. There will be the one who throws sand in the eyes of the other. There will be the one who helps and calls for an adult to intervene. There will be the one who is too vulnerable and reticent even to enter the sandbox. Some will parallel play while others will interact in their game. Some will exit the sandbox crying, others will skip away happy. Some will be refused entry into the sandbox.

This simple box with sand, a shovel, and a pail is designed to foster fun. However, this space can become an environment for complex human behavior to play out. Often it will mimic the primitive ancestral history of these children and foreshadow the emotional and behavioral patterns that will follow them into the workplace.

The manager of this sandbox will have a complicated job because this simple sandbox is just not that simple.

There are unique challenges for those who work in human services. Serving others is beautiful and serving others can be exhausting. Human vulnerability and needs that must be addressed and attended to are unending, and because there is no endpoint to the needs of others, the HHS workforce can often feel as if their job is never done. Feelings of helplessness and hopelessness get triggered when success is unfairly measured by solving problems and completing tasks. Not all problems can be solved, and not all tasks can be completed. As long as we are in service, the need for more assistance continues. We fall into an abyss of perpetual help needed. Service to others must be examined when it creates disservice to self.

People who find themselves working in HHS may be "wired to serve" and possess higher amounts of empathy than the general population. Individuals who, themselves, have suffered psychosocial adversity earlier in life may also be more inclined to rescue others from similar circumstances. Being helpful may compensate for earlier feelings of helplessness. However, sometimes we are unable to rescue, remedy, or even to help at all. Experiencing helplessness when needing to be helpful is a psychologically difficult space. Self-awareness, in order to manage levels of empathy, out-of-awareness personal missions, and other aspects of one's self, is vital in HHS work. We must continually assess the motivations and expectations of ourselves—and those to whom we provide services—in part so we can identify unrealistic expectations. The road is difficult when we want to give to others who are unable to receive or change, and often it is disappointing and frustrating when needs exceed the resources we have to assist others in need.

Workaches extracts key concepts from the latest social neuroscience research to assist readers with understanding the close connection between the impacts of workplace experiences and relationships on different brain regions and the experience of surviving or thriving at work. Some of the topics explored include: how adverse work experiences trigger stress and the threat response; how positive experiences trigger feelings of reward and engagement; how profoundly others impact us because of the social nature of our brains; how secondary trauma can develop from exposure to human suffering; how workaches adversely affect health and well-being; and, how building new pathways in the brain—or "neuroplasticity"—can help us repair the damage of workaches. We address the physical and psychological effects of social pain and the role self-care plays in maximizing health and well-being. And we also discuss strategies for optimal workplace learning, creativity, and productivity and the value of workforce diversity. Finally, we offer advice on constructing organizations to maximize activation of our social-engagement nervous system and to minimize activation of our threat system—to foster thriving, not just surviving.

As clinical psychologists, we often ask people to pause and "take a step back" and examine their lives to gain a sense of how things are going. We encourage periodic reexamination and reevaluation to move from "autopilot"—or just doing things because that is how they were done yesterday—to intentionally reexamining and asking basic questions such as: "Am I happy?" "Is my life going the way I want it to?" This process allows for valuable updates in life assessments, intents, motivations, goals, and behaviors. As organizational psychologists, we also ask organizations to "step back" and reevaluate how things are going.

Work is not going so well for many. People report surviving, but not thriving. The United Nations commissions an annual assessment of the happiness, or well-being, of nations across the world. The World Happiness Report 2018 reveals that, in the United States, income has increased but subjective well-being has decreased (Helliwell et al., 2018). Americans have more money but less social support and connectedness whereas people in Latin American countries (with less per capita income), for example, had significantly higher reported well-being. The findings were attributed to interpersonal relationships that were nurturing and to a culture with less focus on material wealth and objects. In *Workaches*, we suggest that the competitive drive for success (fueled by our primitive brain regions) has been overpowering our social engagement system (fueled by higher brain regions) and resulting in higher stress levels and lower thriving or well-being. Finally, the role of stress in harming the American workforce is receiving long-overdue attention. Both public and private organizations are increasingly seeking to enhance the health and well-being of their employees. Whether it is the customer, client, leader, or employee—the well-being of all matters. The healthier the workforce, the better the community can be served.

Odyssey of Working with Humans

If we look at the space between individuals, it appears empty. Yet this is one of the most complex, ever-changing, and intensely filled spaces in the known universe. Our senses are constantly "taking in" others, whether we want to or not, and we all experience the less-than-pleasant impacts of other people. We introduce the term "workaches" to describe interpersonal assaults and psychological injuries suffered in the workplace. They are experiences that trigger the threat or stress response. Hurt, harm, harassment, and hate can interact with past psychological wounds, which can lead to potentially devastating outcomes. Workaches can range in severity from mild and annoying to catastrophic and disabling.

Too often, we have been psychologically harmed before entering the workforce, so work wounds act upon older family and school wounds. We call this retraumatization. By the time we enter the workplace, we typically have been members of two other very influential groups—the family of origin and the school/peer group. Ideally, the first group that we are part of provides us with protection and nurturance. And ideally, the second group we become part of provides us with education and socialization. Unfortunately, in both these groups as well, "other stuff" happens that is counter to the ideal purpose and goals of nurturance and protection, education, and socialization. This other stuff arises in that interpersonal, relational, or social space between us and other people. We call this space the relational field. And what gets generated by interpersonal problems in this space is relational stress. People psychologically wound each other.

Sometimes we are aware of this interpersonal aggression (whether as perpetrator or victim), while other times it is outside our awareness but still having remarkable impacts. Even if another individual of a past generation aggressed against our ancestor, we may still be affected. Awareness of harm taking place in the relational field can lead to taking responsibility for addressing these issues whether as victim, perpetrator, or both.

Distinguishing physical from psychological harm is becoming increasingly difficult. We know now that psychological injuries cause physical changes. A physical blow to the head is no longer considered the only way to cause brain damage. Emotional blows or traumas physically change the brain (Bremner, 2016). While the psychological wounds we suffer at the hands of one another are often subtle, and sometimes invisible (out of awareness), these wounds are no longer hidden or undetectable to the eye of the latest brain scanning technologies. Mounting scientific evidence reveals how work stressors can and do change the brain. Studies indicate that most Americans are stressed at work. Research is increasingly revealing the adverse impact of job stress on health and well-being, as well as on mortality. A collaborative study between Stanford and Harvard Universities (Goh, Pfeffer & Zenios, 2015) revealed that workplace stressors such as organizational injustice, work-family conflict, and low social support significantly contribute to physical and psychological ailments. Across the human lifespan, an individual can experience multiple and varied psychological injuries and stressors that often compound upon one another.

For ease and simplicity, in this book, we use the terms emotional, psychological, and psychosocial injuries interchangeably (with the understanding herein of the physical component to these wounds as well). We focus on mental, emotional, and social (verbal and nonverbal) relational harm. Because organizations themselves are made up of a group of individuals, we also examine workaches that emerge from this collective group. People can be targeted by an individual or by a group. Groups provide protection, but also can become centers of harm from within-group or between-group conflicts. Our journey together explores the interpersonal field of social combat as it pertains to work. So much destructiveness—and so much healing—can take place in the relational field between people. We must continue to explore and understand that space between us that contains a whole universe of evident and hidden dynamics.

Figure 1.1 offers a non-exhaustive list of the most common workaches we have encountered and addressed in the HHS workforce. Individuals and groups across the country have shared the distress that accompanies these relational experiences.

WORKACHES	
Loss of optimal brain management ("top-down management," or TDM)	Secondary trauma / burnout
Unfairness	Disillusionment
Sexual Harm	Microaggressions / bias
Insecurity / Uncertainty	Bullying / mobbing
Shaming	Work / life conflict
Power / status	Safety concerns
Exclusion	Evaluations
Covering / passing	Loss of control / helplessness
Institutional betrayal	Velocity (work speed / load)

Figure 1.1

An essential goal of this book is to promote the well-being of the HHS workforce or any individuals who serve other humans. To do so, we must first lay some foundation so our recommendations have context, make sense, have appeal, and compel leaders to forge change. To accomplish this, we need to understand:

- How humans evolved to work together (Chapter 2)
- What we are all working with—our human brains (Chapter 3)
- How our brains are impacted and changed by our relationships (Chapter 4)
- The range of workaches that exist in the contemporary workforce (Chapter 5)
- Individual and organizational consequences of harm in the workplace (Chapter 6)

- Healing potential, psychosocial self-defense, and well-being at work (Chapter 7)
- Essential strategies for thriving organizations to foster safety, resilience, growth, meaning, learning, engagement, and productivity (Chapter 8)

Below, we introduce some of the significant issues addressed in this book that contribute to work stress and psychosocial injuries to set the stage for these upcoming chapters. We examine the problems, their history, underlying dynamics, damage inflicted, and strategies for problem-solving and for evolving organizations. Progress does not necessarily mean change happens in a linear or rapid manner. Setbacks, detours, and regressions are natural. Nonetheless, we push on toward our goals in service of evolving HHS organizations.

The graphic below depicts some of the forces impacting HHS professionals at work (Figure 1.2). Most of the underlying forces are human-created stressors (as opposed to stress caused, for example, by a natural disaster such as an earthquake). These issues emerge from our relationships and what we impose upon one another in our contemporary work cultures. Just as it is we who have created these work issues, we can be the ones to recreate and update them. Frequent updates occur with workplace technology. Updating workplace cultures and promoting the emotional well-being of the workforce requires addressing contemporary work pressures.

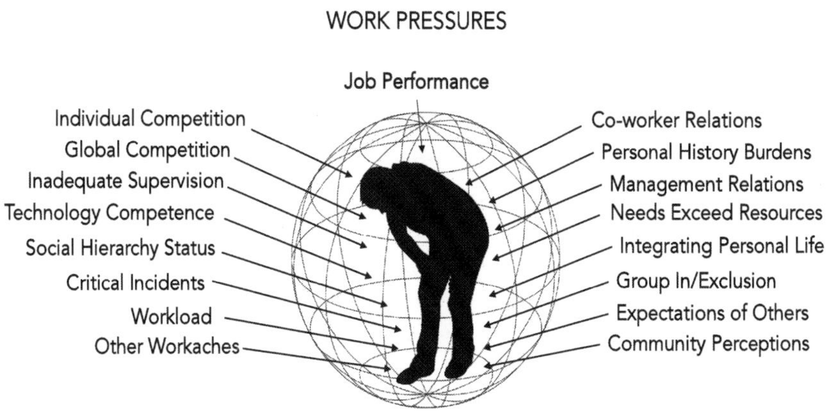

Figure 1.2

Dilemma of the Brain in the Civilized Jungle

The simple goal in the sandbox is to have fun (thrive). The simple goal at work is to contribute to the collective group and receive financial and meaningful rewards (thrive). All energy or work should ideally just go toward accomplishing these goals. Instead, much work goes into negotiating the psychosocial dynamics, such as being included in the group, scanning for danger, and protecting personal space (survive). Just being around other people can exhaust us at work before we even complete the main tasks at hand. These are potential psychosocial costs of work.

Today, we all connect with remarkably greater numbers of people than ever before. Our ancestors only had to hang with a handful of others. Now we even socialize virtually through digital connections. Our ancestors would be overwhelmed in our society—as we often are too, because parts of our brains are the same as theirs were. Our human dilemma is that we have wondrous brain regions that can imagine the future and create all kinds of new possibilities, yet we possess other brain regions that resist change and fear the unknown. Some brain regions offer us unlimited horizons, even facilitating the creation of technology for distant travel and communication. We now can know each other globally. However, our deeper and more primitive regions fear unfamiliar others and prefer staying "close to home." These more primitive regions are wired for survival, not creativity or collaboration, and they are busy perceiving potential threats. So, part of us needs things to stay the same, yet part of us continually changes things and has an eye on the distant horizon of possible futures. Our brains are social and wired to connect with others, yet we are suspicious of and competitive with others. Many people may not understand why they feel overwhelmed by today's expectations, and part of the explanation is that our culture has dramatically changed more rapidly than certain parts of our brains have. Knowing that some brain areas have adapted and evolved to accommodate modern lifestyles, and others have not, may afford us patience and compassion with ourselves and others as we work out our issues. These are just some of the paradoxes of living a human life and working among diverse others!

Humans imagine, desire, create, complicate, destroy, and rebuild. We change our environment. Then we struggle to adapt. For most other animals, the environment changes first, and then they adjust. Mice, for example, are living about the same existence that they were living millions of years ago. They too can learn and adapt, but they adapt to the environment to ensure their survival. They do not change it. When their environments get artificially altered in the laboratory (e.g., crowded), they also get stressed. Humans, though, are able to use stress as an impetus for change and to create new things, often from our imaginations.

One of the relatively newer and unique entities we have created is the workplace. Now we must continue to work out the problems of our creation.

Awareness of what is not working for us is essential. This book promotes the concepts of self-intelligence and crucial thinking because we believe one of the best ways of navigating workplace dynamics comes from understanding ourselves first. Self-awareness is a prerequisite for being able to know another individual fully. Knowing how our own brains function and how we have been influenced, not only by our known relatives but by our more primitive ancestors as well, is essential to creating workplaces where we can thrive. Additionally, being aware of how we affect each other in our relational fields is crucial to understanding our experiences in our workgroups.

Driven to Survive, Not Thrive

We are wired to survive; the thrive is on us. We must develop certain attitudes, beliefs, and behaviors to thrive. Because physical survival is the primary underlying driver of human behavior, psychological survival, or thriving in life, takes a back seat in the brain. Reproduction (ensuring future DNA) and power (ensuring maximum safety against threat) are the principal engines of physical survival. Risk, competition, and status are important mechanisms serving this driver in human life. We may not be consciously aware of it, but it was wired into our brains long ago. Embedded deep in the most primitive areas of our minds is this most insatiable, behind-the-scenes force. We observe a relentless drive when these areas are unbridled in those who cannot obtain enough money, prestige, weaponry—or whatever signifies and supports power in a culture.

Reptiles and lower mammals are not seeking quality of life and peace of mind. They are seeking survival for themselves and their offspring. These animals must compete among themselves and against other groups to survive. These animals must also cooperate some to survive. We share regions of their brains, but we have evolved other areas that offer us hope for overcoming some of these more primitive drivers. These higher regions of our brain facilitate our opportunities for thriving, beyond just surviving.

Primitive brain structures in the lower part of our brain, such as the brainstem which houses our survival instincts, do not care about our happiness. The amygdala, our basic emotion and threat decoder, does not care about our peace of mind. Only our higher brain regions hold our chances for thriving. Once we have judged that our safety and survival are ensured, we can decide with our wiser—that is, more evolutionarily advanced mind—to seek thriving. The prime reason for being aware of our primitive drivers is to be able to manage them. Otherwise, they will drive us, and not necessarily take us to our best places. These structures will drive us to unnecessarily "tell" ourselves we are not good enough, perceive a threat in people who are different than us, and chronically trigger our stress response. How often have we achieved a goal and instead of celebrating, added additional rungs to the ladder? The bottom line is that even though we may not be consciously aware of it, the need to survive is constantly underlying most behaviors in the workplace. Unfortunately, this contributes to some of the least attractive human behavior and creates many workaches. Because the more primitive regions automatically have the most influence over our work relationships, we must intentionally engage our higher regions to navigate effectively.

Many different parts within our skulls must somehow work together to achieve goals. Some of these parts are modern and sophisticated, and others are ancient and quite primitive. As in a good orchestra, if all the instruments are working together and in harmony, they can produce beautiful music. Otherwise, we hear noise. People work best in communication and in concert with one another in an organization. Similarly, our brain regions work best if coordinating and communicating in harmony with one another. We consider this to be when the brain is in its "sweet spot."

An orchestra is an organization like any other, and so is our brain. In this book, we will explore the concept of top-down management (TDM) in our brains. The "top" refers to where the rational and thoughtful brain region is located in our skulls, which is physically higher up than the lower, evolutionarily older, emotional and reactive, regions. We will discuss how to be aware of the signs that suggest you or the other person you happen to be dealing with has lost TDM. Our goal is to understand and welcome all regions of our brain so we can have the most adaptive relationship with our own selves (and others).

Similar to a great manager in an organizational setting, we want to be the best manager of our own mind. This implies accepting and regulating all emotions, listening to all thoughts, and non-judgmentally managing all behaviors toward desired goals.

We address the understanding and non-judgmental management of the more primitive regions lower in our brains that, out of our conscious awareness, scan for differences in others and scan for similarities to those who may have hurt us in our pasts. Differences trigger threat because they indicate an unknown factor and potential danger. Encountering an individual who shares similarities with someone who has hurt you in the past can trigger warning of potential danger. These scans of others not only occur out of our awareness, but in milliseconds. Managing this extremely critical aspect of the brain is vital in our workplaces because reactions can lead to violence. We get bombarded by both verbal and nonverbal social information constantly.

The human nervous system is complex, and its influences extend throughout our bodies: our brains are just one piece of the full picture of what make us thinking, feeling, and acting human beings. This system is quite fluid and designed to change with the changes in our environments—which include other people, with whom we are wired to connect. Our brains are regularly engaged in a fluid exchange with one another. Other individuals have such high impact that they physically and functionally change our brains, as we will address in Chapter 3. If a threat emerges, our whole body is prepared to respond to survive, but different bodily conditions are in place when we are not under threat. When we are in our thrive mode, we are open to learning, creating, and playing (as opposed to battling when in survive mode). So, we are driven to survive, but once our basic survival needs are met, the goal is to effortfully and intentionally calm our threat system (which drives competitive survival) and more fully engage our social system (which drives our relationships with our own selves and others).

Names Will (N)ever Hurt Me

The adage, "sticks and stones may break my bones, but names will never hurt me" does not ring true when we learn about psychosocial impacts:

taunting and name-calling are taken very seriously by the brain and get encoded. The adage "time heals everything" also does not ring true.

Time may change everything, but it certainly does not heal everything. A deep scrape on the knee takes about one to two weeks to heal. The body is quick to send out its repair and immunity troops to heal and safeguard a physical wound. Emotional wounds, however, do not heal in the same way as physical wounds because the brain wants to learn about and to remember the underlying threats of psychosocial wounds.

The brain is built to store what is dangerous to survival in this existence—it is a sponge for collecting scary, shaming, hurtful, and threatening experiences and information. I may not recall what you gave me at the office holiday party, but I likely recall when you humiliated me in front of our coworkers. Stored in a "neuro-vault" are all the verbal and nonverbal socially relevant communications from others that indicate social standing within the group. Though I would prefer to recall the more pleasant memory, specific segments of my brain certainly do not see it that same way. Research has revealed that when asked to remember emotional events, people remember four negative events for every one positive event. We are wired to store the information that is most crucial to social, and thereby once again physical, survival (Baumeister et al., 2001).

Our threat system was designed a long time ago to respond to the occasional threat of the wild animal we encountered in the jungle, or the warrior from the other tribe along the way. We reacted to the danger, and then it was over, one way or the other. However, in the modern workplace, the threat system is more typically turned on by an unfair boss, bullying coworker, or an upcoming performance review. These threats are typically encountered, or at least anticipated, many days per week. We are generally restrained from using our more primitive threat-induced impulses and reactive behaviors to solve these types of issues or stressors, so the repeated and unnecessary activation of our emergency threat response system leads to adverse impacts in our lives.

In a typical work day, others will unavoidably trigger a host of feelings in us, as we will in them. Some of these feelings will be in our awareness, and others will not, but we will still have responses to these feelings. Most individuals can manage these different emotions and practice self-control in the workplace. However, in some instances, triggers overwhelm some individuals' abilities to cope and control their emotions. The potential for workplace violence increases when individuals act out what is termed displaced anger. Understanding how to best navigate workgroups with awareness of all the daily triggers and potential for varied, often irrational, reactions is essential.

Foundational Groups: Home, School, and Work

Groups are fundamental to human life. They profoundly influence our thoughts, feelings, beliefs, and behaviors. Groups can get us to change our minds, sacrifice ourselves, and even kill. People in disfavor of the group suffer tremendously. The "eye of the other" that seems always to be watching us is constructed out of the norms and values of our dominant group. Early on, we become aware of what we should hide from our group, lest we get condemned and banished. We often feel shame about our feelings, thoughts, fantasies, beliefs, and behaviors that we suspect deviate from our group's norms.

The three main groups in our lives are all "hubs" of interpersonal connections that impact us greatly. The first two, home and school, have what we might call "developmental protectors." These are elders who are aware of their roles as protectors of our vulnerabilities. Some fulfill their roles responsibly, and others do not. By the time we enter the workgroup, there are no more assumed "protectors." If we are fortunate along the way, we have a mentor, or we become one to someone else. However, it will never be the same as in Groups 1 and 2.

By the time we enter the workplace, rarely is there an assumption that we are developmentally vulnerable or that we might need care and protection. This blindness to adult vulnerability and needs is one of the primary reasons we need awareness and policy.

As we will discuss, we age, but we still possess the vulnerabilities of our younger selves, though they typically get disguised. Relationships with others continue to be of utmost importance to us. We seek approval (reward) and attempt to avoid disapproval (threat). Those close to us and our therapists typically know about our vulnerabilities, but few others do.

When tigers get released into their own independent lives at maturity, they have been schooled by their mother and siblings on how to work—hunt, gain shelter and status, survive—in the wilderness. Their work is their survival. Their survival is their work. They have banked many training hours since the age of six months in perceiving and dealing with issues within their pack and the myriad threats outside of the pack. They get well trained for the perils of the wild by the time they go off on their own, between the ages of 24 and 30 months. Humans do not receive such relevant training in their first groups. Our brains do not finish developing until our mid-to-late twenties, so we typically leave the nest before we have fully learned how to independently navigate the psychosocial wilderness of adult life. We even leave before the brain connections between our thinking and emotional regions become firmly established. So, our immature judgment which promotes acting on our emotional impulses leaves us vulnerable. We need additional learning and training from mentors, elders, and leaders in the other groups we join.

The additional learning we receive through our relationships with others is loaded onto some basic knowledge that we have when we arrive in the world. Humans are born "pre-loaded" with survival instincts and tools. We enter our families of origin with genetic and epigenetic blueprints which become modified through relations in this first group, and with others after that. Chapters 3 and 4 explore how the brain changes throughout our lifetime. The brain is not a static organ. Other organs, such as the liver, may regenerate cells, but do not learn and they remain relatively the same. The brain, however, changes continuously in response to its environment. It changes when one becomes an adolescent. It changes when one becomes an adult. It changes when one becomes a parent. It changes when one becomes a leader. It changes when one has an adverse experience.

We are not taught, and we do not come in knowing, how to protect ourselves from our parents or siblings in our family of origins. We enter the world vulnerable and "trust and believe" in the benevolence of the people who are going to be our caregivers. Someone from outside of this group (e.g., social worker) would have to enter the family and observe harm to attempt to protect us, if we were in danger within this first group. Our brains are too young and dependent to gain perspective and to defend ourselves. If our injury is subtle, disguised, and protected by the group, it likely will go undiscovered. Nonetheless, the brain changes from these assaults—both in subtle and overt ways (as we discuss in Chapter 6). We similarly are seldom taught how to protect ourselves from our teachers or peers. The harm typically must be apparent and severe enough to come to the attention of others. In school, we do not yet have enough personal power and perspective to protect ourselves independently.

The brain learns about our interpersonal standing and worth in a group from the initial relational experiences in our families of origin. We learn about authority and operations of a group from parents—our first managers. These experiences and learning form actual neural pathways in our brain, as we will learn in Chapter 3. These neural templates in our minds form the basis of what we know about ourselves and others by the time we enter school. Our second managers are our teachers and our second siblings are our classmates. By the time we enter the workplace, clear neural pathways have been laid in our brains that will interact in complex ways with our bosses and coworkers. The graphic below simplifies and illustrates authority and sibling figures' dynamics getting passed to and replicated in successive groups.

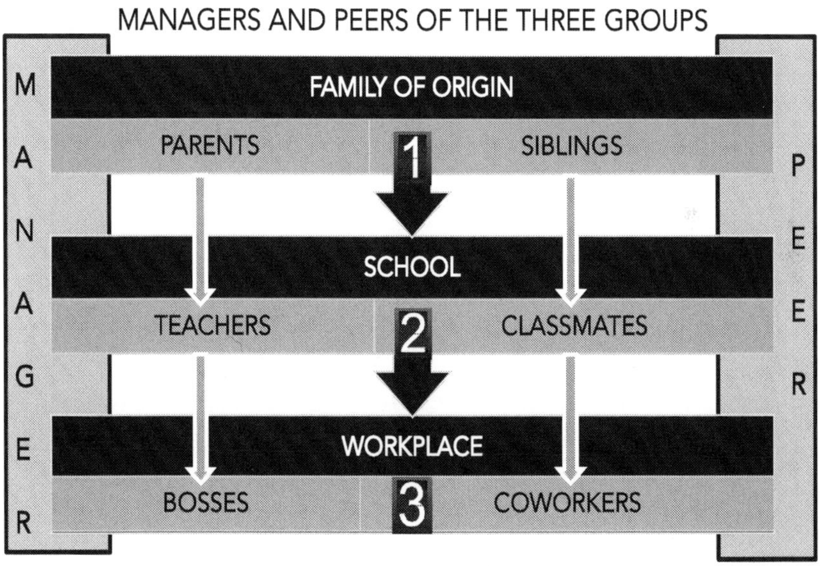

Figure 1.3

People depend on their groups for protection and care. Ideally, we receive this in Group 1. We look to have our needs met with minimal work in return. We also have our needs attended to by others in our school group. These experiences and expectations often get unconsciously transferred on to the employer. We have come to expect our allowance in exchange for chores, some protection from those in authority, and even healthcare (the adult version of the nurse's office in Group 2). These expectations are all out of awareness, but the shadow of the parent gets cast over the employer. Even though we are consciously aware that our employer is neither our parent nor our teacher, unconsciously, in the nether regions of the brain, we do perceive them as such and desire the same protection and security. We get disappointed. Others no longer have that same investment in our nurturance or learning.

When we enter the workforce, we are typically more prepared to do our jobs than we are to take care of ourselves. Others have looked after us in our past two groups. Ideally, we could talk to a caregiver or a teacher if we had questions. They could help negotiate a sibling conflict or playground rivalry. We could complain about our homework load and seek wisdom about friendship. Then it ends. We usually are ill prepared for what we are going to experience inside our organizations and inside ourselves when at work. Typically, no one has advised us on how the witnessing of human pain and suffering is going to impact us. Before this stage in life, many of us are more protected and gradually introduced to the world in our advancing developmental states by our families of origin. We are also progressively introduced to the academic world step-by-step (grade by grade) by our educators. The work world is different. We are expected to perform our job duties and navigate the group dynamic with minimal preparedness.

> Considerable distance lies between theory and practice. What we learn in school is very different from the pain and suffering we encounter and witness in the field. Leaders are invaluable and needed to teach, guide, mentor, protect, and model how best to care for the self when serving others.

Organizations thrive when they protect the well-being of their employees and assist in the development of resilience and growth. The wisdom and support of management can help with coworker struggles and the myriad other organizational stressors. Leaders become the parents and teachers that we have developmentally left behind. Some leaders can fulfill this role, and others cannot. Some staff members can be fulfilled by what they receive from competent leadership, and others cannot.

Workaches and Other Relational Dilemmas

Workaches seem so unnecessary and destructive, yet understanding that they are a part of human nature might allow us to better protect ourselves. The complicated and stressful dynamics that take place inside workforce relations can be emotionally and socially intense. In *Workaches*, we describe how just as we might seek physical immunity from a coughing coworker because we have learned about germs, we might seek psychological immunity from a toxic coworker because we have learned about interpersonal contagions and emotional infections. Learning how to navigate and manage the social and political realms of any workplace is vitally important, yet despite how common relational conflicts are, most of us do not receive training in strategies for this form of combat.

Many are ill-equipped for dealing with the interpersonal struggles and unavoidable battles in which they will be involved in the workplace.

We have a chance to be better prepared for protecting ourselves in our work environments. However, if historically we have not learned self-efficacy, self-respect, and self-care, it becomes more difficult to protect ourselves at work. And if we have not learned how to identify workaches, it becomes more challenging to practice self-care. As interventional psychologists, our goal is to promote understanding of these different issues, as well as to encourage adaptive cognitive and behavioral changes. Acknowledgment and acceptance of the mixed emotions triggered by interpersonal dynamics is constructive. Most are victims and perpetrators of these relational dynamics along the way in one way or another. It takes a lot of work to become aware of how we affect others, as well as how they impact us. None of us gets a pass from the unconscious nature of our brains and the occasional harm it does. Therefore, we are all responsible (as individuals and as organizations) for understanding and managing these dynamics.

In the workforce we have a different kind of dependence than we had in our previous groups. There is a mutual dependence. We need the organization, and the organization needs us. We contract with one another to do our parts. If needs are not met, we can leave or the organization can let us go. We are typically all adults now, which creates a much more equal "playing field," though issues of power and status and nonconscious dynamics can render us vulnerable, nonetheless. To our brains, our survival remains at stake. Most humans, unfortunately and inevitably, have been wounded by others before entering the workforce group. Therefore, we may be either numb or more sensitive to workaches by the time we arrive at work. Trauma can adversely affect our interpersonal gauge (which measures and signals when we get harmed). If we have not addressed our previous interpersonal or social injuries and trauma, we may not be in the best position to protect ourselves from potential emotional hazards at work. Those with trauma histories are more vulnerable to being revictimized and retraumatized. These histories often result in the need for recalibration of the interpersonal dynamics gauge. Just knowing that one's gauge may be "broken" can facilitate more caution when navigating work relations and may also lead to seeking assistance with recalibration. Building our own personal narratives or stories is vital to this process of recalibration because coherent personal narratives facilitate awareness of the self and help us organize our experiences and understand them. One of the benefits to organizing our stories is the opportunity of placing our experiences into historical contexts. It is often a triumph for trauma survivors to gain insight and restructure the adverse experience in memory as having happened in their past; they can "time stamp" that memory to affirm that they are now safe (if indeed the threat is over). We'll discuss this more in Chapter 7, "The Heal."

So why must it be this way? We set out to work with such good intentions. Why do we have to make it difficult for one another? Why do we have to block someone from getting into our lane on the highway? Why does a coworker have to look us up and down when we enter the door and make us doubt our appearance or style? Why does a boss have to criticize us and make us feel oh-so-small? Why do we have to notice that the lunchroom goes quiet upon our entering and get that yucky ache in our gut? Why do we hide our "real" selves at work? Well, we know now that some of the answers lie in the way our ancestors lived. Our brains have both remained the same and evolved. At the core of our motivations is the need to do almost anything, in and out of awareness, to survive. These are the evolutionary answers. Some of the answers also lie in how we fared in the first two groups of our lives—the developmental answers. Our experiences in our early groups influence and lead us to what we believe about ourselves and others. We are impacted and affected by all we encounter in our environments (even by microorganisms).

So, the question of why we "mess" with each other becomes the essential query at hand. There are deep parts of the brain that lend themselves to our psychosocial scuffling. These parts often operate outside our conscious awareness—they are on auto-pilot and directing a lot of our reactions to others. Nonverbal communications are constantly exchanged between people—from puzzled looks to furrowed brows. Intentional and unintentional behaviors are constantly getting interpreted and misinterpreted. People in the workplace are having to navigate through experiences such as rudeness, exclusion, and shame that create tremendous social pain. The more we understand how our brains operate, the more we can work to manage these natural human reactions and behaviors. We tend to see increased levels of interpersonal tension and acting out when there are increased levels of stress in an environment. But the more we bring some of the uncomfortable and sometimes unattractive human behaviors to light, the better our chance of adaptively and more honestly managing them in ourselves and others. These reactions are part of the human nature in all of us; there is no need for shame.

Fitting in with the dominant group is often a major interpersonal stressor. These varied, sometimes distressing, interpersonal behaviors are not unique to humans. If we look around the animal community, we can spot similar relational dynamics. Some animals are dishonest and deceitful. Some animals wear disguises or "social masks" to avoid an attack. All are motivated by the same biological pressure to survive. Seahorse behaviors provide an example of covering one's true self and "passing" to avoid "aquatic bullying" and predation. Some seahorses have adapted and evolved to look like plants. Their authentic or true identities are as seahorses, while their false selves (adaptive, protective personas) are as plants. Marine biologists have named them sea dragons. So, we are not alone in putting on social masks and pretending to be something we are not to fit in with the group and avoid harm. The potential gain of pretending is in service of survival for all animals. The loss is in thriving for humans due to the psychological cost of inauthenticity, experienced as detractions from self-esteem and disengagement from the workgroup. This cost is why covering, disguising, and passing are considered workaches.

Today in the workplace, we are much more concerned that another individual is going to insult us, as opposed to bite us, yet the underlying primitive fear is likely the same. Other animals' growls, strikes, and bites have become humans'

interpersonal, psychosocial aggressions such as malicious words, judgmental looks, exclusion, gossip, and bias.

Competition is a major underlying driver of people "messing" with one another. Humans are continually competing for resources—from siblings seeking resources from parents to coworkers seeking resources from bosses. Underlying even the most seemingly benign and straightforward situations are human social strategies for survival. Humans possess the ability to engage in interpersonal battle with a deceptive smile. Our verbal and nonverbal expressions can be completely different than what our intent and behaviors might reveal. It is so much easier to detect harm when it is undisguised. This ability for deceit creates a level of unease in the workplace. Individuals often report being unsure of whom they can trust at work. Even though in contemporary times there is typically "enough to go around" for all to survive, nonconscious and primitive drivers do not "believe" this and are constantly scanning for threats—often misperceiving non-threats as real threats. Our stressed bodies and minds pay a biochemical price for all these misperceptions. We sometimes assume that we have evolved above and beyond the more primitive reactions and often nonconscious behaviors we observe in other animals. In reality, though, we retain these primitive motivations—survival and reproduction. We have many fancier and more complex ways of disguising ourselves and our motivations, but the "basic instincts" remain and sometimes "hijack" our brains.

Workaches from Digital and Global Pressures

Industrialization carved the current path to how Americans work in the contemporary workplace. Plastics and then computers ignited this path. Machines were supposed to ease stress at work, but things have not turned out that way. Globalization and digitalization have further contributed to tension in the workplace, which is yet another force operating on people at work. Some of the workaches we experience trickle down from increasing global pressure in the sociopolitical competition for survival and status. This type of stress places humans in a battle mode of win or lose. Thrive mode off. Survive mode on. We become myopic rather than creative in this collective state and keep doing things in the same ways. No time is allotted to rethink and reconfigure systems, because creativity has no place on a battlefield. Too much is at stake. The drive here is to work harder and work faster. When the pressure is to compete, it becomes more challenging to step back and reflect on our systems. The brain does not allow for much introspection and wisdom when it becomes narrowly focused on survival. However, when in a thriving mode, thinking and wisdom are potentiated.

The bar of success seems to keep rising higher and higher. A race has been initiated with no foreseeable finish line. The definition of success in life is increasingly narrowing to what someone does (versus who someone is). Mostly out of awareness, in our collective unconscious, is a competition for survival on a global scale. Technology has made it easier to "see" what other groups are doing or having. In the ancient past, if we came upon a tribe that had better resources, we would have a local fight and move on. Today things are different. We can now show our resources and induce envy on a televised global stage, which fuels the race. Survival underlies the dynamics of shame, resentment, status, greed, and power, and these feelings and encounters can become fierce.

Different jobs are valued or devalued based on this context. When survival is perceived as at stake, jobs in the arts, for example, are considered to be less valuable than those that directly impact combat ability and survival. This reality is an important point to remember when struggling with feelings of inadequacy. Assignment of worth can be based on changing social context and perspective. Currently, we see, for example, much more global competition to build the best drone versus to create the best poem. As we will argue in upcoming chapters, it is crucial for us as individuals, and as a collective, to make competitive motivations conscious so that we have more choice in these matters. If not, our primitive wiring for survival will continue to prompt us to build a bigger bomb or improved coding for the destruction of the other group in service of our survival. Working when motivated by survival is remarkably different than working when motivated by the desire to thrive and to make a creative and positive impact in the world.

It appears that we are at a crossroads. We have amassed a great deal of data about the issues of the workplace that are harmful to physical and psychological well-being. Are we going to step back and look at this data and make the necessary changes? Or are we going to keep doing what we have been doing because we resist change? We can blindly continue to compete and sacrifice more and more of our personal lives and health. Or, we can begin to see the workplace from a different perspective. *Workaches* examines these questions and issues from the micro level of a nerve cell to the macro level of the global influences on our work styles.

Looking Forward

Together, we will excavate the psychosocial layers beneath some of the conflicts in the workplace to better understand why we mess with one another. Knowing what is "beneath the surface" can assist in the management of these issues. The ability to uncover and accept all the different layers of one's humanness is part of self-intelligence.

We create each other. We destroy each other. We harm each other. We heal each other. And we learn and grow together. Let us now explore together the biological, psychological, and evolutionary curiosities and paradoxes of our relationships with one another. We hope that addressing workaches through a lens of applied neuroscience makes a difference. And together we shall see that through all the science and other disciplines, the key or essential ingredient to human thriving seems to come back to the human-to-human relationship.

Introduction: Key Concepts

1) Interpersonal dynamics and relational conflicts have significant mind/body impacts, which highlights the need for awareness, understanding, and psychosocial self-defense training.
2) The workplace is a significant life group (after family and school) with its own developmental challenges, rewards, and threats.
3) Neuroscientific and historical knowledge of the brain and human dynamics are necessary for adaptive management of relational stress in the workforce.

2
HUMAN DEVELOPMENT AND GROUPS: THEN AND NOW

We are never "ungrouped." We enter this existence in the context of all the people who are alive and here, and of all those who used to be here. Our ancestors profoundly influence us. Even though we will never have met these folks, they have an enduring impact on us through our genes and how our brains have been designed. Human genetics extend back hundreds of thousands of years. There continue to be remarkable discoveries in the field of genetics that connect us all. New scientific findings suggest that the experiences—especially traumatic ones—of our past relatives impact our biochemistry. Epigenetics is the study of this phenomenon. We just cannot get away from each other, as much as we might sometimes want to. We consider our ancestors as "Group 0." Our brains have evolved in a way that makes group membership pretty much mandatory. Most of our learning in life occurs within groups or relationships. Four major groups in our lives have profound impact on us and include our ancestral (genetic), family, school, and work groups. In this chapter, we have extracted some of the major factors and processes within each of the different groups in human development that later impact us in the workforce. Understanding some of these group factors will assist us in making better sense of how we work today. We will see how each of these groups have already evolved tremendously since we humans have been here. We just need to carry forward the evolutionary baton that has gotten passed to us and do our parts now to continue the positive transformation of the workplace.

Group 0: Early Humans and Their Lasting Effects

The study of human experience through time and space is called anthropology. We only have written records from about the last 5,000 years of human existence. Social scientists rely on fossils and other forms of evidence to put together knowledge of those that lived before that time. Early Stone Age humans (about 85,000 years ago) lived in small groups or bands and were hunter-gatherers who moved from place to place in search of food. They had been evolving for roughly 2 million years from apelike groups. These nomadic people would pick up camp to follow and hunt roaming animals. These hunter-gatherer societies were considered egalitarian; people were relatively equal in what they did. No clear evidence exists that people were placed on any social hierarchy in their small groups. Labor divisions by gender have been noted once hunting strategies advanced to target more massive game such as bison. Females are then believed to have gathered foods such as berries and seeds and to have stayed close to temporary camps to care for the children. The males would travel up to several miles from camp to hunt wild animals and fish. They cooperated to hunt, gather, reproduce, child-rear, and survive all the elements, including defending against other animals. Staying in the favor of the group was essential for survival.

Approximately 10-12,000 years ago, humans began to plant crops and farm in different areas of the earth. Developing agriculture meant they no longer needed to travel from place to place in search of food. They began to stay in one place to take care of their fields—often along rivers where water could be used for farming. Because people no longer had to search for food, and fewer people were needed to do the farming, others could start doing different things. People began to domesticate animals. They formed agricultural groups. They began to develop different types of relationships and share resources and trade. People began to be able to store things, and some started to have more goods than others (Harari, 2018).

During this period, humans began to exhibit power differentials, and eventually, inequalities followed. Social hierarchies started to form. These times mark the emergence of using material possessions as symbols of status and power. When everyone in the group is a laborer seeking shelter and foraging for food (as with hunter-gatherers), roles are pretty much equal. When someone becomes a farmer, they eventually need farmhands—people who do the labor for them. They also begin to possess the land, crops, animals, and the river water in proximity to their land. These resources afforded the possessors more power than those who did not possess them. We begin to see the growing distinction between the "haves" and the "have-nots" with the development of agriculture and living in one place. Nomads minimize what they carry from place to place. People who live in one area can collect and possess more and more objects. The underlying competition for survival begins to fuel the contest of obtaining material possessions to communicate status and power to others. The possession of land and animals became a fundamental differentiating social factor between people. It also eventually required strangers to work for one another and become dependent upon one another. The need for different forms of cooperation emerged, along with different forms of competition. Here we see the dawning of unique psychosocial battles.

Our goal here is neither to demonize our agricultural ancestors nor romanticize our hunter-gatherer ancestors. Evidence exists that the hunter-gatherers also killed others both inside and outside of their groups. If another tribe hunting the same game threatened their livelihood, they fought. If a member of their group was a liability, they got rid of them. However, they are primarily known for working hard and having an egalitarian system. No current historical evidence exists that suggests some tribe members sat back and lived the good life while others hunted and gathered. Why humans began to settle and develop agricultural societies is unknown—some attribute it to climate change, opportunity, and chance discovery. Health declined with the advent of farming.

Nutrients were now limited to what people could cultivate and whether crops did well that season. We begin to see differentials in health and wealth. Social power grew for a few within the groups as they gained control of the resources that other members needed for survival.

Some of these farmers who controlled the river water for irrigation gained power enough to eventually become dominating political forces as well. When humans began to stay in one place they needed to build and organize communities. Customs and cultures began to form. Work roles became differentiated. Workers became further classified by social status and power they held within the group. No longer were humans hunting and gathering for survival. A human group "against" (i.e., competing with) another human group became the norm. Threat and survival competitions were further triggered. Humans wanted to keep their land and animals, so they fought those who threatened their livelihoods. Archaeologists inform us that one in every ten human skeletons during this time show evidence of physical blows. If your village's crops failed, invading the next village became necessary for survival. We were no longer competing with wild animals—we began competing with one another, and there were consequences and casualties along with new forms of conflict and social stratification. We will explore how this all contributes to workaches today.

The agricultural period was a critical turning point in human social history. The collective belief system about the status or worth of people changed. We assume this ignited a significant source of workaches, because beliefs about social hierarchies assign inferior and superior statuses to individuals.

Eventually, about 90 percent of the populations were cast as peasant workers and the remaining 10 percent as elites. Once cast, it was next to impossible to change status. Status was passed on to the next generation. Private claims to land with plants and animals meant that these resources were no longer freely available to all. If I now own the land and resources, you must come to me to get them, and because they are essential to your survival, I am now going to have power over you. You now can possibly work for me to earn these resources, or eventually trade or purchase them from me. I have gotten to the top of the social hierarchy here for no other reason than I now possess the resources you need. If you work for me, I need you, so I will invest some in your surviving, but your thriving is not of my concern.

The significance of this period in our collective history—the beginning of social stratification in the workplace—cannot be understated. Two basic types of individuals emerge at this point in human history: 1) the landowner who needs laborers; and 2) the laborer who needs work. Although we see the interdependence of needs, one of these individuals is going to have greater power and status over the other individual. Hands down, the person in control of resources for survival is going to be "on top." These social and cultural structures that we inherited from our ancestors have major ramifications for some workaches such as modern power plays and status displays in the workplace. No evidence has been uncovered that suggests there was anything inherently "better" about the people who moved into positions of power and then passed this status down to their heirs. We emphasize this point because so much shame and hurt occur in organizations over power and status. Knowledge about the origins of these dynamics can be useful for understanding and managing feelings of inadequacy that get triggered in the workgroup.

Are we inherently inadequate or do we just happen to occupy a role that has social implications based on a primitively constructed and arbitrary hierarchy?

We have witnessed the social pain of individuals who passively accept and do not question social beliefs about status and privilege. They falsely believe that they are inherently lesser than others just by the nature of their job classification, as if dictated by some truth of the universe. We will see how important it is to cognitively challenge and restructure these types of beliefs in Chapter 7.

This period of transition to agriculture, also called the birth of civilization, may also have been the point when what an individual performed as their work began to define their identity. A common question in modern times is "what do you do?" Work in our society has become a remarkable overlay of an individual's identity. This reality can present issues when someone is no longer able to work, has never worked, works in a socially devalued position, or when one is seeking to develop a deeper sense of themselves. The transition to retirement, for instance, is often experienced as an identity struggle due to these social artifacts. Doing and being are two distinct states of humanness. However, just "being" does not ensure survival and thereby affords less status and power, and often results in compromised self-esteem in our culture.

Work roles became further differentiated with the advancement of agriculture. Initially, the adults and children within a clan were the laborers. Eventually, as agriculture spread, others outside the clan were increasingly needed to complete all the work. The elite landowners and resource producers began to work less, and the others started to work more. The domestication of horses and cattle further delineated social class lines between the "haves and have-nots" because farmers could easily access further fields. The opportunity to exploit both animals and other humans for personal gain grew. The days of the more egalitarian hunter-gatherers began to dwindle in most regions of the globe.

The Origins of Workaches

The beginnings of workaches can be seen in the Agricultural Revolution. The new dynamic of one individual possessing socially sanctioned power over another individual both to obtain and bestow resources for survival was a significant shift. If one could not gain the favor of a "higher-up" on the social hierarchy (i.e., a controller of resources), they would not secure the necessary resources to survive. Strangers in hunter-gather days may have become occasional competitors if they happened to be hunting that same wild bison. New dynamics emerged between strangers in agricultural days as some people became dependent on others and those others henceforth gained power and status. The entire social structure and power dynamic changes if I now claim ownership over bison on my land, for example. You must now come to me to buy bison or work for me to earn your living to then buy some bison. Either way, you now need me for your survival and I therefore have power over you. Social power and status begin to reflect the competition for survival. It is no longer the best hunter or gatherer that ensures and maximizes survival. Social dynamics and workaches were thereafter to grow increasingly complex.

Evolutionary psychologists report that the maximum number of individuals these early groups could safely contain was approximately 150. If a group grew much bigger than this, people would be unable to know one another (i.e., predict safety) and organize in the best interests of the group. Even the evolutionary strategy of gossiping to transfer information on people starts to break down if there are too many folks and stories to follow. With the advent of commerce and money, people needed to extend their relations to even more strangers to maximize their profits. This business allowed for growing communities, as well as the exchange of ideas and customs. Accepting whatever the group assigned one as a role or status was adaptive for survival. What remained consistent in the agricultural period was the need of the individual to stay in the favor of the group. This need continued with the development of commerce, industrialization, and technological societies.

Because groups are powerful enough to determine if we are going to survive or not, group dynamics are intense and have a profound impact on us. Picking up the group's intent became increasingly vital to survival. We can begin to see how relevant the experience of shame was to our survival in our early groups. The individual needed to perceive when he or she was losing favor in the group. This need to know how others are experiencing us is a compelling argument for why we are so attentive to verbal and nonverbal signs from others. Shame can be viewed as adaptive, but in contemporary society, it no longer serves the same purpose. If someone devalues another on social media, survival is not at stake. Our ancestors needed to be aware when they were becoming devalued, because danger increased if negative social information about them was circulating in the group. To this day, we retain the impulse to put our ear to the wall when we think others are talking about us in the next room. In those days it might be gossip about who was not contributing to the group or who was consuming too many resources, rather than today's chatter about who might be getting a divorce or having an affair. It was important to know what social information or gossip was circulating so as to decide what one needed to do to retain membership or to prepare for quick exit. The unpleasant experience of shame was necessary for this context. We are wired to pick up that disapproving glance from a parent or judgmental stares from a group. We will later address how our social brains developed and adapted to ensure our survival, including the use of unpleasant emotions such as shame.

Further Differences and Suspicions

Our visceral experience of shame can be viewed as picking up on a potential threat from another individual or group. We possess, and we fear they see, some aspect of ourselves that they seem not to like or possess, and that they judge, devalue, and fear. Shame is such a profound experience for us that no other person has to even be around for us to experience it. Our internalized "eye of the other" is enough to shame us about our identity or behavior. This is most frightening when it occurs in a group in which we are a member. A prime example of this is ethnic identity. Approximately 50-80,000 years ago, ancient humans spread out from Africa across the continents. They were our first pioneers. These people adapted to their environments over time and generations, and their physical characteristics and traits changed accordingly. Their cultures, customs, and psychological characteristics also changed, as different geographical regions promoted the development of different traits. If they were closer to the equator, it was more adaptive to have increased melatonin in skin—which led to darker pigment—to be protected from to the sun. Having paler skin was more adaptive in climates with less direct sunlight available. If they came to live in more tropical areas, they would become tall and lean to lose heat. If they came to live in Arctic and mountain regions, it was more adaptive to be shorter and broader to conserve heat.

The farther groups wandered from one another, the less recognizable they became to one another. These differences would later come to be perceived as threatening. Depending on where communities were established, people began to cultivate and eat foods available in those areas, so even the foods eaten began to change. We eventually forgot that we were once one people. Contemporary humans can now experience shame about how they look or what they eat when the majority group raises that eye of suspicion. We diversified based on our particular environments, which now seems eclectic and enriching—but not to the primitive brain.

> Soon, differences took on negative significance. If appearance, food, clothes, and mannerisms were different, this could signal membership in a competing and threatening clan. So "different" is going to become interpreted deep in the brain as "threatening."

Humans did not develop spoken language until approximately 50-100,000 years ago. They communicated, but their communications were nonverbal. We have inherited from these preverbal ancestors the sensitivity to and keen awareness of nonverbal communications—facial gestures, body language, grunts, etc. We now have language to communicate but continue to use some of these primitive gestures. For example, the open hand gesture of greeting communicates friendliness and reveals to the other that there is no weapon in hand. This inherited sensitivity to nonverbal signs and signals has significant ramifications for nonverbal communications in the workplace. Our more primitive brain regions are suspicious of differences and constantly scanning for these types of threats. Fearing and shaming became close cousins in primitive times and continue to shadow us.

Social Hierarchies: Assigning Rank and Worth

Small clans grew into larger groups that eventually grew into larger communities. More roles and divisions of labor became necessary. Social hierarchies naturally and necessarily grew from the need for organization and role distribution. Hierarchy typically implies the rank someone has within a group in terms of the amount of power, influence, and dominance they possess (Koski, 2015). It is important to note here (for this will become most relevant in Chapter 8) that dominance has been divided into two types: 1) aggressive dominance characterized by achieving and maintaining power or access to resources through antisocial, possibly violent, behaviors; and 2) sociable dominance characterized by achieving and maintaining power through prosocial and cooperative behaviors (Kalma et al., 1993). In contemporary organizations where employee engagement and thriving are goals, aggressive dominance may no longer be needed. Individuals who show the group that they possess valuable traits and skills and are socially generous can attain high hierarchy positions (Anderson & Kilduff, 2009).

Social beliefs also evolved as larger networks of groups got organized—including beliefs about equality and social rank. The belief that some would be considered elite and others commoners or slaves would be passed down through generations. In order to survive in the new agricultural system, those dubbed peasants needed to adapt and adopt a "peasant" mindset to work hard for survival that was now in the hands of the elites. This mindset had to be passed down to future generations who were unlikely to escape this predetermined social status and work role. Social beliefs, however, do not come without consequence. This point is relevant to how we work today. We want to challenge our inherited mindsets if they are no longer adaptive. If we have inherited the mindset that we must work in unhealthy ways in order to survive—this must be challenged. Our understanding of Group 0 is important for this and many other reasons.

Hierarchies are complex and trigger remarkable emotions, from resentment to reverence. Social hierarchies that trigger shame and adversely impact self-esteem ultimately impact group cohesion or organizational functioning in negative ways. Individuals constantly scan for inequalities and unfairness. Social tensions trigger underlying survival battles and move the group away from the potential for thriving. Not all groups in nature exist with aggressive-dominance hierarchies. They may exist with differentiation of roles, but not with a sense of bestowing more worth, status, or resources on one member over another. Sociable-dominance hierarchies have theoretical appeal, but are sometimes harder to establish and maintain, possibly due to the human drive for a competitive survival advantage. Humans have more difficulty sharing equally due to all the nonconscious operations of our more primitive leanings. Our theoretical beliefs about equal sharing for all to thrive come into conflict with our survival instincts and drive for a competitive advantage in all our groups. Dominance hierarchies get created to organize and maintain the social order of large groups. However, they often fail to promote group harmony and fair distribution of resources. People on top are inclined to take more than what others perceive as their fair share, even though those on top may bring unique, valuable, and needed leadership talents to the group. These positions breed envy, jealousy, competitiveness, and aggression because they lower the status (survival potential) of those subordinates in the hierarchy. Awareness and management of these triggers and feelings is imperative. The building of a healthy hierarchy in any group is a delicate construction.

Whereas genetic evolution is slow, cultural evolution is much faster. As a culture and as individuals, we can learn to manage the emotions and social maneuvers we inherited from Group 0—such as fearing differences, devaluing others, gossiping, excluding others, and competing for survival when survival is not threatened. The time and energy that go into these dynamics can be better spent on building optimal and thriving organizations. Our rational abilities afford us opportunity to step back and gain perspective over our more primitive leanings and inherited mindsets. We can remain aware, for example, that brain parts adapted for our primitive ancestors still influence us today. We know the brain picks up social cues of status. A clear example of this is humans' nonconscious positive bias toward height in leaders. This was relevant in ancient times when a leader may have needed to physically overpower another. Today this is not a relevant need for our leaders yet remains a preference deep in our brains. Learning about our nonconscious bias affords us the possibility of managing it in order to choose the most adaptive leader for us today, as opposed to one that may have been needed in primitive times. We can also understand, for example, that differences are adaptive though we are suspicious of them. We can respect all the roles in an organization. We can act based on our wise goals and work to manage how we react based in emotional and misperceived threats.

A crucial goal is to guide our lower brain regions toward our wisest aspirations and ethical ideas and beliefs about equality and social justice. Today, survival is ensured for most, we need not compete and fight as much as we might be driven to by underlying nonconscious motivations. HHS organizations are in unique positions to forge meaningful social change and can lead the way forward in construction and update of organizational work systems. Whereas private industry is built on our financial system of capitalism and the acquisition of capital or wealth, public industry is built upon our sociopolitical system of democracy. This difference promotes a distinct manner of caring for the public, as well as for the worker. Community members or constituents must be educated about the unique potential of HHS for blazing these important and meaningful paths toward well-being promotion and thriving for all and for addressing some of the more adverse fallout from Group 0 on the American worker.

Group 1: Family of Origin (Parents and Siblings)

Just as Group 0 evolved over time, so has Group 1. The family group has evolved from a group of related individuals working together to stay alive and reproduce to a group committed to each members' attachment, engagement, enrichment, and thriving (ideally). Our ongoing connections to Group 1 reminds us how we are forever connected to other human beings throughout our lives—and even before our individual lives began. We all retain the physical and symbolic reminder of our connection to the other: though the umbilical cord cut affords us an individual self, our connections to others remain deeply rooted in the brain. Early life experiences have profound and lasting impacts on brain development and later human behaviors and experiences (Fox et al., 2010). These findings from neuroscientific studies on brain development and childhood emphasize the critical importance of Group 1. Unfortunately, not every family group has evolved to their ideal capacity. Every group still has the potential to be enriching and helpful or stressful and harmful.

We enter this world connected to the first "other"—our biological (m)other. Whether she raised us or not, she has passed on the genes and experiences of her past. She passed us the conditions of her womb when we were conjoined. We arrive into a group of one or more other(s). This group will be called our "family of origin" which is defined as the first social group we belong to. Many varieties of these initial groups exist—some will be enduring, while others will be more transient. For some, families and caregivers will change (e.g., adoptive and foster placements). For ease and simplicity, hereafter we use the terms parents and siblings to denote the family of origin, with the awareness that these terms have varied and diverse meanings and applicability. Whatever the constellation of the initial people in one's life, they will make permanent imprints and records in the brain. This first group will form a template of one's status, role, value, and identity. Experiences and identity in Group 1 remarkably impact future experiences and identities in Groups 2 and 3.

Though the umbilical cord gets cut to create our physical separateness, the invisible "neural" cord from brain to brain is never severed. We are forever connected to others.

In nature, it makes sense to be part of a group, as we saw with our primitive ancestors. We are not alone in navigating the threats of the world as a member of a pack. Many organisms in nature exist in groups. An ant, for example, would not survive alone, because it could not perform all the roles and duties necessary for survival. When we see a lone ant, we assume it is part of a colony, and it is likely out in the world performing its role for the group. It gives to the group, and the group gives back to it—and so they survive as a collective, even if one or more die. The ant colony is protective. We need one another, whether we are an insect or a human.

Relationship Essentials in Human Development

People are going to bring their unresolved issues from Group 1 into the workplace. Understanding some of the basics of development within this group is therefore important. Human infants are utterly dependent on their caregivers. They take a relatively long time to "leave the nest" (they are "altricial"). Other animals use a different developmental strategy and are mature in the womb and are mostly ready to go off on their own soon after birth (they are "precocial"). Some birds, for example, are hatched with their eyes open and can leave the nest within two days. Whales take longer to launch. A blue whale does not reach maturity until approximately 10 to 15 years of age. The longer an animal needs to remain "in the nest," the more critical social relations are due to this dependency. Parents must teach offspring the ways and strategies of physical and social survival in the pack. An altricial animal is preloaded and programmed with basic reflexes and some survival strategies but needs caregivers to provide advanced training and education.

Relationships are more important to those animals, such as humans, that have more extended dependency periods. We need others around us to survive. We need our caregivers to form attachments, so they will stay and take care of us in the best ways possible. We only have about nine months to grow from a single cell and be ready to emerge into the outside world. Human babies do most of their growing outside the womb after birth. Developmental theorists believe that this "early" entrance into the world allows for the brain and environment to interact more so the infant can adapt. The human brain starts learning inside the womb and will continue to learn and change for its entire lifespan.

We now know that the human brain does not reach maturity until approximately the mid to late twenties (Sukel, 2017). Humans' relatively long dependency period is one of the reasons scientists believe we have done so well on this planet to adapt and survive. Our prolonged dependency relationships give the brain plenty of time to learn about the most adaptive survival strategies for the times in which we are born. We really learn a lot before we leave the nest. And even after launching into adulthood, we remain interdependent with other people. The first people or relationships in our lives, however, form the templates in our brains for future relationships.

Studies on brain development identify attaching to a caregiver as a vital part of development (Sullivan, 2017). Neurobiological research on human attachment continues to reveal how much first relationships affect the brain and all future relationships, and researchers have even come to consider failed attachments as creating brain damage in the young developing brain. The process of attachment begins in the womb, but attachment issues or problems can begin even before one's existence, because they can be passed down through the generations (intergenerational transmission of pathology). If a parent had trauma or attachment issues with their own parent, this can impact their capacity to attach to their offspring. Wonderfully, we often see individuals who are capable of stopping this intergenerational transmission and can form secure attachments with their children though they did not have this in their own early experience. Parents who have a coherent understanding and narrative of their attachment to their own parents are able to create more optimal attachments to their own children.

How we make sense of our experiences and put them into words for ourselves and others is crucial to attachment and brain development (Siegel, 2015). We get to know ourselves, and then share ourselves, through our words and stories. A critical implication of this is that what happens to us may be less important than what we do with it and how we make sense of our adverse experiences. For example, this is similar to awakening from a stressful nightmare. We add soothing words, understanding, and context to the experience. The more we add to the experience—such as labeling it as a nightmare, giving it context, and thinking about what elements may have emerged from our real experience—help to make sense of the nightmare and integrate into a larger story of ourselves. We help children make sense of their experiences (such as a nightmare) initially through our relational presence, emotional soothing, and later by helping them place experiences within a cognitive and integrated biographical context. We are a story-telling people. This is an important point to keep in mind when we address managing and healing from workaches in Chapter 7.

The biochemistry of the biological mother changes to facilitate the process of bonding to the unborn child. Oxytocin, the hormone that is considered the "bonding" chemical, circulates in especially high amounts during pregnancy and breastfeeding. The womb is a perfect environment in which to grow and develop safely and comfortably—a nurturing environment where all needs are provided for and all senses soothed. Ideal conditions of a womb create a "bath" of rewarding chemicals for the fetus to develop. If the pregnant mother has adequate support and sufficient resources in her personal and professional life, she is releasing reward chemicals (e.g., oxytocin) that circulate through her and her fetus.

However, like any other environment an individual will find themselves in, there are often less than ideal conditions. Stress that is short-term and can be relieved with address and rest is not considered to have any adverse effects (Dhabhar, 2012). However, if the pregnant woman gets too stressed, due to high-intensity or prolonged stressors, she secretes stress hormones. Research has shown that chronic stress can build up in amniotic fluid and create harm (La Marca, 2017). We are more aware and educated as a society about the harmful effects of a mother consuming potentially harmful chemicals, such as those in drugs, that might affect her developing baby, but we are less educated about the internal chemicals that are manufactured, released, and circulated within the bodies of both mother and child. The implication of this research to organizations is that prolonged and high levels of stress at work can even impact future generations.

Four Remarkable "A's" of Development

Attunement +	Attachment +	Abandonment -	Annihilation -

Four "A-experiences"—attachment, attunement, abandonment, and annihilation—profoundly impact development. The process of a caregiver observing and attending to the child's different states and needs is called attunement. The caregiver is sensitive—attuned—to the child's internal life. The relationship between child and caregiver is a template for future development and relationships. Life stressors occur immediately in the world outside the womb. The birth process itself is stressful to both mother and child. The infant releases stress hormones during birth (internal) and cries for help (external). Ideally, a caregiver soothes the infant, allowing it then to release reward chemicals. The caregiver is teaching the baby that it can go from a body state of distress to a state of calm. The child will eventually be responsible for this process of emotional regulation in times of stress. The individual differences observable in the regulation of emotions in the workplace can derive from these early experiences in Group 1.

The ability to self-regulate emotions is a critical human capacity.

Self-regulation is vital in groups where relationships trigger our threat system. A child is neurobiologically at risk if the caregiver is unable to provide, teach, and model emotional self-regulation. The inability or unavailability of the caregiver to calm the nervous system of the baby is often the beginning of developmental trauma. Nonverbal gestures such as eye contact and touch are vital sources of sensory comfort and soothing. Objects such as blankets and pacifiers become substitutes for eliciting soothing and calming of the nervous system. They are called transitional objects, and we later bring them into our workplaces in the more adult form of knickknacks and photos. When the caregiver is a source of threat or fear, this is remarkably distressing to a child. A baby goes toward the primary caregiver because that is pre-programmed in the brain. However, a baby moves away from a stressor because survival is also pre-programmed. This dilemma can lead to insecure attachments. The stress created in a child by their perceiving that there is no one to take care of them in the world consistently (ensure their survival) is significant. The brain stores these experiences, and this history emerges in future relationships including those in the workplace—especially in relations with authority figures. Stress responses in children are often confused with misbehavior. Stress responses in adults can also be misperceived and misjudged.

Siblings in a family also contribute to complex emotional dynamics. Competition with siblings and, eventually, with schoolmates and coworkers is part of human nature. Some of this competition may be overt, but a lot of it is out of awareness. Our primitive ancestors survived famines and hunting and crop failures that led to scarcity of resources for survival. Many children died before reaching adulthood. While most no longer have to worry about these scenarios, we still experience anxiety as if our survival is threatened. These primitive fears are encoded in the nonconscious regions of the brain. These struggles for resources, as if survival is threatened, are sometimes acted out in the family, school, and workplace.

Secure attachment is needed for optimal brain growth. The caregiver is fully bonded to the child but also establishes that the two have independent identities or selves that are connected through deep bonding. The ideal caregiver models respect for the self and the other, and is attuned to the needs of the other. Abandonment can range from intermittent and temporary to chronic and complete. Annihilation refers to when a caregiver fails to acknowledge the existence of a separate self in the infant. The causes of annihilation can range from the primary caregiver's avoiding the infant to the primary caregiver's having such a narcissistic self that they do not recognize the separateness of the infant. This dynamic can be overwhelming, emotionally smothering, and anxiety provoking for the infant. In either form of annihilation, the independent self of the child is sacrificed and leads to severe psychological consequences. Annihilating behaviors create tremendous fear in children because they imply that the child is unseen or nonexistent. The nonconscious fear is that caregivers may not offer necessities for survival. Occasionally, this is not a fear, but an unfortunate reality. Child welfare staff encounter this when a child is discovered captive, and the guardian has obliterated the self of the child and made them into an object. The child has not been abandoned but has been psychologically annihilated. Of course, different forms of this range from mild to severe, as in the above-referenced example.

In summary, the four "A's" of human development are critical in brain development. Attachment and attunement facilitate optimal brain growth and development, while their opposites can result in psychic and even brain damage. The effects of the first A's are experienced through the lifetime of the individual and have ramifications for future generations. Children and adults share a core need to be valued and cared about within a secure relationship (DeWall et at., 2011). When this does not occur, there are impacts not only on the emotional experience or feelings of that person, but also on their brain. Disruptions in early bonding and attachment to caregivers leads to later difficulty in interpersonal relationships and self-regulation of emotions.

Reflecting on the psychosocial dynamics of our own early experience in Group 1 is essential to promote awareness, understanding, and compassion in our adult selves and relationships. When we look at our behavior through the lens of our childhood, we can make more sense of our actions and reactions in our adulthood interpersonal realm. This understanding and integrating of Group 1 experiences can lead to more adaptive navigating through relationships with other groups and individuals in our lives. Once we look through this lens at ourselves, we can also look at our colleagues through this same lens. Often, we can better understand why a coworker, boss, or client may be behaving in a manner that does not make immediate sense when we have a historical perspective.

Group 2: School (Teachers and Peers)

People bring their unresolved issues from school into the workplace. Experiences in the classroom and on the playground further influence our self-concepts and relationships with authority figures and peers. A major developmental step occurs upon leaving the protection of Group 1 and becoming a part of Group 2. Children typically move from the closed group of parents and siblings to an open group of strangers who become their "managers" and peers. This is a major step for the primitive brain that was adapted to living, learning, and working within a small family clan.

Children enter schools with mindsets shaped by their families of origin, as well as with inherited traits from how the brain was sculpted from Group 0. Group 2 affords the opportunity for social growth and new learning. The classroom and peer group have been shown to influence us significantly. Even though school is considered a place to learn, it becomes much more than that to most people. Group 2 can be a refuge and compensate for adverse family experiences. It can become a secondary source of psychological sustenance and relationship. Much research has amassed over the years on the role school plays not only on cognitive development, but on psychological and social development, including development of self-esteem and self-efficacy (Brooks et al., 2010). Much opportunity exists in Group 2, but the possibility of adverse experiences, unfortunately, exists as well. If Group 1 was adequate and provided secure attachment and resources for positive self-esteem and emotional regulation, a child is better fortified to withstand any adverse experiences at school. If Group 1 was less than adequate, the child might be more vulnerable to psychosocial assaults in the academic and social play arenas. As with any group in our lives, it can be a source of stress and struggle for survival or a source of engagement, enrichment, and thriving.

Moreover, because the playground never ends—as we have all heard and probably experienced—the shadow of these experiences carries over to Group 3. In addition, feelings of likeability and acceptance by schoolmates follow people into the work breakroom and after-hours socializing, as do early social exclusion experiences. Social exclusion has been shown to create significant risk for later problems with work, substance abuse, and overall well-being (Bynner, 1996) due to associated brain impacts (Williams, 2009). Explicit academic hierarchies exist at school, which can be reminiscent of the hierarchies started by our primitive ancestors. Academic measures are typically based on performance relative to other classmates. If you get a grade of a "C" you are pretty much aware that you were less academically worthy than your classmate who earned an "A." Sensitive issues related to inclusion and exclusion, including academic achievement differences, arise in this arena that have lasting impacts on self-esteem and self-concept in students. Feelings of competence and professional esteem often grow out of historical academic success, and academic success has a positive correlation with self-concept into adulthood (Enam, 2006). Academic performance then shadows job performance.

Learning differences also have remarkable impact on self-esteem and self-concept in students. The school group ideally values each of its students equally and respects individual differences (including learning differences) and develops unique talents. Not all brains are the same, and some children learn differently than others. There is a growing notion that the world needs different minds—"neurodiversity"—so that a variety of individuals can meet the variety of issues and needs that arise. However, the historical tendency to equate learning differences with different intelligence levels has assaulted self-esteem remarkably for some individuals. Just the label of "learning disability" has promoted shame and misjudgment about learning differences. We are now beginning to acknowledge the value of having "different intelligences" in the workplace. Unfortunately, most children do not understand this and feel inferior to those who learn in the manner that is typically promoted in traditional schools. Conformity to traditional academic norms (e.g., the three "Rs") has been a significant pressure in Group 2.

Many other social, cultural, and global factors also exert pressure on Group 2. A growing awareness suggests that with increased global competition, the emphasis on STEM fields (Science, Technology, Engineering, Mathematics) is going to alienate those creative students whose talents and interest lie in other areas. We see global antagonism and a race for more and more sophisticated technology for warfare. This contest creates threats to survival and subsequent pressure on citizens to compete and to create better weapons. If the next war is waged via artificial intelligence, competitive pressure exists to produce students who can compete in this realm. We are also in an electronic age and the national and global competitions often occur in this arena. The self-esteem of the students whose interests and talents lie elsewhere are further at risk. The child who can code versus the child who can construct a poem is going to be valued differently in this context. Thriving could be equally and differently served by the poet or the coder. We need both. We need all. Later, in Chapter 8, we will examine how valuable collective intelligence (all the different shared intelligences that diverse individuals bring to a group) is for organizations.

The other significant arena of Group 2 is the playground or schoolyard, where a great deal of play and socialization occur in childhood. The playground has been viewed as an important place for social and emotional development, with opportunities for learning team building and conflict resolution. The American Academy of Pediatrics (AAP) released recommendations for ensuring children have recess, because "recess promotes social and emotional learning and development for children by offering them a time to engage in peer interactions in which they practice and role play essential social skills" (American Academy of Pediatrics, 2012). However, there is another side to the playground that must be identified and managed. A great deal of "other stuff" occurs here too, such as bullying and excluding, that has adverse impacts on development. Social exclusion and bullying extract great tolls on the brains and experiences of children. Recess is dreaded by some and coveted by others.

Social competition, in addition to academic competition and ranking, exists in Group 2. If you are picked last for the kickball game on the playground or not invited to the party, you are aware that you are not one of the "cool" kids. Social exclusion on the playground foreshadows similar experiences in workplace lunchrooms and after-work gatherings. Recess management is crucial. A 2010 Gallup survey revealed that 89 percent of behavioral problems occurred during lunch and recess. Schoolmates serve as mirrors informing (or misinforming) us of our likeability and acceptance. Playground experiences reflect if we are worthy of being picked for the team. The group informs us if we are to lead or follow, and if we are in or out. The group can become a threat or a social haven.

The critical social mirror reflecting if the group approves or disapproves, includes or excludes, or likes or dislikes a member only intensifies in adolescence. Peers have even greater roles and impact on adolescents (Leets & Wolf, 2005) because they typically transition dependence on primary family members to peers. Social acceptance from peers becomes important to self-esteem and an adolescent's sense of self. Adverse peer experiences lead to diminished self-esteem, self-concept, and self-efficacy, which follow the individual into Group 3. Fortunately, Group 2 has also been evolving and students' psychosocial well-being has become a major focus.

Group 2 in its ideal form can be a protective, engaging, and enriching environment in which students can learn positive concepts about self and others, in addition to academic learning. An enriching school group can serve as a great model for a later work group. A great deal of group and team building gets promoted in most school environments. Campuses typically have clubs and other arenas to promote varied interests and identities. Colors and mascots identify group membership. Counselors are present to encourage and support further development and "next steps." Some of these resources may not be available in Group 3.

Our exit from Group 2 comes with significant developmental losses. One of the most remarkable of these losses is the loss of dedicated caregivers who were specifically assigned to us. Our parents or caregivers from Group 1 were assigned responsibility for our care, development, and well-being. Some of this care was then transferred to the school, and our caregivers had to trust in others to be responsible in their roles with us. The term "alma mater" that refers to the secondary school we attended, means "nourishing mother" in Latin. We lose this "parental" oversight once we transfer into the workgroup. There are no longer dedicated adults responsible for our care, development, and well-being. We have abruptly become independent adults responsible for our own care and welfare.

Group 3: Workplace (Bosses and Coworkers)

Leaving one's clan to join strangers in an unfamiliar environment is unnatural (other than for mating) and risky for survival, and this is how the more primitive regions of the brain experience leaving Group 1 to enter Group 2—it is strange. Separation anxiety—exhibited by the child who clings to the parent when entering the classroom—may be an echo of this prehistoric reaction. Leaving Group 2 to enter Group 3 is even stranger. Many individuals report receiving minimal assistance in the transition to work. The expectation is strictly to perform. The tables have dramatically turned, and somehow, we have become the ones to serve, teach, help, and protect others—others we do not really know, others who have not been part of our clan, and who now surround us. We have become a cooperative and interconnected society. Meeting new people and moving in and out of different groups is adaptive to our cultural evolution. With the advent of trade and commerce, the need for socializing increased, because strangers became potential enhancers to survival. Nonetheless, we remain wary, and certain parts of our brain are always on guard. Cooperation ends, and competition ignites with any perceived threat.

Our experience in the social world of Group 3 is complicated by the progressive and cumulative effects of what we experienced and learned and how we were impacted by prior groups. By the time we join a workgroup, we have learned what groups are and how we fit in those groups. We enter with preconceived notions of our own and others' value, role, and status in the group—because we see strangers or other people through the lenses we developed in our previous groups. This means we may sometimes project onto them the ideas we learned about people from our previous group interactions and relations, just as we often unknowingly play our "assigned role" by bringing our previous role identities to our workgroups. If our early families were led by disorganized, incompetent, or immature parents, we might have been the child (adultified and parentified) in the family to become highly organized and responsible. If our work environment mimics our childhood environment, it is easier to assume this role again. We are more likely to compensate for others and take on responsibilities and job duties that really do not belong to us. If we did not have siblings to help us learn how to compromise and negotiate, it might be more challenging to share and cooperate with others on our teams. By now, most of us have learned to present a social façade to accommodate the majority group. We quickly figure out the social norms of the workgroup to increase our chances of inclusion. Most learn to at least adapt to the group culture to avoid moving into disfavor with the group.

The essential provision of group membership is security. Security is essential for survival and is of the utmost importance to the primitive brain, which doesn't discriminate between physical and psychosocial threats. Most individuals will work hard and sacrifice much to obtain and retain group membership. Gangs and cults capitalize on this need for group membership for security. These groups recruit vulnerable individuals with the promise of a "new family" and protection. If the group fails to provide the individual member with security, the automatic threat system is triggered, which results in a significant cascade of biochemical events. Conversely, if the group provides the individual with consistent and adequate protection, the member will have security and feel safe and rewarded with neurochemicals that create a feeling of pleasure. We will detail these neurochemical events in later chapters. As we see, individuals are vulnerable in the workplace and growing recognition of this has led to attention being afforded to the well-being of employees.

A Brief History of Workplace Wellness

Early on, the workplace was not designed to care about survival, let alone thriving. The workplace has changed remarkably over time, in most ways for the better. The exploitation of workers has a long but diminishing history across the globe. Early workers were predominantly perceived as servants, but they were needed so their survival was attended to in part by others. Through the centuries and with industrialization, notions of human rights and social justice led to the formation of labor unions and worker's rights movements. These can be seen as the precursors of workplace wellness cultures.

The first documented proponent of workplace wellness was a physician, Bernardini Ramazzini, who in 1700 wrote about occupational diseases and the need to explore preventative measures for the workplace (Franco et al., 2001). The first person known to advocate for more reasonable working hours was Robert Marcus Owen who, in 1810, proposed the 10-hour workday. He later went on in 1817 to advocate for an 8-hour workday. He is said to have coined the phrase, "eight hours labor, eight hours recreation, eight hours rest" (Donnachie, 2005). The Ford Motor Company was one of the first employers to transition to the 8-hour workday in 1914, and this has been the standard in the workplace ever since. Labor unions in the United States have long advocated for the protection of workers in one way or the other from early on in American history. The Department of Labor was established in 1913, when the federal government formally became involved in occupational safety, wage and hour standards, and other employee rights and protections. As companies were fined more for workers' injuries and fatalities, they began to increase safety concerns and practices. The early years of occupational safety strictly focused on physical safety; psychological health wouldn't be on the horizon for another half-century.

The first Employee Assistance Programs (EAPs) were developed in the 1950s with a focus on the treatment of alcoholism. In the 1970s, financial and cultural pressures led to a rise in EAPs that finally focused on the psychological well-being of employees. Healthcare costs shifted from government to employer, which motivated more employers to attend to the health of employees. Fitness and stress management became important issues, and EAPs evolved further and grew in number across the nation. During this time, we also saw a growing influence of government initiatives, such as one that encouraged employers to identify depression in their employees. This furthered attention to not only physical but emotional issues at work. EAPs began to offer more comprehensive treatment for psychological issues. The need for and benefits of wellness programs in the contemporary workplace is now well documented. We will discuss these issues more in later chapters.

We are witnessing newer generations of people and different groups of workers seeking to work differently. Physicians, for example, have historically been some of our hardest workers in terms of hours invested and efforts dedicated to their services. As a group, physicians have been rewarded financially and socially with high status and prestige. However, we are seeing this is no longer enough. Burnout among physicians is now considered a public health crisis (Harvard Global Health Institute, 2019). Burnout was characterized in this study by emotional exhaustion, sense of depersonalization, and loss of efficiency on the job. Physician groups are demanding wellness and increasing focus on their thriving. Calls for "chief wellness officers" for staff in health care organizations have recently gone out. Increased awareness of physicians' vulnerabilities and resultant interventions have begun to yield positive results (Shanafelt et al., 2019). Physicians are not alone in confronting this issue or in embracing this contemporary consciousness. Forging organizational change based on what is going on "now—as opposed to doing things the way we used to—is essential for evolving organizations. The calls today for thriving in the workplace are now loud and clear. Surviving is just no longer enough to sustain and satisfy the workforce.

The workplace has undergone a remarkable evolution regarding physical and psychological safety. Some groups around the world have done this better than others. Sometimes we do not understand the different cultures of different groups across the globe from the lens of our own culture. However, survival is dependent upon being adaptive. Different groups get structured, function, and change based on very different environmental conditions and pressures. The hope is that continued change occurs in the direction of increased compassion and social justice for all, wherever we are on the globe.

Natural and Cultural Evolution of Groups

The workplace has changed over time because we have changed. Work will continue to adapt to our changing thoughts, beliefs, feelings, and needs. Humans have developed together within groups through the processes of natural and cultural evolution. Natural evolution is the process in which organisms adapt to their environments in ways that maximize physical survival. Some people also label this biological or genetic evolution. Natural evolution has been occurring for millions of years to suit us for our changing environments most adaptively. No right nor wrong or particular direction occurs with natural evolution. Traits are selected to continue or change based in the environment at any given time. Human populations continue to evolve biologically to this day. Our ability to digest milk products is one interesting example (Max, 2017). In prehistoric times, humans only had the enzyme to digest milk as infants when breast milk was available. The production of the enzyme to digest milk was then turned off after that developmental period because there were no milk sources available. However, approximately 9,000 years ago, as some humans moved from hunting animals to herding them, milk sources became available. The herding humans eventually, through the process of natural evolution, developed the enzymes and thereby the ability to digest milk. Other fascinating adaptions in insects, animals, and plants occur throughout our world. Birds who live in the city evolve different beaks than their country cousins in order to eat in the city. Ants in the city have evolved digestive systems to survive on junk food (Worrall, 2018).

The process of natural evolution in nature offers HHS organizations vital wisdom about best practices for making changes. Adaptation in nature is not bound to the bias to do things the same as yesterday. Change is not a threat, but typically a biological advantage to organisms. Natural evolution and adaptations have served us well—we humans are still here. But natural evolution does not concern itself with our life satisfaction or happiness—it facilitates physical survival. It is our cultural evolution that can create our thriving at work.

We must balance our fear and resistance to change with the wisdom of "survival of the most adaptive."

Cultural or social evolution is the process in which human customs, beliefs, ideas, social attitudes, and ways of life change through time in a society. Cultural evolution typically goes at a faster pace than natural evolution. We are much more in the driver's seat of cultural evolution. The HHS workforce contributes each day to the cultural evolution of our society.

Cultural evolution emerges from the most recently evolved and wisest segments of our brains because we can imagine a better future. Many humans are learning that we do not have to be so competitive to survive, that we can cooperate. Indeed, we still witness those who will do almost anything to have a competitive edge and will dominate and use others for their own gain. But the collective has less tolerance for obvious unfairness, especially in civilizations that project images of social justice and respect for the sanctity of each individual life. Learning and imagination fuel cultural evolution.

Technology has propelled our cultural evolution to an unprecedented rate of change. As just one of the most immediate examples, information spreads rapidly, and relationships can be created, maintained, and ended on electronic devices. Our electronic age has also levied a significant impact on the velocity of work. The introduction of machines during the Industrial Revolution came with significant numbers of documented physical injuries and fatalities. We must now be aware and measure both the physical and psychological injuries our technological and electronic revolution may be inflicting on workers today. The speed of delivery of vast amounts of information from these devices comes with a burden on those in possession of them. The utilization of electronic devices, to date, has also not reduced the workload, but actually has increased expectations and pressures, and when these devices go home with employees, so does work. Many employers expect their employees to respond to text or emails when not at work, and the amount of emails in the morning inbox can be overwhelming to many. The use of machines was predicted to reduce the load of work on people during the Industrial Revolution, but it did not.

Figure 2.1, below, illustrates the revolutions that have remarkably changed and influenced human societies, sometimes more rapidly than the brain could evolve and catch up. Every significant change in human society has come with both advantages and disadvantages. What we must watch out for in this newest wave, the Fourth Industrial Revolution, are further inequalities and inequities as well as unforeseen physical and psychological injuries—workaches.

PERIOD	CHANGES	IMPACT ON WORK
AGRICULTURAL REVOLUTION (~ 12,000 years ago)	▪ Small nomadic bands of hunter-gatherers settle ▪ Farming of crops and animal husbandry lead to larger communities ▪ Population size relative to area increases	▪ Creation of hierarchies and inequalities due to division of labor ▪ Land ownership ▪ Necessity of hiring strangers to do work ▪ Increased social divisions between owners and workers
INDUSTRIAL REVOLUTION #1 (~ 1750 in England)	▪ Work becomes more mechanized ▪ Manufacturing of goods shifts from homes to factories ▪ Mechanization leads to mass production ▪ Business and factory owners see	▪ Work moves out of home ▪ 14-16-hour days and 6-day weeks the norm for children and adults ▪ Low wages ▪ High number of injuries and fatalities

PERIOD	CHANGES	IMPACT ON WORK
	workers as highly replaceable ▪ Populations become denser due to localized availability of work	▪ Minimal concern for worker health and safety ▪ Pollution
INDUSTRIAL REVOLUTION #2 (Technological) (1870-1914)	▪ Mass production is the norm (e.g., Ford assembly line) ▪ Petroleum, electricity, and steel industries expand ▪ Urbanization increases as workers seek housing in cities near factories	▪ Labor market expansion ▪ Diversification of jobs ▪ Some jobs threatened by automation ▪ Work hierarchies further established ▪ Increasing pollution with health impacts on workers
INDUSTRIAL REVOLUTION #3 (Digital) (1969-current)	▪ Computer technologies become ubiquitous in work and personal life ▪ Novel materials are invented ▪ The Internet connects the world and enables increasing globalization	▪ Labor specialization ▪ Telecommuting (return work to home) ▪ Increase in need for skilled labor ▪ Loss of certain jobs to machines, computerization, and automation ▪ Loss of certain jobs (e.g., coal-related) due to changes in environmental concerns

PERIOD	CHANGES	IMPACT ON WORK
INDUSTRIAL REVOLUTION #4 (emergent)	▪ Lines between real and virtual blur ▪ Artificial intelligence enters many industries ▪ Technologies increasingly replace people ▪ Genetic engineering is norm in agriculture and expands to other industries	

Figure 2.1

The Divide Widens at Work

Increased need for labor to build, operate, sell, fix, and update machines came with each period of the Industrial Revolution. The production of the first automobiles required many phases of work from inception to maintenance and beyond. The automobile industry employed many people, from engineers to mechanics. Pay was not distributed equally per hour per employee, although all were needed to build a car. Worth was assigned to each role, and pay was set up accordingly. People were assigned their professional financial worth on the job which then ultimately translated to their social worth off the job. Social worth was also determined by other factors such as race, physical appearance, and gender. Money and power increasingly became possessions of a select few who then passed it down to their heirs. Breaking into this system became increasingly difficult.

With each phase of the Industrial Revolution also came increased social stratification, hierarchy, and status differentials. For example, there became the "haves" who owned a car and the "have-nots" who did not. The haves needed the have-nots in order to possess a car, and the have-nots needed the haves to buy the car to keep them employed. Although this may sound like a win-win situation, the psychosocial ramifications of this—including reactions to the inequitable distribution of value, esteem, and respect and underlying perceptions of unfairness at work—were profound. Primitive aspects of the brain do not take well to inequity because it threatens survival. Unequal access to resources creates remarkable social animosity. Envy evolved as an adaptive trait—wanting what other clans had maximized survival when, for example, the possession was a better tool for hunting. Envy in contemporary society is often maladaptive when it becomes part of status battles and fuels perceptions of unfairness. Technology now allows people to "see" what others have that they do not. Different forms of media, for example, that reveal what the "rich and famous" possess may be amusing, but they can breed and fuel nonconscious contests. Humans have a dilemma here—on the one hand the drive for status and rank results in conflicts, but on the other hand, the achievement and maintenance of status does afford significant survival benefits (Fernald & Maruska, 2012).

We sometimes need and choose leaders who possess and project power and status, and then come to resent the power and status we have afforded them. Organizations need to assign different levels of power to certain roles in order to function (Anderson & Brion, 2014). Certain people possess the traits needed to fulfill and maintain these roles. We must remain aware of our very human and nonconscious drivers toward status and power, and counterbalance or integrate them with the wisdom and compassion that can serve all in contemporary culture. Human nature is complex! In the next two chapters, we will explore how these human traits breed underlying resentment and tensions between people, and where these experiences lay tracks in our brains. Hunter-gatherers had equal access to shelter and food. The subsequent Agricultural and Industrial Revolutions changed this. Civilization has improved in many ways, but there have been costs. Economic and social divides have grown remarkably. The distribution of economic reward is beyond the scope of *Workaches*. We do, however, examine some of the underlying psychosocial stress that can result from these divides in the workplace.

People need to feel valued and respected to thrive, and therefore for groups to thrive, relational equality is essential.

Organizational role hierarchies to manage members and achieve group and individual goals are necessary beginning in Group 1. Systems move into disharmony when there are missing organizing forces. However, there is no compelling reason that any member should hold less value or be perceived as lesser than any other. Group 3 is no exception, despite variable pay scales, positions, and responsibilities. We just must keep figuring out better ways of organizing and managing while upholding respect for human dignity. This must be done while we seek increased understanding about what motivates and engages individuals to thrive at work.

Human groups have served different purposes over the course of our evolutionary history. They all began and were organized around the goal of having their members survive. The goal of the group as a source for thriving was long in the coming. It started to happen in Group 1 when children and family members began to be perceived as emotional attachments rather than objects or free labor. It happened in Group 2 when student individuality, engagement, and enrichment became to be prioritized over obedience and rote learning. It is increasingly happening in Group 3.

Forging Compassionate and Evidence-Based Change

Given all the conscious and nonconscious complexities of social interactions and the relatively short period of time that we strangers have been working together, we are not doing that bad of a job. Many are working tirelessly to understand and remedy the issues of a fast-changing workplace that is on the brink of a Fourth Industrial Revolution. We continue to evolve. Hopefully, our collective wisdom (less our global primitive competitiveness) plays a crucial role in progress toward increased social justice. The competitiveness can get out of hand and lead to both psychological and physical damage and annihilation, but when managed well, competitiveness can lead to incredible advances and inventions in all areas of human life.

It becomes crucial to critically examine and differentiate between our survival-based primitive underlying drivers and our higher and wiser leanings.

We must remain aware of the contest between nonconscious fears and lack of knowledge or exposure and conscious wisdom. One of the most important reasons for understanding all these underlying group dynamics and behaviors is to have increased perspective, and thereby more choice and better options with regard to how we want to act. The goal is to assess and to be aware of the dynamics we are entering in order to have a choice about whether to participate in certain social dynamics and games. Typically, when we are first introduced to a board game, we query, "what is the object of this game?" "How do I win or lose?" "What are the rules of play?" You then get to decide if this game is acceptable and if you want to play or not. Then you get to develop strategies that will facilitate your goal, which is typically to win at that particular game.

Humans enter evolutionary games unknowingly and without rules of play. We are programmed in nonconscious arenas to play. We need to consciously gain perspective on the objectives and costs so we are most at choice. We need to stay aware that even if we have the sense that we are winning, what are the costs to the "losers" and is that acceptable. Awareness can lead to managing some of these group or social pressures.

REFLECTION

Think about how you assign worth or status to objects or people. Is gold more important than silver? If you assign higher value to gold, is it because others have assigned it greater economic value? Or do you prefer its color? How do you assign worth to other human beings? By their roles in the world? The amount of money they possess? Is the actor in a film more important than the writer? How do you feel about your own social status in the world? Does it change based in what you possess or what you are doing at any moment in time? Is it based in any way on what other person you are with and the status they possess? Do you ever feel that someone at work is somehow taking away from your status? How do you recover your sense of status or self-worth after it has been damaged or when you have been shamed or humiliated? How would you ideally like to think and feel about status at work?

In the workplace, ideally, diversity of talents and skills within the group would be appreciated and valued. We need different people to contribute and cooperate to make a product or fulfill different missions. Most groups benefit from members not being in the same lane or not being clones of one another. The timepiece in Figure 2.2 offers a meaningful analogy about assigning higher and lower value to members of a group. In this case, mechanical pieces working together to form a whole and achieve a common purpose—offering us an answer to, “what time is it?”

Figure 2.2

We appreciate varied answers and great discussions when we pose the question of the timepiece. Group members are actively utilizing their higher brain regions to rationally and ethically discuss status and worth. We know, however, that more primitive nonconscious regions do have bias and do assign higher value and status to certain attributes of objects or traits of people. We discuss this further in the next two chapters. For now, though, if we return to the timepiece and apply reason, we know that all parts work together to offer us the time of day. We see a cooperative organization of diverse parts. The more “introverted” components work behind the scenes. The more “extroverted” ones display in front. And the protective encasing components safeguard the whole group. No need exists to assign a hierarchy to determine what part is more important than another. If we somehow had to offer more status, power, and pay to each component in a timepiece organization, some might say that the hands and numbers are the most important due to their performance visibility. Others might argue that the inner components are more valuable because they create the displayed time. Fortunately, we do not need to answer this question. We do, however, within organizations of people. Beyond earning less money, individuals who perceive that they are not fairly compensated in their roles may feel less valued than others and this often extends into their personal realms. This is a workache. Shame is a significant symptom of hierarchical systems that assign different worth to each component of the organization.

Acknowledging that a great deal of unintentional shaming takes place in an organization is important. Individuals are having to manage shame when positioned in a ranking system such as a hierarchy because status and its underlying driver—survival—frequently get threatened.

Our primitive human drive is to rise as high as possible in a hierarchy. This is no different than getting to higher land when there is a flood. Survival is at stake. Individuals are valued or devalued based in their assigned or assumed positions. People "know where they stand." They feel it in Groups 1, 2, and 3. Individuals work to reduce the bad feeling of inadequacy and shame. The pressure begins in Group 1 to study and get good grades in Group 2 in order to get the best job in Group 3. We learned that primitive survival drivers favor the acquisition of power in humans. Greater rewards of power and status typically come with competitiveness than with cooperativeness in contemporary society. Especially since the Industrial Revolution, financial security and material objects display status and power in America. Conscious and nonconscious drivers of survival pressure individuals toward climbing the social hierarchy or remaining on top of it. Emphasis gets placed on how to be more competitive versus discovering one's unique talents and strengths.

Families who have status need the next generation to compete and to keep it. Families who do not have status need the next generation to compete to achieve it. Pressure exists on all levels of a social hierarchy. Consider the all-too-common case of suicidal university students, particularly international students, who become distraught if not earning the academic grades needed to ensure they will "make it" in America. The anxiety and fear of being a disappointment to family is profound. Some of these students are not studying to learn in their desired and chosen fields. They are there to shed the shame and raise the status of their families; they are in survival mode. They are typically vying for positions in highly competitive graduate programs leading to degrees in professions that can afford them higher power and esteem. Work, for these students, is often viewed through the prehistoric lens of survival. Work is not about self-realization and expression and personal contributions to the group. We must challenge and crucially examine the social drivers and dynamics in all the developmental groups of our lives. We must question, or we will continue to suffer damaging workaches. As we will see throughout

Workaches, much of what we must manage in our work lives is content that exists mostly beneath our conscious awareness or in our nonconscious arenas. Luckily, it is possible to move nonconscious material to conscious awareness as we will see. And even if we are unable to relocate nonconscious material to conscious awareness, just being aware that it exists in the underground of our minds is important.

America has evolved to have an interesting mix of economic, political, and philosophical ideas and practices. The ultimate question or struggle here becomes balancing or integrating the different components of our complex operating system. Ideas and systems, similar to people, have relationships too. They move through relational periods of compatibility and incompatibility when put into practice. They have conflicts. Sometimes they are more harmonious and can coexist. We have a capitalistic economic system in which private individuals and businesses compete for resources and wealth. Capital accumulation or profit is the goal. Workers power these private industries. At the same time, we have a democratic governmental system that promotes equality and cooperation among its citizens. Workers power public organizations too. The continuing challenge is to balance competition and cooperation. Public service organizations work for people, not profits, but still must be paid. Private organizations typically work for financial profit, but still must concern themselves with humanitarian issues. Whether in the public or private domain, all workers are impacted by how much they are paid and if they are treated with respect and feel valued. This is the common intersection of private industry and public service.

We need each other in all our groups, even in Group 3 despite all our issues and the fact that we are all adults. Needs for social connectedness and inclusion are not age-independent. We have always needed each other, and we still do. In fact, research has suggested that social connectedness is a prime need at work (Kohll, 2018). Our brains have evolved some in an attempt to adapt to our modern social interdependencies and hierarchies, but there are many kinks remaining to be worked out. One of those kinks is the stress that emerges because of all our underlying interpersonal dynamics. Next, we look at some of the ways our brains perceive and react to all this confusing and constant input in all our human groups. We seek to further answer that proverbial query of why we mess with each other in all our groups. We will try to understand how the "primitive" in all of us continues to thwart our wisest intentions for collective thriving.

Below, we briefly summarize the ideal goals of the three main groups and the impacts if these group goals are not achieved:

Group 1 provides a secure home environment and relational attachment for a child to develop and thrive optimally. If a home is unsafe, a threatened brain makes insecure and ambivalent attachments to others and has an adverse impact on development.

Group 2 provides a secure academic environment for a child to learn and play. If a school is unsafe, the brain cannot learn. Instead, it is a threatened brain preparing to fight, flee, or freeze. A feeling of insecurity or lack of safety has an adverse impact on learning in the classroom and playing—and forming relationships—on the playground.

Group 3 provides a secure work environment for the individual to produce and professionally develop. If a workplace is unsafe, the brain is not motivated or productive. Threatened brains are driven to "survive" versus "thrive," which detracts from learning, producing, creating, and feeling fulfilled in the workplace.

Chapter 2: Key Concepts

1) Humans have an evolutionary history of small social groupings where living and working were integrated.
2) Home, school, and workplace are three developmental groups all impacted by primitive survival pressures.
3) The contemporary concept of work is relatively new and evolving, and requires ongoing reevaluation and adaptation to present day cultural and environmental realities.

3

HUMAN BRAIN(S): MANAGER OF THE SELF

"Sitting on your shoulders is the most complicated object in the known universe." —Michio Kaku

A gray, jelly-like mass of protein and fat that weighs approximately three pounds is suspended inside your skull. It makes up only about two percent of your body, but it requires more energy than any other organ. This conglomeration is your brain. It always somehow feels a bit silly to write about "it" (in the third person) when "it" is doing this writing. But then again, who has better knowledge about it than itself? If you had to choose one organ to identify and understand the essence of *you*, it would be your brain. Not your fingerprints, not even your DNA—those are more static. Your brain best represents you because this organ continually changes based on all that you experience and learn and will do so throughout your lifespan. Your brain has also changed based on what your ancestors experienced during their time here. All these varied influences make the brain the most amazingly complex and incredibly fluid human organ.

The more we understand about the brain, the better we can care for our own and those of others. Knowledge of basic human brain functioning is especially vital in work groups where these organs are forced to interact and often come into conflict with one another. Our livers do not seem to perceive or care if our coworker got that promotion, but our brains sure do! Our minds are bombarded by all that is happening around us and inside of us—past, present, and future.

The brain is forever like a child in need of nurturing, a student learning, a team player tirelessly working, and a manager organizing and leading—all in one. It never leaves home, exits the classroom, or finishes work—a perpetual multitasker that is on 24/7.

We know less than we think we know, but we know more than we have ever known before about our own inner workings. Our current knowledge of the brain can really assist us as we navigate both our personal and professional worlds. Some of the nonsensical human behaviors that we all experience in our lives can be better understood today, in part because the last decades have brought about significant advances in imaging techniques (e.g., brain scans) that have offered us the ability to look inside the brain. Before these advances, it took a great deal of guessing about what was in this "black box." Historically, unfortunate accidents involving the head contributed to scientists' understanding of the effects of brain injuries, which also helped them understand the state of the brain before the injury. They were able to assess what function or ability was lost after a specific part of the brain was damaged or destroyed, and so were able to connect specific cognitive functions to physical areas of the brain. We can now better understand brain structures and functions on biochemical, electrical, mechanical, and social levels. For our purposes here, we interchangeably use the terms brain and mind. Elegant distinctions can be found in other writings such as those of Daniel Siegel, MD, who views the mind as an entity that extends beyond the physical substance of the brain. He describes the mind as "the emergent self-organizing process, both embodied and relational, that regulates energy and information flow within and among us" (Siegel, 2010).

We learn basic car operating facts when we learn to drive and are taught about basic signs and signals of the road. We know how to interact with one another at a stop sign or to communicate our intent to change lanes. We are taught to navigate changing and hazardous road conditions. But we rarely receive instruction about how the primary vehicle of our lifetime operates—the one that takes us through the journey of our lives—our brain! Learning general and user-friendly nervous system concepts and operations is imperative if we want to adaptively navigate the winding personal and social roads and rough terrain of the workplace. In this chapter, we describe the most relevant aspects of brain functioning at work. We start by sharing some of the new and exciting discoveries of this expanding frontier.

Expanding Frontiers of Applied Neuroscience

Neuroscientific studies have been proliferating over the past few years and have led to fascinating new discoveries. Some of this new knowledge has been rapidly translated to practical applications in both the personal and professional realms—from neuro-sex (physical pleasure via brain implants) to neuro-spying (brain-wave capture programs). Some overseas employers have employees wear caps with electronic sensors to monitor their brainwaves and emotional states. With the assistance of computer algorithms, the data identifies workplace tension, sadness, and rage from the brainwaves captured by the sensors. Employers learn about their employees and make decisions about whether to send an employee home or schedule their breaks based on their transmitted emotional state (Chan, 2018). We are all living in this neuro-revolution, and we need to remain aware of harnessing this knowledge responsibly and ethically. *Discover* magazine maintains a blog called "Neuroskeptic" in an attempt to keep all in check. *Workaches* examines how emergent findings in the neurosciences can help working individuals and organizations.

Our brains are intimately interconnected with our bodies and our external environments. For example, researchers have discovered clear connections between the brain and the gut (microbiome), as well as other organs. We are not just groups of human cells—we all are composed of different groups of microorganisms. In fact, we are made up less of human cells than of other types of cells. There are findings that suggest some of these microorganisms are even influencing our behaviors. Even more stunning is the fact that researchers using human stem cells can now grow little brains about the size of lentils in lab dishes; these *brain organoids* have working neural features of a life-size human brain, enabling scientists to conduct various experiments on different features of the human brain.

In addition to advances in stem cell therapies and other gene therapies, a new frontier called "electroceuticals" or "bioelectronics" that use electric signals rather than chemicals to assist neurons inspires hope for more effective interventions and treatments. With continued research and advances in imaging and other techniques, scientists will be discovering more and more about this wondrous organ that makes us unique creatures on this earth. The brain remains a mystery even today, just less of one.

For our purposes here, these research breakthroughs have many implications for how we work. Brain studies not only provide organizations with templates to build thriving workplaces, but they also help us understand the significant adverse impacts on employee productivity and well-being of specific workplace cultures and dynamics. The neuroscience is supporting the need to address how workplaces are managed and operated (Rock, 2013). In Chapter 8, we review Rock's NeuroLeadership studies and strategies for managing employees' needs to feel valued and engaged in the workplace.

Our Ever-Changing Brain

Our genetics and environments, along with their interactions, profoundly impact us. We now know that the question of nature versus nurture is too simple. Human share about 99.9 percent of the same genetic make-up with each other, which means that genetically we are only about 0.1 percent different from one another (Genetics Home Reference, 2018). Some of the genetic difference is a result of our human ancestors adapting to varied environments as they migrated and spread out across the globe. What creates much of our diversity as humans are the unique mixes of our genes, the unique experiences of our ancestors, and the different experiences we have from conception onward. Every human organ is affected by life experiences, but our brains appear to be the most sensitive to the impacts of our surroundings. We create our unique individual brains by having experiences, storing memories, learning new things, and forming various connections between brain regions.

Our brains store our journeys and hold our stories.

The brain at birth arrives ready to learn and comes pre-loaded with some basic and essential data. One example is a newborn's ability to take nourishment by pursing its lips and sucking. Some reflexes that newborns possess get lost as development advances. Infants, for example, are born with an automatic ability to hold their breath if submerged in water. This capacity, called the "diving reflex," is one we share with some aquatic animals like seals and is believed to be a leftover survival instinct from our oceanic origins. Data gets rapidly added to what is "pre-loaded" in the brain. Infants take in about every experience and are absorbing and differently storing the good and bad experiences. The strong emotion-provoking experiences are more likely to be remembered because of their perceived threat to survival.

In the last chapter, we addressed how natural and cultural evolution influences us. These processes change us by modifying our brains and other organs to fit our environments better. Our brains grew larger as we humans began to live in groups (Radford, 2011). Today our brains are three times larger than they used to be millions of years ago. Early humans needed to learn to communicate along with other social skills, not only for the functioning of the group but also to outsmart lower animals. Humans needed to become more reasonable in their negotiations with one another, so the more rational parts of the brain were naturally selected for and evolved over time.

Not every person or organism in a group naturally evolves at the same rate or to the same degree. Not all of our primate ancestors lost their tails at the same time. Not every human in a group culturally evolves at the same time either—we see this with acceptance of new cultural ideas or practices, which happens at different rates.

Sometimes this variability is frustrating for those who have gone first and view things differently. For example, it was cultural evolution in America that afforded workers labor rights. Not every person at the time believed in the idea behind these labor laws and went along with the concept and change in rules. Over time, however, we often see more people from a culture joining and accepting a dominant cultural viewpoint. In the case of more just labor laws, this is progress and a good thing. However, if a dominant majority joins together to marginalize a segment of people, this is an unfortunate thing that is most typically based in a nonconscious perception of a threat to survival.

People learn ideas, beliefs, behaviors, and skills from other people. Humans are also capable of what looks like devolving. There is no clear and consistent direction in either genetic or cultural evolution. The influences on any one individual are vast and extend from way back in time and from vast geographic and cultural variations.

On the next page is a simplified flow chart (Figure 3.1) of how your brain has come to be:

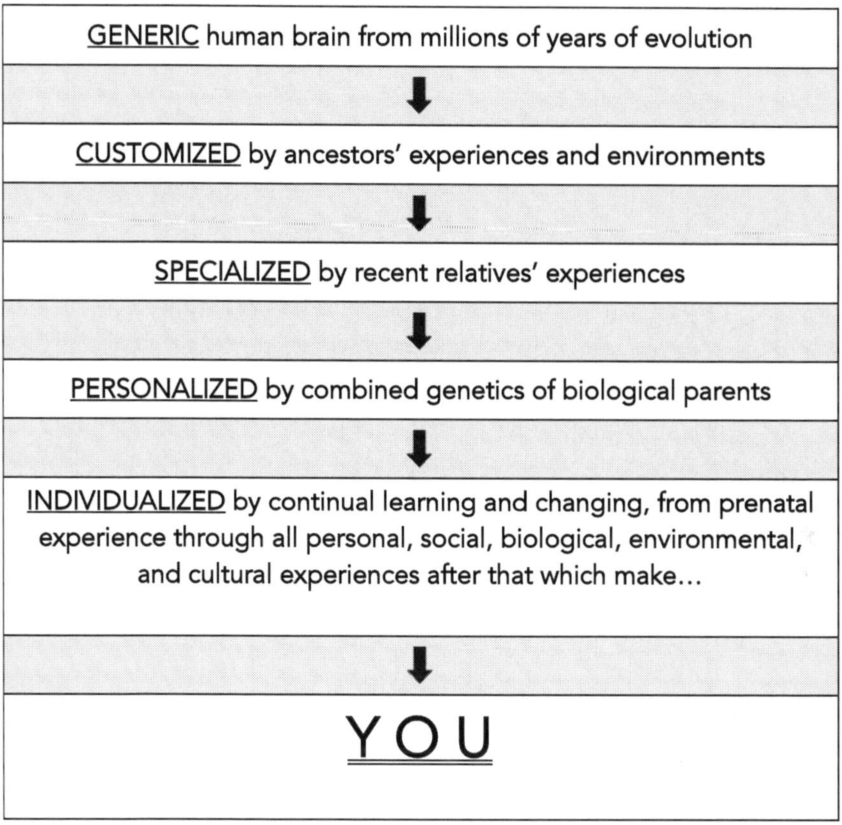

Figure 3.1

Human Brain as a Group of Connected Parts

The master control center of human civilization and organizations is the sum of all the brains that collectively make up the system at that moment in time and space. This system is always changing as individuals are added and subtracted but constantly reestablishes itself and remains a consistent and coherent whole. As if one solitary brain is not complicated enough, once we add all the other brains, and then add their interactions—we have complexities and complications galore! The individual is a collective of parts, the group is a collective of individuals and their interactions, and the world becomes a collective of the sum of all those parts. We are all part of endless groups and interconnected systems.

The human brain may be anatomically classified as a singular organ, such as a heart or pancreas, yet it really seems to operate much more like a "plural" than a "single" entity. If we look at a graphic of the brain, it does not necessarily appear as one single organ. Brain cells are found beyond the skull and nervous system. Some have been discovered in the lining of our guts (Underwood, 2018). Our brain is made up of many different interconnected parts, regions, and groups that contribute to its complexity. Many express that there are multiple voices and decision-makers up there. Some refer to it as their "committee." The architecture of the brain is more like a collective "grouping" of multilayered, evolutionarily distinct regions, right/left halves, with multifaceted parts and inter-connected systems ranging from conscious (in awareness) to nonconscious (out of awareness) in nature.

The blueprints of some brain parts were created millions of years ago. Some parts are newer. The ancient parts were designed for very different circumstances in our evolutionary pasts, which we learned about in the last chapter. Those parts do not "know" this, and resist being "updated" to contemporary realities. A job of our "newer" parts is to help the more primitive regions in their struggle to negotiate modern society. The ancient parts of our brain are not removed and replaced—rather, they are built upon. The newer structures have evolved and grown above the old parts. Can you imagine if your new computer was composed of a Stone Age tool and a typewriter that were connected together to a cutting-edge microprocessor that worked as one whole unit processing constantly changing software in the modern office space? Operating it would certainly be a challenge!

The first system that we must learn to coordinate and manage in our lives is that challenging neuro-grouping of our own brains. Becoming competent stewards of our brains facilitates our being able to best interact with the brains of others. HHS professionals become intimately involved with both the conscious and nonconscious regions of the brains they serve, as well as with those in their organizations. As we outlined in Chapter 2, living and working in groups has been essential to human existence. The managers of our first two groups (parents, teachers) assist us in managing our immature brains. After the assistance from these two groups, we are pretty much on our own. It is essential to have a working knowledge of the operation and optimal care of our brains to support and coach ourselves.

All through nature, we find inter-connected systems—both internal to us and external. The United States of America can serve as an analogy to an external system that is made up of individual and diverse parts yet has some organizing principles and connections that keep it whole. Our country is consistent, connected, and coherent through space and time, and so is our brain. Yet, both are continually changing and adding and subtracting individual components. The United States of America is composed of individual states that have unique identities and distinct styles and goals. However, they each follow an over-arching set of governing principles. The Federal Government is the agreed upon overall manager. Each state has its own management, however. Additionally, each individual state is further broken down into smaller divisions and regions to form counties, and cities, etc. Each city is made up of the individuals that reside within its boundaries (which is always changing as people move back and forth across state lines).

We build physical roads, bridges, and different forms of communication between all the different areas—the more, the better—for information sharing and enrichment. The system works, in part, because there are consistent federal guidelines to follow. Even though individuality is preserved and promoted within specific locations, overall adherence to national guidelines exists most of the time. When this adherence is disrupted, we witness discord and conflict and sometimes attempts toward disruption and remarkable change of the system. Of course, there have been points in time (e.g., Civil War) when the parts were so far apart that break-down occurred and we saw a war in the system. We can make an analogy to mental illness with these same points. When the different parts of the brain become so opposed to the operating system (e.g., thinking versus feeling), a systemic breakdown in communication occurs, and there is difficulty operating by the guidelines. America was able to reconstitute as an evolving system and return to the coherency of fundamental purpose and goals after the Civil War, but the internal struggles and conflicts continue. The disputes are natural parts of any evolving system and are to be expected. The integrating and resolving of the conflicts are the crucial pieces and determine whether the "whole" can remain coherent and intact, yet still change and evolve. The system requires fluidity and adaptability while keeping its overall integrity. The Constitution articulates our overall purpose and goals and thereby affords us an operating manual to manage and guide each citizen in the American system or organization.

Neurons and Neural Pathways Form Our Brain Trails

The basic building block of America is each individual. The basic building block of the internal system of our brain and nervous system is the nerve cell or neuron. It receives, processes, and transmits information via chemical, electrical, and mechanical means throughout the body. The human brain contains about 90 billion nerve cells that make about 100 trillion connections in our bodies. As the graphic (Figure 3.2) below depicts, the neuron has a cell body with dendrites branching out from it that communicate with other neurons in the spaces between the cells, called synapses. The dendrites are like receptors that pick up messages for the cell.

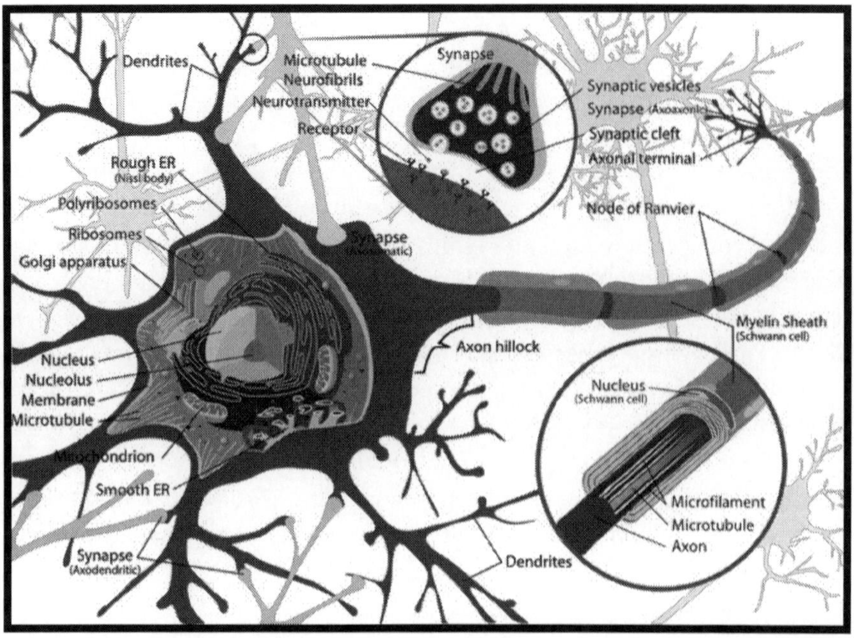

Figure 3.2

Dendrites interconnect with other dendrites to create relationships among all the different neurons of the nervous system. Also, branching out of the cell body are axons; these are considered the managers of the neuron and determine whether the signal or message will travel down the cell body to the synapse and get communicated to the next cell. The neuron will either fire and send the signal on or it will not. If it fires, the axon "hands over a baton" to another neuron, but through a chemical neurotransmitter at the point of the synapse. Motor neurons control the muscles of our bodies. Sensory neurons receive information from our senses and send this back to the brain for processing; inter-neurons are the cells that connect to other neurons. Neurons come in all shapes and sizes. Neurons and their connections make up what we call the connectome.

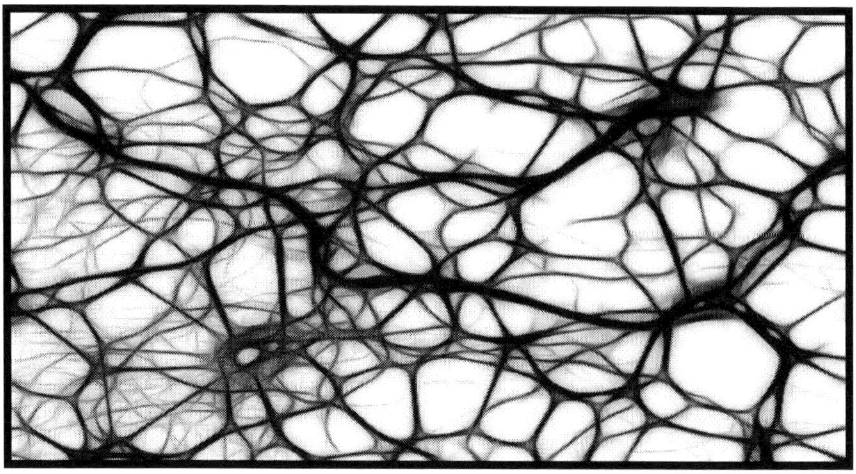

Figure 3.3

A neural pathway is a made up of clusters of neurons (communities) that are linked and communicate directly with one another. Neural pathways process and control information flow and form networks that allow us to do things such as learn, think, and feel. They make up the neural correlates of our mental experiences. When you see something for the first time or learn something new, a brand-new neural pathway gets formed, neuron by neuron. Let us take the example of when we learned our multiplication tables. When we learned that 2 x 5 = 10, we began a new and relatively weak connection (neural pathway) in the brain. The more we rehearsed and practiced, the stronger the pathway got and the better we became at this multiplication problem. We strengthened the neural connections of this pathway. After many repetitions using different learning methods, we got that rewarding feeling of mastery, and it became easy to come up with the answer of 10! Figure 3.3 depicts many connecting neuropathways.

More Neuros: Neuroplasticity and Neurogenesis

Neurons grow, connect, and change. Neuroplasticity refers to the capacity of the brain to change over time. As opposed to other animals who are ready and set to go at birth (born with mature brains), we have the opportunity to learn from our current environment. This immaturity of the brain at birth allows the maximum possibility to learn about, and adapt to, the current environmental and relational conditions. This learning causes the open and fluid organ to be further sculpted by its environment, as the brain learns how to best survive in the environment to which it has been birthed. Our minds become personalized and specialized to our first environments. So, if the brain enters an abusive or neglectful environment upon birth, this will be the original learned template about the world. If the brain enters a rejecting environment and learns to view itself as useless and unimportant, this view will become an original template about the self. Although the original templates resist change and can seem rigid when we try to change our habitual ways of seeing things, our neuroplasticity also allows for new or "re" learning. In effect, neuroplasticity allows people to update their brains. Both individuals and groups of individuals can evolve. This fluidity is one of the greatest freedoms we have as humans—the capacity to grow and evolve from our experiences. Neuroplasticity affords us choice and the ability to monitor and manage our more primitive impulses and reactions and to learn from our mistakes. It also affords psychological mercy for many individuals who have learned unfortunate things about themselves and others early on, because we can re-learn, re-create, and re-gain perspective and safety.

Another process, neurogenesis, is when new neurons come into existence through cell division. The capacity to generate new cells is good news because neurons also die. Neurogenesis is an active and ongoing frontier of study. Researchers continue to identify brain structures (e.g., hippocampus) where the birth of new brain cells take place, and some studies have been conducted on factors that might promote or optimize neurogenesis, such as exercising and engaging in novel brain activities ("neurobics") (Harvard Health, 2016).

Alert and at Ease: Human Nervous System

Just as individuals join with other individuals to form teams within an organization, neurons join together to form neural networks. Neural relationships or systems form our nervous system, which can be divided into two basic parts: 1) central nervous system (CNS); and 2) peripheral nervous system (PNS). The CNS includes the brain and spinal cord. The PNS comprises the rest of the nervous system—all the nerves that branch out from the brain and spinal cord and extend to different parts of the body. The PNS is divided into the autonomic nervous system (ANS) and somatic nervous system (SNS). The ANS and SNS are involved in communication between the CNS and all our different sensory organs and body. The ANS has two branches: sympathetic and parasympathetic nervous systems.

The ANS is most relevant to our discussions in *Workaches* because it is so connected to our stress and relaxation responses. The sympathetic nervous system manages the activation of the nervous system and body in response to threats. It controls our fight, flight, or freeze reactions. The parasympathetic nervous system counterbalances the sympathetic branch and is sometimes referred to as the "rest and digest" or "tend and befriend" branch because it conserves energy. This system relaxes and calms us. Sometimes the parasympathetic nervous system is referred to as the body's "braking" system and the sympathetic nervous system as the "accelerating" system. The sympathetic and parasympathetic nervous systems are meant to work in rhythmic coordination or alternation with one another. We will learn how chronic stress and trauma disrupt their balance and create neurochemical imbalance and problems.

These two major aspects of our nervous systems developed in response to our primitive ancestors' survival needs in early environments. The fight-or-flight response, or sympathetic nervous system, is adaptive when reacting to physical threats in our environments. Our parasympathetic nervous system is adaptive for our social bonding and nurturing of our young and others. Some of the structural and functional aspects of these systems are outdated for our modern world. Knowing this, we do our best to understand and manage them, because there are many obsolete human traits.

Unnecessary Physical Organs and Psychosocial Traits

There are a number of human physical structures that we still possess called vestigial organs. They have no known purpose or benefit to humans in modern times. Vestigial organs include the appendix, wisdom teeth, body hair, tailbone, third inner eyelid, and male nipples. These organs are residuals or remnants of organs our long-ago ancestors may have needed, but we do not. There are also vestigial behaviors such as getting goosebumps and hiccups. Other animals have vestigial organs and behaviors too. For instance, an ostrich has wings but can no longer fly.

Vestigial psychosocial behaviors and traits are "left-over" attributes from our primitive ancestors that they developed as they evolved and adapted to their environments. These traits are no longer useful adaptations in our modern-day environments. Some of these psychosocial traits and behaviors

that we discuss include gossiping, nonconscious judgment and bias, public humiliation and shaming, and rage reactions.

Tens of thousands of years ago we needed to be stressed by and suspicious of differences because they would have signaled a potential clan intruder and threat. We then also needed to feel shame and try to hide our differences as a result, lest we be eliminated. We no longer need these traits just as we no longer need our wisdom teeth. We no longer have to tear apart uncooked and coarse foods such as roots and animals with our jaws and teeth. Many people have wisdom teeth removed because today they are more bothersome than helpful when they erupt. Some of our brain parts, such as the amygdala, also continue to erupt unnecessarily. We are unable to remove them so we must understand and manage them. For example, we know from genetics that distinct racial groups no longer exist as before because humans have diverse genetic backgrounds now. Nonetheless, we continue to see racial animus. We consider this a psychosocial vestigial trait in need of acknowledgement, understanding, and management.

Resources were limited, differences in others were potentially lethal, and physical bravado was necessary in the environments of our primitive ancestors. Evolutionary psychologists speculate that many of our modern-day biases took root in primitive times and hang on in our lower nonconscious minds. They helped us survive back then; now, they just makes us less than ideal "co-humans" sometimes. Possible manifestations today include scanning for those obtaining more than their "fair share" and discriminating against those that are perceived as "unfit" for physical battle. We will later discuss how many of the frustrating and annoying behaviors of our workmates emerge from leftovers in our brains from our primitive ancestors.

Reptiles, such as chameleons, still need to be able to hide or camouflage themselves and change colors to blend with their environment because there are still active predators just waiting to eat them. Higher brain regions have not evolved in reptiles as they have in us. We have evolved brains that create civilizations with alternative resources and safeguards against cannibalism and predation. Certainly, we still need to remain wary of threats, but no longer to the same degree. The same needs to be true for psychosocial vestigial traits when they are more maladaptive than adaptive in modern times. We must first understand the evolutionary history of the human brain to understand these vestigial psychosocial traits.

Models of the Human Brain

The human brain has been evolving for millions of years. Single-cell organisms in the ocean do not have brains per se but have structures enabling them to sense and respond to their environments. Our nervous systems started there and grew and changed as organisms moved to land, where different brain structures were needed and evolved. The most primitive brains are made up of bundled nerve cells. As animals further adapted to different environments and conditions, brains continued to differentiate and change. So, let us take a brief journey into a long history, after making a stop in an anatomical model.

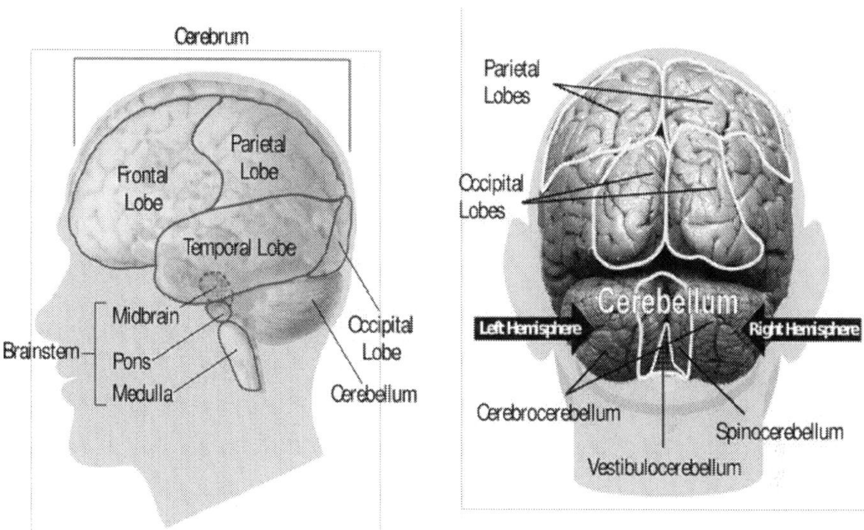

Figure 3.4

Most of us are familiar with the notion that there are two halves of the brain—right and left hemispheres—connected by fibers. This is a two-part (side to side) model of the brain. We commonly describe the right hemisphere as housing creative thinking and the left hemisphere as housing our more mathematical, analytical thinking. The brain is now known to be so complicated that this simplified view is increasingly challenged. Nonetheless, this model is still widely used to describe different aspects of brain functioning. There are two (a pair) of most structures in the brain. Conventionally, however, we tend to refer to structures using the singular form of their names. For example, we write a lot about the amygdala below (a more famous part of our brain today due to its central role in our psychosocial functioning), but the plural is amygdalae.

In addition to the two hemispheres, there are five lobes that have some differentiated roles (Figure 3.4). We now know, however, that these regions are not as distinct as previously thought, and they can even compensate for each other after brain injuries (Gazzaniga, 2012).

The cerebral cortex, which is the outermost portion of the brain that we see, is divided into four sections or lobes: 1) frontal; 2) parietal; 3) temporal; and, 4) occipital. In brief, the frontal lobe is the center of higher cognitive functioning and motor skills. The parietal lobe is associated with processing the body senses. The temporal lobe is associated with interpreting sound and processing language. The occipital lobe processes visual stimuli and information. They all do much more and we are learning more each day about how they are able to pitch in for one another.

Tripartite or Triune Model of the Human Brain

A less familiar depiction of brain division has been called the tripartite or triune (meaning "three-part") top-to-bottom model of the brain. We use this model in *Workaches* because it illustrates how the architecture of our brains has evolved from our early beginnings. A pioneering neuroscientist by the name of Paul MacLean developed this model in the 1960s and introduced it in his book, *The Triune Brain in Evolution* (MacLean, 1990). This model has also been shown to be too simplistic to comprehensively and adequately describe the complexity of our brains. However, science often utilizes simplified models to understand and summarize complex systems. The tripartite model is user-friendly and assists with our ability to conceptualize, and thereby most adaptively manage, what goes on inside our skulls.

Our brains have an evolutionary history that the triune model depicts. Some parts are ancient and others are newer. Think about a three-story house that started as a one-story house approximately three million years ago. The ground floor does not get remodeled, but a second story is added on top of it about 1 million years later. Then, again without remodeling of the second story, a third story is built on top about 200 thousand years ago. Because it needs to function as a whole house, connections must be placed between all three stories. Our genetic codes form the blueprints that can replicate all three distinct regions ("stories") in modern humans. Other animals have only one or two regions, and only a small portion of the third region, if they have any at all. Humans exclusively have the whole "top floor" which contains higher order thinking, language, and perception of time (our exclusive ability to be consciously aware of a distant past and imagined future). Because we have all three regions that best function as a whole unit, the goal is to build as many passageways or neuropathways as we can between regions to maintain communication and coordination. Figure 3.5 illustrates this evolutionary structure or ladder.

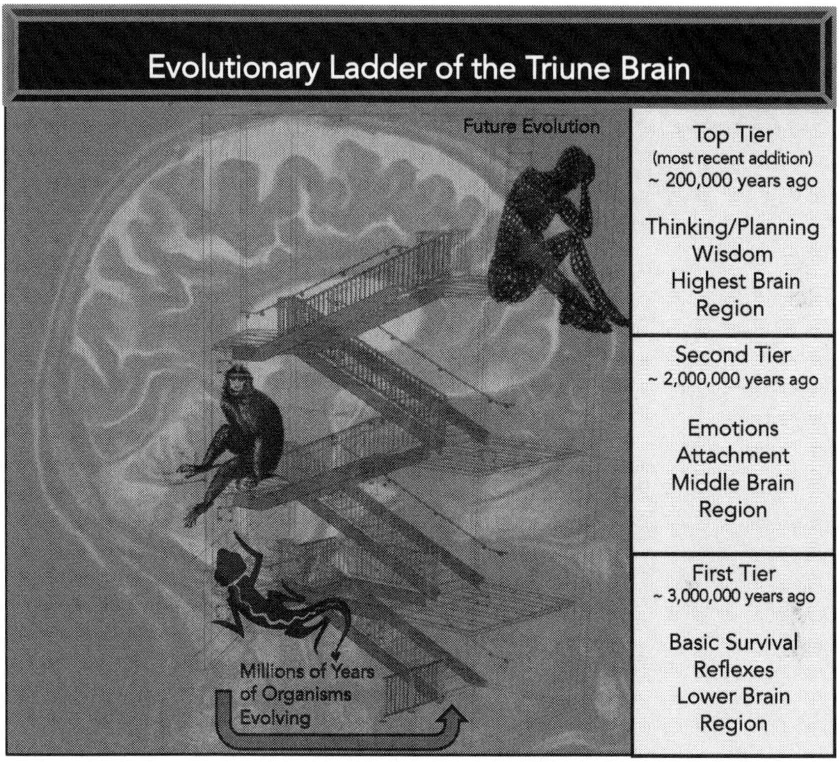

Figure 3.5

Though the outside may appear as a modern structure, the foundation is ancient and dictates a great deal of the internal life of the structure.

The good news is that we can intentionally remodel some of the structure by adding new passageways between floors and more complexity between the top two stories.

Counseling and therapy, as we will address later, attempts to remodel and create more communication between floors. Humans possess more cortex—the most evolutionarily recent part to develop—than any other animal on the planet. Dogs, for example, have all three levels, but have much less of the top tier or cortex than a human, as can be seen in the cortex folds in the images below (Figure 3.6).

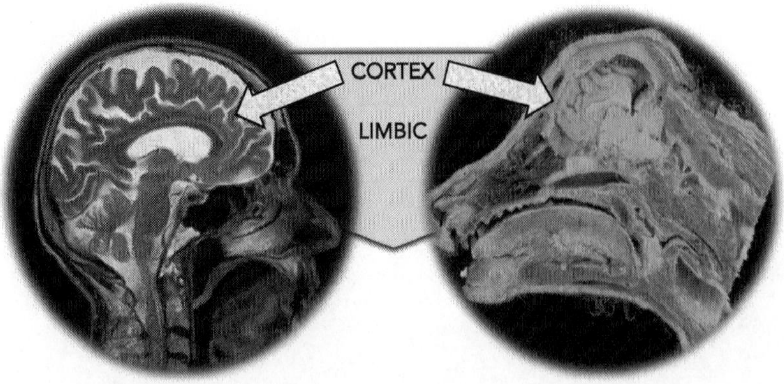

Figure 3.6

Primitive Brain (Oldest): Bottom Floor

Approximately 300 million years ago, the brainstem (inner core of the brain) grew at the top of the spinal cord and allowed for the survival responses of fight, flight, and freeze, and reproduction. This lower part of our brain is concerned with self-preservation—in other words, survival. Reptiles have been able to live their lives and survive well with this brain configuration. Thriving, however, is irrelevant to their existence. This region only supports surviving. The cerebellum is another part of this region that receives sensory information and regulates our motor movements and balance. The brainstem and cerebellum control essential functions such as breathing, reproduction, motor behaviors, heart rate, and attention. The brainstem controls the flow of internal information between the brain and body and is mature and ready to go at birth to promote survival. This region does not need early caregivers to nurture it. This region is often referred to as our "reptile" or "lizard" brain but is a bit of a misnomer because modern reptiles do have some higher brain regions or cortex.

The brainstem is reactive and rigid, and it does not learn and evolve like the other two parts of the brain that get further "sculpted" by both positive and negative interpersonal and other experiences in the environment. Because this region of the brain has remained so primitive, it still pressures us to act as if our survival is threatened (as it was when this region adapted to life millions of years ago). If you watch a lizard, you can see this survival pressure in action. You may just want to observe, greet the lizard, perhaps even pet it, but it reacts as if you are going to kill it and flees. Humans must rely on our newer brain regions to help us manage these same primitive reactions.

Lower Mammal (Paleomammalian) Brain: Middle Floor

Approximately 200 million years ago, we saw the emergence of the limbic system over the brainstem in animals. This growth gave rise to the first mammals. The limbic system works with the brainstem and body to produce feeling and motivational states and facilitate memory formation and attachment. The amygdala, hypothalamus, and hippocampus make up its major components. The amygdala is involved with fear, aggression, social bonding, and other emotions. The hypothalamus helps regulate body functions such as hunger, thirst, and temperature. The hippocampus is the organizer of memory between the amygdala and cerebral cortex. It has direct connections to the amygdala, and this may be why specific memories can trigger significant emotions. Overall, the limbic region is central in processing social information, activating arousal if threat is detected, and coordinating the brain/body response to our world. We also refer to this region as part of our primitive brain because it too is millions of years old.

The hippocampus is closely connected to the cortex and helps encode and retrieve memories. Many of our alarm circuits are grouped together in the amygdala and collect direct sensory information about our environment. The amygdala is an ancient structure that directs a great deal of our behavior as if we were still living in prehistoric times. For example, many humans have a fear of snakes. Yet, in modern times, the risk from cars is far greater than from snakes. Reasoning with the amygdala is next to impossible! It does not possess necessary cognitive capacities, such as a sense of time or rationality, to update itself. This area is reactive and does not envision the future. We often end up regretful, apologetic, and making amends when this region gets triggered, activates, and overwhelms or hijacks our more advanced brain regions. No planning or envisioning of consequences of actions occurs in the emotional heat of the moment.

The amygdala receives a great deal of information from all senses and other brain structures that trigger emotional responses. In addition to dealing with danger and fear, the amygdala is active in perceiving food availability, sexual partners, and other people who might be competing for the same resources (threats). Later, we will discuss building neural pathways from our logical centers to the amygdala, which allows for some communication and management. We can blame our bottom two reactive regions of the brain for triggering us to say and do things that we later regret! We can also thank these regions for keeping us safe, though they are unnecessarily over-protective in contemporary times.

Higher Mammal (Neomammalian) Brain: Top Floor

As more time passed on earth, the brain continued to grow and diversify to adapt to new environments and circumstances. Approximately 200 thousand years ago, we see the emergence of a third layer of the brain called the cortex (entire outer layer of the brain). It grew above the limbic system and allowed for more sophisticated and complex thinking on the part of our ancestors. The cortex is the gray matter and the outer wrinkled and folded layer of the brain. It contains billions of nerve cells and trillions of connections between these cells. Today the genetic blueprints passed on to us program the building of all three stories (regions) when assembling the contemporary human brain.

The neocortex makes up the majority (approximately 90 percent) of the cerebral cortex. The neocortex has six layers and is responsible for capacities such as insight, morality, intuition, empathy, response flexibility, fear extinction, language, attuned communication, and time awareness. The first layer of the neocortex is called the prefrontal cortex (PFC). This region carries out executive functions which involve planning and decision making. This area is much more proactive and able to envision the future. The PFC was the last part of the brain to grow in the process of evolution. Oxford University researchers have identified a segment of the PFC that may be unique to humans. This area is identified as connected to our capacity for strategic planning, decision making, and multi-tasking (Neubert et al., 2014).

The PFC is also the last part of the brain to finish growing and connecting in an individual's development, and often the first part of the brain to start to decay with aging. Before the advent of car airbags, we used to see PFC damage from drivers hitting their foreheads on steering wheels and sustaining head injuries. Family members would often report that these individuals had lost their unique personalities, more sophisticated social nuances, and judgment. Research suggests that this part of the brain is not completely developed or fully connected with lower brain regions until a person is in their mid to late twenties. Parents serve (or at least attempt to) as the "prefrontal cortex" for their children and adolescents—assisting with impulse control and judgment. Our early years and relationships with our primary caregivers have the most significant impact on the last two regions of our brains—limbic system and cortex. The neural pathways that form in these early years will impact us for the rest of our lives. Some of these areas are preverbal and sensation-based or visceral, so our access to them as adults will be more difficult because they are out of conscious awareness and without time perception. The early pathways form a major core of the self or identity.

The cortex becomes individualized and specialized within each unique person. Healthy interpersonal relationships and nurturing are critical to optimal brain growth. Unhealthy and traumatic interpersonal relationships lead to disrupted and disorganized neural networks in the brain. Our social worlds have a significant impact on the cortex. We will learn more about this later and will address how the cortex can get "shut down," leading us to react to things and people in our environment without our typical judgment and empathy. In times of stress and fear of unfamiliar or dissimilar people, the compassion circuitry (specific brain structures) in the neocortex goes off-line, and these unfamiliar people are at risk of being dehumanized and treated like objects by the more primitive brain. When our capacity for empathy and thinking diminish, we may act out our fears in both personal and professional environments. The optimal goal is to have access to (along with optimal management of) all the amazing capacities of our complex and creative minds.

Because of our highly sophisticated neocortex and ability to fantasize, humans have been able to create artificially intelligent machines and robots. Robots do not have a human brain but operate off the human mind via artificial intelligence. Next, a cross between a human and a robot is predicted that will contain both our unique brain components and artificial intelligence components. Artificial body parts already exist for organs such as hearts and hips, so the leap to artificial patches in the brain is not completely outside the realm of possibility. This hybrid humanoid will likely not include some of the more primitive and confusing (and often conflicting) elements of our current human brains. Artificially intelligent beings could result as the next evolutionary step of brain "growth" that is "atop" our neocortex. Figure 3.7 depicts a futuristic evolutionary chain that illustrates the last imagined brain as even existing outside the human body. Artificial intelligence appears unbounded.

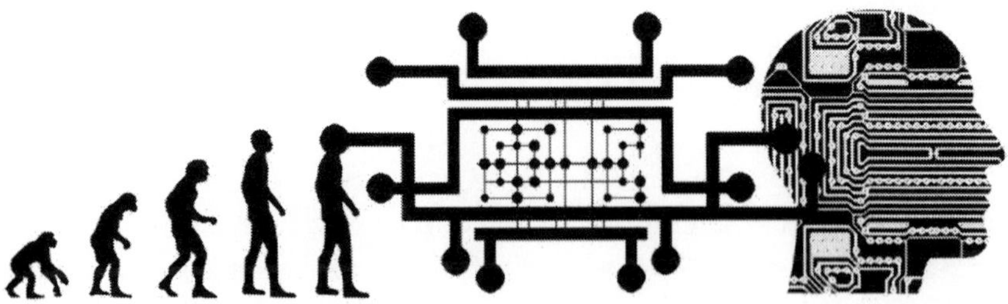

Figure 3.7

Today we know that the brain is really a mosaic of interconnected and ever-changing areas. Quite a challenging organ to understand and manage most adaptively. Until the time AI can become our brain decoders and navigational systems, we will likely continue to utilize different and simplified models to understand the vast terrain of the brain. In the contemporary workplace, we continue to use pretty much the same brains as our ancestors of long ago and continue to coordinate all "three brains" on the vertical plane, along with our two horizontal halves, plus all the neural connections and networks extending throughout the entire brain and body. This is all on top of the constant and transient neurochemical changes taking place in response to impacts from other people to microorganisms! We are also changing due to all our experiences each day. All this responsibility and challenge supports the case to offer ourselves much compassion in navigating alongside others with such an interesting and complex leader called our brain.

Threatened Brain: "On Alert"

Threat detection is so crucial to the brain that it reacts to both accurate perceptions and inaccurate or misperceptions. Better wrong than sorry, according to that primitive brain. The processes of generalization and discrimination are pre-loaded into our brains. We are wired to be drawn toward others, yet we are also wired to detect unsafety quickly, and then to store that information deep in our brains. What is familiar is going to be perceived as safer than what is unfamiliar. This human trait has important implications in the workplace. Diverse strangers are all around us at work and our primitive brain is constantly scanning for differences as potential threats in our environments. The potential for the misperception of a difference as a risk or threat is high. In the face of significant threat, the PFC is unnecessary and goes off-line, so we can react as quickly as possible to survive.

This system of threat detection that goes directly to the limbic area for quicker reaction is our fast track for information processing. We have both fast and slow tracks for processing the information that our senses take in from our internal and external environments. Think about how fast you can spit out something that, upon first taste, seems spoiled or tainted. Now think about how slowly you also can savor a taste. If something tastes, looks, smells, feels like a threat, it is going to be fast-tracked! The information bypasses the thalamus which is typically the structure of the brain that relays sensory information to the higher region of the cortex. The thalamus and the cortex stay in close communication unless presented with an imminent threat. Please keep this fast-tracking system in mind, because later we will explore how this adaptive fast-track system that evolved to keep us safe, now in contemporary society, can make us suspicious of differences and fuel unnecessary biases and disharmony.

Beyond the Skull and Throughout the Body

The brain has "operatives" throughout the body. The HPA (hypothalamic-pituitary-adrenal) axis has the major responsibility of carrying out our stress response. The hypothalamus, pituitary gland, and adrenal glands work together on this. This system is also involved in other important, but separate, bodily functions. When a threat is perceived (that tiger or that upcoming job interview), this system triggers the release of certain chemical messengers that result in the release of cortisol—often called "the stress hormone"—from our adrenal glands (which sit above our kidneys). There are connections from the amygdala, hippocampus, and the PFC that feed into and communicate with the hypothalamus. Cortisol raises the sugar levels in the bloodstream to supply energy and prepare the body for battle—fight or flight. The adrenal glands also release adrenaline, which has the effect of increasing heart rate and blood pressure to facilitate fighting or fleeing. This system was designed to enable us to take significant bodily action against threats. However, in modern life, these threats typically no longer exist, and these chemicals that remain in our bloodstreams ultimately do damage because they are not used or metabolized as quickly.

We are aware of the world around us through our senses, which are on duty 24/7. Our five basic senses are facilitated by our ears, eyes, mouth, nose, and skin. They are like radar that first and foremost informs the brain about potential threats. Even when we are asleep, our brain is processing our senses. These brain regions are tireless. The audible alarm we set to wake us up in the morning capitalizes on this. We alert to the sound, but there is already a neuropathway built from our cortex that immediately reminds us that the purpose of this sound is to awaken us and no real threat exists that requires address. Our higher brain regions come online to help us decide if we want to hit the snooze button.

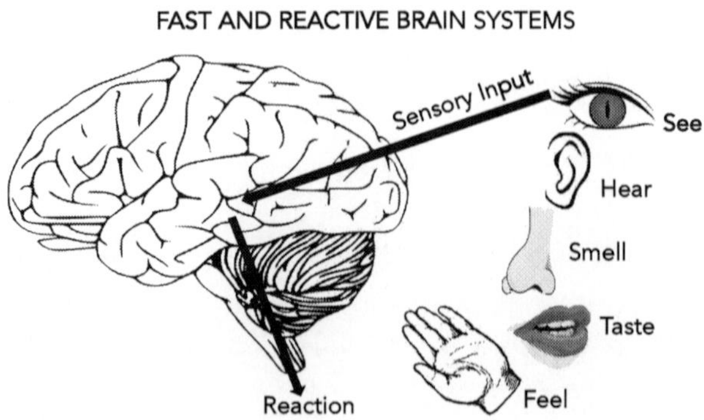

The amygdala lies in wait for potential threats and will react in fractions of a second to signal down the brainstem and to the spinal cord with the message to fight or flee or freeze. The neocortex goes mostly off-line when a potential threat gets detected. If we do not have to battle the threat, we want the neocortex to return to full functioning as soon as possible. Misperceiving false alarms as real is a waste of energy. All data that are not immediately scanned as potentially threatening are processed by the slow track (through the thalamus to cortex). Preserving energy for when we genuinely need it is adaptive. Anything at any time can get paired with fear by the amygdala. Sometimes we do not understand why another individual might be afraid of something we are not; often it is because for some reason that person's amygdala has gotten wired to sound an alarm when the senses perceive that entity or experience. Some of these alarms are pre-wired while others are learned and individually built. Social threats are particularly complex and diverse. For example, one individual can perceive the manager's invitation to come to their office as a threatening experience, while another can perceive it as a rewarding experience. Figure 3.8 shows why we really do not have access to rational thinking when under threat. Other functions such as digestion go off-line as well.

BRAIN IN THREAT MODE

REGIONAL ACTIVATION	ON-LINE	OFF-LINE
Fight, Flight, Freeze	●	○
Thinking	○	●
Logic	○	●
Learning	○	●

Figure 3.8

Below, we share a story that illustrates behaviors that people exhibited when some regions are turned off and others on. This story is one that resulted in no significant consequences. That is not always the case when specific regions are activated, and others deactivated.

A couple of years ago, we conducted a seminar on how the human brain functions in the workplace and elicited stories from participants about times when they felt their neocortex had gone off-line at work. James shared an amusing—from his vantage point months later in our seminar—story of breaking the screen of his cell phone. His boss had just denied his vacation request. James was angry and immediately texted his wife to commiserate with her about the now ruined dates for their trip. The only problem was that he mistakenly texted his boss. Almost immediately after tapping that send icon, James realized what he had done and, in a reactive flash, tried to undo the send and threw his phone in fear. He described the millisecond of relief he felt in casting away the phone (threat). James soon realized his reaction was going to cost him and also did not solve the problem, once he saw his shattered screen. If we analyze James' incident through a neuroscientific lens utilizing the triune brain model, we see that the anxiety or threat of what James had done in sending the text triggered a threat or stress reaction. His neocortex temporarily went off-line, and immediate reaction was taken from the limbic region sending a message to the extremities to react. James throws the phone to rid himself of the threat. There is an immediate reward in taking limbic action. However, once the neocortex came back online, James realized the consequences of his reaction. He now had a financial cost for his reaction and no adaptive solution to his problem. Once the balance of the brain had returned, James wisely knew that he would have to take corrective action with his boss. He waited a day and then communicated with his boss, who fortunately responded appropriately. Whether we pound the steering wheel or throw the phone, we are all subject to limbic reacting versus acting wisely when under perceived threat. Unfortunately, not all reactions are as benign as James' was.

Whatever the perceived threat (real or imagined), the stressed brain expends significantly more energy and requires more fuel. The brain uses glucose as its main source of energy. During increased periods of stress at work many people consume sugary snacks. Brain researcher and diabetologist, Achim Peters, has reported that reaching for sugars and carbohydrates may not necessarily be due to lack of self-control, but attributable to the brain's legitimate need for quick fuel during times of stress. Even if the rest of the body has enough energy supplies, there are lower brain regions that signal the need to consume food in order to supply glucose exclusively to the brain (Peters, 2019).

Traumatized Brain: "On Chronic Alert"

The traumatized brain is the threatened brain on over-drive. The entire body is involved because the deeply disturbing or distressing experience sounds the alarm that sets off the neurobiological "troops" secreting stress hormones that circulate widely and engage most organs. The body and brain are integral parts of the same system. They continuously change each other. Similarly, emotional, physical, and cognitive aspects of our selves are constantly interacting and changing one another (Lewis, 2008). Both body and mind are inextricably connected by trauma. The words we use that separate body and brain imply they are more distinct from one another than they really are.

Workaches can create stress and trauma within organizations, and thereby change bodies and brains. Awareness of the effects of chronic stressors and trauma is essential in organizations. The Substance Abuse and Mental Health Services Administration (samhsa.gov) states "individual trauma results from an event, series of events, or set of circumstances experienced by an individual as physically or emotionally harmful or life-threatening with lasting adverse effects on the individual's functioning and mental, physical, social, emotional, or spiritual well-being." SAMHSA has led the way for organizations to become trauma-informed, which we explore in Chapter 7. When one has experienced trauma, especially developmental trauma, the brain maintains a high-alert status or hypervigilance. If at least one other person has caused harm, generalizing to others to protect oneself from threat is adaptive. Other human beings and relationships become a source of danger to the body and those regions of the brain that hold the trauma memories, even if these memories are entirely out of awareness.

Figure 3.9 summarizes the roles of the main chemicals that get released with an extremely stressful or traumatic event.

Catecholamines	Cortisol	Opiates	Oxytocin
trigger fight/flight/freeze reaction	makes energy available	reduce physical pain	reduces emotional pain

Figure 3.9

The neurochemicals that circulate in the body during trauma are significant to how and where the trauma memory is going to get stored or encoded in the brain. These chemicals also change how individuals react during and after adverse events. These reactions can be misinterpreted by both victims and bystanders. Some of the hormones secreted by the body have anesthetizing effects—both physically and emotionally. Self-inflicted trauma or injury, such as cutting, has been linked with the release of opiates (Sher, 2008). Due to these neurochemicals, some individuals have delayed perceptions of being physically shot by a gun or psychologically harmed after a traumatic emotional experience. Assessments of the impacts of trauma must therefore be made over time due to the possibility of delayed effects and recall.

Memory in general is a complex human process, and memory of trauma is even more complex. Because we are wired to survive, anything that perceptually threatens survival has high value for memory—by our primitive regions. With no verbal capacity or time perception, storage here is complex and hard to get at. Another complicating factor of memory is that non-experienced (experiences that did not actually happen) recollections can sometimes be integrated with experienced recollections (experiences that did happen) (Roediger & McDermott, 2000). Memories can get stored as fragments versus whole events. Different senses can be stored in different memories. An individual may not visually recollect an adverse experience but may recall the smell at the time (Buchanan, 2007). The trauma sits (gets encoded) in the limbic system and remains there unless managed. Trauma disrupts the typical process of the amygdala and hippocampus and neocortex working together to both consolidate memory and later retrieve it (Phelps, 2004). The likelihood of trauma-related symptoms and diagnoses such as PTSD increases.

Evolution did not seem to care as much about how we were going to make sense of trauma or grow from it. Consequently, our higher brain region is not too involved with reacting to, processing, or remembering trauma. We must consciously invite this region to assist us with adverse experiences.

For example, it is the neocortex that can help us weave together the past, present, and future in order to gain perspective (and hopefully relief) when trauma is over. This can help us move the trauma from being a pre-verbal visceral or bodily experience to an integrated historical experience, and it can also help us manage triggers and decrease unnecessary stress reactions. There are areas of our higher brain that can help us put our adverse experiences and memories into words and form our personal narratives. With engagement of the conscious and higher regions, we can reflect on our experiences and better regulate our emotions with TDM—top-down management. Other people who engage us and make us feel safe facilitate this healing process even when we are unaware that it is even happening in the relationship.

It was evolutionarily important that we store adverse experiences in ways that would keep us suspicious and quickly reacting to all potential threats. Once again, better safe than sorry when survival (and reproduction) is the main goal. Our memory assists our learning of both cognitive and emotional material. Generalization is an aspect of learning. As an example, if a dog bites a child, fear of all dogs—not just the offending dog—can occur. The child is then likely to avoid dogs. The brain wants to keep this child safe and has extended this scary learning in the most general ways to all dogs. This defensive strategy protects the child from a physical survival vantage point. However, the brain has overdone it here because most dogs do not bite. The brain has generalized, and the child is deprived of this pet option if the limbic part of the brain remains in control of this learning and decision. This region of the brain does not care about the thriving potential in having a dog as a pet, but cares about the surviving potential from avoiding all dogs. New learning (with dogs) is necessary to extinguish the learned and remembered fear. We will later see that this same type of new learning through the caring and compassion of other people helps individuals who have been harmed at the hands of other people to recover.

All the senses of the body serve as "guards in the look-out tower" to transmit findings of potential threats to the brain for command operations. The hypothalamus lays in wait to deploy our biochemical troops. Chronic misperceiving of false positives or false alarms takes its toll. Imagine having a guard that never gets to sleep and alerts to both real threats and misperceived ones (false positives). A guard stationed in a high-stress environment eventually begins to exist within a constant state of danger and high alert. Sometimes this guard is just stressed all the time. Sometimes this guard can eventually become resigned, feel helpless and hopeless, and ultimately shut down. Sometimes this guard surrenders and just dissociates from the reality of both real and false threats.

Unintegrated and unresolved trauma remains encoded and isolated in the limbic region where no time perception exists, so the body is on guard as if the threat is current (even if it occurred in the distant past). It is only after the trauma gets linked (neuropathways built) to higher regions through language, for example, that it can gain the benefit of perspective and time perception. This allows for the parasympathetic nervous system to become more dominant to calm the body down.

As we saw in James' phone-throwing story, when faced with a perceived significant threat, the neocortex ramps down. Activities such as thinking, calculating math, or being verbal become unimportant. The limbic system and brainstem become most relevant. Fighting or fleeing the threat is most adaptive. With the rational region removed, the memory of the experience gets encoded and stored with high priority to survival in the limbic system. We may have survived the threat or trauma, but we are going to have longer-term psychological issues if that trauma is left unaddressed and unintegrated. The trauma gets stored in the hippocampus, which has no cognitive wisdom or time perception. When adversity is unaddressed and left in this region of the brain, we often see emotional dysregulation, hypervigilance in environments, and hyperarousal of the sympathetic nervous system—as we saw in the behavior of the guard who reacted to all possible alarms, both real and false.

Harm from a natural disaster, accident, or another animal is undoubtedly traumatic, but when another human being has perpetrated harm, it typically becomes more complex trauma. Part of the complexity is that other humans are everywhere, and we need them. For people to become a source of danger is tragic but all too common. The social nature of the brain makes relationships with others necessary and desired. A psychological dilemma results when harm comes from another person, especially another with whom one has a relationship. The brain generalizes and learns that other people are dangerous. The harm is even more complicated when perpetrated by a caregiver or authority figure whose genuine role is protection. This type of harm is not only done in childhood but adulthood too. Just as our brains remain vulnerable to physical injury at any age, they remain vulnerable to psychological injury at any age. Adults are vulnerable and sensitive beings too.

The concept of epigenetics, introduced in Chapter 1, explains how we are wired to learn about and remember that which is dangerous to our survival. Here's an illustration of that concept in action. A laboratory research study with rats was conducted which paired electric shock with a chemical scent of almonds. Rats like almonds, but each time they smelled them in the study, they were shocked. They learned to associate the smell with being shocked (pain). The smell of almonds became a threat. Their offspring (which never met their parents) avoided almonds! In fact, the fear extended to their children and their grandchildren. The fear got transferred genetically (DNA modified) within one generation (Dias & Ressler 2014). We, like these rats, have definitely been designed to stay vigilant of danger. Stressful and traumatic experiences are deeply learned and stored. Bad experiences create imprints in the sub-cortical areas of the brain. Ideally, in safe and secure environments, all regions of the brain become linked and integrated. The traumatized brain often is dissociative, and neural networks are unlinked. Unresolved trauma remains secluded in limbic pockets of the brain.

Healing is possible when the associated sensations, behaviors, and emotions of the trauma become integrated with cognition. The addressing of the stored trauma facilitates the development of perspective and restoration of safety and allows for the verbal ability of the individual to form a coherent narrative of the event. The neural networks formed as a result of the trauma can connect, integrate, and communicate with the higher regions of the brain. Interventions for trauma survivors must create neuronal growth and integration to be successful. We will discuss more of the complexities and ongoing nature of healing in Chapter 7.

Rewarded Brain: "At Ease"

Once the brain has determined that threats and risks have passed, and safety is ensured, it can begin the process of deactivation and inhibition of the limbic structures that promote the fight-or-flight response. When we are no longer in danger, it takes approximately 10 to 20 minutes to calm down and restore our prior state of mind. We feel better and can engage in different tasks once our threat system returns to the background and our relaxation network becomes dominant in our nervous system.

One nerve deserves special mention here: the vagus nerve is critical to counterbalancing the sympathetic nervous system or fight-or-flight activation. When this nerve gets stimulated, it triggers the release of a neurotransmitter called acetylcholine. Acetylcholine serves to counterbalance the stress hormones and reduce inflammation throughout the body. The vagus nerve has been identified as the major driver of our parasympathetic nervous system, which regulates the "tend-and-befriend" or "rest and digest" responses. Twelve pairs of nerves—our cranial nerves—emerge from the brain. The vagus nerve is the tenth cranial nerve and the longest nerve that is part of the autonomic nervous system. Each side of the body has one vagus nerve that starts in the brainstem (reptilian region) and runs down to the abdomen. The vagus nerve bidirectionally connects the brain to organs inside the body and communicates unconscious body functions such as the beating of the heart and digestion. It carries parasympathetic messages between body organs and the brain and is responsible for interoception (perception of the inner or visceral feelings of the body). Research into this nerve is an ongoing and represents an exciting ever-expanding horizon. Stephen Porges introduced "Polyvagal Theory" after his experiments with this nerve. He identified further depth and complexity (beyond calming and counterbalancing fight-or-flight) in our parasympathetic nervous system that he described as our social-engagement system (Porges, 2009). Engagement of the social engagement system and prosocial behaviors and reward seeking can return once the vagus nerve is engaged. Therefore, the vagus nerve is implicated in feeling safe in the workplace and engaging with others in the group.

Workaches focuses on the underlying survival drives of humans and resultant relational contests and stress. However, like most other aspects of human nature, the neuroscientific story is unfolding as rather complex. If it is all about survival, why do so many humans give to charity or participate in selfless acts of kindness with strangers? Well, an identified brain region exists that is responsible for altruistic behavior which likely evolved as it became increasingly adaptive to cooperate with larger groups of strangers. Additionally, the reward center of the brain activates with altruistic behavior and dopamine gets secreted. There is another aspect of the nervous system that facilitates another reaction—staying to help, or going toward a risky scene to assist, rather than running away. We worked with a manager who sustained a stab wound for an employee by placing himself in front of her during a workplace assault. His threat system was obviously triggered, but nonetheless, he went toward his employee to protect her. We expect that initial stress neurochemicals were later replaced with reward neurochemicals as a result of his heroically attending to another human being.

Feel Good Neurochemicals

Dilemmas occur when we avoid other people because they have hurt us (flight neurochemicals) and then need other people because they make us feel better (befriend neurochemicals). Humans enjoy being acknowledged, liked, and rewarded. These experiences activate the brain's reward system, which is a series of structures associated with motivation and reward and with the production of dopamine, which is a neurochemical or neurotransmitter that produces a pleasurable feeling. When the brain gets presented with something rewarding, it increases the release of dopamine. Structures and systems associated with the reward system are the mesolimbic pathway, mesocortical pathway, the ventral tegmental area, and the cerebral cortex. These systems and the release of dopamine have been identified as being key to motivation. Dopamine has also been shown to play a role in encoding memories about a reward. Just as the brain remembers what is threatening and stressful, it recognizes the sources of pleasure and dopamine production. These sources can thereby become addictive. We begin predicting, anticipating, and even enjoying our rewarding feelings before we even possess the actual rewarding source, which explains in part why we become highly motivated to seek these experiences and feelings.

Simply stated, we avoid unpleasant experiences because they make us feel bad, and we seek rewarding experiences because they make us feel good. Employees avoid work when it becomes associated with threat and stress. It makes a remarkable difference when there is at least one rewarding source at work to look forward to upon arrival. Just one coworker, task, client, can sometimes be enough to change the emotional valence of the workplace. The diversity of responses of what is reward or punishment to each individual in the workplace is complex. One person can be filled with dopamine and enabled while giving a presentation while another can be filled with cortisol and disabled from giving that same presentation. This is why it is so important for individuals to fulfill the work roles they are best suited for; otherwise, the stress of incompatible roles can be biochemically taxing, disabling, and counterproductive for the organization. Some examples of what employees report as rewarding include being recognized for their contributions, salary increases, public awards, experiencing team synergy, professional development, valuable project completions, and interpersonal connection and acknowledgement. To simplify...

REWARD → MOTIVATION → ENERGY GOES TO ... PRODUCTION

PUNISHMENT → THREAT → ENERGY GOES TO ... PROTECTION

Brain States and Contests

Our bodies and minds are active 24/7 and constantly changing in response to our environment. There are struggles and contests with other people. There are struggles and conflicts within our own selves—our thoughts may be in conflict with our feelings, and our behaviors may be in conflict with our goals. There are struggles between regions responding to a perceived threat and those seeking to pursue a reward. These intrapersonal struggles may occur more frequently than interpersonal struggles. Even though we remain consistent human beings over time and retain the same brain, our mind or brain states are constantly changing. Different internal states and external environmental factors, from viruses to hormones, change us. The varying amount of activity and energy in the various lobes and regions of the brain can create such remarkably different mind states that our actions and feelings may surprise others and even ourselves. One may ask how a brain region such as the limbic system that does not have verbal ability can get us to shout profanities or words that are later regretted. Our brain areas are not entirely isolated and independent of one another. The neuro-connections allow for communication, and the limbic system can "hijack" the higher brain centers and use the verbal ability of the neocortex to carry out its own will.

REFLECTION

Think about some of the contests or conflicts between the different regions of your own brain. Do you ever struggle between impulse or temptation and wisdom? Which part typically wins? Which part do you usually want to have win the contest or struggle? If you consciously decide to hold your breath (a decision from the higher conscious part of your brain), how long does it take your lower nonconscious brain region to win so that you are forced to breathe again?

Breathing is an easy example of a brain battle because it is one physiological activity that is both consciously and nonconsciously controlled. But you see that if you choose to hold your breath, you can only do so for so long. The lower primitive region will always win the battle, and you will be forced to breathe against your conscious will or choice. Automatically ensuring survival is non-negotiable to our reptilian, or most primitive, brain region. Our nonconscious regions do not always win, however. We can also see the changes and challenges in our varying degrees of willpower. Sometimes we can resist that last doughnut, and other times we cannot. Frequent contests and challenges occur daily in the workplace between all the different regions of the brain that interact with others. Sometimes the conflicts and contests that occur within us lead us to behave uncharacteristically or in ways that can make us fail even to recognize ourselves. We sometimes exclaim, "I lost my mind," "I snapped," "I don't know what came over me," "I just lost it," and "I went crazy." Different brain states likely underlie our uttering these phrases. Next, we introduce a brain-wise organizational system to assist with managing the very different regions of our brain. We may not be able to hold our breath for longer than our primitive region allows, but we do have more choice in other matters and can manage other aspects of our more primitive parts.

Top-Down Management (TDM) of the Brain

In adulthood we become the managers of our own selves. Prior to this we are in training by our caregivers who are typically trying to get us to the developmental point of being our own independent life managers. As adults, we become not only our own managers, but also our own board members, thought leaders, supervisors, and workers. We are pretty much "it." This multi-faceted role is important, because the adage of "too much of a good thing" applies to our reward system. Even reward seeking can go too far and must be managed. The seeking of pleasure from sugar or other substances and objects can have adverse consequences. Top-down management, or TDM, of the brain implies that higher cortex is managing most of the reactions, reflexes, impulses, emotions, and other behaviors generated by the limbic system and the brainstem. The cortex must be able to use its capacity for reason, time, and goal-directed behaviors to process, organize, delay, or inhibit the impulsivity of the two lower brain regions.

TDM is not always possible. Primitive and nonconscious arenas can overwhelm or "hijack" the neocortex. TDM is a simplified technique that follows a simplified model (tripartite model of brain), so it has its limitations in applicability sometimes. The primitive brain can exert nonconscious and overwhelming control over our higher regions. Our higher regions do not necessarily hold more power. Circumstances, disease, age, and other individual variations are examples of things that can impact our capacity for TDM. Loss of TDM is the "it" of the phrase "I lost it." Individuals who have suffered frontal lobe or PFC injury often exhibit impulse-control issues that they did not have before injury.

Children and adolescents do not possess enough neuropathways and connectedness to do as well with TDM as most adults. Individuals with dementia often lose capacities from higher regions first (e.g., ability to think before ability to emotionally react). Additionally, when our survival is at risk, our ability for TDM is affected. When our primitive regions deem it is not adaptive to think, we really cannot! So, as with any supervisor, manager, or leader attempting to effectively control certain situations—some situations are just unmanageable, though we try our best.

The tripartite model of the human brain aids our understanding of how a person (whom we would never predict to harm another) would come to assault a fellow human being. Once again, this does not excuse antisocial behavior, it just helps us explain what we might see in others, ourselves, and on the news. This model is useful to help us grapple with the discovery that our sports hero has committed murder, our coach has committed sexual assault, or that we, ourselves, have done something we now feel ashamed about and wonder how we could have done it. When the neocortex goes offline—in any human—that individual may act remarkably different than when their brain is integrated and in TDM.

Figure 3.10 depicts some of the dynamic interactions or communication patterns between the different brain regions. Once again, we are managing quite a dynamic and complex organization that we call our brains!

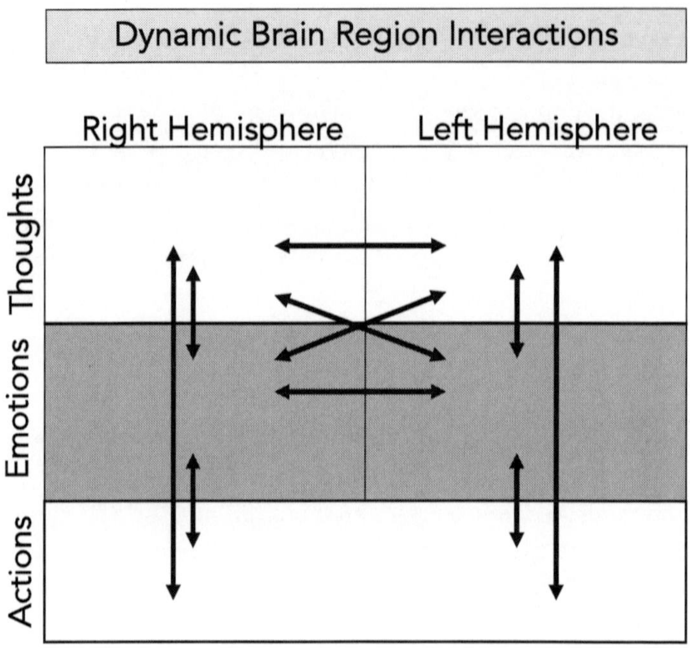

Figure 3.10

We aim to hire the best managers for our organizations, but first, we must engage the best managers for our own brains. Figure 3.11 summarizes the tripartite model of the brain and the three parts to which we have assigned names based on their functions. So, would you hire T.D., Amy, or Liz?

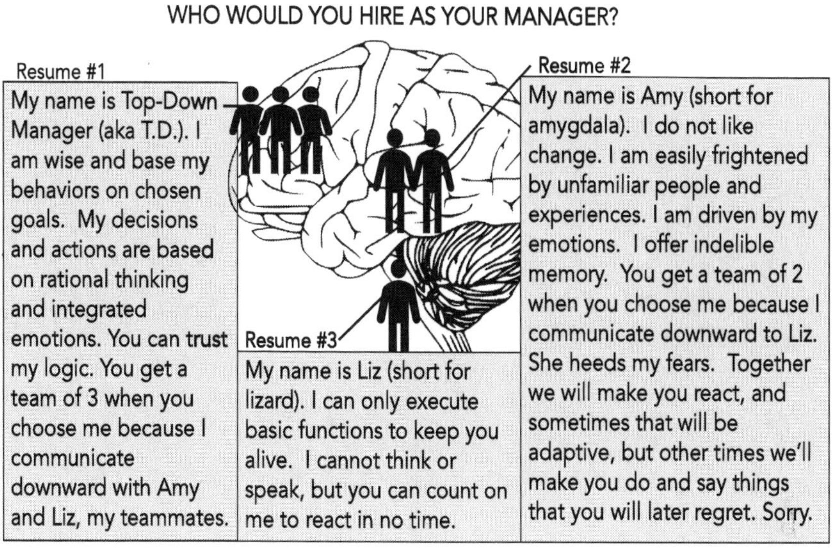

Figure 3.11

Most likely, you would hire T.D. because resume 1 indicates that T.D. utilizes all resources of the entire integrated brain. Hopefully, T.D. can delegate authority to the others below on the team who possess a quality needed at the time. Liz brings her fast reaction time to the team. Amy brings her sensitivity and emotionality to the team. However, Amy needs supervision because she is so rigid and zealous due to how she was designed to function millions of years ago. Amy is a workaholic and scanning 24/7 for threats in the environment. Amy often misfires and alerts to false alarms. Liz reacts whether true or false alarm, and therefore requires supervision as well. Unfortunately, in modern society, this is a biochemically costly endeavor because this system utilizes the same resources for a false alarm as it does for a real threat alarm. Amy and Liz both require adaptive and compassionate management and deserve all due respect as dedicated and hard workers.

Let us consider another example of the role different emotions play in our self-management, or lack thereof. With increasing congestion and competition for resources, we are aware of increasing incidents of road rage. We cannot underestimate the increased stress employees endure on their way to and from the workplace. The tripartite model fits nicely with our understanding of road rage as illustrated more generally below.

Event (cut off in traffic) → fast brain activation (survive challenged) → threat → anger defense → reactive violence → perception of self-protection (dopamine release) → neocortex comes back online and TDM returns→ ambivalence ("what did I do?") → recognition behavior was not in line with values and goals (thrive of existence) and likely led to maladaptive outcome → stress hormones → regret

The goal, if there is no real threat, is to keep the neocortex online and maintain an integrated brain with TDM. If this is impossible, then we want to regain TDM as soon as possible. The goal of treatment with road rage is strengthened pathways to that "top-floor" of the brain which allows time and perspective to come into play. The prefrontal cortex is an ally and can organize and soothe the other regions.

Bottom-Up Processing in the Brain

TDM is not always necessary or indicated. Sometimes we want the manager (PFC) to go away so we can be free to experience and linger in good sensations and feelings. We do not want to be thinking or doing math or employing logic. We are safe and secure during these times and just want to indulge our senses, not our thoughts. The wise mind at these times is similar to an attuned and fluid manager in the workplace—it knows when its presence and direction is needed, and when to retreat and trust. People with trauma histories have more difficulty with this. The trauma memories are stored on limbic and somatic levels that can make these individuals experience the body as unsafe. A crucial part of trauma intervention is to facilitate the body's feeling safe, or at least as safe as possible.

We do not need the neocortex to experience the smell of a flower, watch a sunset, or pet an animal. This is when we invite bottom-up processing. The practice of mindfulness, which we address later, involves bottom-up engagement, as well as higher brain regions. Different areas of the brain are never completely turned off, but intentional and active disengagement of higher brain regions has its proper time and place.

Emotional Regulation and Dysregulation

We typically do not perceive the work environment as the place where emotions are the primary content of the day. However, given all the above-ground triggers and underground reactions, intense feelings can be there despite our best attempts to avoid them. Emotions are especially active when work involves other people and serving other people, such as in HHS. Our feelings and emotions are a characteristic aspect of our humanness.

There are specific areas in the brain that when stimulated produce corresponding emotions. However, as we develop, we learn which places are safe for emotional expression and which are not. We are overtly and covertly given culture-based, gender-based, race-based, and hierarchy-based lessons on emotions. Emotional ranges and nuances are part of our individuality. New employees typically "look around" to observe what the display rules are for emotions in a workplace. Of course, everyone wants to appear "in control" of their feelings. The management of emotions is yet another challenging task at work. This challenge especially holds true in HHS where emotional triggers abound in work content. Later, we will address the strategies for the acceptance, recognition, and optimal use of emotions in the workplace. Our feelings are a vital gauge and form of psychosocial information for us and others.

Six basic emotions have been commonly identified in humans (and other mammals): sadness, happiness, anger, fear, disgust, and surprise. Newer research has suggested there are only four emotions—grouping fear-surprise together and anger-disgust together (Beck, 2014). All other feelings, then, are a mix of these emotions, which is similar to the primary colors making up the full spectrum of colors. When we assess someone's emotional functioning, we look at specific dimensions including range, expression, intensity, duration, regulation, transitions, cultural displays and restrictions, triggers, and capacity to reflect on emotions and communicate them in interpersonal relationships. Emotional intelligence (EI) refers to the ability of individuals to be aware of their own emotions and those of others, to manage the emotions adaptively, and to be able to empathize with the feelings of others. Later, we will see how particularly important it is for leaders, managers, and supervisors to possess EI.

Human Brain and Its Hidden Stories: You Never Know

We end this chapter on the brain with some simple illustrations of the notion that although our bodies change remarkably as we grow up, our brains do not change in the same way. The early experiences remain stored in the brain and can be triggered and reactivated at any time throughout adulthood. The clinical notion of the "inner child" has been validated by neuroscience in that early experiences are stored in the emotional areas of the brain and shadow our adult selves in what are called synaptic or neuronal shadows. These unseen shadows are there when we interact with colleagues. For example...

The coworker who noticed the silence upon entering the office may have been the subject of lethal gossip in school.
That employee that you are giving feedback to may have been shamed by an authority figure as a child.

We all remain vulnerable—especially to one another. Adulthood social disguises may mask childhood vulnerabilities, but the brain and body remember. We are all struggling human beings despite our titles, roles, and social personas.

The next chapter further explores how social and connected our brains truly are and the impacts we have on one another.

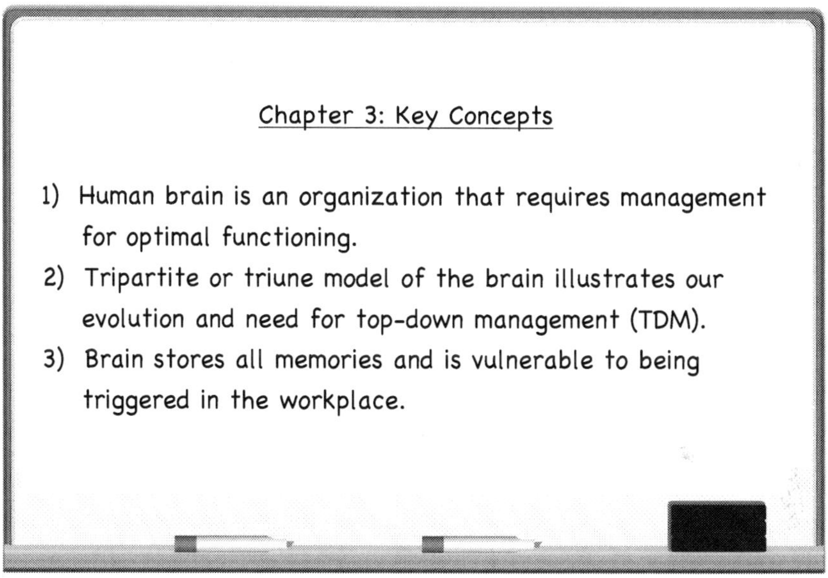

4

RELATIONAL FIELDS: OUR SOCIAL BRAINS AT WORK

The psychosocial space between us is not empty.

The force of gravity has a constant and pervasive influence on us, though we do not directly see it. Viewing the absence of this force when astronauts float in space is amusing. Children enjoy playing with magnets for similar reasons. Invisible forces often fascinate us. Some magnets attract, and others repel each other in the magnetic field. Major invisible physical forces have been identified in the universe and studied for a long time.

Another force exists, however, that has received much less attention over the years. This is the omnipresent psychosocial force of the relational field. These interpersonal forces have constant and powerful influence on us, though we do not directly see them either. Just as we study the effects of gravitational forces, social scientists study the effects of interpersonal forces in those spaces between and within us.

The relational field is full of some of the most intense and dramatic forces in the universe. They have profound impact on us and have significant implications for our work relations.

So, whether it is a gravitational, magnetic, or relational field, to best manage these forces of nature, we must get to know them. Modern technology has been able to reveal the first two kinds of forces. We are now able to "see" relational forces, too, with our newest brain imaging techniques.

As we described in earlier chapters, our evolution has wired us to survive best in groups. Scientists believe that our brains grew larger because we had to cooperate, coordinate, and communicate with others in our expanding clans. We became safer together. This worked—we have survived as a group. Yet, we also harm each other in our groups. Quite an evolutionary paradox exists here. We help each other and harm each other. We create each other, and we destroy each other. We have intense reactions to one another, yet we have this keen ability to pretend we do not. The relational field is yet to be fully understood. Nature has selected or chosen us to form pairs and groups, and then to have conflict within and outside our groups. In this chapter, we explore some of the dynamics of the social brain and its vulnerability to other people. We additionally explore the social learning brain or how we learn from observing each other. We learn about ourselves and others from others. So those apparently judgmental glances, rumors, gossip, and various other communications negatively affect our own identities and self-esteem. Acceptance, validation, and respectful communication positively affect us. We are wired to learn what others think of us and often believe their assessments (even if they're inaccurate). Bottom line: other humans are deeply impactful in our lives.

This chapter serves as the bridge from the basics of the human brain and social anthropology to interpersonal dynamics. When we finally arrive at the organizational level, we will appreciate the complexity of human interactions and the inevitability of relational complications.

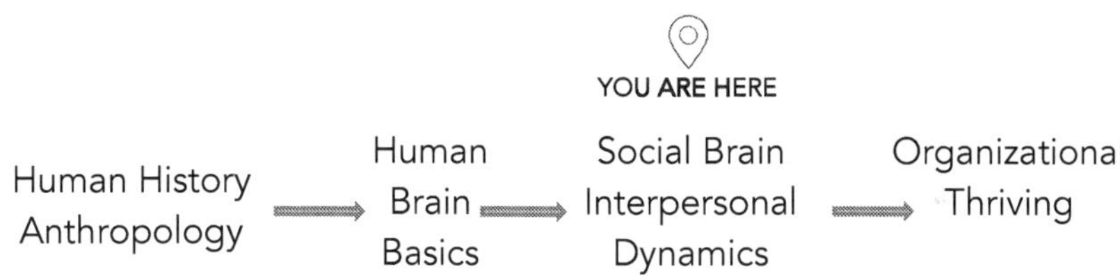

We include this chapter on how social and connected our brains are to underline and better appreciate the amount of energy that goes into working on the human relations incidentals of work, especially in health and human services. In any given work day, sometimes the energy required for these job incidentals can be greater than what we put into the work tasks themselves. For some, just getting to and from the workplace is taxing. Add to this negotiating work relationships and experiences, as well as the accumulating effects of all the emotions that accompany tending to the pain and adversity of others.

It takes a finite amount of time and energy to remove a foster care child from their fifth foster home placement and return them to the temporary county facility during a work day. This is a mere fraction of the ultimate toll that this takes on the social worker. The emotional effects extend well past the end of the work day.

We now know that emotional effects have enduring neurobiological ramifications. As we have learned, it may be impossible to separate professional from personal, or work from life. Our ancestors did not have to. We do. Or at least, we try to. We are tasked with completing our work responsibilities in our allotted work hours. Employers calculate our pay based in part on our work time or product. The issue with this is that a great deal of work is going into managing all the daily emotional triggers and other psychosocial experiences of our work. There are 80 organs in the human body. The brain monopolizes approximately 20 percent of the body's energy, and with psychosocial burdens, it needs even more. This has significant implications for our need to refuel energy supplies when output is so great.

Psychosocial Injuries: Bloodless Wounds and Invisible Scars

Our brains are very vulnerable to injury through acts of commission (what someone does to us) and acts of omission (what they do not give us that we need, such as acceptance into the group). While the skull protects the brain from physical injury as best it can, it unfortunately cannot protect the brain from psychological or social injury. We now know that other people—from our ancestors to the new people we meet—contribute to the building of our brains throughout our lives. The brain learns and changes with interpersonal interactions by forming new neural pathways and connections. The brain is wired to be social.

To set the stage for the chapter on workaches, we first explore relational or group social aggression. Stress that is created by people and between people causes significant neurochemical changes in the brains and bodies of all those involved. The changes particularly occur in the brain areas most associated with emotions, including the amygdala, hippocampus, and prefrontal cortex. Studies have suggested that inflammation, which has been implicated in many disease processes, is triggered by stress. Both psychosocial and physical injuries cause inflammation, which is physically harming, so the distinction between them is diminishing in the literature (Liu et al., 2017).

Interpersonal violence of a physical nature has been estimated to account for about 2 percent of human deaths consistently throughout history and 1.43 million deaths per year across the world (Siever, 2014). We do not have any clear statistics for the incidence of interpersonal psychological violence, much less its correlation with deaths, but we know it is pervasive. Throughout the workday, many individuals are getting psychologically slapped, punched, and poked. Despite our defensive armor, there is cumulative damage that occurs as a result of these interpersonal dynamics. Psychological injury is mostly invisible to the human eye. None of our known senses detect covert emotional injury unless the victim emits a distress call, such as crying. Some individuals, however, do "sense" emotional distress more than others.

As clinical psychologists, we often have hypothesized about the potential value of "visible" psychological bleeding. Would it trigger more self-awareness and empathy? Would people stop emotionally harming if they "saw" their immediate impact? Would we have a better measure of the harm being inflicted on others and ourselves?

Blood and bruises in the physical world reveal acts of commission. Acts of omission can also be revealed in the physical realm. If a child is not provided necessary nourishment, he or she physically starves. Others can see when someone is physically starving or failing to thrive. Detection of acts of omission in the emotional realm, unless they are quite severe, is more challenging. Often, signs of emotional neglect or social exclusion do not manifest until much later in the development of the individual. They manifest eventually in a physical manner too—in the brain. Depriving another individual of their personal integrity and self-worth—what we refer to as annihilation—does great harm.

These experiences are not particular to childhood. Acts of commission and omission occur at work just as they do in other life realms. Relational fields in the workplace are laden with intense and ever-changing emotions and accompanying neurochemical reactions. Other people throw us off of our TDM navigation throughout the workday. They especially trigger our middle brain by stimulating feelings such as anger, love, disgust, lust, envy, shame, desire, etc. These feelings come with changes in brain and body chemistry, which make them extra difficult to manage. Staying aware of these emotions is adaptive in the workplace. We just cannot be neutral in this zone. Humans have evolved to disguise psychosocial injury in order to appear invulnerable and unaffected, and thereby continue to appear viable to the group. People are often unaware of the psychological harm they are doing to one another. Sometimes we are unaware of the psychological harm being inflicted upon ourselves. Our human ability to hide our psychosocial pain or injury can be adaptive at different times and places, but maladaptive in other circumstances. Great need exists for increased understanding of psychosocial damage from unhealthy workplaces, because all people get triggered at different points, no matter how they socially appear. Once personal triggers are identified and explored, we can learn to better manage them.

Mirror Neurons and Empathy: "I Feel Your Pain"

We have observed that a great proportion of the individuals who find their way to HHS work have remarkable levels of empathy. One of the reasons, for example, the social worker transporting the foster care child would be so affected is the existence of a certain type of brain cell called a mirror neuron. Mirror neurons are believed to facilitate our social ability and capacity for empathy. These neurons were discovered in monkeys in the 1990s in a neurophysiology laboratory in Italy (di Pellegrino et al., 1992). Their discovery has led to continued research and fascinating findings about the social nature of the brain, because mirror neurons were shown to fire when we perform an act ourselves in the same way as when we observe another person perform that same act. That's how they got their name—they mimic or replicate like a mirror. So, whether you observe an action or perform it yourself, corresponding neurons fire, and for this reason, they allow us to experience and imitate the intentions, actions, and feelings of other people. It turns out that I may not need to "walk a mile in your shoes" to understand and feel for your plight. I may just need to hear your story or observe your life. I may even come down with the symptoms of trauma after learning about yours.

Mirror neurons also facilitate learning. For example, if we observe another touch a hot stove and pull their hand away with pain, we learn not to touch a hot stove from this one-time observation, because observing the reaction builds the same neural pathway in our own brains as experiencing it ourselves. Like most other aspects of human experiencing and brain functioning, mirror neurons may not fully explain our capacity for empathy and compassion, but nonetheless, to date their study has led to remarkable clinical implications.

As with most any other human trait, things are a bit more complex than just having the trait or not. Empathy, like many traits, falls on a spectrum. Individuals exhibit different levels of empathy throughout their lives and in different circumstances. In his intriguing book, *The Science of Evil*, Simon Baron-Cohen (2011) examines individuals who range from high to low on the trait of empathy and poses the idea of an empathy quotient (EQ). He describes some individuals as possessing no ability to empathize with another (Level 0). These individuals have no awareness of others' feelings or how they themselves come across to others. They lack the capacity to anticipate or predict the feelings of others, which results in extreme self-centeredness. Others at the opposite end of the spectrum (Level 6) possess such significant capacity to empathize that they remain in a state of hyperarousal because they are constantly taking in others' feelings and anticipating their reactions. Dr. Baron-Cohen provides The Empathy Quotient test at the end of his book for those interested.

Daniel Goleman (2014) has described empathy as divisible into three different types:

TYPES OF EMPATHY	
COGNITIVE:	<u>Know</u> what other is feeling or thinking
EMOTIONAL:	<u>Feel</u> what the other is experiencing
COMPASSIONATE:	<u>Help</u> other based in feeling/understanding their needs

Possessing all three types of empathy at the appropriate times is important for parents, teachers, and leaders. The importance of empathy in leadership will be discussed in Chapter 8.

Beauty and Burden in Caring

Many of the HHS professionals we have met over the years appear to have a high empathy quotient (EQ), which may be why they find themselves in fields that serve the needs of others. While their empathy may be an important ability on the job, individuals on the higher end of the empathy spectrum often require practices and instruction to "turn off" or "tune down" their empathy in order to rest and let down. We address workaches such as compassion fatigue and secondary trauma in the following chapter.

Individuals who find themselves in helping professions attending to the pain and adversity of others may have more mirror neurons and empathy. As wonderful as these traits are, they come with costs to their possessors.

Some individuals have such a high empathy quotient that they somatically experience the feelings and symptoms of others, which means these individuals are bombarded constantly by the experiences and pain of others, in addition to their own. Judith Orloff, MD has written extensively about these individuals and labeled them as empaths (Orloff, 2017). In her book, *The Empath's Survival Guide: Life Strategies for Sensitive People*, Dr. Orloff offers valuable strategies for managing these traits. She addresses how compassion can be exhausting and emphasizes the critical need for self-care. *The Highly Sensitive Person* by Elaine Aron is another good read on the trait of sensitivity and empathy. Alice Miller, in her book, *The Drama of the Gifted Child*, captures the plight of a sensitive child growing up in an environment lacking empathy and sensitivity to the child's needs, for example with an individual with a lower degree of empathy who may have difficulty offering unconditional love.

The capacity for empathy is considered to be part of "emotional intelligence" (EI). Next, we briefly review emotional intelligence, as well as other forms of intelligence and styles of personality. We encounter the full spectrum of individuals in most workgroups, and being familiar with these different traits comes in handy.

Diversity: Natural and Needed

In the workplace or any other environment, we are going to find people possessing varied traits and characteristics. Individual brains bring different ways of thinking, creating, feeling, relating, building, and behaving. Evolution favors diversity, as much as we might be wary of differences. Diversity of characteristics allows for greater possibility that some will be more adaptive in different and changing environments. If some organisms have gills and others have lungs, and the environment turns aquatic, at least those with gills will carry on. This applies to psychological characteristics as well. Awareness and appreciation—even if one cannot get to acceptance—of different styles can assist in the workplace. Having accurate impressions of the unique traits of others helps to minimize disappointment and unrealistic expectations, but it also assists with appreciating what the individual does contribute.

Recognizing the need for and the value of diversity is crucial, because we need different types of intelligence in most workforces. In fact, diversity has been shown to increase productivity and creativity in the workplace (Altman, 2017). Having teams that are made up of the spectrum of individuals lends itself to increased creativity, different perspectives, better potential matches with clients and customers, and the possibility of solving problems by looking through different lenses and having diverse approaches. Because we have been designed to be suspicious of traits and characteristics that are different than our own, staying mindful of the value of diversity may help counteract some of the nonconscious fears.

When we think of intelligence, we typically think of cognitive intelligence quotient (IQ) which is measured by standard intelligence tests that assess ability for verbal and nonverbal reasoning. However, IQ may not be the most impactful type of intelligence in the relational field of the workplace. It may be important for completion of work tasks, but emotional and social functioning have greater relevance in interpersonal functioning. Emotional intelligence (EI) involves the ability to understand, perceive, manage, and utilize emotions within oneself and others (Salavoy & Mayer, 1997). Social intelligence (SI) is defined as the ability to successfully build relationships and navigate social environments (Goleman, 2006). Like other human traits, social intelligence can be measured on a spectrum from very low to very high. Whereas IQ is considered to be a relatively fixed and stable attribute, SI and EI are considered to be more fluid and have more potential for being learned.

We also see diverse personality characteristics in the workplace that range from well-adjusted and adaptable personality styles to personality disorders. Not all human traits are positive ones. Some are more antisocial than social. A recently studied personality trait, labeled the Dark Factor or D-factor (Moshagen et al., 2018), is associated with more malevolent aspects of personality, including revengefulness, selfishness, narcissism, sadism, manipulativeness, and evilness. Overall, the person with a high D-factor is self-centered and places his or her own goals, interests, and needs above all else. This type of individual gains pleasure from the misfortune of others (schadenfreude). Identifying and gaining immunity from these types of individuals is vital in the workplace. We must not pretend that individuals with selfish or evil intent do not find their way onto our teams.

Awareness of these different traits and styles can lead to increased immunity and protective actions.

Collective intelligence (CI)—the combined and shared group intelligence that results from the collective efforts of collaborating individuals (Woolley et al., 2010)—is brilliant. Having a room full of diverse minds bringing in all types of intelligence to consider an issue or solve a problem is powerful and optimal. We have seen CI at work with the wraparound approach in social agencies, for example, when diverse individuals from service providers to family members are brought together to think about and create interventions for a client. Team members work together to enact the plan of action. The concept of intelligence has evolved over the years. Intelligence and academic achievement are no longer considered one and the same. Developmental psychologist Howard Gardner proposed the theory of multiple intelligences, which breaks down intelligence into seven categories, as shown in Figure 4.1 (Gardner, 1993).

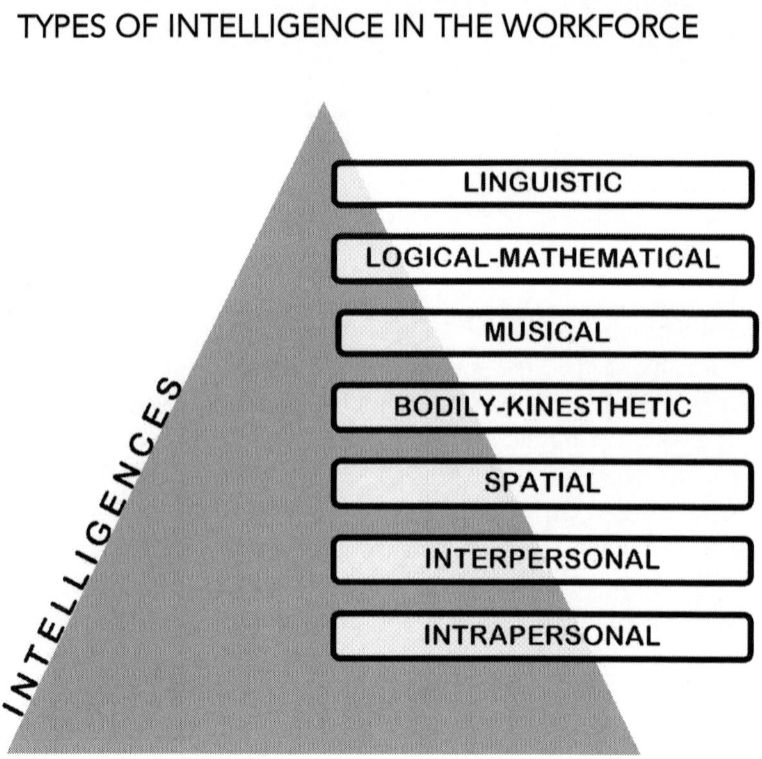

Figure 4.1

Managers who recognize the varied forms of intelligence in their staff will greatly ignite their engagement and development, as well as benefit the organization. Recruiting for emotional and social intelligence is important due to their value to interpersonal relations in the workplace. Workaches are often a consequence of a lack of fit between person and role in the workplace. We want to match as many of the traits needed for a job position to a person who possesses them. We have spoken with countless distressed employees who have been placed in roles that are not a good fit for them. Job duties were often not disclosed clearly enough in job descriptions. We have addressed the more introverted employee who is mandated to give public presentations. We have spoken to the artistic and creative individual who has discovered that a part of their job role is to maintain a statistics-based database. We have communicated with the employee with minimal SI who has been told to coordinate the holiday party and gift selections. Mismatches result in stress for the employee and loss of quality performance for the employer. The more compatibility between needs of position and traits of person, the better the relationship and potential for thriving in the position. Being aware of what specific types of intelligence may be needed for specific job descriptions is useful. This assists with interviewing and hiring individuals who are likely to be good fits for their positions. This diversity of intelligence is essential for a workplace to be successful because it allows for an array of strengths and talents needed for different tasks and jobs. We do not want to hire staff who are all in the same lane.

Social Strategies and Illusions: Charm and Deception

Our social world is incredibly complex, and navigating it is often perplexing because things are not always what they seem to be. People are not always who they say they are. When we see another person, we see a unique face. Each person also has an accompanying brain that is even more unique. An individual's brain has been sculpted by their environment beginning in the womb, and brains have more variability than faces. The brain stores every moment and continues to learn and change. The human face can be deceptive but also can give away what an individual might be feeling or planning through nonverbal signals such as diverted eyes. Our ancestors needed to develop varied social strategies to gain entrance into more and more groups. They needed to learn how to charm and sometimes deceive others. They then needed to learn how to decode disguises and discover other ways to "know" a stranger. It certainly was simpler in the early clan with only a handful of people living together throughout their lives.

Social strategies have serious implications for employee recruitment and hiring. Screening potential employees is critical for competent employee selection. However, to date, no foolproof method exists for doing so. There will always be those individuals who are more deceptive on their way in, and we currently have no way of measuring this. Our brains possess the ability to make us imposters or chameleons, and even to fool ourselves into believing we are qualified for a position for which we are interviewing. We can manipulate and adaptively make ourselves appear to be the person others might want us to be. As hiring authorities, we can only predict up to a point how any given brain will operate and socialize in the workforce. Chapter 8 furthers our discussion of the inevitable challenges of recruitment and hiring.

While it may be expedient to the individual at the time, social deception erodes trust and feelings of safety within groups. It creates fear and mistrust in our own ability to assess whether someone is friend or enemy. That may be one reason we continually scan one another for consistency and predictability. The threat system scans for that snake in the woodpile at the same time we want to believe that we are safe and protected. Horror story writers know how to scare us when the parental, consistent, and trustworthy character unexpectedly turns out to be the psychopathic killer. We were predicting and projecting what we needed on the character (as we know our brains like to do) and finally felt comfortable, when the author switches it up on us—quite frightening!

The social underground of humans is vast and intricate. As we have described, more nonconscious material lies beneath the surface than conscious material. The iceberg is often used as a metaphor of how much more of our minds are "beneath the surface," yet powerfully present. If we refer back to the triune brain model, we can think of the exposed part of the iceberg as the neocortex. Beneath the surface lie the other regions, including the limbic system and brainstem. Stored beneath the surface in nonconscious states are the emotional and relational memories that shadow people into the workforce. Our employers and coworkers do not see below our surfaces and do not know of the neuronal shadows that are cast upon them in our relating to them. We do not see their shadows on us, but we can sometimes feel them—as when we feel misunderstood or sense they are projecting their unresolved issues onto us.

The more connections we can make between our nonconscious and "above the surface" conscious realms, the better our communication and coordination of emotions, thoughts, impulses, actions, and behaviors. These connections are made by neuropathways connecting deeper limbic regions to higher cortical regions. The more pathways we have integrating our brain regions, the better our perspective on others and ourselves. Having many lenses from which to perceive our world is an adaptive quality. In Chapter 7, we discuss how counseling and other strategies can facilitate these connections. With better connectedness, we have a greater chance of stepping back and reflecting on interpersonal events to gain perspective—which will make us less likely to act on nonconscious reactions. We can only do this imperfectly, however, because of the architecture of our brains. The challenge is that a great deal of our exchanges with others continue to take place in the social underground—out of our conscious awareness. Our own emotions, stored experiences, and more primitive motivations lie beneath conscious awareness. As we navigate our social worlds, the ideal is to remain aware that we have a social underground and struggle to gain as much conscious awareness of it as possible. And we can only hope that others do the same.

The brain is the organ that we tend to view as the "smart" one of our bodies. Yet, this organ can easily be tricked and made to believe something that is not necessarily true. We are wise to remain aware of this in the workplace. All our senses can be fooled. We have blind spots. We make inaccurate attributions. We perceive stuff that is not really there. Magicians and comics make use of this vulnerability in us. Our eyes are the sense organs that bring the visual world to us, but it is our brains that ultimately determine what we see. What do you first see in Figure 4.2? Who you are, the time of the year, and other factors will determine what you see. This figure was created by an anonymous illustrator in 1892 and later popularized by Joseph Jastrow (Jastrow, 1900), a psychologist who studied human perception. The fast brain perceives a duck or rabbit first, but then most people can see either. If it is close to Easter, people are more likely to see a rabbit first. In October, people are more likely to see a duck first. This ambiguous figure reminds us how our brains are vulnerable to perceptual distortions and illusions. Not all illusions are visual ones.

Illusion Credit: Anonymous.1892. 'Welche Thiere gleichen einander am meisten?' Filegende Blatter. Braun & Schneider.

Figure 4.2

The other side of illusions or trickery is the unamusing use of the brain's vulnerability to manipulation and control by others. We refer to these as social illusions. Some of the dynamics underlying certain workaches are caused by this vulnerability to be duped or made to feel something based on another person's agenda. For example, we can be made to feel worthless by means of "neurodeception" or "neurotrickery." This kind of manipulation is often used to convince a vulnerable brain to join a street gang or terrorist organization. We know that cult leaders can gain power over certain regions of the brain and can even get members to harm themselves—an extreme example of the social influence one human can have over another. Hypocrisy is also a form of neurotrickery to remain aware of. The loss prevention specialist in an organization can be the one siphoning funds. Roles are not always ethically fulfilled by those who occupy them.

Sometimes the trickery is out of awareness of the trickster. If the trickster needs status, they may humiliate the other to gain status for themselves without being consciously aware that they are even doing this. Leaders may have no awareness of how they are using their power to sometimes make others feel disrespected and inadequate. Children as young as three years old are capable of trickster behaviors, as many parents know. This is why that child is typically never the one who ate the cookie (even though the crumbs are clinging to their chin). We learn early on how to manipulate others—or at least make the attempt—in order to secure our own safety and resources.

Perceptual Distortions: More Social Illusions

Sometimes we need someone to be something to us so badly that we "see" them in that way. Sometimes we do not "see" something in someone or cannot receive something from them because they remind us of someone from our past. We described the phenomenon of neuronal or synaptic shadows in the last chapter. Perceptual distortion is a psychological term used to describe this social phenomenon. We do this with one another outside of our own awareness, and this phenomenon is not yet fully understood. When this happens within our awareness, we typically can identify a physical resemblance or a similar sounding tone of voice that triggered our feelings or experiences about someone from our past. When this happens outside of our awareness, it is much more difficult to detect. Sometimes someone else may need to bring this to our attention.

In some forms of counseling, this shadow phenomenon is called transference. It occurs when the client "transfers" onto the therapist nonconscious feelings and desires from childhood (Sayin, 2013). Countertransference is when the therapist does the same thing to the client. Neither can perceive the other as they truly are. Neuronal or synaptic shadowing also describes how we do not necessarily perceive others completely free of the templates we store in our brains about people from our pasts. Another term that is used is parataxic distortion. When we adopt an abused animal from a shelter, we soon realize that they are perceiving us through their lens or previous template of the abusive human. We must proceed sensitively and help them learn that some humans are not dangerous. We want them to form and strengthen a new neural pathway between human and safe, versus human and unsafe. Most animals generalize in this way. If it happened once, it can happen again.

Staying aware of how we might distort others is important in the workplace. Just as we make corrections for distortions of vision by wearing glasses, we must attempt to make corrections for our perceptual distortions. It also becomes critical to be aware of when others may be distorting us based on their past histories. We are often quick to personalize interpersonal nuances, but sometimes other's reactions to us have little to do with us. An example of a sensitive perceptual distortion at work is in the offering of feedback. Most of us desire to be perceived in a favorable light. Some employees have great difficulty receiving any commentary on or criticisms of their work. Sometimes this is due to a boss truly being critical and offering feedback in a maladaptive way. Other times, it may be because of a neuronal shadow of a critical parent or devaluing teacher cast onto the boss. In this case, the employee receives and perceives the feedback as threatening because it is filtered through the neuronal shadow. This triggers nonconscious regions to become protective and defensive, which in turn can inhibit valuable learning from the feedback.

Our Social Underground: Maneuvers and Communications

Distortions abound at work because of inaccurate perceptions, shadows from our past, projections, judgments, complicated reactions, and the personas we create. Most individuals are socialized enough by the time they enter the workplace to translate their true feelings and thoughts into socially appropriate words and behavior (at least when in TDM). Most people have learned to "neutralize" and "normalize" their social self—from what they wear to the content of their speech. Typically, this is done to remain under the social radar of the group. The presence of just one other person influences us greatly.

REFLECTION

If you were the only person on earth, what would you do differently because nobody else would be around watching you? What would you wear? What would you drive? Which objects would you possess? Where would you live? Would you wear makeup or jewelry? Would you shave? How would you wear your hair? How would you spend your days? Reflect on other pressures from which you might be relieved. If you could choose to introduce others back into your life in this scenario, what types of individuals would you allow to reenter your social world? How would you design living and working?

Social Observational Learning: We Watch Each Other

We watch each other. We watch each other to learn. We watch each other to compare and compete. Ultimately, we watch each other to survive. I need to stay aware of any advantages you may be gaining over me. I may be threatened if you are out to lunch with the boss. Survival is at stake. But you may be noticing something that I do not. This is considered an adaptive trait because if you spot a threat that I do not, if I am watching you and your actions, I am safer too. We watch each other not only to assist with threat detection but also to discover resources. In our more primitive days, you may have noticed a stream of water or patch of berries that I did not. Your gaze would have alerted me to something valuable for survival. In contemporary times, you might notice it in stores when people follow others' gazes and footsteps to that last good deal or that last coveted object. It can even get dangerous because it is such a primitive survival response. At times, we hear utterances such as "I saw it first" and see actions such as body blocking an object or blocking a parking space. We have evolved notions that the first "spotter" versus the second "gazer" is more ethically entitled to the resource. But people do not always follow that moral line.

We scan facial expressions to detect emotional states too. A baby can learn from observing others engaged in social interactions. For example, it has been shown that even at 18 months of age, if a baby observes an adult getting upset with another adult for doing something the baby typically likes to do, the baby will no longer engage in that activity (if that adult who previously got upset is in the room). This is a prime example of social-emotional learning. More obvious is that example of watching someone else put their hand on a hot stove and be injured. I will learn to not touch that stove when it is hot. This is single-trial social observational learning. This happens often between people, whether we are aware of it or not.

Gaze is a very important social cue for detecting danger. Accurate social reading or perception of how someone is looking at us is essential. This is important to remember with cultural differences in eye contact. We can misread a lack of eye contact with people from different cultural backgrounds. We may become suspicious of a gaze style and misinterpret it as being threatening. This data gets fast-tracked to the amygdala—no time to bother with the PFC or reason! The workspace is fertile social detection ground. We are watching who is hobnobbing with whom, engaging with the boss, and "in the know" of potentially crucial information. Gossip facilitates this information collection too. We collect social information through all of our senses.

REFLECTION

You can try your own informal social neuroscience experiment on observational learning. See how many people follow your gaze when you shift the direction of your gaze to another focal point in a room. Notice what happens. Do some age groups follow you more than others? Do you notice any differences with people following and tracking your gaze if they are known individuals or strangers? Does it make a difference what expression you have on your face when you shift your visual attention? Does it make a difference how fast you shift your gaze to a new location? Do you too follow shifts in the eye gaze of others?

We watch one another to detect threats and calculate risks to survival. Much of this is fueled by the nonconscious drives. We may believe it is out of curiosity, but it is more out of anxiety. We seek to catch a glimpse when the other is not watching to view the "real." We want to see through a weak spot in the social armor that reveals what the other is "really" like. It may reduce our own anxiety to see vulnerability—the person without the social mask or make-up. Perhaps knowing that they are imperfect like us makes us okay. We also want to reduce our anxiety about the threat of the "unknowns" about others. We want to feel certain about other people and be able to predict their behaviors. We know, like us, they are not sharing everything and are disguising aspects of who they are.

Individuals are also driven to group together to discover and share information through the use of gossip. People are collecting individual pieces of the puzzle and come together in an attempt to put together a more complete picture of the other. Much of these group social maneuvers are also fueled by anxiety. Today, people have another way to find about the other—the Internet can be utilized to discover the "truth" behind the social mask or facade. We know that digital reputation is important to people. Online reputation management professionals are available to scrub unflattering digital data and restore social reputations. Online personas and digital masks are just cutting-edge technological strategies to manage our age-old fears and shame. Privacy is a major issue in contemporary society.

Once we settled down in one place to build agricultural communities, we could build shelters where we could close doors and block windows into our personal lives. We no longer really knew each other as in our small clans. Suspicions grew about what was lurking in others. We needed more privacy for

ourselves through social façades, and then more ways to snoop behind the façades of others. Many of these social strategies are maladaptive today, but we remain driven by our fears and continue to utilize them.

Social Communication Beyond Words

We have learned that our social brains are bombarded by the psychosocial aspects of the workplace. Communication is a major aspect of the workplace. Especially without words, we are constantly sending out and receiving communications and signals. There are studies that reveal we subliminally smell, for example, one another's immunological statuses, signs of disease, and hormonal cycles. We are continually reading and interpreting (or misinterpreting) these nonverbal signals. Overt talking is just a tip of that proverbial iceberg. Most communication is being exchanged in the underground. Even if we cover our ears, we take it in. Even if we cover our eyes and ears, we still take it in. All our identified senses and those waiting to be identified and named take it in.

The anthropologist Gregory Bateson coined the term "metacommunication" in the 1970s to refer to the underlying messages that we send to one another in addition to what we actually say. These metacommunications send nonverbal information along with the spoken words that can enhance or invalidate those words. An office mate can respond with, "I'm fine," to your "how are you?" Her response may communicate that she does not want to share personal information with you, or, if said with a certain tone, that she is angry. There are many possible interpretations of her two spoken words. One possibility is that she really is fine. If you know your coworker well, you may know how to more accurately interpret her words. Much room exists for misperception and misinterpretation in interpersonal exchanges. In some forms of couple's counseling, communication is the basis of the interventional strategies because so much relational conflict occurs due to miscommunications, not listening, and misperceiving what the other has said.

Some metacommunications place people in double binds in the workplace. Double binds occur when an individual is presented with two conflicting messages or choices to act on. For example, a manager instructs her supervisor to model better self-care for his staff. The supervisor calls in sick, but the manager permits staff to call the ill supervisor at home on a difficult case matter. When the supervisor returns, the manager communicates all the problems the team incurred in his absence. The message to the supervisor is confusing and places him in a bind—he should care for himself, but his team needs him. What message should the supervisor follow?

Individuals fear rejection from groups and are sensitive to verbal and nonverbal communications of it from group members and those in power. In the book, *How the Way We Talk Can Change the Way We Work*, Robert Kegan and Lisa Lahey address the importance of how and what gets communicated—including metacommunications—to staff. One theme is that individuals of all ages are vulnerable to abandonment threats. We do not want to threaten children with being thrown out of the house when they are behaving inappropriately; we want to teach and guide them toward more socialized behavior. We do not want to threaten removal from a classroom if a child is struggling to learn the alphabet; we want to figure out how teach them. We do not want to threaten an employee with termination when they have failed to meet a deadline; we want to work collaboratively with them to address and problem-solve the issue. We want to encourage personal and professional growth. Underlying all these stressors is the threat to survival from being rejected by the dominant group that holds the power. "You are a valued group member and we will do all in our power to work with you to keep you in our group" is the sentiment most people want to perceive when harboring this fear.

Our brains are way too social to play with the social umbilical cord without significant consequence. Threats to the interpersonal and social bonds that people make across their lifetimes—which can come in the form of making someone feel expendable and threatening the certainty or continuity of the relationship—create significant distress. As we have seen, attachments to other individuals and groups sustained our ancestors and remain vital to us. The social fear of being cast out shadows us today, even though we survive group ousting. Loss or disruption of a relationship in any of the groups of our lives leads to remarkable emotional upset.

Information about social standing or status is some of the social data we are bombarded with in the workplace. A telling example of the subliminal operations of more primitive brain parts comes from a recent study of monkeys (who share these brain regions with us). Although this study has clearer implications for understanding how we are swayed by advertising, it has ramifications for navigating status competitions in the workplace. Scientists paired advertisements featuring brand logos with pictures of 1) high-status male monkey; 2) low-status male monkey; or 3) female monkey genitalia. Results of this research indicated that the monkeys "preferred" objects that were associated with female genitalia and high-status males (Platt, 2018). We know when advertisers are marketing to humans, similar preferences hold true: high-status celebrity endorsements are incredibly valuable, and advertisements for products from cars to cleaning products feature eroticized women. "Rubbing elbows" with high status individuals at work can also be incredibly valuable for this same nonconscious reason. The implications for the workplace will become clearer when we address sexual harm as a workache, because our subliminal "preferences" also involve the drivers and dynamics of sex, power, and status in the workplace. The drive for status, once again, is the disguised drive for survival, as are the drives toward being a certain way for others.

We are all influenced and changed by one another in all aspects of our lives. Individual people are not the only ones to miscommunicate or to project an inaccurate image. Organizations do it too. We have seen organizations and agencies that are in crisis or dissolving, and employees are not given any warning prior to the arrival of pink slips. We know how our social brains and keen senses scan for signs of danger and threat. Individuals often pick up on organizational anxiety and sense feelings of unease and pending danger. Organizational authenticity is therefore important and delicate in nature. Organizations must balance the needs and privacy concerns of the organization with the needs of employees, including the potential for causing significant anxiety.

Switching Teams: Changing Social Affiliations

The human brain has evolved to use groups as a form of protection for survival. Group loyalty is often dependent upon an individual's conscious and nonconscious assessment of the protective factors of the group. If we think another group will better ensure survival, we may make a change in group affiliation. People often report feeling shocked and betrayed when a coworker takes a position with another group or a boss leaves to join a competing organization. Our brains in groups are curious entities that sometimes behave in strange ways, and if we remember our primitive drives for survival, some of these behaviors make more sense. Whether in wars between countries or disputes between individuals, the primitive aspects of our brains drive a great deal of our feelings and behaviors: survival is imperative; loyalty is optional.

Humans also act out these dynamics in play and recreation. Although categorized as sport, team affiliations and loyalties can be fierce. Sports fans identifying with a specific team can carry out extreme violence against fans of opposing teams. Team members themselves form deep bonds and are committed to their team winning. However, if drafted by an archrival team, these same team members will go on to form bonds and goals with their new team. The brain can change affiliation quickly, and even move on to turn against previous team affiliates. There have been cases throughout history of soldiers in war changing sides in battle. One of the pains of childhood is when a best friend joins another social circle and is no longer even a friend.

Our brains reaffiliate depending on what is most adaptive at the moment. These adaptive evolutionary traits can be emotionally striking when played out in our lives. We see it in the workforce when a coworker is promoted and no longer lunches with us because of their new circle or team affiliation. Individuals must manage a great deal of feelings and reactions behind the social façade, and negative feelings accumulate and take their toll if they are not acknowledged, addressed, and attended to appropriately.

Socially Threatened: Differences and Suspicions

In the previous chapter, we learned about brain function and structure. We identified the limbic system structures that get triggered when there is a perceived threat to life and the resultant functions that are alerted to ensure survival. We want to avoid pain and injury. As we noted in Chapter 2, if our primitive ancestors were thrown out of their tribe, this was equivalent to death because they could not survive the elements or predators on their own. As an evolutionary result, the brain system equates physical and social threats. In fact, people have reported that their fear of psychological pain in the future is actually worse than their fear of future physical pain.

An interesting finding shows that acetaminophen assists to make us feel better after psychological pain (e.g., social rejection, hurt feelings) just as it does with physical pain. This can be explained by the logic of evolution: when it came to danger, it was adaptive to include accurate perceptions and misperceptions alike—just in case. Better wrong than sorry, according to that primitive brain. We are wired to be drawn toward others, yet we are constantly scanning for threats in our environments, so we very quickly learn if we are unsafe and then store that information deep in our brains. It is worth recalling that with trauma, especially developmental trauma, the brain maintains a constant high-alert status. If at least one other person has caused us harm, it is adaptive to generalize to others to protect oneself from threat. Subsequently, other human beings and relationships become a source of threat to the body and those regions of the brain that hold the trauma memories, even if these memories are completely out of awareness. Relationships with others are necessary and usually desired, so this presents a distressing psychological dilemma.

Avoidance is typically the easiest antidote to anxiety. However, it is quite difficult to avoid other people, for they are all around. So, we see individuals utilize different forms of defenses and strategies. One of these strategies is to avoid or deny the differing aspects of one's own self to gain or remain in the favor of the dominant group. Just as others are scanning us, we are scanning ourselves for differences so we can decide what to do with them socially. Both acts of scanning use a great deal of brain resources.

Many individuals successfully integrate themselves into the majority group—but often with psychological cost to the self. For example, being in the in-group when you are aware that you most likely would be cast out comes with a host of protective and harmful dynamics and consequences. For example, a gay male (whose sexuality is adaptively undisclosed) in a workgroup of all non-gay males may have socially protected himself but has psychologically harmed himself. Covering and disguising will be addressed as workaches in the upcoming chapter, but let us briefly examine this phenomenon. It is biologically clever to be the chameleon who can change colors to best adapt to the environment. However, as we have learned, reptiles do not have all the brain regions of humans. They do not have the known ability to reflect on their circumstances and identity. We have been afforded this opportunity by the growth of our neocortex. We ponder existential questions such as authenticity and meaning in a way that a chameleon cannot. We feel shame. So, we have a human dilemma. Some of us can be the chameleon and pass, but we pay a psychological cost for this.

Social Chemicals and Other Forms of Intoxication at Work

Daily work interactions with others create biochemical shifts and body-wide changes. Others present in the environment, and even in our memories or fantasies, can change the biochemistry of our brains and bodies. We can become intoxicated by the chemicals of human experiences and interactions such as love and hate because our feelings are accompanied by biochemical shifts. The chemical forces of human relationships are strong, and people change us when we attach to them and form relationships. Whether someone is a friend or foe, they have remarkable impacts on us. The different chemicals can make us feel good, bad, worried, and calm. And they can distract us from our work.

We typically view an individual who is intoxicated as being under the influence of a chemical, such as alcohol, and we may view them as impaired. They are not their usual self, as when all brain regions are integrated and optimally operating—they have lost TDM. The definition of intoxication can be extended to other chemicals, even the ones that we produce internally in our bodies. The brain can be "intoxicated" by a variety of chemicals and substances such as sexual hormones, adrenaline, endorphins, and cortisol, to name just a few. The biochemical balance in the brain can get thrown off at any time by many different emotional elements and interpersonal factors such as power, shame, threat, jealousy, and anger (Figure 4.3).

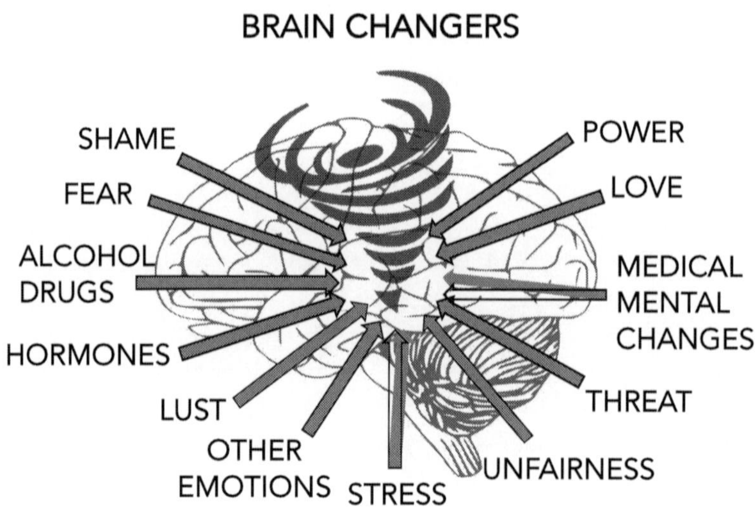

Figure 4.3

Knowing what factors change one's own brain is important. Being aware of where, what, and who changes the brain of a manager or coworker can be vital as well. Behaviors may be reactive, impulsive, and risky when one is under the influence. Words may be caustic and hurtful. Judgment may be impaired. Awareness of others' triggers and habitual reactions can facilitate our taking precautionary measures when we are around someone we deem to be intoxicated. The designated driver program has saved countless lives. No equivalent to a breathalyzer exists as of yet for neurochemical intoxication, so we must use our own judgment in determining our own and others' levels of brain imbalance.

Figure 4.4 lists eight chemicals (and brief descriptions) that are circulating in all of us at any given time. We will later see how some of these chemicals fuel workaches. Like other drugs, these neurochemicals must be managed so we do not become too "intoxicated" to maintain TDM and thereby honor wise goals and ethics. Just as we know not to drive when under the influence of alcohol, we should know not to do or say something when, for example, under the influence of adrenaline.

HAPPY HORMONES FOR THRIVING	STRESS HORMONES FOR SURVIVING
Dopamine – anticipation of pleasure / reward	**Cortisol** – released with stress
Oxytocin – social bonding / attachment	**Adrenaline** – fight/flight activation
Serotonin – positive mood state	**Norepinephrine** – assists with threat system
Endorphins – mask pain / emotional anesthesia	**CRH** – another chemical soldier

Figure 4.4

Chemicals have significant impact on our interpersonal relations. For example, oxytocin—one example of a "feel good" chemical—has been identified as the chemical that facilitates the formation of social bonds and attachment. This neurochemical gets released in the brain in higher amounts during birth and breastfeeding to encourage bonding. Oxytocin has been shown to reduce anxiety and fear, which allows the mother to be less afraid and more aggressive toward others who might threaten her offspring. Perhaps the effects of oxytocin are a reason we sometimes observe mothers able to take better care of their offspring than themselves.

We may subliminally sense the presence of this chemical, and this may underlie why we feel comfortable and safe with certain individuals and not with others. Some people—for instance "earth mothers"—may more generously exude these neurochemicals, we do not yet know. Even though we are not necessarily aware of it, through our sense of smell, we are also assessing one another.

Cortisol and adrenaline are examples of "distress" chemicals. Stress hormones commonly circulate in people, especially in stressful workplaces, because they fuel the threat system, but they were not designed for office dramas—they are for battle. Yet, when a supervisor approaches with a performance evaluation, an employee is likely to get a rush of adrenaline. Managing all these chemical influences is a considerable task in and of itself, and only one of many during the typical work day.

Our biochemistry changes when a threat or stressor passes. Cortisol levels drop in the bloodstream. However, if there are continued threats lurking in the workplace and stress is chronic, the levels of cortisol remain high. Our nomadic ancestors had specific and time-limited threats such as encounters with a charging wild animal. They foraged new land if edible plants or wild animals became scarce. They took action and did not experience long periods of helplessness and chronic stress. The threat system, with all of the accompanying biochemical changes, was not designed to be chronically activated, and we are now seeing increasing stress-related symptoms and illnesses because contemporary stressors are more chronic and stable. Another problem with the prevalence of stress hormones in the workplace is that they do not lend themselves to learning, creativity, and productivity, so in addition to creating physical symptoms and other workaches, overactivated stress systems can inhibit our thriving at work cognitively and socially.

The reins get passed from the sympathetic to the parasympathetic nervous system and the body relaxes when a threat passes and stressor ends. However, if there is chronic stress, this process is disrupted. The sympathetic nervous system must work overtime, which is biochemically expensive. Additionally, many people begin to fuel their own chronic stress by continuing to collect data, for example, about unfairness in the workplace even though they have enough evidence already to confirm their adverse experiences. Stressed individuals may also enlist others for battle, and the stress spreads. These actions can create a chronic state of vigilance and cause the threat system to continually release stress hormones.

Sustaining and fueling a chronic state of stress and anxiety does not serve to change the problems in the work culture but does increase the potential for adverse effects on bodies. Wisdom typically goes out the window with any form of intoxication. Battles, of any kind, tend to fuel conflicts and debates versus discussion and collaborations toward change.

Triggered: Identifying Limbic Flashpoints

Another social reality is that we can trigger rage in each other. Our threat detection capacity and aggression has made us the longest surviving human genetic line. R. Douglas Fields, PhD is a prominent neuroscientist who has studied and written about the limbic system and the rage circuity in our brains (Fields, 2015). His work relates to our discussion of interpersonal conflict and aggression. Dr. Fields describes the rage circuitry as a threat-detection response system that is out of our awareness and that leads to our "snapping" or behaving in ways we typically would not if our conscious motivations and goals were in charge—in other words, when we lose TDM. Dr. Fields identified nine interpersonal threats that are triggers of rage and created the acronym "LIFEMORTS" to summarize these triggers (Figure 4.5):

LIFEMORTS
LI FE OR DEATH: threats to life or limb / survival compromises
INSULT: being socially humiliated
FAMILY: protection of family members against attack
ENVIRONMENT: safeguarding home, own territory
MATE: getting, keeping, and protecting of mate
ORDER IN SOCIETY: unfairness, social injustice
RESOURCES: obtain, keep, and protect valued property, money
TRIBE: defense of one's group (e.g., country, ethnicity, or religion)
STOPPED: being restrained, trapped, blocked

Figure 4.5

Dr. Fields has offered us another view into the brain to gain understanding and management of these reflexes. A key point is the value of knowing our own vulnerabilities and being able to identify personal rage triggers and circuits. Additionally, it is valuable to get to know the triggers of others to best protect oneself. This allows for the potential prediction of reactions before "the point of no return." What and who are we most vulnerable to? What are our coworkers most triggered by? Whatever the specific vulnerabilities, it becomes critical to remember that all humans get triggered no matter how well they hide their vulnerabilities or disguise their reactions. Every individual has a threshold that when crossed can cause them to act out in rage and violence. Dr. Fields cautions that our neural rage circuitry was not designed for modern living and can get triggered when indeed no real threat exists to livelihood. He cites road rage as triggering all nine of the LIFEMORTS. Because we are driving with the same brain that we had tens of thousands of years ago, we misperceive being cut off in traffic, for example, as a major threat to survival, which triggers rage in some. Typically, this only lasts for a brief time, the neocortex returns online, and we continue to our destinations. Road rage is a common human trigger, however, each individual brings their own unique histories, sensitivities, vulnerabilities, and therefore individualized triggers into their environments. Below, we offer a case that illustrates how some of these issues can get triggered in at work.

A few years ago, we consulted on a case where a manager, Colin, was confronting an employee, Gabriel, about a performance issue. Gabriel was aware that his manager wanted to address the issue and was actively avoiding Colin. Gabriel was about to step out of his office when Colin arrived and stood in the door jamb, essentially blocking Gabriel's passage. He told Colin he needed to leave and did not want to address the issue at that time. Colin persisted in speaking about the issue anyway and used his body to communicate his unwillingness to have it any other way. Gabriel was essentially trapped in his office and became agitated and stressed. Gabriel filed a complaint with Human Resources. Colin was disciplined for his behavior. He felt that he was treated unfairly because he was the manager and needed to address an issue with his employee. Colin was insulted by the actions of his employer. When he applied for a promotion the next year, he was turned down due to this incident. Colin was further triggered.

This case exemplifies the "S" of "Stopped" of LIFEMORTS for Gabriel. When someone blocks the free movement or passage of another individual it is a very serious limbic trigger. The threat of this can lead to significant conflict. Colin did not realize that he was using the power of his position and body in the door jamb to block his staff member from leaving. This case also exemplifies the "I" of "Insult" and the "O" for "Order" for Colin. He was triggered, too, and felt that he was disciplined unfairly, and that justice was not served. Both individuals were emotionally triggered. We encourage individuals to keep LIFEMORTS in mind so as to minimize risks of triggering them in others, as well as staying aware of when they themselves are being triggered.

Human Brain on Power: Hubris Syndrome

The power afforded a leader by a group comes with great responsibility and stress. Many hold their power with dignity and humility and use it for the good of the group. Others hold their power differently. Hierarchy status, and the power that goes along with it, is a social construct that that has a high potential for abuse. Gaining, possessing, and retaining power creates a certain mindset in those who possess it. Power is offered by the group to assist with organizing and meeting the mission of the group. But some begin to use this gift based in their own self-interests and to exercise control over others. A very curious neuroscientific finding that is highly relevant to the workplace is how the brain changes when people attain power and leadership positions in a hierarchy. The phenomenon has been labeled the Hubris Syndrome (Owen & Davidson, 2009). In Greek mythology, hubris is characterized as excessive self-regard—when a person in a position of authority becomes so taken by or proud of their own achievements and characteristics that they begin to perceive themselves as gods, or at least as superior to others. In the myths, those under the sway of hubris are ultimately punished. In real life, this is not always the case, and many people and organizations suffer from the leadership of such individuals.

Owen and Davidson identified fourteen characteristics of the Hubris Syndrome. They indicated that only three of the fourteen, and one of the five symptoms with an asterisk, need be present to make the informal assessment of Hubris Syndrome:

- Propensity to see the world primarily as an arena in which to exercise power and seek glory
- Predisposition to take actions which seem likely to cast the individual in a good light—taken in part in order to enhance their image
- Disproportionate concern with image and presentation
- Messianic way of talking and a tendency to exaltation in speech and manner
- Identification with the nation or organization—to the extent that they regard the outlook and interests of the two as identical*
- Tendency to speak of themselves in the third person or use "the royal we"*
- Excessive confidence in the individual's own judgment and contempt for the advice or criticism of others
- Exaggerated self-belief, bordering on a sense of omnipotence, in what they personally can achieve
- Belief that rather than being accountable to the mundane court of colleagues or public opinion, the real court to which they answer is much greater: history or god
- Unshakeable belief that in that court they will be vindicated*
- Loss of contact with reality; often associated with progressive isolation
- Restlessness, recklessness, and impulsiveness*
- Tendency to allow their 'broad vision,' especially their conviction about the moral rectitude of a proposed course of action, to obviate the need to consider other aspects of it, such as its practicality, cost, and the possibility of unwanted outcomes*
- Incompetence in carrying out a policy, where things go wrong precisely because too much self-confidence has led the leader not to worry about the nuts and bolts of a policy

Awareness of the Hubris Syndrome is important for leaders, so that they have a better chance of managing it within themselves if it emerges. Subordinates also need to be aware of this to identify and understand what they might be dealing with when it is encountered in management. We will address organizational awareness of this in Chapter 8.

Power is like fire. If handled appropriately, it can be highly constructive. If handled inappropriately, it can be highly destructive. Once the group assigns an individual a position of power, it is thereafter difficult to remove that empowered individual from their leadership position. Dacher Keltner is a professor of psychology at the University of California, Berkeley, who has studied and described how the brain changes as individuals move into greater positions of power and hold these positions over increasing amounts of time (Keltner, 2017). Dr. Keltner offers a great perspective on power and leadership. He observes that the most adaptive way to hold power is to use it for the greater good. Sharing power by empowering others and fueling compassion are some of the ways that power can be offered by those who possess it. When people see that the power held by their leaders is being used to help, there is much less tendency to compete for that power and engage in power struggles. Dr. Keltner is one of the founders of a vital organization and resource center at University of California, Berkeley called the Greater Good Science Center, which publishes a user-friendly newsletter entitled "Greater Good Workplaces."

Just as individuals with power handle it differently, people under those in power also have different ways of responding to power or leadership. Some individuals in the workforce had authoritarian parents or teachers who used their power to intimidate and subjugate, rather than to protect and empower. They may bring preexisting defensive postures to the workplace. Some will be more likely to withdraw if a boss is more authoritarian and controlling in style. Other will engage in conflict with such an authority figure and there will be power struggles. Some of the best role models for "carrying power" are masters in the martial arts. They have power in the sense of self-defense, but they do not display it to others except when necessary. Others are thereby less likely to engage in power struggles with them because they are not inviting contests. The power of these masters is held with humility, discipline, and respect. They are typically training others in also attaining their level of "power."

Social Brains United: Power of the Collective to Thrive

Individuals can unite and form into powerful groups, but they can also divide, break apart, and lose their collective power. United versus divided groups are quite different. United and harmonious groups possess incredible power that can be directed to assist those on the outside, as well as their own members. HHS organizations are essential to communities and offer vital resources. Those that provide these services deserve to also experience the power of their group and to be rewarded and thrive. Figure 4.6 simplifies some of the research that helps facilitate moving toward the goal of thriving at work. Unless there are real threats to survival at work, the goal is to contribute to the team and thereby contribute to the self.

LEADING THE SOCIAL BRAIN TOWARD THRIVING AT WORK

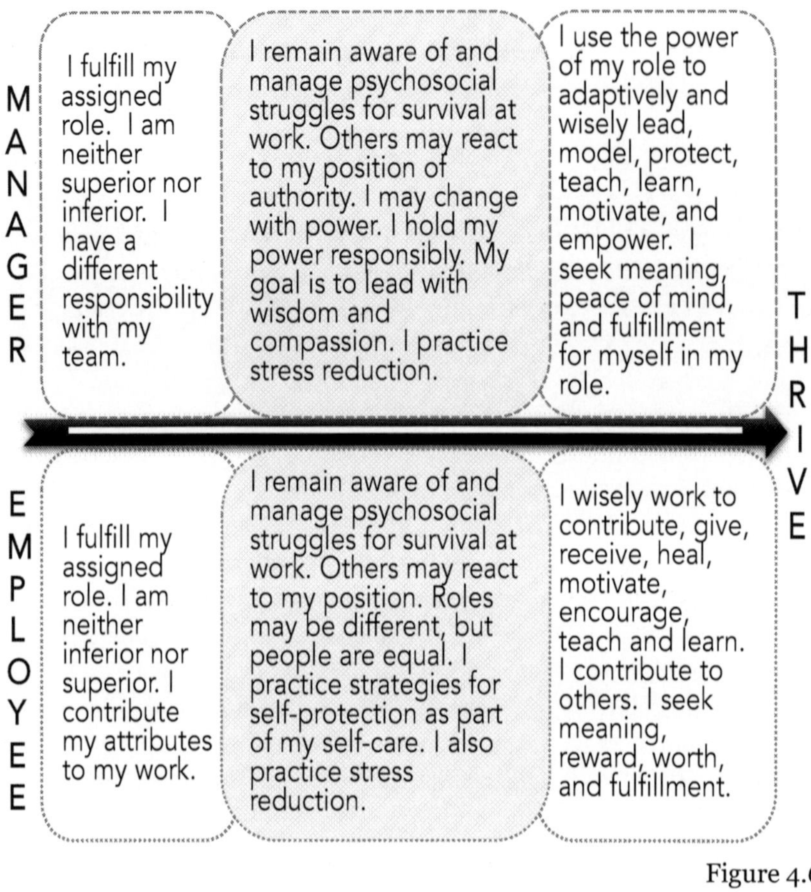

Figure 4.6

Groups divide when stressors or workaches overwhelm internal resources. A great deal of the overwhelm results from nonconscious factors in individual members that are related to survival threats. Fears and suspicions about factors such as member differences, inequities, and internal competitions can diminish the power of the collective alliance and divide members. Self-interest trumps concern for the group-at-large mission when threats lurk. When group members are stressed, the whole group can be distracted away from the collective mission. The more we can weed out some of the more primitive social struggles, the more we can thrive. We can compensate for our nonconscious dynamics with conscious efforts by being aware that they are lurking and by dedicating ourselves to rational strategies. We can emphasize cooperation over competition. We can appreciate the value and different responsibilities of all roles in the group. We can recognize that our collective force is mightier than our individual force.

When individual members perceive fair distribution of resources in a group, survival threats and competition diminish. Resources that can fuel thriving are unrestricted and unlimited. Enough inner peace, meaning, love, people, animals, nature, creative pursuits, and other good feelings and experiences exist to go around. When the group is perceived as safe, both individuality and group membership can be supported and enhanced. Each individual serves the group mission, but also gets to define and personalize what thriving means to them. Each individual is offered a "blank canvas" for this to create from their uniqueness, talents, and inspirations. All are in their own lanes on this one. Kurt Goldstein introduced the concept "self-actualization" in 1934 (Goldstein, 1939), and it was later elaborated by Abraham Maslow (Maslow, 1943). Dr. Maslow defined self-actualization as "growth of an individual toward fulfillment of the highest needs, those for meaning in life, in particular." He described self-actualized individuals as creative and resilient. Self-actualization is the fifth and ultimate phase of Maslow's hierarchy of needs (Maslow, 1943). We view this phase as thriving. The lower, more survival-oriented needs of the hierarchical phases, such as those for food and shelter, must be met in order to move up the hierarchy toward self-actualization. The ideal group facilitates both self-actualization (thriving of the individual member) and group-actualization (thriving of the group). Both the community and the HHS professional win when threats are minimized and rewards are maximized in an organization.

The more dysfunctional the workplace, the more an individual's time and energy goes toward navigating and negotiating the social politics. We have consulted in organizations where only approximately 40 to 60 percent of employee energy was going into work tasks because so much time and effort got diverted to managing interpersonal and organizational dynamics. The next chapter is dedicated to identifying those issues that interfere with performing work at work—the workaches.

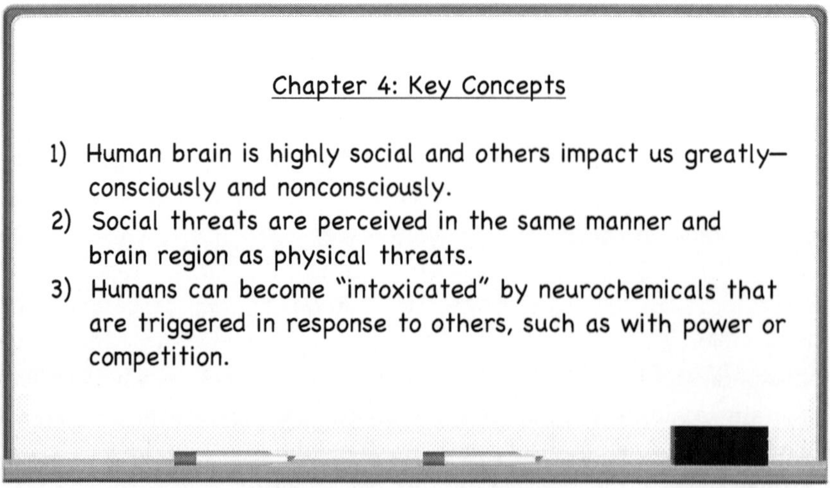

5
WORKACHES: WHEN WORK HURTS

It takes approximately 500 pounds of force to crush a human skull, yet a mere glance from another can crush a human soul.

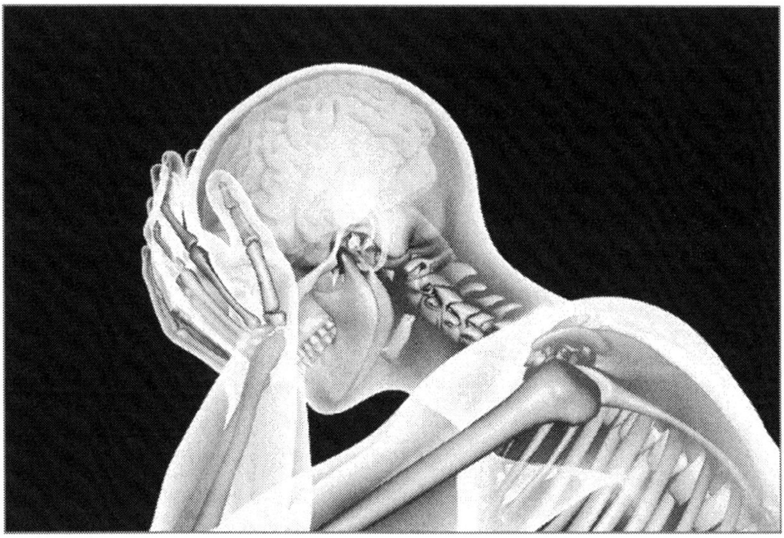

The skull is hard. The brain is soft. The skull protects the brain as best it can from physical assault, but it is unable to protect it from psychological assault. We now know that psychosocial wounds eventually create physical changes in the brain. Besides its hard skull, there are even more ways the human brain has evolved to protect itself from physical intrusions. The blood-brain barrier is a prime example. Unwanted and harmful substances are filtered out before even reaching the brain. With psychological intrusions, however, we filter *in* versus *out*. We compile psychosocial threats. Our dilemma is that each one of our senses is designed to take in and store the information it is receiving from others in our environments, especially if something is perceived or misperceived as socially threatening. The brain wants to learn what is dangerous and remain vigilant for signs of hostility and other interpersonal assaults. We are so much better insulated from physical than psychological assault. Interpersonal conflicts and relational stress take up a great deal of space in our bodies and minds.

Workaches are defined as work experiences that trigger an individual's threat or stress response. They range from acute single episodes to chronic repeated incidents. Workaches are not relative, they are absolute. To illustrate this point, we offer an analogy. If one individual is stabbed and another shot, their pain is not relative to one another's. They both absolutely hurt. In addition, a mere physical poke can appear trivial, but if the poke is delivered to a previously injured or particularly sensitive area, the experience of it is more painful. The absolute experience of pain is important for leadership to remain mindful of, especially leaders who themselves have trauma histories. Staff complaints or experiences that seem trivial relative to a leader's own adversity can sometimes be comparatively minimized by the leader. Therefore, we emphasize the importance of keeping in mind that the harm of a workache is absolute to each individual who is experiencing it. Often, we are unaware of any trauma history or vulnerability that someone brings with them to the workplace.

We classify workaches on a spectrum from mild to severe; the scale applies not to the workache itself, but to the experience and perception of the individual involved. We have intervened with staff who have remarkable triggers and reactions to being stared at, for example, while others could not care less about being in a coworker's fixed gaze. We see tremendous variability across people in triggers and reactions, from annoyance to significant interpersonal violence. Some of this variability can be attributed to brain development and individual experiences with others. The preceding chapters provided the neuroscientific, psychosocial, and anthropological foundations upon which we now examine workaches.

Where there are people, there are conflicts. Where there is a workplace, there are workaches. Because there are no built-in psychosocial assault protections afforded us by our evolution, we must build our own protections and defenses. Leadership must create the organizational culture, policies, and practices to prepare and protect staff from inevitable conflicts. Individuals must also stay mindful of best strategies for navigating the interpersonal world of the workplace to survive and thrive.

The workplace is getting better. Many individuals have been tirelessly working to create safer and healthier workplaces. We are evolving due to growing social awareness and our ability to identify and collectively address unfairness in the workplace. Social awareness and activism to protect adults beyond just their physical lives is increasing, and significant improvements have been achieved in the treatment and rights of employees. Social justice is inherent to our cultural evolution: preventing physical harm and death in the workplace needed to be given priority, while now, identifying and preventing psychosocial harm is in order. We have come a long way from American sweat factories, but studies show that as working conditions improve, people do not necessarily update their perceptions.

Sometimes work situations appear as if they are getting worse because we are probing and looking "under the rug" and discovering new areas that require updates. As we do this, let's remember that when we find ourselves at a point in history when we are scrutinizing the workplace in this way, we are well on our way to improving working conditions. We are moving to addressing finer and finer details of psychosocial justice at work. Just the fact that we can identify nonverbal assaults, for example, as a workache suggests that things have improved. Individuals and organizations must manage a great deal of underground interpersonal impulses and confusing dynamics. This task is neither straightforward nor easy. We carry on the work of others who have blazed the paths toward more humane and healthier work environments.

The psychosocial blows we sustain in the interpersonal field of the workplace take their toll and deserve address, especially as more and more neuroscientific data come in about their adverse effects—on both emotional and physical well-being. To date, metrics on the incidents of the various psychosocial assaults are lacking. We do have increasing attention paid to some workaches, such as occurrences of blatant sexual harm. But we certainly do not yet have enough knowledge of the full spectrum of adverse psychosocial experiences in the workplace, especially those that tend to fall more under the radar and come in disguised forms.

We are increasingly addressing occupational psychosocial safety at work, but more focus is needed. There are guidelines for wearing hard hats in construction zones to protect from brain damage. We also need to protect this same organ from psychosocial impacts that can cause harm and damage.

A review of the data collected and statistics on the USA.gov website and the Bureau of Labor Statistics (BLS, 2017) reveals the lack of data collected on most psychosocial stressors in the workplace. The more we can appeal to federal and state officials with our neuroscientific data on how psychosocial stress impacts physical health, the more hopeful we are that we will increase motivation and see even more positive change. Significant consequences are in place in most civilizations for physically harming another human being. There are remarkably few consequences for most of the social combat that occurs. Perhaps this will change as the public receives more and more scientific documentation that social aggression and harm ultimately create physical wounding too. We are seeing some shifts in holding individuals accountable for actions that may contribute to others' ending their own lives due to psychological assaults such as bullying.

Workaches: Human Nature at Work

We now address a spectrum of issues related to workaches that range from minor to major interpersonal assaults. Some of these transactions and transgressions are in awareness and intentional. Others of these workaches are out of awareness to both perpetrators and victims. The harm, nonetheless, still occurs even if the actions are unintentional. If I unconsciously step on your toe, it still hurts and may cause injury whether or not it was on purpose. This underlines the importance of self-awareness and the need to continually self-assess how we ourselves may be "stepping on toes" and to stay aware and take constructive action when others are stepping on ours.

The list in Figure 5.1 is non-exhaustive but meant to highlight some of the more common interactions and dynamics in the workplace between coworkers, superiors, and those served. They represent only a few of the multitude of interpersonal stressors and psychosocial obstacles that individuals encounter at work. (We have constructed a preliminary version of an inventory to further refine workaches called the Workaches Screening Inventory (WSI) which is shown in Appendix D.) These workaches do not represent distinct categories because there is overlap between them, so, while we do not specifically address each, we briefly address their common psychological underpinnings. We offer most depth on the workache of sexual harm, or what is more commonly termed sexual harassment. All the workaches that we describe have the effect of triggering the threat response and making the workplace a site for biochemically costly experiences, rather than a safe, rewarding, and meaningful arena for thriving. Because our brains change when we are around others, at any time, there are countless factors in the workplace that can impact and disrupt our TDM and throw us off our chosen paths. We describe some problem-solving strategies for workaches in Chapter 7. But first, we must identify and name the problems in order to address them.

WORKACHES	
Loss of optimal brain management (TDM)	Secondary trauma / burnout
Unfairness	Disillusionment
Sexual Harm	Microaggressions / bias
Insecurity / Uncertainty	Bullying / mobbing
Shaming	Work / life conflict
Power / status	Safety concerns
Exclusion	Evaluations
Covering / passing	Loss of control / helplessness
Institutional betrayal	Velocity (work speed / load)

Figure 5.1

REFLECTION

Examine the list and identify those workaches that you or others in your organization have experienced. Think about those you experience or have experienced that are not listed. Have you shared these issues with anyone? Have you received assistance for addressing workaches? Where would you go to seek assistance?

Brain Gone Rogue: Loss of TDM

The loss of TDM is first on our list because we believe that it is a major issue in the workplace and underlies most other workaches. The maintenance of TDM in all individuals is essential to fulfill the roles and mission of organizations and to provide a consistent sense of predictability and safety. Throughout history there have been examples of leaders characterized by frequent loss of TDM and subsequent departure from expected styles and conduct of leadership. Since the acquisition of a nuclear arsenal, many American have feared a reactive "finger on the button." Luckily (because every human is vulnerable to loss of TDM), there is no button that could be readily pushed. However, because of lessons learned in history when the reactive emotional regions overthrow the rational regions, some have called for more layers of safeguarding in the decision to launch such a strike. Although it is not typically discussed in neuroscientific terms, the loss of TDM is essentially what is most worrisome (Goldman, 2018).

We frequently hear complaints of unease and stress in the workplace when leaders are experienced as volatile and unpredictable. People feel safest when their leaders and managers present with consistently calm and rational thinking, which typically leads to predictable behaviors. Additionally, if we reflect back to our discussion of mirror neurons, we can understand how our social brains pick up anxiety in another, especially a leader. If one individual in a primitive clan picked up a threat, it was adaptive for others (who had not directly noticed the threat) to at least notice signs in the individual who did perceive the threat. Loss of TDM can occur in one individual but can also occur on a larger scale in groups. Loss of TDM can be contagious. Collective loss of TDM can lead to mass hysteria. If a social contagion gets triggered and spreads to increasing numbers of individuals in a group, this situation can become quite risky and out of control.

Groups can be ominous and intimidating when not collectively navigating with integration and reason. If someone moves into disfavor with any group (even one in which they are a member), psychosocial survival is threatened. If a group gets destabilized by even one event, member, or leader, members are at risk of losing TDM or being targeted by those who have lost it. Most of us will go to great lengths and try hard to remain in favor with the group and to fit in. Our brains have evolved to pick up threats in groups for good reason. Groups can protect, and they can place people at tremendous risk.

The workplace is in a safer and more predictable state when all are in TDM. Emotions are being triggered, but reason is guiding the actions that people take in response to them. When people are interacting, TDM is variable throughout the workday. The brain is still vulnerable and going to be reactive to varying interpersonal dynamics no matter what position on the hierarchy an individual occupies. Individuals are at risk for departing from prescribed roles when triggered. When individuals act in ways that are inconsistent with role expectations, it can be frightening. The professional roles and boundaries that we assume in the workplace can be overwhelmed when personal issues get triggered. Our more primitive impulses and issues (especially unexamined ones) spill over and overwhelm our ability to cope. Numerous external and internal factors throw off our brain's balance during a typical work day.

Occupational Hazards: Secondary Trauma and Burnout

Humans can become intoxicated by physical or emotional factors, just as they can become infected by these factors. Trauma is contagious. Though there may be physical gaps between us, our social brains have wired us together. We both emotionally and physically experience each other in the visual gaps through the work of mirror neurons. As we pointed out in Chapter 3, individuals who seek to help others may have a higher number of these specialized neurons and have increased levels of empathy.

> You serve in the most meaningful of ways.
> If you bear witness to the hardships of human existence,
> you are at risk for burnout and secondary trauma.

This beautiful attribute of empathy comes with some costs. The costs increase when one's work is to help, heal, and rescue others from their problems, pain, and other dilemmas. The more empathy one has, the more risk one has for becoming emotionally infected by seeing or hearing about another's struggles and stories of pain and adversity. Another risk factor for secondary trauma is having unresolved personal trauma (SAMHSA, 2014). We address this workache more fully in Chapter 6 but mention it here because it is a significant risk factor in HHS.

HHS staff are typically attending to suffering versus joy in others. Contrast their jobs with those who are employed to serve ice cream to others. Those served are typically in a good mood and looking forward to enjoying a tasty treat. The server's mirror neurons pick up the good feelings of those looking forward to their creation. This activates reward circuitry in the server's brain, creating pleasant feelings. Beneficial infection occurs.

This cascade of work experiences is very different for a first or second responder, for example. Most citizens can turn off a newscast or put down a newspaper if the information is emotionally overloading them. If you are someone who is charged with addressing adverse events in some way, you cannot turn it off or look away.

Sometimes burnout spreads like fire. A particularly virulent strain of an emotional contagion that often spreads between coworkers in a workplace where burnout is prevalent is the belief that work is "bad" and the only hope is to "survive" it. The workplace is perceived as a threatening place, and the notion of thriving at work is not even considered a possibility. People engage others to get buy-in to their belief system about the workplace because of the inherent need to seek acknowledgment, support, and comrades. If these mindsets spread, we can find systemic disengagement and dissatisfaction, which serves neither the organization nor the individual.

A secondary infection that often spreads in HHS organizations is the erroneous belief that the experience of burnout comes with the job or is somehow a sign of commitment and hard work. Once an organizational culture is infected, it becomes difficult to remedy. Staff and leadership come to believe that they need to be without needs of their own to participate successfully in the culture. Management often models this poor self-care. Staff begin to feel discomfort and guilt about leaving work for medical appointments, taking sick leave, and even disconnecting from work during vacations. Psychological immunity to these types of contagions is vital. Stepping back and gaining perspective to resist joining in with these types of mindsets is important if we are to move from surviving to thriving.

Another stressful dilemma in HHS systems is the unintentional infliction of pain and trauma in clients and customers served. Most HHS staff choose the profession to relieve suffering, not to cause it. However, some organizations that are developed and designed to help inevitably participate in the retraumatizing of those they serve. For example, children sometimes need to be removed from parents or separated from siblings in order to secure urgent foster placement. These actions, in and of themselves, can be traumatic to children who have already been traumatized at home. Agents of these systems are caught in a very unfortunate psychosocial web. We have treated individuals who have long been psychologically haunted by pain that they unintentionally inflicted upon others. The served and the servers all sustain consequences and complications within systems that are intended to help. Sometimes our helping hurts:

- Social workers do not want to have to pull a terrified child from a neglectful parent's arms.
- Law enforcement agents do not want to shoot another person.
- Firefighters do not want to restrain someone from entering the blazing home to rescue their loved one.
- Healthcare workers do not want to inflict pain on a patient during a procedure.
- Eligibility workers do not want to deny their customers the resources they desperately need.
- Physicians do not want to inform their patient of a terminal illness.

These are the tremendous burdens and costs of helping. Fallout occurs from these experiences on all involved. These and other inevitable situations add to the trauma load and take their toll. These are in addition to the adversity encountered in personal lives, including watching the evening news.

Some medical facilities offer X-ray technicians "radiation monitoring badges" that compile cumulative radiation exposure. These devices are important because of the risks associated with certain levels of radiation exposure. Our government has established standards for exposure limits. Technicians are monitored and interventions taken if cumulative doses of radiation exceed certain limits. We envision a time in the distant future when a similar device becomes available to monitor doses of psychosocial exposures so that interventions can be enacted to protect staff. Until that time, we must, as individuals and organizations, look out for ourselves.

Disillusionment: Role Fulfillment Fails and Disappointments

In most organizations, we find a chain of command, some type of leadership hierarchy to organize the group into roles with varying degrees of status and power. Once there is more than one individual in a group, the group requires some organizing of roles, duties, etc. to best adapt to the goals of that particular group. It becomes inefficient if two people assume that they have to answer the phone at the same time or complete a specific task, so roles require differentiation. If we are soldiers in an army, we must be trained to heed commands from superiors lest the whole group be in peril. The group gets organized—goals are determined, tasks are assigned, and leaders and subordinates emerge. Ideally roles are distributed in a group based on capacity for and desire to fulfill that role, but individuals who genuinely have the best qualities to fulfill a certain role do not always get that role.

We assign certain attributes to personal and professional roles such as parent, teacher, clergy, doctor, supervisor, manager, or leader. The brain is searching for safety in the environment and that often leads to a search for safe people who will assist and lead from birth onward. Dorothy and her pals along the way on the yellow brick road in *The Wizard of Oz* desperately wanted to believe that there was a wizard more powerful than they to care for them and grant their wishes. They were disillusioned and sad when the wizard was a mere man behind the curtain. The loss of this belief in or wish for a leader or guide can be scary and disillusioning for many people. Differentiating a person from their role is essential. Imposters and impersonators exist in all arenas and forms of nature. We often rely on titles or authoritative designations to feel safe with someone and trust them. For example, a leader can emerge in a group because they authentically possess the necessary qualities to best fulfill that role or a leader can emerge because they have mastered the art of manipulation and have an unhealthy need to control others. These people can mimic leadership qualities to move to positions of power. This is a natural phenomenon that is not unique to humans. There are genuine monarch butterflies and there are imposter monarch butterflies that are able to mimic the genuine physical qualities for their own survival benefit. If one really looks closely at the butterflies, the imposter can be distinguished from the authentic monarch. Similarly, most people begin to distinguish an authentic from an inauthentic leader.

We consider disillusionment and disappointment at work to be threatening experiences. Disillusionment can occur when someone is let down and disappointed by an individual in power, an organization, a workgroup, the integrity of an agency, or even their own ability to fulfill the mission of their position. Children sometimes experience this with a parent or teacher. Those who have a history of disappointing and disillusioning experiences with others may bring increased vulnerability and sensitivity to the workplace. Expectations get shattered and reality strikes hard in disillusionment. The threat trigger is the loss of an anticipated guide or leader or belief. People often report a sense of profound disappointment when their belief in someone or something "higher" than their own self is lost. During a trauma-informed care training, a military veteran recently shared getting triggered when a superior at work would not "stand up and do the right thing" for his workgroup. While stationed in the Middle East, he witnessed a higher-ranking officer retreat when his unit was ordered to advance. He had the insight to recognize the emotional parallel between these two separate events and was able to internally manage the emotions that emerged for him. Nonetheless, his feelings of being unprotected by the individual assigned to this were profound.

A role may afford power, trust, and respect, but the person who occupies that role may not be trustworthy, rational, or act in alignment with the parameters of that role. They can also change while in the role. Studies have revealed to us that power itself can change the brain of an individual and result in decreased empathy and ultimately poor leadership. Dr. Sukhvinder Obhi studies the neurobiological changes (obhilab.com) and Dr. Dachner Kelter studies the functional results of these changes in individuals with power (bsil.berkeley.edu). We know that there are certain personality factors that contribute to an individual emerging as a leader. We also now know, however, that once an individual is in a leadership role, their brain can change. In organizations, we often have heard "what happened to her after she got promoted, she is like a different person that I no longer recognize or like." We address this further in upcoming chapters.

Personality traits or factors that have been found to protect those who attain power over others from coming down with maladaptive power issues or diagnoses, such as Hubris Syndrome, are: 1) retaining personal modesty and humility; 2) staying open to constructive feedback and criticism; 3) possessing a degree of cynicism; and 4) having a well-developed sense of humor. These factors appear to help leaders maintain rational perspective about their role in the group. When leaders need too much control, we see staff morale decrease and feelings of helplessness increase. Micromanagement is "macro" or big to our brains. The loss of control that micromanagers trigger in most employees ignites the threat response. Anxiety and fear get associated with the micromanager who gets amplified in importance in the brain. Too much anxiety renders employees less productive and efficient. Employees are much more proficient if their social-engagement system is turned on in relation to their manager, rather than their threat system. Maintaining respect, dignity, and role appreciation and fulfillment in a hierarchical system is a challenging but necessary pursuit, because disillusionment with specific individuals in power can become generalized to the entire organization.

Institutional Betrayal: When Systems Let Us Down

Organizations, like families and schools, are systems that individuals form and then comprise. Interpersonal violence takes place between individuals within these systems, and sometimes it is the systems themselves that harm members. Sometimes the systems deny, avoid, and become complicit with the harm perpetuated by members. Like individuals, systems also have defense mechanisms to avoid conflict, disgrace, loss of power, and shame. We see families in denial and rationalizing difficult emotions. Denial and accompanying lack of support often add an additional layer of trauma to the victim. When an organization promotes a culture of bullying, fails to protect individual members, and invalidates sexual harm or microaggressions, we call this institutional betrayal. The concept was developed by psychologist Jennifer Freyd, who described it as, "wrongdoings perpetrated by an institution upon individuals dependent on that institution, including failure to prevent or respond supportively to wrongdoings by individuals (e.g., sexual assault) committed within the context of the institution" (as cited in Platt et al., 2009).

Institutional support is important as are family and classroom support. We see these same forms of betrayals when a parent "looks the other way" with regard to sexual abuse in a family or when the yard duty teacher "looks the other way" with regard to bullying on the playground. It feels unfair when individuals or organizations are not fulfilling or are abusing the roles assigned to them.

Unfairness at Work and Its Effects

The detection of unfairness triggers remarkable neurobiological changes and reactions, not only due to ethical or moral factors, but because it is a significant threat to survival. Anxiety gets triggered if someone cannot predict fair distribution of resources, especially in return for work performed. This would be the triggering of the "R" for resources and the "O" for order in society in Dr. Field's LIFEMORTS mnemonic. Non-favored siblings are picking up the signs and indicators of the status of the favored child in the family in Group 1. Classmates are perceiving who the teacher's pet is in Group 2. Favored group members potentially gain an advantage over other members. A favor bias affords the chosen individual a greater possibility for securing resources from managers of these groups. Group 3 members are motivated by the same nonconscious drivers as sibling rivalry and classroom competition. Staff are constantly nonconsciously scanning for signs of favoritism. Cooperative behaviors evolved from our larger and increasingly socially connected clans. Cooperation requires fairness in order to work. Violating fairness and equity rules evokes emotional responses in others, even in non-humans. Staff perceptions of favoritism, such as the offering of special privileges to certain employees, are some examples of triggers around fairness.

A study of fairness in capuchin monkeys yielded fascinating data about aversion to inequity and unfairness (Brosnan & de Waal, 2003). Humans are not alone in their aversion to unfairness and their constant scanning for indications of bias. This study also yielded great visual footage where Dr. de Waal illustrates a monkey's response to seeing that she received a less attractive reward (cucumber) for performing the same task as another who received a grape. The footage can be accessed and viewed on YouTube at https://youtu.be/meiu6TxysCg and is usually also good for a chuckle. This study, which has been replicated in other animals, reveals just how reactive the primitive brain becomes when perceived unfairness is detected.

Unfairness abounds in all arenas of nature. We find opportunistic viruses in the microscopic world. We find parasitic creatures in the ocean. We find biased apes in the primate world. We find ants that don't pull their weight in the insect world. And we find it all in the human world.

All are trying different strategies in the struggle to survive. Because gaining power in a group affords such a competitive edge for survival, many examples of unfairness emerge from the misuse of it by those who attain power—from the "glass" ceiling to the "class" ceiling (Pinsker, 2019). As humans (possessing the greatest amount of neocortex), we are fortunately attempting to work things out and evolve toward increased fairness and cooperativeness. Until these "grabs for survival" are fully worked out, we must navigate with the unfortunate reality that they exist and protect ourselves most adaptively when they cross our paths at work.

In years past, people would do unfairness or injustice collecting by watching who was spending "too much" time at the water cooler or in the break room and not doing their work. One of the issues that our technological revolution has brought us is access to the Internet at work. Some employees do "leisure surfing" in order to de-stress and enjoy periodic and needed distraction or "recess." However, over the years we have heard increasing complaints by individuals who are triggered by seeing their coworkers and supervisors excessively "cyberloafing"—the personal use of the Internet during work hours (Pindek et al., 2018). Besides accounting for significant economic losses to businesses and organizations, cyberloafing and personal cell phone use during the workday is a significant unfairness trigger for some in the workplace. The feelings and behaviors that get triggered with perceptions of unfairness, such as with cyberloafing, have remarkable relevance to organizations because of the biochemical resources diverted to scanning for and reacting to these triggers.

Awareness of what gets perceived as threatening is vital as employers look toward reducing threats at work. We will expand upon these issues in Chapter 8 where we translate some of these research findings into practical solutions for the workplace.

Psychosocial Assertions and Aggressions

Workaches, such as bullying and mobbing (bullying by group), highlight underlying competition for dominance, power, and control in the workplace. Ancient battles occurred to secure new resources and opportunities for reproduction. These drivers still exist in contemporary society, but usually in more sophisticated and disguised manners. Psychosocial aggressions arise out of battles for resources—sometimes love, money, offspring, power, and or social status—with survival optimization underlying all. We are complex creatures struggling to manage our primitive brain parts alongside our wise and ethical leanings. Bullying behaviors have been defined as "persistent and repeated negative actions that are directed at individuals who have difficulty defending themselves" (Einarsen et al., 2003). Aquino and Thau (2009), in a review of the literature, identified personal and organizational variables that can predict which individuals may be targeted in the contemporary workplace. Bullies may need to target vulnerable individuals because the bullies themselves are struggling nonconsciously with feelings of inadequacy. Bullying behavior can take on more disguised forms such as intentionally giving someone too firm of a handshake. They thereby engage contests to win power in the group.

Awareness of the possible underlying drivers of antisocial behavior is important because the less startled we are by these occurrences, the more energy can go into minimizing them with preventative and interventional strategies. Social media shaming and other forms of cyberbullying are some of the newer high-tech forms of capitalizing on the vulnerability of our primitive brain regions. The cyberbully attempts to gain power (nonconscious survival advantage) by stealing it from the target through humiliation. This is a form of social capital robbery. We protect our money (financial capital) because we are aware of pickpockets and embezzlers. We also must guard our self-esteem by being aware of psychosocial thieves. The aim is to make others feel badly about themselves and their social standing. Whether it is electronic bullying or face-to-face, the underlying dynamic is the same. We predict that psychosocial robberies are more frequent than robberies for money; certainly this is the case in the workplace. Power and social status are much more in play at work as social commodities and they can lead to financial rewards as well. These types of maneuvers are just much more beneath the surface, disguised, and difficult to hold perpetrators accountable for. If I can get social capital from you, I do not have to work for it, and now I have more clout in the group and am more likely to survive. We should point out that theft is not the only way to gain social capital; as humans we can legitimately earn it. We can also trade, marry, share, inherit, and barter social capital.

There are no ways, to date, to fully quantify the specific and direct impacts of workaches such as bullying or exclusion, but we find it useful to conjecture possibilities. What we can assert is that it is costly in many different ways. Figure 5.2 suggests some emotional equivalents to physical strikes to drive the point of the harm of psychosocial aggression.

RELATIONAL VIOLENCE EQUIVALENTS

PSYCHOSOCIAL	PHYSICAL
Lack of acknowledging greeting	Poke
Judgmental, dirty look	Punch
Mobbing, rejection from group	Assault
Annihilation, feeling invisible, non-existent to group	?

Figure 5.2

It felt pretty bad, often like a "kick in the gut," to be the one tagged, last one picked, or the lone kid on the playground with cooties. It still feels bad to be the excluded one, the one not invited. Social shunning causes unnecessary pain and complication in modern society where survival is pretty much ensured, whether our coworker likes us or not. These different types of experiences make us feel pretty bad when we are the victims because we retain that primitive section of the brain that perceives a social threat as a physical threat to our existence and initiates the release of stress neurochemicals. These experiences make us feel powerful and socially superior when we are the perpetrators because we retain the primitive section of the brain that perceives a survival advantage over others when we bully and humiliate. Bullies perpetrate significant harm. We need to increasingly call awareness to how the body "translates" these psychosocial injuries into biochemical and ultimately physical injuries.

Games typically have an objective, strategies, and winners and losers. Psychosocial games do as well. Some of the roles, maneuvers, and games that are acted out in the workplace are listed in Figure 5.3.

SOCIAL GAMES EXAMPLES IN THE WORKPLACE

GAME	STRATEGY	OBJECTIVE
Social Posturing	Outdo and Shame	Status
Sexual Dominance	Break Down Boundaries	Reproduction
Hierarchical Manipulation	Micromanage	Control
Kiss Up to the Boss	Mirror and Placate	Favored Child
Competence Competition	Outshine Outdo Race	Alpha
Fear Me	Bullying Behaviors	Intimidation
Popularity Contest	Exclude and Rise	Better Liked

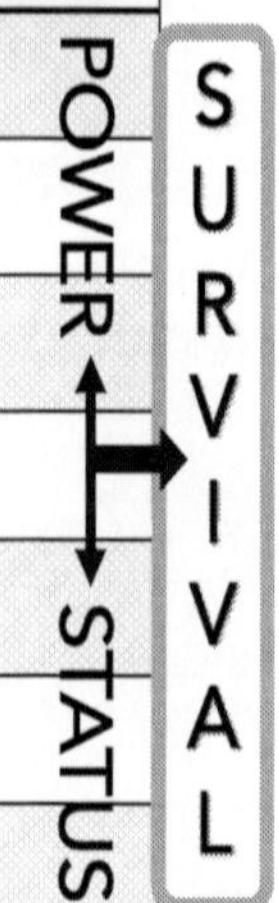

Figure 5.3

Because so much social gaming gets played out by the primitive and nonconscious brain regions, individuals are often unaware that they are even a player in a game. Occasionally, some are even unaware that they themselves have initiated or instigated social game play.

Gossiping is viewed as an evolutionary tool for group conformity, power, and control (Kurland & Pelled, 2000). Some of the adaptive survival strategies that we inherited from our ancestors seem to have morphed into other forms and taken on different purposes. Gossiping, shaming, and threatening have extended beyond forms of social control and order. What might have been adaptive thousands or even millions of years ago may be maladaptive today in their new manifestations. Language helped humans cooperate and communicate to form larger and more complex societies. But today...

- Necessary adaptive information sharing has turned into maladaptive gossiping leading to social devaluing, humiliating, and excluding ("shame on you for being different")
- Necessary adaptive role division and differentiation has turned into social and work status hierarchies ("I am more important or better than you")
- Necessary adaptive use of shaming (nonverbal disapproving and warning glance at behaviors that were non-conforming and potentially threatening to the clan) has turned into exclusions to the point of social annihilation of others that fuel some suicides ("you are worthless and unwanted in our group")
- Necessary adaptive abilities to wage battles with threats to survival have turned into intragroup conflicts and fighting, from road rage to project sabotage ("we hate you")

Evolutionary psychologists believe that gossip grew out of a need for the spreading of information as groups got larger. Similarly, the development of language is also believed to have grown out of the need to coordinate and organize group living. Individuals in the workplace often feel uncomfortable and harmed over becoming a topic of gossip. The function of gossip was to gain information about other individuals to stay on top of potential threats and possibly to inform role competencies and performance. Gossip is now a prime vehicle for carrying and transmitting shame, humiliation, devaluation, and exclusion.

Humor is another vehicle for transmitting shame and gaining power. Making fun of people at work can be one of the most insidious of workplace interpersonal assaults. The amount of interpersonal pain that can be packed into a joke is remarkable. Humor and laughter have been scientifically shown to have many benefits to well-being, including lowering stress hormones in the body. However, when someone is made the object of a joke, or hears a joke and laughing about a disguised aspect of themselves, the result is psychosocial harm (and sometimes people feel they must join in to pass and remain undiscovered). Individuals who "pass" (meaning their particular difference from the dominant group is unperceived by the group) often feel incredibly distressed by forms of group humiliation.

Differences: Uniformity Versus Diversity

The first thought that might pop into your head at the notion that this individual in the adjacent picture is different is a curious question: how are they different (from me)? We often become uneasy when we do not know how someone is different, especially because nonconsciously, the difference may place us in harm's way. Is he like me or not? Is he of my clan? It is easier on me if my brain's scan of him can pinpoint the difference(s) immediately because then I know I can take action, even if just to label and place him into some category. Think about your own initial thoughts, suspicions, and questions about this "different" individual. You likely would need and seek others to find out about this guy. Gossip would then become a tool.

Initially, it can feel too risky to get close and discover this individual without a comrade. We are more likely to engage in gossip to seek the information of how someone is different. The questioning and gossiping may gain us access or cement our ongoing inclusion and possible entrance into a protective group. This person is on the outside, especially because we do not know what makes him different. His unknown difference is fear inducing and anxiety provoking. However, if we ourselves have been marginalized from the dominant group because we are different, his difference may be a psychosocial opportunity. We may hope that his difference is our difference, which may mean we have a comrade and potential group member.

Humans will try many things to fit in with a dominant group. Unfortunately, one foolproof way to get into a group is to find a common enemy, because people like fellow comrades to join them against a threat. It is often striking to see someone who had previously been marginalized be welcomed into the group when there is a new perceived threat and thereby a need for more group members (fellow social soldiers). However, groups thrive evolutionarily with diversity. The more differences there are in organisms in a given environment, the greater potential for survival when the environment changes. If all organisms are the same, let's say they all have limbs that make them ground-dwellers, and the environment becomes water-based, survival is threatened. Survival is maximized if some, for example, had fins or wings. However, as organisms have grouped for survival, one with fins may be threatened by one with limbs. The difference indicates another group which could spell trouble and demise.

The dilemma is that as we separated out further into the world and formed larger groups, diversity was no longer favored because we needed uniformity. We needed to be able to predict each individual. Evolutionary pressure is toward diversity. Group pressure is toward uniformity. The paradox is that we want to fit in, yet we also long to be ourselves. But where do we fit in? What aspect of ourselves should we identify for group admission? Or should we just neutralize ourselves, so we are some average conglomerate and therefore have a better chance of blending in? Our individuality and uniqueness are built upon our differences, yet our differences get detected by the nonconscious radar of others. While a reproduction of great art goes for a fraction of the price of the original, a "one-of-a-kind" person can easily become marginalized by the majority and considered peculiar and suspicious, and their perceived worth may go down. Ideally, we would look at each individual as a unique work of art.

We can also look around the world to see the confusing nature of group identifications. To use a simplified example, if someone does genetic testing and discovers they are of Korean heritage, and they seek to join their ethnic group in the world, where do they go? North Korea or South Korea? We do not know because this ethnic group has divided and is now identified by political and geographical divisions. Sometimes group admission and acceptance seem to operate by primitive and arbitrary rules. When negotiating rejections and acceptances from groups it is valuable to keep this arbitrariness in mind. We want to think about and gain perspective on the power of group membership. This cognitive perspective (which we will describe in Chapter 7) is vital when negotiating group identifications and maintaining self-esteem and social worth. The in-group at work may not be what we have made it out to be when we step back and examine it rationally. However, it is difficult to gain wise perspective when the powerful nonconscious force pushes us to gain membership in the group that appears to have the status and majority. Remember, status equals power, which equals survival. And we want to survive above all else.

An adaptive trait is to be able to discriminate when to share or not share one's differences or diversion from the norm or majority group. Fear and anxiety can lead to aggressive acts. It is wise to assess the culture of the dominant group and to then calculate the risk-benefit ratio while in TDM. Of course, this is only in the case where differences are not directly perceived by the dominant group. Cultural and individual pioneers often must weigh personal sacrifice and safety with compromise and authenticity. There are individuals that can be identified throughout history who have sacrificed their own selves in service of the cultural evolution of their groups. We want this to be a choice versus a reaction from the threat system. Often when an individual wants to be liberated from their oppressive past of psychological sequestration and announce to the workgroup their particular uniqueness, they are acting in reaction to this past. But when we are behaving reactively, we are typically no longer in TDM, and there are higher risks attached to our actions.

Though unrecognized differences no longer mean the same, we still see the vestigial remains of our primitive fear response in our contemporary world. We still retain a segment of our tails from long ago, so it is any wonder we still retain behavioral and other characteristics of our ancestors?

To illustrate this point, let us consider an employee of a large organization who lost TDM when in the staff restroom. He was unable to categorize the gender of an adjacent individual and became enraged and verbally violent. At that moment, a traditionally binary categorization for the primitive fast brain could not be calculated and triggered his threat response. Threat led to a defensive reaction of verbal violence. Once again, education (once TDM is restored) becomes the goal. In this case, we did an autopsy of the incident. The goal was to dissect what happened in his brain to elicit such anger and contempt. Education about the triune brain and his personal triggers for loss of TDM was important. While this particular individual was disinterested in learning about the updated non-binary nature of gender, his motivation to manage his brain was to avoid the consequences of his rage in the future.

Freeing ourselves from binary categorizations and gaining spectrum perspectives represents a major progression in our current stage of cultural evolution emerging from our higher brain regions. We often use the analogy of the color spectrum to educate people that most human traits fall on a spectrum. Appreciating a spectrum takes more time and energy than our primitive brain affords us. The data from our environment entering our brain through our senses are processed first for threats to survival. We can rapidly spit out a bad-tasting food before we even have time to think about what we just ingested. We can quickly duck if we detect something buzzing above our heads. Our primitive brain regions make rapid (fractions of seconds) detections based in simple and often binary categorizations, which can lead us to judge people we haven't even met yet. We are called upon to non-judgmentally and compassionately understand, educate, and manage these aspects of ourselves. Individuals have learned to hide some of their differences when they can. This may be adaptive, but it can often come with high psychological cost. With the scanning for differences, unnecessary resources get expended for all—the individual who has detected a difference and nonconsciously feels they have been invaded and threatened, and also for the individual who bears a different trait (apparent or hidden) and fears that their physical and psychosocial safety is threatened. We address in Chapter 7 how to get a message to our partly obsolete brain regions that we are safe and need not be so reactive and controlled by our more primitive leanings.

Bias and Microaggressions Are Big

The full spectrum of diverse individuals exists in the workplace, though some may be passing or hiding:

- The woman who has been diagnosed with a degenerative disease but must pass as vital to keep her position
- The man who has nobody to bring to the company picnic so avoids it out of shame
- The coworker who lives in his car at night
- The eldest individual in the group who feels like an outsider
- The youngest member of the group who fears she has nothing to contribute
- The non-techy individual who is afraid his lack of technical sophistication will be discovered
- The coworker who avoids the get-togethers because of her social anxiety
- The new hire who just lost 100 pounds and listens to weight shaming at lunch

- The man who grins along with the homophobic comments but returns home to his husband each evening
- The woman with a sexual abuse history who withstands the flirtatious comments of her supervisor
- The coworker who skips the oral presentation because of his fear of public speaking
- The individual who listens to the racist comments of coworkers but returns home to her spouse of a different race each evening
- The woman who smiles when taking on the extra duties and staying after-hours but who was the parentified child in her alcoholic family, always compensating for others
- The man who raises suspicions when he slips away from the office (to urinate off-site) because he has anxiety about using public restrooms

Remarkable neurobiological cost is involved in keeping secrets (Slepian et al., 2017). The experience of carrying around concealed information is correlated with diminished well-being. The research has shown that it is the process of one's mind wandering to the secretive information which results in loss in feelings of authenticity and relationship connectedness. We are all vulnerable to being shamed (and thereby trying to avoid it) about some aspect of ourselves in one way or the other, even if we are not in a protected class. Disguised individuals are in families, schools, and eventually in the workplace. Disguises are just typically better developed in adulthood. Many have learned to hide, mask, diminish, dismiss, and even deny workaches in fear of loss of group membership, position, and job. It is realistically impossible to be aware of, knowledgeable about, and able to accommodate all the differences and sensitivities that each individual brings to work. The best management navigates with the assumption that all are masking diverse and unknowable vulnerabilities and differences. Even if an individual appears to be of the privileged majority, we assume they are human and thereby vulnerable. If we treat each individual with respect and without assumptions, we are relating in the best possible manner.

Humans have a nonconscious implicit bias in favor of those who are more similar to themselves (in-group) and a bias against those who are dissimilar (out-group). Brain studies have shown activation in the amygdala when subjects view out-group members signaling fear and distrust (Henderson, 2018). A growing body of literature is showing that microaggressions are remarkably strong social determinants of both physical and psychological health (Wallace et at., 2016). Microaggressions are derogatory verbal and nonverbal communications (often subtle and nonconscious) toward people with marginalized social statuses within the dominant culture. Historically, microaggressions have targeted race, gender, sexual orientation, gender identity, religion, and disability. Individuals and groups who have been marginalized over the years are often keenly aware of the threats inherent in bias, misinformation, stereotyping, discrimination, ignorance, and fear. Those targeted typically are aware of their precarious position within the group and their threat system revs a bit higher on a daily basis. However, when an actual microaggression occurs, it still is jarring to be reminded of one's vulnerable position and the threat system gets further triggered. We have collected many personal stories about microaggressions and their effects over the years. Microaggressions often get disguised and communicated in nonverbal ways (e.g., looks, behaviors, and attitudes), as well as through verbal communications. Below, in Figure 5.4, we have compiled some verbal quotes that have been uttered in the workplace as examples:

OFFENDED	MICROAGGRESSION
Older Caucasian Female	"Good morning young lady!"
Asian American Male	"I suspect you can calculate that in your head for us."
African American Female	"Please know your race doesn't matter to me."
Hispanic Male	"Where you from?"
Male on Autism Spectrum	"We didn't invite you because we knew you wouldn't want to come."
Gay Male (non-disclosed)	"That's so gay."
Introverted Female	"Why do you have to be so loud all the time?"
Male with Learning Difference	"Don't you have spell check?"
Lesbian	"I would never have guessed you were gay!"

Figure 5.4

Microaggressions Embedded in Work Communications

What we have discovered in our discussions with those affected is how intensely these micro-aggressive comments and questions fuel the primitive threat system. Often, microaggressions are nonconscious on the part of the offender, and then they are communicated to the nonconscious arena of the offended. Communications such as those in Figure 5.4, above, can serve to remind an individual of the unsafety of the group and the need to remain vigilant so as not to get thrown off guard by believing they have been genuinely included. Each microaggression then serves as a poke of sorts to the threat system. Our anxiety system "collects" threats to keep us safe and remind us of our vulnerabilities to ensure survival. These threats accumulate and begin to generalize and interact with other threats stored in our minds. So, though our conscious and wise mind may know that microaggressions are sometimes committed out of ignorance versus intent to harm, our nonconscious threat system does not dismiss these threats. Our threat system has specifically evolved to take action to protect our survival and not to discern nuances of intent or ignorance.

A couple of years ago, we conducted a series of seminars entitled, "Cultural Misunderstandings," and one participant, Amara, shared her experiences with microaggressions that illustrate some of the adverse and interactive effects of these experiences. Amara was a first-generation immigrant from Angola. She disclosed how her grandmother would frequently remind her not to get "too comfortable" at work lest she forget that she was not of their tribe and get hurt. Amara reported that the microaggressions she experienced in her workgroup confirmed what her grandmother had warned her about, but that she had never really wanted to believe as a child. She had resisted the notions from her grandmother who had lived at a very different time in history than she, but nonetheless, these admonitions went in and shadowed her and ultimately interacted with her experiences at work. Amara reported that she never felt completely comfortable and at ease with her workgroup. Lurking threats were always in the shadows no matter how nice coworkers were being. Amara eventually entered private counseling to address the issues.

Figure 5.5 illustrates the intergenerational transmission of threat via stories by elders, in addition to epigenetic transmission of trauma as we discussed in Chapter 2. We can see that what seem like minor, sometimes harmless comments, are significant communications to the nervous system to remain on guard and to remember "this is not your clan." As we have reviewed, the threat system is already heightened in harmed individuals and its neural radar is actively searching for potential threats through direct contact and from other sources such as stories of others. If we place this in the context of how social the brain is and thereby how important other people are and group membership is, we see how devastating microaggressions can be. Once again, we calculate a significant biochemical cost. These costs that seem so unnecessary today take away from the energies that could be going into creativity and productivity.

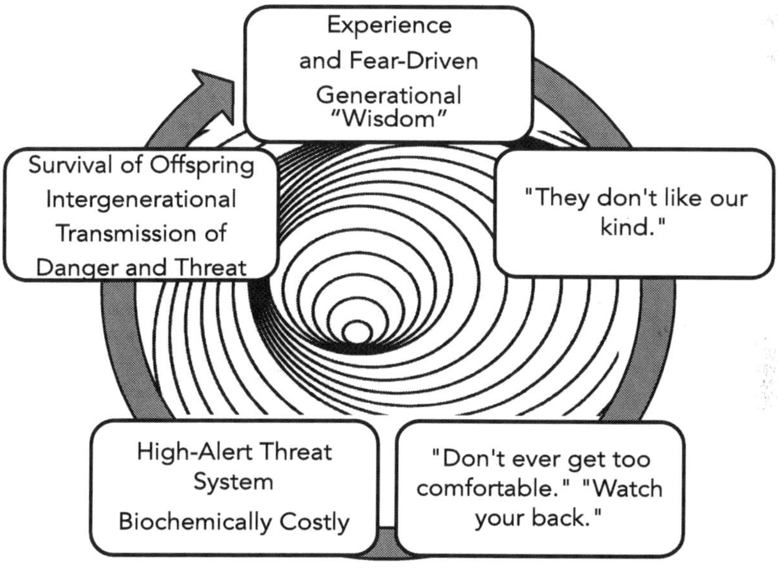

Figure 5.5

We have been admonished by some leaders that today we are too sensitive and politically correct about these "harmless" comments and that by focusing on them we are creating more of an issue than they deserve. However, we find that once we educate these organizational leaders about how the brain works, particularly the nonconscious regions, we typically can achieve consensus that there is no place for microaggressions in the workplace. If we view prejudice as a neurobiological issue (versus politicizing it), we can possibly all be "on the same side" to address it. The more leadership understands that the threat system disallows engagement and creativity, the more they see that microaggressions adversely impact their bottom line of efficiency and productivity. Diverse teams are the best teams and offer different styles and perspectives to the benefit of the collective. Microaggressions keep the threat system active in those targeted, as well in those passing and hiding from being targeted. The threat system is also active in those committing the microaggressions. Nobody wins here. We know that the best antidote to fear is information. When we are exposed to and learn about others who are different than us, our threat system typically deactivates, and our social engagement system activates. This is a win for all individuals and the organization at large.

It is worth keeping in mind that what might annoy one, may even enrich another. One staff member may become irritated by listening to the sound of chewing and another might trigger to the steps of the boss approaching. Some might not even take in these sounds. Each perception, though taken in by similar-looking organs such as a nose or ear, goes to its corresponding brain region for interpretation. Because each individual's path has been different, the brain regions assessing the meaning of these sensations will be too. Figure 5.6 offers examples of historical experiences that may be potential triggers in the workplace.

PERSONAL HISTORY FACTORS AND WORKPLACE TRIGGERS

Vulnerability	Workplace Experience
Childhood sexual molestation	Sexual Harassment / Harm
Exclusion from adolescent peer group	Lunch room cliques
History of social anxiety	Mandatory public presentation
Early learning differences	Criticism of work sample

Figure 5.6

We encourage staff and leadership to neither minimize nor dismiss the perceptions of another as measured by one's own response to workplace events and experiences. We also encourage individuals to not judge their own perceptions if different than those of the group. Identifying one's own unique annoyances, irritants, and stressors provides useful information to add to a personal narrative. Small irritations can add up and have a cumulative impact, so awareness is important and facilitates taking adaptive action.

Some individuals bring their childhood family roles with them into the workplace. Pigeon-holing is another potential stressor for some in the workplace. Our brains naturally classify and categorize. While one person may be categorized and seen as the go-to person in a workgroup, another person may be categorized as the incompetent one. The brain is lazy in this way and, after categorizing others can fail to update impressions, so we begin to see people through only one lens. Here, we enter the realm of "that person is always..." generalizations, which often become unproductive and even harmful. Another variation of this categorizing and generalizing is what we call "the terrible toos"—where people are categorized and rigidly perceived as "too nice" or "too mean." Individuals who are "too nice" have shared with us the burden they feel as the "most responsible" or "nice" worker of the group. These are the people who are asked to cover shifts, answer questions, perform off-job tasks, stay late, etc. They are helpful and make it easy for us to ask them to meet our needs. These individuals are safe to approach with a need. Some of these individuals have an early history where pleasing others was a necessary survival strategy. Their interpersonal dynamics gauge, which helps them discern when to say "no," may be broken or in need or recalibration. We must remain aware that for some, being "too nice" is a workache. There is a cost to picking up the slack or compensating for others in the group. People have emotional reactions to perceived unfairness or a sense of being taken advantage of. Kindness, performance, talent can all be over-utilized in a work group and must be monitored by the individual and the organization. Difficulty setting boundaries and saying "no" often accompanies this type of personality. Individuals of this nature often feel overburdened and sometimes resentful despite their outwardly appearing good nature.

Shame and Humiliation: Profound Impacts

Earlier, in Chapter 2, we addressed the developmental issue and potential harm of parents using shaming to socially control children. Shame is used by individuals and by groups for social control because it is such an intense experience in the brain. It creates unpleasant visceral sensations. We learned that shame was the equivalent to physical death when once upon a time group membership meant survival for our ancestors. Clans needed to keep group members in line with behaviors and actions in favor of the survival goals and rules of the group. A disapproving glance from the tribal head could communicate that a member was veering too far from group ways. This was adaptive for that member—it gave them a chance to adjust their behavior to be more in alignment with the group and retain membership and, therefore, survival.

Shame is so powerful that we can experience it even if no other individual is around to know what we are feeling, thinking, or doing! The ominous "eye of the other" is always at work within us. Shame is differentiated from guilt by a simple difference in self-statement: with guilt, the statement is "I've done something wrong"; with shame, the statement is "I'm bad." Humiliation is thought of as occurring between people. An individual can experience shame alone. An individual humiliates another to induce shame in that other person. Humiliation (to be "lowered" in the eyes of the other and/or self) has been linked to depression and aggression against others. The aggression on the part of the humiliated may be an attempt to restore their sense of dignity. Anthropologists and historians have even identified humiliation and shame as contributing to war and terrorism. Terrorist organizations capitalize on this underlying neurobiological response by recruiting in impoverished communities where men, especially, feel shame and anger (humiliated by other groups, societies) that can be manipulated (McCauley, 2017). Shame and humiliation are such intense experiences that they have been linked to interpersonal violence of all degrees. Humiliation is thereby a risky and potentially dangerous emotion to elicit in others.

HUMILIATION → SHAME, ANGER, AND VIOLENCE POTENTIAL

Shame is embedded in all families, groups, and cultures to differing degrees across the globe. In America, we have a financial score (FICO) that informs others of how reliable we may or may not be when it comes to lending us money. We may or may not feel shame when we discover where our score falls compared to others. Other countries have even extended it further with a "social" score. Instead of a comparative financial status, there is a comparative social status designed using shame as the underlying mechanism to achieve social control. We see this in groups even without a formal social score. Some people are aware of who they want to be seen with or not based on the social status of the other. Some fear that their own social status will be lowered if they are seen with someone who is devalued by the group. Being shamed and devalued by the group, once again, is a threat to survival to that primitive brain. This is a potentially dangerous artifact of our brains that we need to stay aware of and manage.

We were consulted as an outside source by an Employee Assistance Program manager to assist a man, Oscar, who was struggling with shame, humiliation, and rage. Oscar had been raised in a very religious and traditional family that had immigrated to the United States when he was seven years old. He was taunted in elementary school for being in special English classes and having an accent. Oscar quickly learned English and excelled athletically. By high school, he was admired by peers and shed the shame he had initially felt at school. Oscar eventually rose professionally to a high level of a law enforcement agency. But Oscar had a problem. His 19-year-old son had begun the transition to be a transgendered female and Oscar needed to report a change in gender to Human Resources for insurance and other purposes. Oscar was a dedicated father above all else and this facilitated his moving through what was quite a difficult process for him. Oscar had a history of being "against" LGBTQ rights and causes. He held rigid notions of masculinity and felt tremendous shame about his transgendered daughter. Nonetheless, he plowed through and tolerated being educated about and discussing issues of gender and shame. He tolerated examining his own early shame and eventually recognized that his transgendered daughter's journey would be difficult too as was his due to his early differences from the majority group. Oscar had to question the entire fabric of his historical beliefs or mindset. He ultimately recognized that ignorance and prejudice deserved more of his anger than his daughter. Oscar's attachment and commitment to his daughter facilitated his being able to override his early learned prejudices, his personal shame history, and his own internal neurobiological response to differences.

Interpersonal to Intrapersonal: Worst Infection of All

A most unfortunate outcome of group hate is when it infects the targeted individuals themselves. The group has power enough to sometimes make the targeted person believe what the group believes, which can lead to the worst attack of all—the self-attack. When people begin to believe that they are inferior or defective based on the dictate of the group (mobbing) or due to another individual (bullying), the victim may self-attack, in what is called intrapersonal aggression (within an individual). We emphasize interpersonal aggression (between people) in *Workaches*, but it is intrapersonal aggression that occurs when the nonconscious bias and aggression is turned inward. Buying into and personalizing some workaches such as racism or homophobia can lead to self-devaluation, self-hatred, and self-attack. An inner voice against the self that joins with the "voice" of the dominant or majority group can begin to narrate terrible things that attack the self. As we have described, the group is very powerful to certain regions of the nonconscious brain, and if the group makes us feel that our "difference" is "bad," this is very dangerous. Self-attacks can be as lethal as attacks by others, sometimes extending to the point of murdering the self (suicide).

Psychosocial self-defense is crucial in combatting verbal and nonverbal attacks from a group. In Chapter 7 we introduce the notion of crucial thinking that employs TDM of the brain and scientific knowledge to counteract and challenge both conscious and nonconscious attacks from others.

Gender Contests and Struggles

Gender is increasingly a fascinating and complex subject, as our understanding of it evolves. Rather than viewing gender as binary (one is male or female) our culture is moving toward seeing gender—like most other human traits—on a spectrum. Nonetheless, primitive contests and gender displays are sometimes exhibited in contemporary workplaces. Both males and females are objectified and nonconsciously triggered to work in unhealthy manners. Gender non-conforming individuals are subject to others' nonconscious biases in both personal and professional realms. More studies and data on specific issues faced in the workplace are needed.

Nobody is immune to the discrimination of nonconscious preconceived and primitive biases, though some are more protected by the power associated with the status they are afforded by the group. Some females find themselves in conflict over being home and raising their children and balancing their time at work and professional identities. Some females find themselves labeled as leaders but not necessarily perceived as such. They sometimes find their assertiveness perceived as aggressiveness and judged. Occasionally, it is difficult to say which gender is most offended by a microaggression. Consider a lunch meeting between a male and female coworker. The server hands the bill to the male making the male feel uncomfortable because he does not want to pay and making the female feel unempowered because it is assumed she would not.

Some males find themselves in conflict over the primitive force of competition and survival and desire to spend more time at home. Peter Glick has researched and written extensively on male and female sexism in our work cultures. Here we address the primitive pressures on the workforce and the resultant workaches and impacts on organizational culture by illustrating what men in the workplace face (Glick, 2018). Glick describes four cultural pressures on males (Figure 5.7):

Figure 5.7

Men must do battle in this arena to survive and advance in these types of workplace cultures. Women too must psychosocially weaponize in order to compete. Some of the factors acting on men are dramatically illustrated in the male-dominated gaming industry. "Crunch" is the term gamers use to describe 20-hour work days and work weeks that can extend to 100 hours. Tremendous pressure exists to perform and compete and to show no pain. Bathroom breaks, eating, and certainly going home to families are frowned upon. Eyebrows are raised if someone needs time off. There is an eager newbie awaiting an open position, so even talented people feel replaceable. And job loss, due to moving game development overseas, is a looming threat. Even though this illustration is one from private industry, these styles of working occur in public service as well, where employees often feel expected to "go above and beyond."

The social pressures on males to be "strong" and suppress emotions have often historically begun in Groups 1 and 2. Without the benefit of emotions and feelings, however, self-care becomes more difficult. People who go through life with the inherited condition of being unable to feel physical pain are at risk for physical injury. People who numb feelings with alcohol and drugs are also at risk. It is dangerous to be unable to experience emotional pain. Males are often socialized that the only acceptable emotion is anger. Females too have increasingly consulted us for techniques to dampen their emotions in the workplace; they especially want strategies for not showing tears at work. Gender-specific workaches harm all genders.

As we discussed in the section on intoxication in Chapter 4, even neurochemicals that make us feel good can also be hazardous and make us behave in maladaptive ways. For example, as we will see with sexual harm below, judgment becomes impaired when we are intoxicated with oxytocin and dopamine. When these "good" feelings combine with power and rage, the risk to others increases. And when these feelings combine with the need to please, or the familiarity of being taken as an object, the risk of revictimization increases. Awareness of when we are intoxicated by "feel good" or "feel bad" neurochemicals is important so that we can be aware of any changes to our decision-making capacity and actions.

Sexual Harming: More than Harassment

Before discussing the workache of sexual harassment or harm, let us recall that our primitive ancestors developed, played, learned, worked, and died within a small network of clans. Anthropologists believe that males and females would sexually prowl other small clans within their local network for reproduction purposes. The physical power of males would likely have afforded an edge or advantage for sexual conquests. We have evolved since then, but as with other traits, we still see residual primitive behaviors. Not every human evolves at the same pace—some are more or less evolved than others. This applies to both natural and cultural evolution. We see a spectrum of social evolution traits in the workplace, just as individuals are on a spectrum with respect to TDM capacity in the workplace. So, it is going to be more difficult for some individuals to manage their feelings and impulses and not act out their sexual and power inclinations. Because the workplace is a microcosm of the world at large, what goes on outside the office is going to take place inside the office. Using power to facilitate a sexual contest is no longer just related to physical power; in modern society it is often related to the power afforded by status.

We have observed that staff in some organizations have become increasingly desensitized to the term “sexual harassment,” and the requisite sexual harassment trainings in organizations are perceived by workers as unrelated to them and are attended reluctantly. Let us remember, the brain is soft—it is vulnerable to impacts from external factors of many kinds. After sexual harm, the brain changes. When it changes for the worse, we typically call this brain damage. Here, we substitute the term “harm” for “harassment” in order to drive home the notion that the brain is often harmed in these types of situations—both psychologically and physically.

Humans typically reach sexual maturity while they are members of their first two developmental groups. Group 2 typically becomes the ground for experimenting with sexuality, exploring romantic possibilities, and developing a sense of a sexual identity. Others in this group are scouted for possibility, compatibility, and opportunity for sexual connections. Flirting and sexual posturing become part of this developmental ground. Teachers and other staff who are employed to work in Group 2 must not participate in this developmental aspect of Group 2 membership. The players in this group (students) must be differentiated from the managers of this group (teachers/staff). When there is role confusion, there is higher risk for inappropriate participation in and exploitation of the sexual exploration of students. The developmental and power differences, as well as the taboos, between parents and children and between students and teachers are well defined in our culture. The necessary boundaries are thereby clearer in Groups 1 and 2 than they will be in Group 3, which is a completely different arena.

Some view Group 3 as providing an “equal playing field” for sexualizing, but it does not. Power differentials in roles make it unequal, though all may be sexually mature adults. Most individuals in the role of parent or caregiver, or in the role of teacher or educational staff, are aware that sexualizing a child is harmful to that child, but those with more power in organizations often do not perceive this same level of taboo. The rationalization is that everyone now is an adult and responsible for themselves and their choices—an inaccurate and harmful premise. This may be due to assumptions we make about adults and invulnerability. As we learned in Chapter 3, the brain changes with power. The brains of subordinates also change due to their dependency and need for survival.

Survival or financial needs increase vulnerability to victimization. Research has revealed that sexual harassment occurs more frequently in workplaces that have clear and strict hierarchies (Oertelt-Prigione 2018); we will look at the power dynamics which offer some explanation of why this might be.

Over the years, we have worked with individuals who have been charged with sexual improprieties in the workplace. Many (earnestly) do not understand how their behaviors have been harmful. They often have viewed their sexual interests and behaviors as a positive comment on the victim. One of our first tasks is to educate them about adult sexuality, power, and vulnerability. Many believe that sexuality is only about play and good feelings. Human sexual behaviors and communications are easily misinterpreted. Flirtatiousness is sometimes confused with consent to engage sexually. As with physical harm, social harm, or emotional harm—sexual harm changes the brain of the victim—and of the perpetrator. Sexual harm is never play. We propose a four-pronged model of factors that we have seen enable sexual harm in the workplace (Figure 5.8). We named this model using the acronym "PONT" because a pont is a bridge that facilitates movement between points. In the case of sexual harm, it is a bridge that can facilitate the slippery slope of perpetrating of sexual harm.

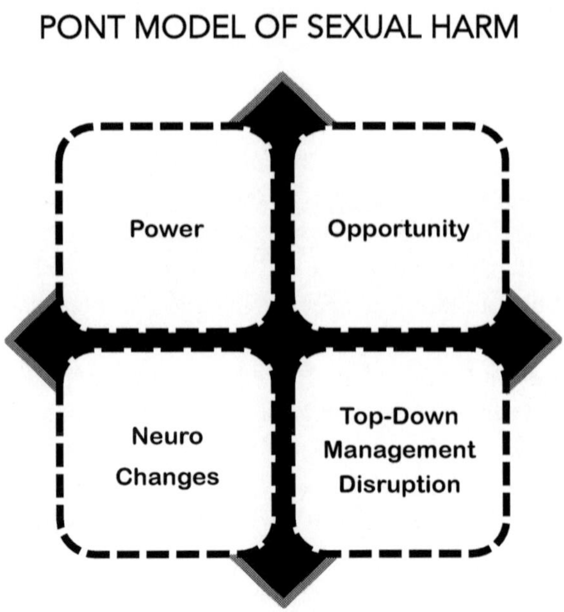

Figure 5.8

POWER gained over another individual by means of: 1) strength differential; 2) possession of a weapon (e.g., gun); 3) intimidation; 4) position of power, status; 5) intoxication of victim; 6) inability of victim to consent due to physical, psychiatric, and/or intellectual disability; 7) oppressive cultural and/or religious beliefs; 8) neediness of victim; 9) psychological coercion; 10) entrapment of victim; and/or 11) incapacitation of victim.
OPPORTUNITY that emerges from: 1) presence of victim; 2) vulnerability of victim; 3) perception of immunity or protection from consequences; and/or 4) belief one will not be caught or held accountable.
NEUROCHEMICAL CHANGES that result from transient neurochemical reactions: 1) drugs/alcohol intoxication; 2) hormones; 3) intense emotions; and/or 4) other variables such as infection and other brain assaults.
TOP-DOWN MANAGEMENT DISRUPTION and emotional dysregulation that results in impaired judgment leading to maladaptive decisions leading to reactions (versus rational actions) and harmful behaviors.

An individual who is in TDM is less likely to act on these impulses and desires. However, if these impulses have hijacked the neocortex, and sound judgment is out the window, the risk is more likely to be taken. The reward chemicals in this case are quite powerful and addictive. When we observe people in high positions of leadership risk their status for a brief sexual experience, it often makes no sense to us. It does not compute that they would risk their career, family, livelihood (harm self) and act out on a subordinate (harm other). We are typically viewing their actions when our brains are in TDM; their brains were likely not at the time of the incident. The brain events are not dissimilar to those that occur when we eat that candy we vowed not to or yell that profanity we later regret once TDM is restored. We all do things that are not in alignment with our identity, chosen ethics, empathy, compassion, etc. A spectrum of harm is committed in these acts (and loss of TDM) from minor (e.g., petty, derogatory comment in reaction to petty offense) to major (e.g., reactive violence). In the realm of sexual behavior in the workplace, without the guidance of the neocortex, there is a risk of pursuit behaviors including predatory and stalking actions. Risk of coercion and rape exists. These are primitive behaviors from our primitive past that we can still view in the sexual/reproductive lives of other animals. This is why awareness of TDM is crucial and the ability to manage the brain so vital.

Risk factors have also been calculated regarding who may be sexually targeted in the workforce. As one might imagine, the first factor is being a subordinate and having less power. Jobs ensure people wages to cover living expenses. Fear of loss of employment triggers that same underlying threat to survival. A history of sexual abuse and having been taken as a sexual object in the past is another risk factor.

SONT MODEL OF VULNERABILITY TO SEXUAL HARM

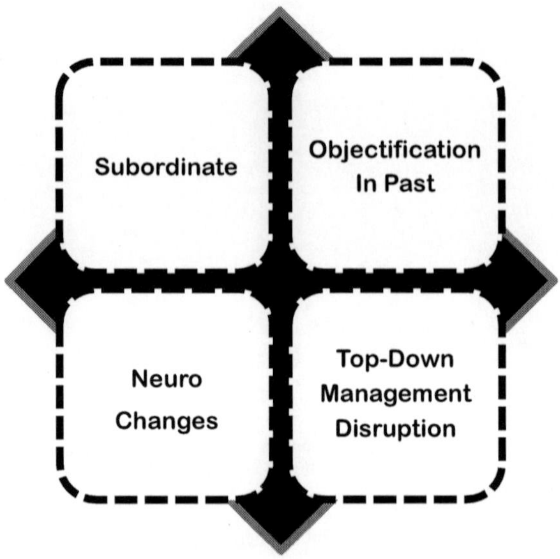

Figure 5.9

The dynamic between a PONT and a SONT creates a high risk for exploitation. Both individuals need to be aware of their risk potentials and take protective steps so as not to act this out in the workplace. If someone knows what they are working with inside themselves, they have a better chance of managing their feelings and behaviors. Non-judgmental education is the first step. We are wired to feel and have primitive regions of the brain triggered that lead to diverse desires and impulses. Some of these desires and impulses can lead to harmful actions. We have yet to discover some of the underlying reasons humans possess certain sexual proclivities. We do not judge the feelings and impulses—rather, it is the actions carried out that can be judged as harmful or unethical. In fact, as psychologists, we are relieved when a perpetrator of sexual harm discloses their maladaptive, antisocial, or atypical impulses. Creating a safe space for disclosure and discussion gives us an opportunity to work on these issues, and possibly keep another vulnerable individual from being harmed.

Velocity: Speed of Nature versus Modern Technology

The speed at which information passes through the workplace and the speed at which some work functions are expected to take place has dramatically changed. Our brains have not. The tools we are using and the speed at which they work are remarkably different than those of our ancestors. Our ancestors were confined to the speed of nature. The digital age has sped up our machines exponentially. Technology is bringing us information that flows in and out of our daily lives constantly. Machines win. Humans can make them, but not outpace them.

Some of the stress employees report comes from the need to keep up with the proverbial desk pile, which now is an inbox growing fuller each day, sometimes even more than our electronic cloud can hold. This electronic shadow creates stress, and must be adaptively addressed in the workplace, especially as information flow continues to speed up. There are some futurists that have predicted that our AI robots of the future will experience their version of depression when they too cannot keep up, compute, and complete the algorithms, or find the information that is requested of them! Although the digital age is an expression and product of humans (part of nature), it has moved beyond some of our grasp and speed. When we ask people to complete tasks that they may not have the internal resources to be able to do, we stress them. The inability to keep up can trigger feelings of helplessness and powerlessness. We must acknowledge this out-of-control experience as a workache requiring address.

One of the biggest differences dividing individuals in the workplace is in technological knowledge and capacity. Proficiency with electronic devices, varied communication methods, and versatility with software varies tremendously.

An ever-increasing workache in organizations is due to the growing divide between the "cans" and the "cannots"—those who can work the newest software and hardware, and those who cannot. Employees who are unable to be "technologically relevant" often feel shamed and threatened.

This divide triggers the threat response and is sometimes based in age differences. The technological bar is rapidly rising, and each generation of employees is recognizing the significance of the differences they bring into work based in their generational membership. A goal is to try and move this divide out of the realm of competitiveness and into that of cooperativeness where each generation shares their unique talents.

Caring about Workaches in the Workplace

Humans of all ages need support and protection from something larger than themselves, such as their groups. The group that most individuals belong to in adulthood is the workgroup. Research has revealed the importance of employees perceiving that their organizations support them, similar to how a parent, teacher, or coach would. Organizational support theory (OST) describes how employees project human-like traits onto their organizations (Eisenberger et al., 1986). Because we used to work within small clans, there were identifiable elders to guide and support us. Organizations now take the place of our work-life clans. Individuals often assign the organization, especially on nonconscious levels, a family-like valence. Some people think of their superiors as "being the organization itself." These individuals may or may not well represent the organization, but needs get projected upon them. Employees form an opinion as to whether the organization recognizes their contributions and cares about their well-being. Studies have confirmed the ideas of OST and shown that perceived organizational support (POS) has a positive effect on employees' commitments and job satisfaction (Riggle et al., 2009). The need for another to "have our back" continues throughout our lives. When organizations fail to protect members, we see the effects of organizational betrayal in diminished morale, productivity, absenteeism, and high turnover.

Organizations must address workaches, so employees perceive that they are cared about and protected. HHS organizations are committed to caring for and protecting the public, and it is just as essential that they give the same level of awareness and commitment to caring for and protecting staff. Employers must recognize the win-win nature of providing employees what they need, which then facilitates employees' providing what their employers need. The responsibility of the organization is to care for the employee. The responsibility of the employee is to fulfill their role in the organization. Both organization and individual can thrive when missions are executed responsibly. Caring about workaches and addressing them is part of this mission.

Chapter 5: Key Concepts

1) Workaches are defined as work experiences that trigger the threat or stress response.
2) Workaches can overwhelm an individual's ability to cope and lead to symptoms, illness, and trauma.
3) Some staff are more vulnerable to specific workaches based in their histories. Workaches can interact with past trauma.

6

THE HARM: NEURAL HIGHWAYS OF ADVERSITY

If emotional wounds bled, you would realize.

The rings of the tree in this picture tell a remarkable story of its life. At points in its long history, it sustained fire, fungal invasion, harsh weather, and other unidentifiable conditions that made it unlike any other tree. Despite its adversities, it kept growing, until someone cut it down. Prior to that final cut, we can see that its "tree identity" was "bigger" than any of its competitors, attackers, or parasitic relationships, and it held its place. If we were not able to look internally, behind its protective outer bark, we would not know from its outside appearance what it had gone through and survived in its lifetime. What we do know and can assume is that no path in nature is free of pain and adversity. The existential philosopher, Jean-Paul Sartre, wrote about the "coefficient of adversity" which was originally introduced by philosopher Gaston Bachelard. In mathematics, a coefficient is a constant quantity or number that shadows and multiplies the number to which it is connected. In philosophy, it is metaphorically extended to be a factor in all lives that carries with it a level of pain and distress. Acceptance of this "given" in existence is seen as lessening the impact of adversity when it does occur. All experiences, good, bad, and in-between, become part of our complex story as we carry on. Behind the persona or outer covering of another human is a complex being with a unique narrative that includes adversity. Similar to the tree facing a chainsaw, every human is vulnerable and has a breaking point where they too can no longer withstand the blows and fall. Unlike the tree, however, most of the time we can and do get back up. The inner vulnerability and complex pain history of each human we encounter may be unknown to us, but that everyone has one is an essential assumption with which to navigate the workplace.

We do not have visible rings carved in bark that tell our story. Our stories get etched in our brains. In previous chapters, we learned that our psychosocial injuries have carved neural pathways that get stored for future use in the brain's attempt to keep us safe. Relational harm and violence lead to long-term behavioral, emotional, and physical changes. Healing from interpersonal harm is an active, ongoing, and integrative process. The learning that comes from being harmed by another human is complex because it often generalizes and gets projected onto other people.

We may not be able to unlearn, but we can relearn. It becomes essential to learn that even though some people have harmed us, we can also be healed by people.

Our neocortex assists us in the choice to either fuel cynicism in the workplace or to fuel acceptance and safety with our colleagues and managers. Rather than seeking to discover who presents a threat, with effort we can find those who offer kindness and compassion. This new learning is possible because of the process of neuroplasticity, which we introduced in Chapter 3 and which is an ability we can harness throughout our lives. We can learn. We can change. We can update. We can heal within the limits of humanness. The implication of all this is that there is always hope. What we have been most moved and impressed by in our work with stressed and traumatized individuals and organizations over the years has been the incredible resilience we have witnessed. Because we have never been able to eliminate all existing workaches in an organization, or stop new ones from cropping up though we promote prevention and intervention, our biggest wish is always for resilience. Resilience, however, is not a passive or effortless activity. It must be cultivated and relentlessly pursued. First, though, let us look at the harm that occurs from the interpersonal injury inherent in workaches.

This Cache Cannot Be Cleared Either

Be it a tree, human, or computer, no true erase function exists. We do our best to clear our Internet tracks, but most of us have come to learn that our digital footprints exist somewhere even after we think we deleted our account history. We no longer see it, but it is somewhere in or out there. As humans, we also try to forget things, delete episodes that we feel shame about, suppress events that harmed us, dissociate from interpersonal relations that scared us, and deny activities that we regret. However, they are all still there lurking between those neurons.

There will most likely be a time in the distant future when humans have the choice to erase certain unwanted memories. There have already been fictional depictions of such events. The difficulty with this futuristic notion is that it entails the loss of what makes us unique as individuals and often inspires us. Those who have moved on from their adversity and are safe eventually come to consider these pain-based memories to be motivating, evolving, and enriching aspects of their true identities. The totality of life experiences—both good and bad—form our personal narrative and unique life journey. And as we will highlight below, growth after pain and adversity can be life altering. Editing out the pain is a compelling idea as a futuristic endeavor, and it will no doubt generate much ethical debate. Until that time, let us briefly review what we typically come to do on our own, before we learn how to confront and integrate some of these experiences.

What Is Learned and Remembered: Post-Traumatic Cognitions

We have learned that adversity arises in the workplace from the trauma histories individuals bring, workaches experienced within the work environment, and sharing the traumas of those served (in HHS). We then have all the interactions of the different adversities between and within individuals. When the bad experiences have been with other people, two primary messages get stored in the brain:

> I am unsafe and vulnerable.
>
> Other people pose a threat to me.

These types of thoughts have been studied and labeled post-traumatic cognitions and are a significant part of the harm that emerges from adverse experiences (Ehlers and Clark, 2000). However, these types of ongoing beliefs disallow the bad experiences from becoming part of one's past history and keep the stress and threat "live." Other types of post-traumatic cognition involve self-blame, guilt, and shame and include beliefs about being responsible for bringing bad things upon oneself. Beliefs can be haunting and shadow people throughout their lives unless challenged and updated.

Experiencing adversity at the hands of other people and the subsequent ongoing hypervigilance in interpersonal encounters can be both acutely and chronically stressful. Stress-inducing beliefs about other people and the world are biochemically costly. Individuals who enter the workplace with these beliefs selectively collect reinforcing evidence to perpetuate their beliefs about being unsafe. Our threat or anxiety system does not concern itself with collecting counter evidence that could disprove our anxieties and suggest our safety. It does not matter if a workplace is the safest place in the world—if an individual feels unsafe, that will be their perception, experience, and biochemical response to being there. The corollary to the above messages or cognitions about the workplace become:

> My workplace is unsafe, and I am vulnerable.
> Coworkers and management pose a threat to me.

Thoughts and beliefs are not isolated in the brain. They connect to emotions and the entire biochemistry of our bodies and minds. Living with these types of distressing thoughts whether they are accurate or inaccurate comes with cost. If the mind perceives and believes it, the body goes along. But anxiety does not typically create enhanced safety. Energy is better spent on adaptive problem-solving in truly unsafe environments.

Psychosocial Threats are Physical Threats

What relatively recent research has shown is that our bodies respond to different threats in a similar manner (Eisenberger, 2012). The brain does not distinguish between physical and social threats. The same underlying neural pathways get activated. Social rejection or exclusion is painful in and of itself but can also lead to other illnesses. For example, individuals who have a history of being socially excluded and rejected by a group have a 22 times higher likelihood of becoming depressed (Kendler et al., 2003).

Both the "shaming" finger and the gun depicted in Figure 6.1, below, result in the stress response and a cascade of biochemical events. These findings emphasize the importance of acknowledging the harm that results from some workaches that have historically been considered to be benign and ignored by management. Interpersonal threats have remarkable consequences.

SAME BRAIN REGIONS ACTIVATED BY PHYSICAL AND SOCIAL THREATS

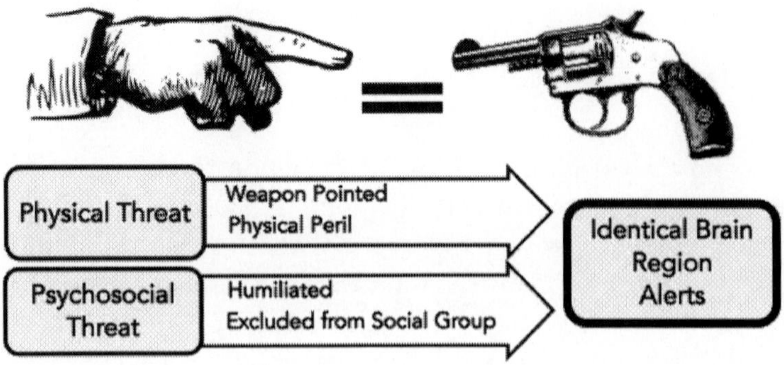

Figure 6.1

This research has significant implications for those who work serving the public as well. Many people have been harmed and traumatized by other people. The Adverse Childhood Experiences (ACE) study, initiated by Kaiser Permanente and the Centers for Disease Control (CDC) in 1995, has demonstrated that many individuals will have ongoing issues in adulthood due to harm they experienced in childhood. Below we elucidate some specific findings of this landmark study. In Chapter 4, we discussed Dr. Field's LIFEMORTS triggers. Here we see further how profound a response someone can have with, for example, the "I" of Insult or shame. If an eligibility worker must deny a customer's request for emergency assistance, the response could be beyond the immediate disappointment of not getting needed resources. Just the shame or "I" alone that someone is already experiencing by needing help can trigger a threat response that is amplified due to a history of trauma. The research data showing that the brain can interpret these threats on the same level as a death threat is profound and underscore the importance of remaining aware when we ourselves or those we are interacting with have lost TDM.

Body and Mind Under Stress: From Ache to Disease

Individuals with histories of adversity and trauma often live in a chronic state of arousal and stress—and they often do not know any different. Many are unfamiliar with the visceral feelings and psychological experiences of completing activities of daily living from a relaxed state facilitated by the social-engagement or parasympathetic nervous system. When soldiers return from war, it often takes much time and work to transition to a balanced state between the threat and reward systems. When stressors remain in the current environment, it is that much more difficult, and sometimes impossible, to get to that "soldier at ease" state of being, making individuals who work in HHS particularly vulnerable.

Just as our brain does not distinguish between real and perceived threats, it also does not distinguish between the primitive threats our early ancestors faced (getting eaten by a wild animal) and contemporary threats (being late for a meeting due to being stuck in traffic). No matter their source or reality, all threats are costly to our bodies. We have discussed what happens during both acute and chronic stress. It is also important to consider what does not happen during these times. Energy that would typically go to non-essential functions that are not vital to the immediate need to fight or flee to stay alive is diverted to functions for battle. Figure 6.2 shows some of the different bodily functions from which energy is borrowed for times of battle, or at least perceived battle.

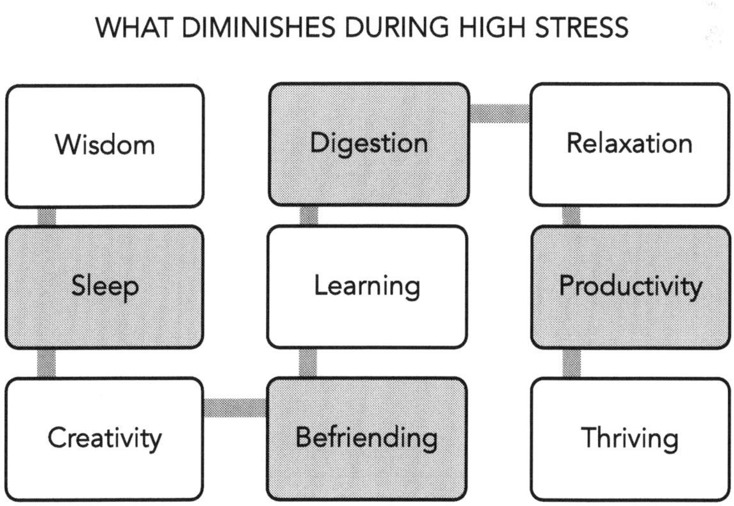

Figure 6.2

The chemicals that get triggered by perceived threats due to the stress response travel to every cell of the body. Once the amygdala perceives potential threat it tags the hypothalamus. The neural pathways between the amygdala and hypothalamus are so well laid and efficient that we do not even know this is occurring. The hypothalamus activates the sympathetic nervous system, which signals the adrenal glands to release the stress hormones cortisol and adrenaline—the body is in fight-or-flight mode. Breathing becomes more rapid and the respiratory system is now involved, as the brain needs extra oxygen to stay alert and focused on the danger. The heart beats faster and blood pressure increases, and now the cardiovascular system is involved. The liver produces extra glucose to give you more energy, and therefore the digestive system gets involved. The stress response also stimulates the immune system—in a response from primitive times for healing battle wounds. After the first surge of adrenaline subsides, the hypothalamus activates the second stage of the stress response—via the HPA axis. This axis, which includes the hypothalamus, pituitary gland, and adrenal glands, keeps the sympathetic nervous system activated if the threat is still lurking. If and when the threat passes, cortisol levels fall, which results in deactivation of the sympathetic nervous system and reactivation of the parasympathetic nervous system. The HPA axis (stress response system) remains active with chronic low-level stress.

Working hard is significantly different from working stressed. The reward system of the brain is turned on when working hard for a desired monetary goal or non-monetary reward (e.g., praise or meaning). The threat system of the brain is turned on when an individual is working in fear (e.g., in order to avoid disapproval or other negative consequences).

Excessive stress does not facilitate engagement at work or completion of work tasks. The primary goal when working stressed becomes avoidance of punishment. The fear results from anticipating adverse consequences and penalties ranging from reprimand to job loss. This type of concern is also set up when there is unhealthy competition between individuals. When researchers give test subjects a task to perform in a lab and set up a punishing system of feedback (e.g., electric shock if not fast enough or error-free), both quality and quantity of work decline. Physiological measures of stress via brain imaging and other measures such as blood cortisol levels, skin perspiration, and heart rate reveal a physiological state of fear in subjects. In this state, performance was impaired in contrast to when subjects were offered a reward as motivation for task completion. Some organizations have moved away from performance evaluations because of the threat or psychological "shock" of being evaluated. Some research is suggesting that these types of assessments induce fear and reduce employee engagement, commitment, and productivity (Rock et al., 2014). The use of performance evaluations is currently an area of debate and investigation.

SEEKING REWARD → WORKING HARD

AVOIDING PUNISHMENT (THREAT) → WORKING STRESSED

Neuronal shadows of early criticism only serve to exacerbate the stress of re-experiencing this type of leadership in the third group. Individuals in leadership positions who use their power to lead based in threat may gain a sense of immediate control, complacency, or obedience from their employees. However, intimidation of others rarely leads to thriving or optimally contributing to the goals and purpose of the workgroup. Individuals are disabled with regard to learning, creativity, and productivity when working in the threat mode. As we have learned, energy and resources are diverted to threat management and survival.

Hans Selye introduced the concept of the "general adaptation syndrome" to describe stress responses to perceived threats (Selye 1936). His original findings emerged from autopsies of stressed rats and studies of ill patients. Selye showed not only that stress was an unpleasant experience but that it involved physiological changes and states in the body based in perceived environmental stressors. His legacy is remarkable. Decades later, his early findings have been confirmed and furthered with cutting-edge technology. The stress-response system prepares the body for self-preservation, which could involve battle or retreat. Bodily functions unnecessary for fight or flight are shut down, including digestion, immunity, and growth. However, they are remarkably affected (later) due to biochemical impacts during the stress response. As Dr. Selye stated, "every stress leaves an indelible scar, and the organism pays for its survival after a stressful situation by becoming a little older."

Mounting research data indicate stress creates significant inflammation in the brain and body, and inflammation is implicated in many disease processes (Liu, Wang, & Jiang 2017). Figure 6.3 illustrates a pathway from workaches to a few of the body systems vulnerable to disease as a result of stress and the chronic activation of the threat system.

WORKACHES STRESS RESPONSE

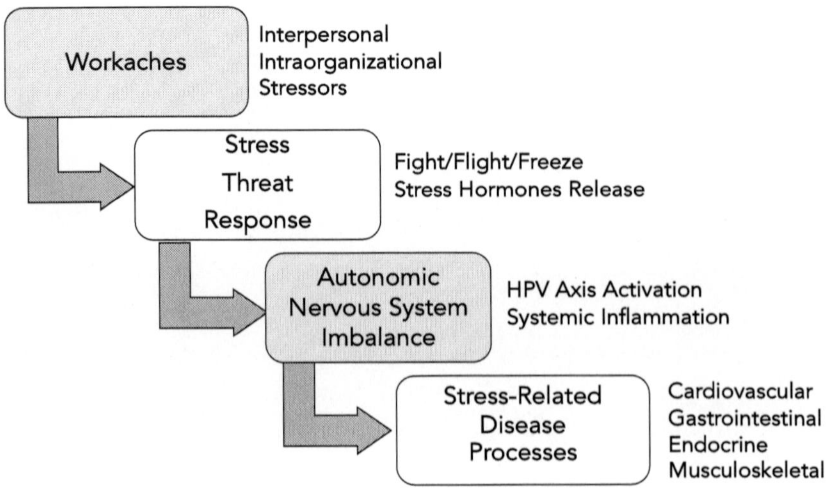

Figure 6.3

Although he was one of the first to describe the adverse effects of stress, Selye made a point to acknowledge that to have a human life is to have stress. He believed, and other scientists have come to agree, that adaptively managing adversity is key to mitigating the effects of stress. Not all stress is considered to be bad. We have been discussing "bad" stress or distress that results in often unnecessary and adverse impacts. Positive stress is called eustress. Examples of eustress include being promoted at work or starting a new challenging project. Eustress can motivate and fuel productivity and engagement. Sometimes we can intentionally transform distress into eustress by reframing problems as challenges.

Ways We Try to Escape the Pain

Because stress is uncomfortable, most people develop personal adaptations and defenses. Sigmund Freud introduced the concept of unconscious or nonconscious defense mechanisms in the nineteenth century. Freud believed that humans deploy defense mechanisms to push feelings and memories into the unconscious arena of the mind to avoid the anxiety that the conscious mind would have to deal with. Neuroscientists have since studied defense strategies via brain imaging and inform us that there is scientific evidence to support their existence (Berlin & Koch, 2009). Defense mechanisms can be adaptive or maladaptive at different times in a person's life. For example, a child might employ displacement and act out their anger on dolls and other toys because they have learned that anger is an unacceptable emotion in the family. Displacement may be adaptive in this individual's childhood but likely will be maladaptive in adulthood if anger gets acted out and displaced onto others. Some of our defense mechanisms interfere with our ability to form close and authentic relationships. This is especially true when the defenses have been developed to protect against threats from other humans. Avoidance of interpersonal intimacy after childhood abuse as a defense against the anxiety from being close to another human is often tragic. Defensive strategies can have remarkable impacts on human relations across a lifetime.

Whether they happen during childhood or adulthood, after they have passed, bad experiences remain with us and we continue to try to "get away from them." This happens in both the personal and professional realms, and the psychosocial armor that we wear as a result is emotionally heavy and biochemically costly. Relief comes when we can escape or subdue the anxiety we feel and the unwanted and uncomfortable thoughts and memories we have. Sometimes it seems more comfortable to avoid our problems and emotions at work and to carry on with business as usual. We may pretend that they are not even really happening, because when we feel drained of our energy by workaches, we do not have a whole lot left over to address uncomfortable issues.

Anxiety is uncomfortable and unsettling, and when it is chronic, we do not want to experience it anymore, so we employ different strategies that push the unwanted aspects from the conscious arenas (in awareness) of our brains to the nonconscious (out of awareness) deeper regions. While our defensive strategies sometimes just help us avoid adverse realities of our existence, they do not remedy interpersonal problems and they stress the body further. In the next chapter, we will discuss "the heal"—adaptive ways to address stress, problem-solve workaches, and engage our relaxation response and social engagement system.

Some of the defensive strategies employed in and out of workplaces include:

DENIAL: The ability to deceive the self, as well as the other, is viewed as adaptive. Remember, we are programmed to stay in the favor of the group and to avoid consequence. We will do what is necessary for inclusion, even if it means denying an experience, even to ourselves. This defensive strategy makes it easier to carry on in the social milieu than to disrupt and possibly compromise our position. Victims of abuse often do not step forward, initially or sometimes ever, in part due to how our brains operate and employ defensive strategies. Abuse is sometimes not consciously registered. Abusive experiences may not get transferred to memory storage in the manner that more neutral experiences do.

DISMISSAL: When we minimize the bad experience and its effects, or come up with an excuse such as, "it will never happen again, so I don't have to worry about it," we are practicing dismissal.

DISPLACEMENT: An individual has a bad day at work with a boss, for example, and returns home to take out frustrations on an innocent, less intimidating, family member or pet. The bad feelings are discharged and displaced onto another object.

HUMOR: We sometimes attempt to place a funny or ironic spin on bad experiences to laugh them away and move them to a more casual, less anxiety-provoking, realm. If we laugh something off, we do not have to necessarily face the internal conflict it creates.

INTELLECTUALIZATION: We may attempt to use higher order thinking to explain actions taken in response to a bad experience, or to avoid the emotional components of an issue or experience. Some people get perceived as "cold," "distant," or "clinical" when this defense is employed.

RATIONALIZATION: We often attempt to excuse or blame away the emotions and feelings involved with an adverse experience. For example, a person who utilizes this defense who gets turned down for a job may then remark, "I didn't want that job anyway."

<u>SUPPRESSION:</u> We may consciously push away or place aside unwanted memories, experiences, thoughts, wishes, needs, desires, feelings.
<u>PROJECTION:</u> When we ascribe our own feelings, thoughts, desires, and motives to another person so as not to own them (and thereby avoid the anxiety and shame of possessing them) we are projecting.
<u>REPRESSION:</u> Similar to suppression, repression occurs when we nonconsciously inhibit a feeling, impulse, desire, or need so as not to confront the tension that might accompany or get associated with these human experiences.
<u>DISSOCIATION:</u> This occurs when we fragment or separate out feelings, sensations, thoughts, memories, and experiences and isolate them away from other parts of the brain. Severe forms of dissociation result in dissociative personalities—often called multiple personality disorder or dissociative identity disorder. In the workplace, you sometimes may witness this in meetings when the person you are addressing is physically present but psychologically absent.
<u>REACTION FORMATION</u>: This refers to when we transform unwanted feelings, thoughts, and impulses into their opposites. For example, when a boss experiences a deep repulsion to or dislike of an employee, and cannot tolerate these feelings (and is unable to accept and explore them) the boss might excessively and disingenuously shower praise and adoration on that employee.
<u>COMPARTMENTALIZATION</u>: We compartmentalize when we separate out certain actions and emotions that may not align with our own ethical or value system so as to spare the self the anxiety that would typically be attached to such feelings or behaviors. For example, in the workplace, when a typically ethical and honest employee feels taken advantage of and perceives unfairness, they might take home a stapler to reduce the anxiety of the unfairness they are experiencing.

Unwanted thoughts, intolerable feelings, unacceptable desires, and guilty misbehaviors in the workplace all create anxiety and are thereby vulnerable to being whisked away from consciousness by a defense mechanism. Sometimes, it is difficult to differentiate between lying and denying—or conscious and nonconscious defense mechanisms. Is that individual lying and not taking responsibility for an action, thought, or feeling, or has she thrown up a defense mechanism against an action, thought, or feeling that is now no longer accessible to her conscious mind?

We often do not allow ourselves the opportunity to explore and integrate workaches—and thereby heal and grow—when they get barred with defensive strategies, but when people make attempts to address an issue, they often feel more empowered. Self-efficacy, which is the belief in one's own capacity to manage environmental experiences and achieve goals, is an important aspect of self-esteem (Bandura, 2012). Excessive use of defense mechanisms, which can contribute to feelings of helplessness and powerlessness, can thwart the building of a sense of self-efficacy. One strategy in counseling is to identify the defense mechanisms that an individual employed as a child, and then to discover what they needed to defend themselves against. This understanding becomes part of their personal narrative. We check to see if these mechanisms are working to an individual's advantage or not in adulthood, and we then consider updating these defense mechanisms to more adaptive coping strategies and problem-solving techniques.

But sometimes stressors and workaches in adulthood continue to be defended against with the same childhood mechanisms. Because the individual did survive their childhood, these strategies get reinforced and coveted. These defenses become difficult to surrender because life, of course, continues to bring threats. Why would we shed our armor if we do not see an alternative that will protect our vulnerability to attack? When someone has been harmed, it is difficult for them to trust again. Recovering is typically slow, and we must offer new adulthood coping strategies that the individual can come to trust as protection, or they will continue to use unrevised defenses that emerged from childhood.

Let us take a brief step back to childhood to set the stage for understanding how workaches can have different impacts on different individuals, especially those who have been harmed earlier in life.

When the Harm Starts Early in Life and Continues

Past interpersonal trauma is a risk factor for future vulnerability and for significant impacts resulting from compounding stress. Most of the comprehensive research on the effects of bad life experiences at the hands and wills of other people has focused on childhood. The ACE study was limited in the types of adversity queried. The researchers only included the ten most mentioned childhood traumas from a relatively small group of 300 individuals who were Kaiser members in San Diego, California. Certainly, there are many more traumatic experiences that children face that were left out of the ACE Questionnaire but that nonetheless contribute to significant adversity and negative outcomes as well. But the ACE study has been expanded and diversified over the years and is now a significant compilation of data about the lasting effects of childhood trauma into adulthood (Felitti et al., 1998), and the CDC continues to follow research participants and generate data. No comparable comprehensive studies, similar to the ACE study, have been conducted on the long-lasting effects of adversities sustained exclusively in adulthood, such as in the workplace.

Many individuals enter the workplace in their youth and remain until retirement age. Given that work is typically such an extended part of a person's life, it is imperative we gain a deeper understanding of the potentially debilitating psychological and physical effects of adulthood interpersonal harm. Indeed, the most striking and repetitive findings of the ACE study have been the link between childhood adversity and adulthood disease and psychosocial problems. As an ACE score increases, so does an individual's risk of disease and symptoms (the ACE assessment can be taken online, and the results are then calculated to generate an ACE score—cdc.gov/ace). The adverse childhood events all include person-to-person or interpersonal dynamics, including being directly harmed and witnessing interpersonal violence. The ACE has facilitated increased public recognition of the devastating consequences of early interpersonal violence. The many papers published from the study have indicated that childhood trauma and stress lead to serious risk to later emotional, cognitive, behavioral, and social development, and physical health. The evidence generated by the ACE study has even revealed the risk of premature death for those harmed. A stunning statistic is that with an ACE score of 4 or more, the risk of suicide increases 1,220 times (acesconnections.com).

Over the years, the definition of what constitutes trauma has been updated and expanded. Examples of what can create childhood trauma include: inability of primary caregivers to bond with child; having a mentally ill or alcohol/drug dependent parent; prolonged separations from caregivers; early emotional/verbal abuse; physical/sexual abuse; being bullied at school; having learning differences in classroom; and premature deaths/losses of attachments. The trauma is extraordinarily complex when it occurs inside the home. Healthy attachments and relationships inside the family of origin are viewed as having a protective effect and helping children manage trauma that is sustained in outside environments. If the stress is inside the home, this does not occur. When the threats are inside the home, we see chronic activation of the threat response. The child is in a bind. They need the family and home in order to survive, yet it is the home life that is the source of the anxiety and threat. Often, feelings of helplessness and surrender are exhibited. We can extrapolate from this to the subsequent major groups of an individual's life. The third group, workplace, is needed for survival, yet if the stress or threats are occurring there—we see yet another remarkably difficult bind.

ACE research has provided remarkable data on the impacts of high ACE scores in the workforce. Researchers have found significantly higher rates of unemployment, absenteeism, financial problems, and other job issues.

ACE is just one of many studies that have raised our awareness about how most people have neuronal shadows from the past that impact their present. The threatening memories are especially haunting because the brain evolved to store scary memories and remember threats in a most amplified manner. Even brief threatening experiences get converted into structural changes in the synapses between neurons to create long-lasting memories that shadow us thereafter in our lives. These memories remain in the subcortical brain regions, often until they are triggered from the neocortex. Workaches or stress at work often interact with these synaptic shadows and can trigger them in unfortunate ways and often at inopportune times. The following vignette illustrates psychological trauma sustained from combat when this individual was in his early twenties (and therefore his brain had not even finished growing and connecting, as described in Chapter 3).

Clarence had been a pilot during the Vietnam War, decades before we met him. He feared his upcoming retirement from social services because his work had long distracted him from what he called "ghosts of his past." Clarence's combat experiences still haunted him. We share Clarence's situation because it illustrates the complexity with which the human brain stores and processes trauma. His experience also demonstrates the role of rage and the threat response, and how we can depersonalize others. Clarence described how it was much more difficult to fire artillery from his aircraft when he was closer to the ground. His "targets" became real people to him if he could see them, and it became harder to carry out his mission. If he was higher in the sky, he could not necessarily make them out as distinct human beings. Clarence also relayed that when his sergeant would "fire him up" against the "enemy," it was also much easier to carry out his missions. One day Clarence spotted a water buffalo on the ground from his helicopter. He flew closer and realized an enemy soldier accompanied the animal. Clarence failed to respond as trained. We believe his affection for animals disrupted his focus on his task at that moment. Additionally, the human and animal brought up relational feelings with other beings, and Clarence could no longer perceive them as "enemy objects." That human face he "locked eyes with" and the water buffalo were imprinted in his memory and became the content of Clarence's flashbacks and nightmares.

Studies of combat soldiers have informed a great deal of our understanding of traumas sustained in adulthood. Clarence's story illustrates some of the profound impacts of what we ask of our soldiers. Clarence remained pretty isolated and was unable to establish any desired long-term relationships even though many years had passed since his service. He used street drugs to self-medicate in his attempts to escape his memories and bad feelings. The subcortical regions of the brain where these memories got stored were unaware of how much time had passed. Sometimes it seems as if these adverse experiences get "frozen in time and place." Clarence stayed away from most people and had difficulty managing the relations he did have because some of the typical conflicts stirred his past experiences and stressed him. He chose self-medication, distraction, and avoidance because they were familiar to him. Clarence feared that not using these familiar defensive tools, and trying new and more adaptive coping skills, would render him too vulnerable to the pain and horror of his combat experiences. He had been using his maladaptive defensive strategies even before he had been deployed to Vietnam.

By the time a coworker, employee, or boss arrives in the workplace

(Group 3), their brain has been sculpted and personalized to their specific experiences in Groups 1 and 2. Neuroscientists can now pinpoint links between specific types of abuse and specific brain changes (Patoine, 2018). A person maltreated in Group 1 or 2 will bring different defenses and psychological postures into the workplace. With maltreatment at the hands of others, the brain's sensory systems often get desensitized. Sometimes, this process is merciful because it reduces, filters out, or numbs the overwhelming sensory experiences of trauma, but if too much sensory information is filtered out as an adult, it is more difficult to advocate for oneself and assess stress and needs.

Most parents would never intentionally inflict damage on a child through absence, inattention, distractions, and omissions. Often there are no immediate and clear signs of the adverse effects of these experiences, making it difficult to recognize the harm perpetrated. Similarly, employers are typically not consciously intending to harm their employees. However, nonconscious emotional states, communications, and behaviors can be active and cause harm. For example, a manager might unknowingly be threatened by, competitive with, and dismissive of their employee because they feel insecure in their own position. What gets communicated in the psychological underground of that relationship may affect the employee. A sense of workgroup safety, performance, and engagement can become significantly impacted. As psychologists, we can attest that psychological injuries are some of the deepest and most devastating of all.

Relational trauma emerges from stressful events that occur between people that exceed the capacity of individuals to cope and/or defend against the incidents and injuries. These events typically include shame, humiliation, exclusion, and other threats to psychological integrity and self. Annihilation and abandonment are prime examples. Chapter 2 revealed how these disruptions to the attachment process could impact the developing mind of an infant. These experiences extend beyond Group 1. The brain remains social and plastic, and therefore vulnerable, in all future groups. For example, if a teacher annihilates a student who does not take to arithmetic and does not "see" that same student's outstanding talent in art, harm occurs. If a boss overlooks the talents of an introverted employee, this omission can be annihilating and cause harm. The four "A's" of development (attachment, attunement, abandonment, annihilation) in Group 2 apply in the workplace too. Leaders are encouraged to create social attachments and stay attuned to staff experiences. They are also advised to remain aware of staff that might be feeling unimportant and invisible in the workforce (abandonment and annihilation). In Chapter 8, we address "stay interviews" that facilitate conversations with employees that can potentially reveal such experiences and emotions in the workplace.

Past threats and traumas interact onward with future stressors and adverse experiences. On a positive note, however, future resilience also interacts with past threats and traumas. A less well-known research project that emerged from the ACE study (Rains & McClinn, 2006) provides an excellent study of resilience. *The Resilience Questionnaire* developed from this study examines protective factors that possibly counterbalanced some of the traumatic experiences of study subjects. Many measures of resilience now generate a factor labelled the Resilience Quotient (RQ) that reflects how one recovers and adapts after remarkable stress. We will consider some of this research on resilience in Chapter 7: The Heal.

Adulthood Trauma and Its Impacts

As a society, we have focused a great deal on childhood trauma, which is extremely important. However, as we have discussed, no magical invulnerability gets bestowed in adulthood. Some adults are even more vulnerable than children due to the cumulative effects of trauma. Adulthood trauma data have traditionally come from comprehensive research on soldiers returning from combat and with the diagnosis of post-traumatic stress disorder (PTSD). The PTSD diagnosis has since been extended beyond combat veterans and placed on any individual who meets PTSD diagnostic criteria. PTSD can occur at any age after a threatening event or experience. The National Institute of Mental Health (NIMH) defines PTSD as a disorder that develops in some people who have experienced a shocking, scary, or dangerous event (nimh.nih.gov). Cumulative trauma effects result in higher rates of PTSD. Some key symptoms of PTSD include:

Intrusive Memories / Flashbacks	Withdrawal / Avoidance / Numbness
Mood Issues	Hypervigilance / Hypovigilance
Anxiety / On Edge	Sleep Issues
Anger Outbursts / Irritability	Exaggerated Startle Response

Many more diagnoses and symptoms are attributed to maltreatment, adverse experiences, and trauma. Many symptoms that are not formally characterized or clustered into diagnoses nonetheless remarkably impact an individual's life after adversity. Post-traumatic stress (PTS) is characterized as a common response to an adverse or extremely stressful event and includes more transient symptoms such as shakiness and bad dreams (Bender, 2013). Symptoms of PTS typically subside after a few days as opposed to PTSD which can last a lifetime. Some additional signs, symptoms, and issues that we have seen across individuals include:

Depression	Avoidance of Others
Mood Shifts	Fear of Others
Distrust	Diminished Self-Esteem
Feelings of Impending Doom	Shame / Guilt

We need more studies on how adversity and experiences such as workaches impact adults. As we have seen, the brain remains vulnerable in adulthood. Stress and trauma accumulate as an individual develops, and past experiences interact with current stressors. While one individual can deal with a situation without stress or pause, the same situation can trigger a cascade of old trauma in another. Our work with court-mandated road rage clients illustrates this point.

Leonard was a compassionate leader of a public service agency. He was known as a champion of his employees and fairness in the workplace. Leonard was mandated by the court to attend anger management sessions after a road rage incident. Leonard was a soft-spoken, personable, middle-aged man who was remorseful about injuring another man after smashing the driver's car window. He was a father, husband, and respected community leader. Colleagues had no clue that Leonard had a history of trauma.

The freeway exit Leonard took daily to get to work had gotten crowded over the years, and this was stressful. What was more stressful for Leonard was when some drivers did not start their exit at the back of the line but would move over at the last minute just before the exit. Unfairness was a trigger, to begin with, for Leonard. That day, a driver did just that one car up from Leonard. Leonard took it upon himself to get out of the exit lane and proceed to dangerously cut off this driver. Leonard was no longer heading to work—his initial and conscious goal. An aggressive verbal exchange ensued. At some point, the other guy used a derogatory term insulting Leonard's manhood. This slight was the final trigger.

Leonard is an unfortunate example of an individual with unintegrated trauma (who had never built a personal narrative and coherent understanding of his life) who temporarily lost TDM and got into trouble. He had for years prior utilized the defense of repression and denial in order to get by. The road incident triggered the buried trauma, the neocortex went off-line temporarily, and then limbic rage directed a violent reaction downward to get carried out by extremities and a body filled with cortisol and adrenaline.

We use Leonard also to illustrate a point that sometimes only mere fractions of seconds may separate us from regretful reactions that harm others and land people in prison. This reality is yet another aspect of the nature of our complex brains, trauma, and stress. Anyone can lose TDM at any time and any place. If we work on our issues, we have a better chance to form or strengthen neural pathways from the limbic system to the neocortex. That was the goal with Leonard. Together we built his story and understanding of his triggers. We also worked on behavioral strategies to disengage the threat system and engage the relaxation system, especially on the road. And to minimize triggers, Leonard agreed to spend a few minutes extra on the road to avoid the more congested exit which was a specific trigger.

Leonard was genuinely motivated to grow and remained in counseling beyond the court's mandated ten sessions. With such time limitations, we can typically only educate and help build some behavioral strategies to manage anger, but we do not have enough time to develop the insight necessary for deeper change and growth. Neural pathways require repetition in order to build, strengthen, and connect with other pathways.

Because Leonard was willing to continue the work of counseling, to better understand such a significant trigger, we explored his childhood—one that had been buried in the middle brain due to intense feelings and lack of opportunity. The best Leonard was able to do was suppress the traumatic events and emotions to survive his childhood. In brief, Leonard had a father who had severely humiliated him because he was very slight as a child. His father had shame about Leonard's appearance and would physically strike his calves and call them "girlie legs" and often forced Leonard to "work out like a man." The insults and challenges to Leonard's masculinity went on from there. When the other driver insulted his masculinity, that was Leonard's "last straw." Leonard was eventually able to connect the road rage incident to his personal narrative and also to update his own definition of masculinity from that of his father. Acknowledging and understanding shame became key. The underlying dynamics and aim of the counseling became verbalizing, emoting, identifying, and understanding the issues so Leonard could build new neural pathways between buried traumatic childhood memories, intense feelings, and behaviors. These new pathways and insight could offer him a better chance for emotional and behavioral management when he encounters future triggers.

Many considerations and ramifications exist regarding the commutes that employees have on their way to work. Quite a bit of variation exists in the nervous systems of individuals by the time they walk through that office door. Leonard is an example of someone who was utilizing his childhood defense of suppression (which can only go so far in adulthood) to mask his intense feelings from inside his car. Nobody really knew him at the office until his extended absence due to his incarceration.

When Service to Others Results in Disservice to Self

Helping others is one of the noblest of endeavors in this existence. This is why we must calculate the costs of human service to stay as healthy as possible. Otherwise, we harm ourselves—and then nobody benefits. We introduced secondary trauma in the last chapter as a workache, noting its higher risk in HHS professionals. Here we explore this HHS hazard in greater depth and examine the potential harm it levies.

As we have reviewed, we are social beings with specialized neurons and brains that are attuned to other people. Individuals who find themselves serving in health and human service positions are often well-endowed with mirror neurons, empathy and compassion, and the motivation to help others. Compassion fatigue, burnout, and secondary trauma are all clusters of symptoms that result from the brain and body being in a sustained state of vigilance and empathy resulting in depletion of mental and physical resources. The service to and chronic witnessing of adversity and suffering extract a remarkable toll and result in harm to the service provider. Some individuals manifest the damage of stress and workaches by internalizing pathology—others externalize it. Internalizing pathology comprises less apparent symptoms because these individuals withdraw and keep their issues to themselves, but the signs are just as essential to address and treat even though they are less apparent. Externalizing pathology manifests as symptoms exhibited as maladaptive behaviors such as engaging in coworker conflicts or drug/alcohol misuse. Secondary trauma is defined as indirect exposure to a traumatic event by hearing about it from another. Other terms used to describe this secondhand experience include acquired and vicarious trauma. Primary trauma is defined as direct exposure.

A firsthand account from a victim can lead to trauma symptoms in the listener similar to those experienced by the victim.

The newest criteria for post-traumatic stress disorder (PTSD) in the *Diagnostic and Statistical Manual of Mental Disorders* by the American Psychiatric Association indicates that one no longer has to directly experience the trauma to receive the diagnosis (DSM-V, 2013). Our understanding of what constitutes trauma and how it changes the brain has evolved tremendously over recent years. The PTSD diagnosis in the previous 2010 edition of the *Diagnostic and Statistical Manual of Mental Disorders* (DSM) was reserved for those who directly experienced significant military combat or life-threatening events. We now recognize daily work experiences and exposures as potentially traumatic, which facilitates acknowledgment, awareness, and interventions that were not present before. We now know that 10-20 percent of people who hear about another person's trauma will get infected (Wolf, 2018). Those infected can experience PTSD symptoms similar to those of the victim, including hyperarousal of the nervous system, increased startle response, sleep disruptions, nightmares, numbness, existential angst, dissociation, anxiety, depression, and other anxiety-related issues.

Many individuals who serve others have their own primary trauma in their backgrounds and, indeed, may have been motivated to help others because of their personal histories of adversity. When HHS professionals themselves have directly experienced or witnessed a traumatic event, traumas can interact and create complex psychological issues in the workplace. As we saw with the examples of Clarence and Leonard, above, addressing and integrating one's own trauma into a personal narrative can promote growth and assist with the helping of others. However, if one's trauma is unresolved, working with the suffering of others can further traumatize the self. Warning signs of secondary trauma are different for each person, but generally they may include some of the more common signs and symptoms listed here:

Exhaustion (physical / emotional)	Self-Medicating
PTSD / Other Diagnoses	Avoidance / Vigilance
Headaches / Physical Symptoms	Sleep Issues
Hyperarousal	Numbness / Detachment
Absenteeism	Presenteeism*
Mood Issues	Hopelessness / Helplessness
Cynicism / Attitude Changes	Attitude / Outlook Changes
↓ Concentration / Attention	↓ Productivity / Engagement
Self-Doubt / Fear Incompetence	Job Dissatisfaction
Illness / Disease	Leave Position / Desire to Leave

*Presenteeism = being physically present at work but too ill or exhausted to competently perform duties

REFLECTION

Please pause now and reflect on these signs and symptoms of burnout and secondary trauma. Which, if any, do you recognize in yourself or coworkers? Do you experience any additional signs or symptoms that are not on the list? Do you need to speak to a professional counselor for assistance? How would you know if it was time to be concerned about yourself?

Our brains have evolved to take in the trauma of others. If we think back to our evolutionary roots, it makes sense that if early humans witnessed someone else sustain a bad experience, it would be adaptive for them also to take it in and remember it for their own future safety.

Anxiety is contagious in this way. If you sense a threat, it is adaptive for me to detect what you are sensing, even if I do not directly see, hear, feel, taste, or smell the threat.

We watch each other for signs of danger. We learn from one another.

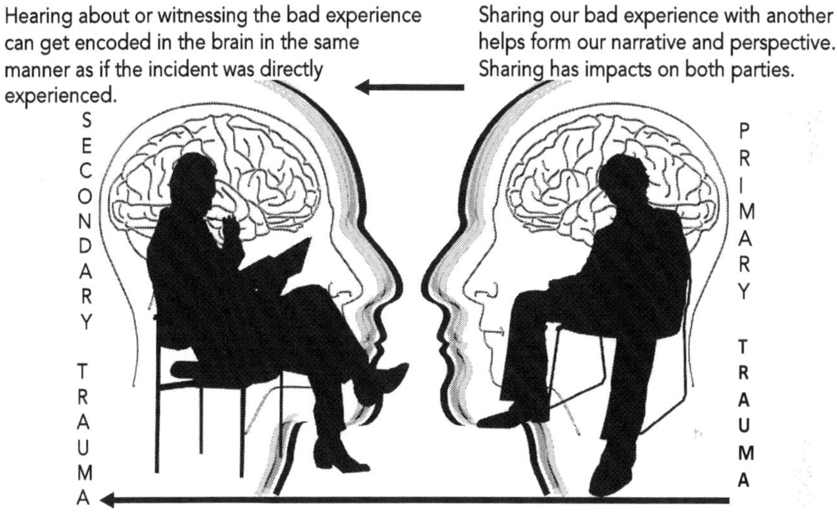

Figure 6.4

We also watch how others work. Burnout can also spread within a work group. For example, a belief that one must work tirelessly can become infectious. Any notion of care of the self is looked upon unfavorably by the group as departing from the norms. Social contagions are powerful and individual immunity strategies such as employing TDM becomes important for perspective and intervention.

Self-sacrifice is not necessarily a badge of honor.
Selflessness may not be a sign of commitment.
Working stressed is not typically working hard.
Self-care is not a sign of selfishness.

Harm to the self, by any means, must be addressed, especially when it has infected and spread throughout the culture of an organization. Self-care actually fortifies us to work hard and compassionately. We do not need to prove our worth at work by becoming ill. Significant harm occurs when shame lands on self-care—including leaving work to attend medical and other essential appointments, for which employees should not feel guilty. We will discuss the value of leadership in modeling self-care to remedy this contagion that has infected many HHS organizations.

Trauma Triggered: Excavating Below the Surface

When there has been significant discord and psychosocial battles experienced or witnessed in Groups 1 or 2, we are more vulnerable to Group 3's psychosocial battles and crossfire. The harm is more complicated. Our primitive evolutionary history continues to shadow contemporary work roles and create some of the harm. For example, we still have the "blue" versus "white" collars and the projected status differences afforded each. A frequent complaint we hear in organizations is feeling devalued by and lesser than others. Most of us have a hard time not feeling that emotional ouch when we are singled out to go fetch the coffee or do the copying while others are socializing in the office.

Here, we share another real-life example to illustrate the concept of the traumas that live in those synaptic shadows and sometimes emerge in disguised forms but can eventually hold essential pieces of the puzzle or story. This illustration also foreshadows the next chapter, which emphasizes the need for traumatized individuals to put their stories together with perspective and in the context of the passage of time. This case study also has implications for employers and leaders regarding the potential for triggering staff with inadequate or insensitive leadership and policy regarding psychosocial functioning in the workplace.

Linda was a well-respected, hard-working, 58-year-old female who was an event coordinator for a large public service agency. She was referred by her manager because she was complaining of feeling increasingly anxious at work and was uncharacteristically beginning to miss work days due to anxiety and insomnia. She denied any prior mental health history. She was allotted eight external employee assistance sessions. During the first session, we reviewed her childhood history and assessed her current functioning. Linda denied any remarkable childhood and adulthood events. She described her childhood as "good." She recalled that her paternal grandmother had suffered from excessive worry and remarked that these symptoms were "probably in my genes." We spent our sessions learning relaxation techniques and practicing other cognitive coping strategies to facilitate her treatment goal of returning to work. She also began taking an anti-depressant medication after a psychiatric evaluation. Linda was able to return to work successfully.

This is not where Linda's story ended, but we save her story for the next chapter because it exemplifies so well some of the ways we can heal.

Shame struggles take a great deal of energy because they are so nonconsciously tied to survival. Challenging shame with perspective and wisdom is critical in the workplace. In the next chapter, we introduce crucial thinking—a way of rethinking, reanalyzing, and revaluing inherent beliefs that are maladaptive and certainly do not facilitate thriving. Our discussion now transitions to the potential for healing and thriving after adversity and workaches.

Chapter 6: Key Concepts

1) Stress response is a biochemically expensive and primitive system that responds to false alarms and can be chronically activated with adverse consequences to health.
2) Workaches in adulthood have remarkable impact.
3) Our brains change even when seeing, hearing, and just knowing about others' trauma.

7
THE HEAL: NEURAL HIGHWAYS OF RECOVERY AND GROWTH

After the strike and the fall comes the opportunity for the rise and the call.

Healing and harming share timeless aspects due to how our brains process and encode them. Recovering from adversity is an active, intentional, effortful, multidimensional, ongoing, and non-linear process. Even though a harmful experience may have ended, the cascade of mind and body processes that follows has not. We address recovery as a mindset or outlook that seeks resilience, strength, and integration. No mindset is rigid and static. Humans question, lose faith, struggle, get triggered, and become disillusioned. Specific brain regions overwhelm and hijack our more rational processes. Losing sight of the desired goal or wisdom mindset is part of the process. Recovery of the core, intended, and most adaptive mindset each time it eludes us becomes the goal. And this mindset will, again and again, move off our radar. Self-compassion is critical in recovery. It anticipates and generously makes room for going off the path, and gently guides us back toward our desired destination and chosen goals.

Healing is as complicated a process as the harming has been to our brains. For some, aspects of recovering fuel a passion for helping others. These are the more inspirational and triumphant aspects of healing.

Nonetheless, helping others with their adversity can lead to exposure to one's own trauma triggers. Remaining mindful of this and practicing self-care become essential for those helping others with their traumas who also have their own personal trauma histories. Otherwise, this beautiful aspect of recovering can become a workache rather than part of healing. Recovering and healing are verbs—they are action words. Just as no human being is ever "finished" growing, no experiences just end, finish, or go away. We want our learning and experiences with others to get distributed to and integrated with higher regions of the brain where we can then gain cognitive and temporal perspective. This process of integration facilitates feeling less fear, being less stressed, engaging life more from the social engagement system (than threat system) and developing a life story that includes *all* learning and experiences—both good and bad.

Adversity becomes a challenge to have to reckon with rather than a threat to have to fear.

In the last chapter, we introduced the defensive strategies individuals use to function at work. Sometimes, we just need to avoid or distract ourselves from our emotions and experiences to make it through the day. Strategies such as these are typically imperfect because, although our anxiety may be reduced in the short run, our memories and issues remain stored in our brains, shadow us, and emerge in disguised ways and symptoms. In other words, the psychological costs of our not directly facing problems can accumulate, making defensive strategies maladaptive in the long run. Some defenses can make us vulnerable to revictimization if we "forget" what has happened and how we need to protect ourselves.

Value of a Personal Narrative

Let us return to Linda's story, with which we closed the last chapter. She made contact with us three years later, and she was very distraught. Linda was desperate to return to treatment. She reported that she was now experiencing panic attacks and feeling severely depressed. Deeper excavation and examination of Linda's life history ensued. During a session exploring childhood adversity, in a barely audible whisper, Linda began to repeat the phrase, "purple knees." After many sessions, Linda finally disclosed how schoolmates taunted her about having purple knees—they were stained from kneeling in the fields while picking grapes.

Linda's childhood had been far from unremarkable, as she had initially reported. Both parents were migrant farm workers with minimal resources. There was significant food insecurity in the household. Linda and her siblings helped in the fields and resided in a mobile home on the farm. Nobody at school ever knew where she lived or what her parents did. Linda carried her family's shame. At some point in her schooling, she was forced to wear a uniform that exposed her knees. Peers mocked her knees. Linda experienced remarkable humiliation and shame. The trauma was buried so deep that Linda herself did not even "remember" or think her childhood experiences would be relevant to her adulthood symptoms and job performance. However, the humiliation at school was encoded as traumatic.

As Linda's story unfolded, the connection between some additional job duties and early experiences became clearer. The supervisor had assigned Linda the role of refreshments server at a weekly agency-wide staff meeting. She requested that Linda wear a badge on those Thursdays and take the requests for refreshments. Linda was triggered by humiliation. She was the only one wearing the badge (symbolizing purple knees) and identified as having a "lower" position (shamed and excluded from group) from her perspective. Uncovering the trauma and bringing it into conscious awareness facilitated Linda's working through the issues.

Below is a simplified diagram (Figure 7.1) depicting the primary shame trigger involved in this case study:

Figure 7.1

If we could have hooked Linda up to a brain-scanning machine, we might have seen new neural connections grow as a result of gaining insight and making the connections to her work experience. Integrating the suppressed memory of humiliation from childhood into a new, more complex personal narrative was of utmost importance for Linda's ability to heal. Later, Linda was able to go on and have a garden in her home that she enjoyed tending to—it was no longer "beneath her" or humiliating to work the land because she had integrated that trauma and built new neuropathways, reducing the power of the triggers.

As Linda's story demonstrates, we can counteract neuronal shadowing through conscious acknowledgment and by putting words to both good and bad experiences to form our personal narrative. Awareness and verbalizing form the neuropathways between the emotional, fear-based regions of our brain and the more rational, time-aware regions. These pathways allow for the acknowledgment of our adversities and their integration inside our brains. This process then allows us to gain perspective, including placing a historical time stamp on bad experiences, so we can move ourselves to a safe and calmer state. TDM and neural-connectedness between brain regions afford us merciful opportunity to say to ourselves "even though I am feeling scared again because I have been triggered (in my limbic system), that terrible experience happened ten years ago—it is not happening now. I am safe." We must "know" this in the neocortex to best navigate through difficult times. Knowing that we can create and restore our own safety builds self-trust. When we have been harmed by another, even if only once, that harm has laid a neural pathway that can be felt and retriggered in the future. Harming and hurting are verbs too. They are ongoing, even though the initial harming occurrence has ended. Our insight and perspective, when in TDM, walk us through the frightening sensations and feelings of threat. When we remove children from abusive homes, their learning and ultimate healing come from the kindness and safety of other people. They learn that some people are not threats. These children build new and strengthen neural pathways that encode that others can be loving and supportive. Paradoxically, we are harmed by other people, and we are healed with the help of other people.

It Also Takes a Village to Care for an Adult

Adults remain vulnerable beings and require care too. There are many resources available to those who have been harmed. Adults, however, often must seek this assistance on their own. Appendix A lists a few organizations and agencies that provide assistance after traumatic events.

Increasing numbers of organizations are working to prevent harmful workplace incidents. Their goal is to reduce and prevent workaches before they occur. Federal and state protections, as well as state and other regional labor unions and programs, are also in place to support workers. Appendix B lists the federal agencies and programs that afford protection and can assist workers. Just as there are child labor laws, there are adult labor laws. Other people do care and can be reached if needed. Witnesses who observe and recognize workaches occurring with coworkers or others can also be instrumental in seeking help for victims. Whistleblower protections are typically afforded those who bring needed attention to workaches in an employment setting. People can anonymously call or provide an online account about abuse observed. We are strong advocates of internal employee assistance programs (EAP), which we discuss in Chapter 8. Providing impartial and caring counselors in a confidential setting can make all the difference to scared and affected staff. Human resources departments are sometimes not perceived to be as safe as EAPs due to concerns about political and confidentiality issues. EAP counselors can serve as the third group's "parents" and "teachers" who care, educate, and soothe. Bottom line: there are other people available and waiting to help you too, even though you are now an adult.

Sometimes it is more difficult for those who are considered the healers, such as those who serve in HHS, to recognize their own need for healing. So much focus is placed on attending to others, that the assessment of one's own needs is incomplete at best. Invulnerability in those who serve others is a societal and often self-imposed myth. Those who serve others must also be mindful that helping others can sometimes be a strategy to avoid one's own pain and issues. People who have suffered unimaginable traumas often emerge as inspirational role models, but first they must attend to the needs deep inside themselves.

Healing as an Intentional and Effortful Process

There are many paths to healing. Recovery is very much an individualized and personalized process. Here, we explore some of the paths individuals can take to address workaches and other relational traumas. We cannot emphasize enough that it is never a linear path. Relational events, nonconscious factors (e.g., nightmares), and other life experiences may trigger and return us to the deep emotional place of our trauma pain. The body may react as if it is back there. Reexperiencing sensations and thoughts does not necessarily imply one is regressing or going "backward," as some often fear. Triggers are a part of an ongoing process of recovery and integration. Once we experience our own resilience, it becomes easier to see and return to it again, and again. Here, we explore **re**envisioning, **re**silience, **re**covery, **re**storation, **re**habilitation, **re**building, and **re**newal in the aftermath of adversity. We are all different—in how and when we get here, get back here, and in what we need as assistance along the way.

When we awaken from sleep, the brain has not gone from off to on. Instead, different regions come back online and go off-line to varying degrees. Shifts in brain regions occur. We can "wake up" in our wakefulness state too and achieve different levels of alertness. We can encourage different brain regions to come back online and discourage others from being unnecessarily active. We view the restoring of TDM as underlying the many different paths of intervention and recovery. Getting the brain back to its integrated and harmonious state is the aim, whether stated or not, of many clinical strategies. We inevitably lose TDM as a result of life interactions and experiences. When imbalanced or out-of-sync brain regions cause harm, the goal is to return to TDM as soon as possible, whether we are victim or perpetrator. We offer a brief example of the distressing experience of a nightmare to elucidate this point.

When an individual is asleep and having a post-trauma nightmare, there is brain activity in the amygdala that is similar to the activity that occurred during the trauma itself. An effective intervention, called image rehearsal therapy (IRT), directs individuals to write down the disturbing content and then to creatively rewrite the nightmare with a positive ending. IRT has shown good results (Krakow, 2001). TDM is evident here in engaging the creativity and perspective of the neocortex, which moves the activity away from the amygdala. Most of us can attest to the return of TDM upon awakening from a nightmare and the relief that comes from the neocortex coming back online and being able to verbalize:

"That was a bad dream." (acknowledgment, acceptance)
"It is over." (time stamp)
"I am safe." (recovery)

When TDM returns, our sympathetic nervous system activity decreases and our parasympathetic activity increases. Nervous system balance is restored. Recovering from workaches follows a similar, albeit longer path. Just as nightmares are part of being human, so are interpersonal conflicts and aggression. We define recovering after workaches as a multidimensional and ongoing process that integrates the adverse event into one's personal narrative. Building a narrative assists in placing a historical time stamp on the bad event that asserts it occurred in the past and that safety, dignity, and calm are restored. Counselors sometimes call this "narrative reconstruction" when a client is assisted in retelling and reintegrating their narrative of an experience in a more adaptive manner than when it was first encoded in fear and threat (Peri, 2014). With the initial recovery of TDM, energy can more adaptively go into problem solving if the threat is ongoing. What an individual is recovering is the feeling (biochemistry) of safety and integrated sense of self; this restoration of self-efficacy is the sense an individual has of their own ability to problem-solve or control their environment (Bandura, 1997). The individual is recovering a revised version of safety that includes the history of their issues and traumas. We do not go back toward previous versions of the self. Rather, in this process of reenvisioning, a new self arrives that knows and understands there is only moving forward. Nonetheless, this renewed self understands that triggers will return the past and require reprocessing and reintegration. New information is added to one's life story. Recovering comes from intentional and effortful actions, decisions, and practices, as well as other natural and spontaneous processes. Each developmental milestone or life event presents a new opportunity for reprocessing, reintegrating, and recovering.

Healing comes from varied and sometimes unexpected places and relationships. Different times, places, people, and developmental periods offer different recovery possibilities. A compassionate leader can unexpectedly be just what it takes to trust another again. One of the most important elements for optimal brain growth and healing—interpersonal relatedness—is free of financial cost. Attachment, acknowledgment, attunement, and affection are all free.

Often, no fancy technology or intervention is needed, just human-to-human kindness and relatedness.

Recovering becomes the ongoing and fluid process of integrating all life events to move toward enrichment, empowerment, and a sense of safety. For once safety is restored, and survival ensured, we can move toward thriving in this existence. We consider thriving to be achieving a creative, meaningful, authentic, and enjoyable existence. Integrating workaches and other adverse life events includes being able to place that time stamp (the gift from the neocortex) so that adversity takes its rightful place in its historical context. And if and when the experience or memory gets retriggered, we can label the trigger for what it is in the current moment. Once we believe survival is ensured, we can put our energy toward thriving.

Counseling and Other Interventions

The underlying and fundamental goal of the different interventions in counseling is the building of new neural pathways (Cozolino, 2017). Earlier, we addressed the concept of neuroplasticity and the capacity of humans to learn and make changes throughout their lifespan. Neuroplasticity underlies the process, goals, and changes that an individual makes in counseling. New pathways built in a therapeutic relationship can serve to facilitate and restore well-being.

Physicists teach us that for every action there is a reaction in the physical world. Social scientists are aware that this also holds true in the psychological realm. All emotional experiences have impact and influence. Adverse psychosocial actions often lead to adverse psychological reactions. Counselors attempt to help with adverse experiences by creating new learning and restoring a sense of interpersonal safety. Given the social nature of our brains, we can never underestimate the therapeutic and healing elements of the counseling relationship alone.

Reducing fear and restoring faith in at least one other human being may be the most therapeutic act of them all.

In Figure 7.2, we offer a model of the brain region targets of some different interventional strategies. As with any model attempting to simplify some of the most complex and not yet fully understood material, it is only to serve as a guide to further reflecting on our different brain regions and our different strategies for engaging them most adaptively in our quest for recovering from adversity. We learned about the distinct structural and functional regions of the brain that we have from our evolutionary past. As psychologists, we are aware that we must attempt contact with different parts of the brain because verbal and reasoning centers often shut down with recall and discussion of remarkable stressors and traumas (Van der Kolk, 2006). We can attempt to divide interventional strategies per brain region most targeted and impacted from different therapeutic interventions.

"TOP-DOWN" & "BOTTOM-UP" INTERVENTIONS PER BRAIN REGION

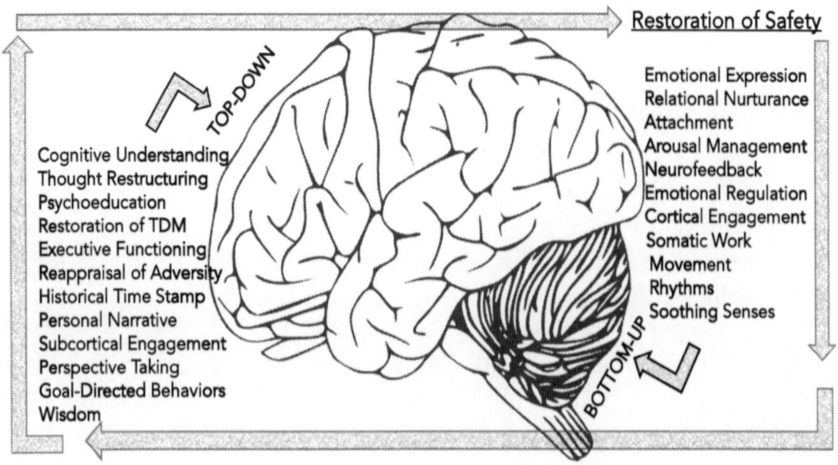

Figure 7.2

Restoration of the feeling of safety is key to beginning the process of recovering, whatever route is taken to get there. Returning to that internal body sensation of safety becomes essential to continuing the process of healing whenever fear or bad visceral feelings get triggered again. Trauma expert Peter Levine makes an important distinction between "reliving" versus "revisiting" trauma. He highlights the use of somatic or body-assisted strategies for revisiting the harm and pain within the context of a safe environment and relationship (Levine, 2008). Dr. Levine developed a treatment for chronic stress and post-traumatic stress called Somatic Experiencing (SE). SE is referred to as a "bottom-up" intervention (as opposed to a "top-down" cognitive intervention); its focus is on getting a client to adaptively restore internal bodily sensations. SE targets core subcortical brain regions to restore balance and self-regulation that positively influence higher regions (rather than the other way around). Counselors assist clients with noticing positive internal sensations. A goal is to restore parasympathetic-sympathetic balance. Cognitive reevaluations and reconstructions are viewed as secondary to, or spontaneous outcomes of, this body-focused intervention (Payne, 2015). Whatever the point of entry into the body or brain, the goal of intervention is to restore a sense of safety internally, and ultimately to exist in the world again with that sense of safety and openness to experience. We want the social engagement system on, rather than the threat or fight-or-flight system (unless there is a true threat).

Living in (returning to) the social engagement state of the nervous system is key to thriving. Living in the threat system state keeps the body in a chronic state of perilous surviving.

Despite the graphic above, we know that it is impossible to determine which brain region is consistently dominant in each treatment strategy because of the interconnectedness of brain regions and other mechanisms. Just the making of an appointment with a body-intervention counselor engages a higher cortical region—it is a cognitive process to acknowledge that you are safe enough with another human to seek assistance. Even in cognitive therapy, one is going to have somatic reactions and have varied feelings triggered despite the intervention targeting higher cortical regions. Different techniques emerge from different theories. Different people benefit from different interventions at different times in their lives. And different symptoms avail themselves to treatment with different techniques. A wide range of interventional strategies exists to help people, ranging from psychotropic medications to various types of talk therapy to body-focused and meditative practices. We have increasingly seen newer forms of treatment options, including different somatic therapies, eye movement desensitization and reprocessing (EMDR), self-regulation, neurofeedback, and sensory integration interventions. Various trauma experts believe that before a stressed individual can utilize higher brain regions or thinking to address their trauma, they must be somatically and emotionally regulated first (van der Kolk, 2014). *Workaches* focuses on cognitive-based strategies that follow from TDM. However, we emphasize again that there is not one path to recovering and healing. Each person is unique and deserves a personalized and integrated treatment plan. Whatever path one takes, the ideal goal is to achieve or restore a sense of safety (secured survival) in order to allow for thriving.

Why Therapists Nag You About How You Feel

The goal of counseling interventions, from a brain-based perspective, is to facilitate the building of new neural pathways. The strategies include navigating one's history, beliefs, mindsets, emotions, actions, and choices in order to assist recovery. The aim is to move from a state of feeling out of control and helpless about a workache, to feeling empowered enough to problem-solve and advocate for oneself in the workplace. First, however, we acknowledge and facilitate the expression of all the feelings. One of the stereotypes of counseling is the therapist's query of "how do you feel?" A rational basis exists for this! If we are not in touch with our own emotional states, it is difficult to gain clarity about our needs, actions, as well as optimal remedies. Sadness can be used to illustrate this point. Crying often serves as a discharge of sadness. Research has suggested that crying can lead to the restoring of balance between the sympathetic and parasympathetic divisions of the nervous system (Graeanin, 2014). It has also been shown to increase social bonding by signaling distress (Vingerhoets, 2016). These studies imply that the suppression of sadness and resultant crying can result in adverse impacts. This is especially relevant for many males who have been socialized to suppress such emotions and affect, particularly in arenas such as the workplace.

The experience of anger (along with its adaptive expression) is another example of what is often facilitated in treatment. Anger can be viewed as the psychological equivalent of physical pain. If we did not feel pain, we would not know to remove our hand from a hot stove. The experiencing of anger provides an individual with the information that something is not okay in a relationship with another or in their environment. This allows for possible corrective and self-protective action. Some individuals have learned to suppress anger because it was not permitted in their household or it was confused with violence due to the early witnessing of domestic abuse. Often in these cases anger is perceived as bad and a threat rather than as valuable interpersonal information. Emotions on their own are not good or bad. They just emerge. Typically, it is the reactive actions we may take in response to our feelings that may be subject to our own and others' judgment. Differentiating between an emotion and a behavior is important. For example, anger is not violence, though violence can often be seen as emerging from anger. But they are quite separate experiences. For those where anger and violence were modeled as one and the same, it might be difficult to accept that anger is an adaptive emotion and a valuable part of a psychosocial self-defense tool bag in the workplace. Verbal and nonverbal reactions that emerge from some of our feelings are sometimes not aligned with our thoughts, values, ethics, or social rules. When there is no actual threat, it is typically most adaptive not to react based on feelings, but to act upon them after they have been processed and integrated by the full brain. Emotions provide valuable social and interpersonal information in the workplace.

We enlist the aid of the neocortex to assist us in looking at feelings and experiences from different perspectives. We additionally use our knowledge of human behavior and anthropology to understand some of what goes on in the workgroup to help us navigate. Understanding our own behavior and that of others promotes perspective—the ability to look at the same thing from different angles, or through different lenses. Sometimes, however, there are maladaptive thoughts that interfere with our more reasonable and rational selves. Feelings are our friends unless they fuel maladaptive thinking and behaving.

In cognitive therapy, there is a technique called cognitive restructuring or reframing that can be useful for examining and updating self-defeating and non-productive thoughts. For example, when I feel sad that my coworker did not include me in the conversation, I might think "nobody likes me here." An alternative or reframed thought might be, "last week that same coworker brought me coffee, I may have looked away when the others were talking because sometimes I assume people don't want to talk to me." This type of thought might lend itself to facilitating a more adaptive behavior. Reframing the thought to one in which one takes responsibility and constructive action toward participating in workplace conversations might lead to "next time I am going to try to spontaneously add something to the conversation to include myself."

We have learned that not all communications exist in our conscious awareness. Often in the workplace, dialogues are taking place out of our awareness and triggering uncomfortable feelings. Part of the emotional life of the workplace is the nonconsciously acting out of different primitive survival impulses and maneuvers. Some individuals are more vulnerable and sensitive to certain triggers than others. Some individuals have a greater need than others to use the work setting as ground for acting out their own traumas and needs. We described status competitions as a workache that can trigger the threat response. For example, let us deconstruct a competitive colleague boasting (not just sharing) about their new car. On a superficial level, not a big deal. If we excavate to a deeper level, however, this relatively unimportant social exchange could trigger a survival competition (nonconscious), especially if the receiver has a history of being humiliated or has even had a recent similar social exchange. This is illustrated in Figure 7.3.

NONCONSICOUS UNDERLYING DYNAMICS OF SIMPLE SOCIAL EXCHANGE

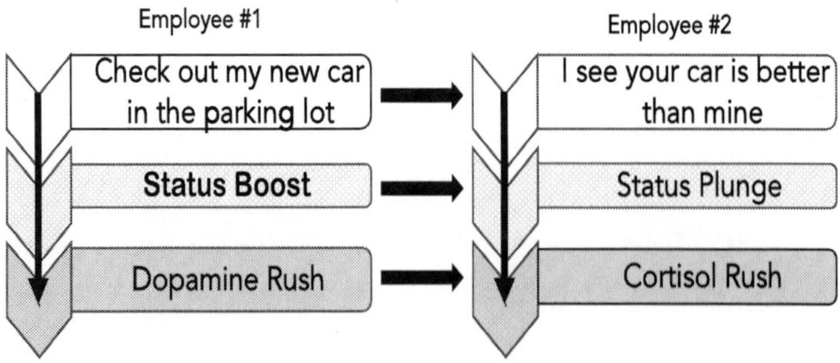

Figure 7.3

These types of events and challenges occur daily, most of them on nonconscious levels, and have a cumulative impact. A maladaptive thought that could emerge from this interaction is, "I am inferior to my coworker." This reactive thought is irrational and deserves cognitive restructuring. Unless you genuinely believe that a newer or more expensive car makes someone better than you, it is important to recall the anthropology and social neuroscience about survival and status—this knowledge facilitates perspective taking and cognitive reconstruction of this interaction. Also, here we remind ourselves of our goals or desired "GPS" destinations—peace of mind and thriving are quite different goals than winning an unhealthy competition. If you truly choose to compete for a higher status car, go for it. If you do not genuinely want that, effort must go into supporting thoughts that are more aligned with and move you toward your chosen goal. If you are ultimately released from an underlying competitive reaction by consciously working the issues through, you may be able to genuinely admire the car and be happy for your coworker. However, if it all remains underground, it becomes a nonconscious and unnecessary competition for survival. It becomes easier to celebrate the successes and objects of others when they are not perceived as a competitive loss for oneself. Unexamined reacting can lead to going out and purchasing an expensive car that one really does not need. Cognitive restructuring can possibly save us money! We do know that it can save us the biochemical costs of ruminating on our inferiority amongst our workgroup. Retrieving ourselves from these more primitive and reactive feelings and thoughts is often merciful—yet another arena where knowledge of anthropology and the brain comes in handy.

Crucial Thinking: All Brain Resources Online

The ability to access rational and reasonable thoughts when we are triggered or healing from adverse experiences is essential. Crucial thinking refers to a form of adaptive thinking that is multidimensional and depends on four key contextual factors: 1) establishment of safety and removal of threats; 2) access to and integration of thoughts, feelings, and actions; 3) wisdom about self and others; and 4) adaptive, goal-directed actions. Crucial thinking is characterized by the following:

CRUCIAL Thinking	Prefrontal Cortex as Designated Driver for TDM
Calm	body and mind in relaxed state
Rational	logical, coherent, time-aware thinking
Unified	all regions coordinating and communicating
Creative	open-ended, fluid, multidimensional perspectives
Integrated	thinking / emotions / behaviors coordinated
Aligned	actions aligned with ethics, values, and goals
Leading	chosen wise manager for "mind organization"

TDM is one of the best navigating systems on the human market that we have seen to facilitate crucial thinking. And it is free of cost. To discover and recover that sweet spot in our brains and experience that harmonious integration of all that makes us who we are, we must know ourselves in as many ways as possible. What threats am I most sensitive to? What throws me off balance in my workplace? What adverse earlier experiences get triggered in my workgroup? Can I translate my self-talk to a more adaptive internal language? What can I do at the moment to return to a more comfortable state? Once TDM is restored and we have access to our full cognitive capacity, we can begin the process of adaptive problem solving to best take care of ourselves and achieve our goals. TDM is a prerequisite for crucial thinking.

The designated driver in the workplace ought to be the neocortex, unless otherwise specified!

If you recall or imagine an admired, trusted, and wise leader, you might recognize these same attributes in their guidance, which probably made you feel safe and comfortable. If we view the brain as an organization of different parts, we can assign the neocortex as the wise and compassionate leader for all.

REFLECTION

Imagine a trusted and wise leader (if you have never worked with one, fantasize about an ideal leader). What did you admire about them? How did it feel to be in their presence? What are three adjectives to describe them? Do you possess any qualities of this leader? Do you trust your "internal leader" to wisely guide you toward your goals?

If you have access to all seven crucial dimensions above, you can be pretty assured that TDM has been restored and you can carry on to problem-solve, communicate, and act most adaptively with others. Creative thinking is flexible and fluid. The property of fluidity in physics describe substances that can flow. If we imagine water flowing down a stream, we can imagine it flowing around rocks and other obstacles in its path. If we throw a stone into it, it is impacted momentarily but reconstitutes and flows on. This metaphor reflects a useful attribute or ability in life. Like water, however, in some states, we are going to be rigid (solid ice) (fight, flight, freeze). When reasoning is fluid, it is multidimensional and can traverse the full spectrum of options and opinions—it is unrestricted. Moving away from binary thinking toward multidimensional thinking (unless there is a threat in doing so) is to our advantage at work.

Having multidimensional perspective on time is also crucial. For example, progress must not only be conceived of as linear and going in one "forward" direction. Time can be perceived as a sphere in all directions rather than as a straight line. We want to allow ourselves the freedom to go in any direction that is most adaptive. Progress can be made sometimes by seemingly "going backwards." In *Workaches*, for instance, we go back and seek wisdom from our primitive or past days. We go back to the speed of nature over the speed of modern technology when we want to relax. Progress does not have to mean going faster, it can mean going slower. Progress need not always be linear.

Crucial thinking differentiates between independent versus collective decision making. As we have learned, others have a significant influence on us that often disrupts our independent thinking. Even if you are making a decision with and for the group, it is sometimes useful to first identify your own thoughts and decisions, before collaborating with the group. Crucial thinking helps people take responsibility when addressing workaches—a necessary step that reduces feelings of helplessness. Even recognizing we did not take the best care of ourselves or set the necessary boundaries with somebody is part of taking responsibility. For example, if I am typically the target of the joke in the office, am I possibly devaluing myself and therefore communicating to others that this is acceptable? Even if one determines that they bear zero percent fault, it is a useful exercise to take this perspective and to engage in this examination. Blame—whether of the self or another—rarely facilitates growth and problem-solving. Even if we have been victimized and are not to blame or cannot be considered at fault, we still have to take responsibility for our own healing. Moving forward and problem-solving is my responsibility. Remaining a long time in a blaming phase can perpetuate feelings of helplessness and does not encourage growth. We want to allow ourselves space for our emotional reactions, but a crucial part of recovering is gently moving ourselves toward integrating these emotions with adaptive thoughts and behaviors. Even if our actions yield disappointing results, just the act of trying and taking any action is valuable to our brains. Crucial thinking leads us to behaviors that can help return our sense of control and self-efficacy.

Adaptive and wise self-talk is a key component of restoring and maintaining TDM. Even though we have been given quite different brain parts, we have been given language to help us connect those brain parts. Just as we use language to resolve problems with others, we can use internal language (self-talk) to address issues of the self. We all have been talking to ourselves from very early on in our lives. This inner talk is constant, and we believe it. So, what we tell ourselves at work and what we tell ourselves about adversity is significant. We can brainwash ourselves just as someone else can brainwash us to believe untruths based on emotional reactivity. But when an individual is engaged in crucial thinking, inner self-talk is deliberately different. Instead, it is mindful and adaptive, which means the self-talk is without judgment and filled with understanding and compassion. Crucial thinking engages a wise inner narrator. The choice of narrator is based on reasonable goals and how one wants to feel about their story. We can take a fictional book and change its genre based on how the story is told by the narrator. The narrator can tell the same story to sound tragic, scary, dramatic, or funny. We can do the same with our internal dialogue. Our inner self-talk carries us through the varied experiences in our lives and can add a unique emotional spin to our different storylines. When we are depressed, the narrator may tell more of a sad story about our life. When we are feeling sorry for ourselves, the narrator might personalize what is happening. When we are in a more light-hearted mood, the narrator might make us laugh. When we are anxious, the narrator may tell more of a threatening and scary story.

Choosing a wise, calm, and compassionate internal narrator is important when recovering from stress and healing from adversity.

This voice combines those of the empathic parent, enriching educator, and trustworthy leader into one integrated and adaptive language for the self.

Mindsets: Perspective, Perspective, Perspective

When we use words such as cognitive, rational, thinking, logical, and wise, we typically are once again speaking about brain activities that emerge from the neocortex. When something bad initially happens, the threat system in the brain amplifies it. As we discussed in Chapter 3, this is due to this survival system wanting to focus on whatever it perceives or misperceives as dangerous to us. Things are up close and personal. Upon threat, we need reaction, not wisdom and perspective! Wisdom never fought off a saber-toothed tiger that we know of. However, in our lives today, we can pretty much count on perspective and thought as being our allies. Time in and of itself does not heal. It does allow for the brain to move back into TDM, affording us access to our "full-brained" selves. Once again, when we use the term "off-line," we do not mean this literally. What it implies is the significant energy and activity shift to a different brain region. We can view experiences from varied perspectives once our neocortex is fully back online.

When we think about being awake and possessing full cognitive perspective from a neuroscience lens, we consider all brain regions as active and communicating. We illustrate this notion here with an analogy to a physical injury—a finger cut. I must "step back" enough to gain perspective that I have cut my finger. I cannot be under anesthesia (numbed), in denial, or avoid the fact that I have gotten hurt. My awareness leads to an assessment of the degree of my injury that informs my actions. This is the physical equivalent to the psychosocial injuries of workaches. One cannot be dissociated, in denial or avoidance, to best take care of the injury. As we described previously, our psychological defenses sometimes anesthetize us to sensing the harm being inflicted by others. This may sometimes seem like salvation from emotional pain, yet it does not place us in the most awake position to attend to our needs and to proactively prevent or minimize further workaches. Figure 7.4 describes the four "A's" of being consciously awake:

FOUR "A's" OF BEING "AWAKE"

ACKNOWLEDGMENT:	I acknowledge injury happened whether I felt the pain of it or not
AWARENESS:	I am aware of the extent and consequences of my injury
ACTION:	I take action to take care of myself and to heal
ANTICIPATION:	I anticipate that I remain vulnerable to triggers and I take necessary actions to prevent and minimize future harm

Figure 7.4

If you reflect about an individual in your life whom you consider wise, you likely admire their perspective on life and work. Neuroscientists have studied wisdom (Meeks et al., 2009) and concluded, "wisdom may involve an optimal balance between functions of phylogenetically (evolutionary stages) more primitive brain regions (limbic system) and newer ones (prefrontal cortex)." This returns us to the value of TDM when we are seeking to be wise leaders and wise followers. If we could image the brain of that wise person you admire, we would likely see increased neural connections between the different regions of the brain facilitating their ability to integrate their thoughts, feelings, and actions. Wisdom is often born of adversity. Some of our most beloved leaders have suffered traumas in their pasts. They possess wisdom about resilience and strength. They are inspirational. These wise individuals have come out on the other side with renewed strength, conviction, and trust in themselves. And like most other aspects of existence, we must work for wisdom. We must seek it. Those neural connections require energy and commitment to build and maintain. We never know where we are going to find the wise from whom to learn or what circumstances are going to increase the natural development of our own wisdom. Seeking it is valuable. Learning comes from all kinds of places, people, and experiences.

Awareness and acceptance are elements of wisdom. The wise leader accepts that there is no way to eliminate workaches. There are, however, ways to acknowledge, understand, minimize, and perhaps even prevent some, using the techniques in the psychosocial self-defense toolbox, described below.

SUMMARY OF BRAIN-WISE STRATEGIES FROM THE PSYCHOSOCIAL SELF-DEFENSE TOOLBOX

⇒ Restore TDM (or at least be aware that you have lost it ASAP) before taking action

⇒ Move from help<u>less</u> to help<u>ful</u> state (even if with one small step)

⇒ Identify stressors (what seems particularly threatening?)

⇒ Recognize personal triggers and responses (what are you experiencing?)

⇒ Identify historical vulnerability to these stressors (have similar events happened before?)

⇒ Distinguish historical defense mechanisms from adaptive coping strategies

⇒ Take adaptive action to promote or restore a sense of personal efficacy and safety (e.g., documenting in a personal journal, even if work stressor cannot be eliminated)

⇒ Utilize stress-reducing strategies for each stressor (some people walk, others meditate)

⇒ Verbalize, talk, or write about the stress (words are actions to the brain)

⇒ Assess internal strengths and activities that have worked in the past

⇒ Identify external support systems such as programs, groups, apps, and individuals

⇒ Establish adaptive perspectives and wise, empowering, and compassionate self-talk
⇒ Engage the parasympathetic nervous system (breathing, soothing senses)
⇒ Invest in thriving activities, divest from survival focus once safety ensured
⇒ Learn and engage resiliency skills (addressed in Chapter 8)

Self-Intelligence: Assembling the Puzzle of the Self

> "My friend... care for your psyche... know thyself, for once we know ourselves we may learn how to care for ourselves."
>
> —Socrates

Part of healing from adversity is fortifying the self with knowledge and compassion. We all have a universal human history and a very personalized individual and family history that have sculpted our unique brains. Workaches interact with both our basic human and more personal histories. Any comprehensive manner of understanding the self is complex and ongoing. Each day, more research data emerge that allow us to understand ourselves better. We are pre-loaded with ancient genetic codes that leave us with some of the same primitive parts from millions of years ago. Knowledge about this and how it affects us is crucial. We also learned that we are forever impacted by what we experience from the neural pathways that form. Self-awareness is a prerequisite for other-awareness. Self-intelligence is frequently considered to be a vital part of emotional intelligence.

Self-knowledge is ongoing because we change each moment of our lives—we change with each person we meet and each experience we have. Curiosity can motivate us to seek understanding of ourselves and others. When we meet someone new, we can learn about them and ourselves by asking ourselves: What do they trigger in us? What does that mean about us? What does that mean about them? Do they remind us of someone from our past? Is their perception of us distorted due to someone in their past? Our limbic functions tend to personalize experiences and make them about us. Crucial awareness of self and other allows for a different lens and for curiosity.

Self-knowledge can be facilitated by understanding the history of your family and of the world as you have developed. Have there been wars? Have resources ever become scarce? What were the impacts? Consider the history of your parents or caregivers. What were their challenges? What significant events occurred in their lives? Did they live through economic hardships that threatened their livelihoods? What was their style of parenting? Did they perceive the world and others as safe or unsafe? Did you have siblings with whom you competed? Ask questions of your contemporary self too: What is my typical social style and how do I interact with others? What is my typical emotional style and how do I interact with others? What are some of the obstacles for me in taking action? Where do I derive my motivation from? What is my guiding life philosophy or beliefs? Who in my life drains my energy? Who in my life boosts my energy? Where are my emotional blind spots? What makes me lose TDM? Can I identify my emotional triggers? What are my limitations and strengths in the workplace? Am I able to hold myself in ambivalence, in other words, evaluate myself accurately? Am I socially generous or withholding? How does this impact my social relations? How do others perceive me generally? What are my morals, ethics, and values? What are my temptations? Where is my point of no return or edge when it comes to my impulses? What workaches have I perpetrated on others? Which have been perpetrated against me?

In addition to knowing one's own triggers, it is also crucial to be aware of one's thresholds: how close one can get to each trigger before losing TDM. Often, when someone is in a 12-step program such as Alcoholics Anonymous (AA), we map out how close they can or cannot get to alcohol before arriving at that slippery slope of loss of TDM. This awareness is important to maintaining sobriety. Questions facilitating awareness often include: "Can I go into a bar without drinking? Have alcohol in the house? Smell a drink? Be around others who are drinking and not lose TDM?" Different people have different thresholds.

Asking oneself different questions and exploring and reflecting on aspects of the self can lead to forming a general life picture or story. A coherent and evolving self-narrative becomes a crucial touchstone of personal identity and self-intelligence. Everything that happens in the external environment is filtered by, and integrated into, this larger core of self-identity. We aim to have this identity be "larger" than the workaches in our path. A well-rooted tree is stronger than a wind that rattles it. If it is not, it falls. The creating of a personal narrative is an ongoing process of assembling the "puzzle pieces" of new experiences in our lives, as well as those pieces that may emerge from our pasts that have moved from nonconscious awareness into our conscious awareness. Sometimes when a piece from our nonconscious moves into awareness, as it "thaws," it can bring back all the feelings that were around it when it happened to us. When this happens—reliving, rather than revisiting—it is important to perform that part of the recovering process of placing a current time stamp. This reminds us of its historical context and returns us to our present-day reality.

A prerequisite to self-care is becoming self-aware. Self-awareness is key to psychosocial self-defense and well-being. Sometimes when we have suffered adverse life events in our past, we move in the opposite direction of self-awareness. We avoid ourselves and stay distracted from and shut down to ourselves. We become afraid of our own stories and our truth.

> One of the most distressing anxieties that we have seen in our practice is the fear of one's own true self. If someone enters treatment based on a fear of public speaking or spiders, these types of fears are much more readily dealt with than when someone enters with anxiety about their own being, thoughts, behaviors, feelings, fantasies, and experiences.

When one has been relationally injured, one often dissociates from some of these aspects of the self and does not feel much of anything. But we must allow ourselves to feel at least a bit of anxiety to acknowledge our harm. The better we know ourselves, the more we might understand our past issues, reactions, motivations, and behaviors. Recall the way Linda was able to discover the true source of her anxiety, integrate the past name-calling into her personal narrative, and deal more easily with her workaches. We often navigate through rough psychosocial terrain in the workplace. All that is reasonable to ask of ourselves is to do our best to manage ourselves and move toward our goals. Self-knowledge can assist with the gaining of perspective on workaches.

Stepping Back to Move Forward

When we are safe, in TDM, and able to employ crucial thinking, we can assemble a fuller picture of a workache we may have endured. This is part of healing. The more we can step back from and divest from a workache, the better perspective we can have about it. Higher regions of the brain can come into play to integrate the adversity. An adverse event is typically amplified and is "front and center" to the first regions of the brain that perceive it. Once we are safe, it is usually adaptive to move toward a less personalized point of view—in order to gain distance and rational perspective. We want to promote recovering by time-stamping the offending event as ended (if indeed it has) and do our best to minimize increased future scanning for potential threats in the environment. We are not suggesting that individuals minimize or dismiss their adverse experiences. Certainly, they are very personal and must be addressed, remedied, and then become part of one's personal narrative. It is unfair, however, if workaches or the potential for workaches continue to block someone's potential for thriving in their work environment.

An aspect of crucial thinking is using reason and information to understand and help us navigate the workplace. This is where knowledge and understanding of seemingly unconnected topics of anthropology, neuroscience, and social psychology come in handy at work for our psychosocial self-defense toolboxes. Because of all the potential workaches, an important goal is to conserve energy and preserve our sympathetic nervous system for when it is truly needed. A major aspect of reducing stress in the workplace is reducing the unease, discomfort, and biochemical costs associated with continually scanning for threats. Once someone has been subjected to a workache, the lower brain regions are going to promote focusing even more on potential threats. Perspective can be built from knowledge and information.

Earlier in *Workaches* we discussed vestigial physical organs, such as the tailbone, that remind us that our primitive ancestors used to have tails. They needed tails. We do not. We then introduced the notion of vestigial psychosocial traits. Psychosocial vestigial traits were relevant and needed by our ancestors. We do not need them as much. But we still retain them in the primitive parts of our brains where certain of our interpersonal reactions and behaviors emerge from. Our ancestors needed to pay close attention to nonverbal characteristics and later spoken gossip, disguise their vulnerabilities, be biased against strangers, and hide their differences. Some were truly at risk for being cast out of the clan and physically perishing if they were not sensitive to the rumblings and shaming looks of the group. The clan could not risk the invasion of someone different, possibly from a competing clan, just as they could not risk a vulnerable or aged member not contributing and becoming a burden to the group. Resources were limited. They needed to eliminate those who threatened the survival of the clan. Their lives depended upon it. Ours do not.

Nonetheless, we sometimes personalize the smallest of interpersonal interactions—a seemingly judgmental glance, a broken lunch date, or coworkers whispering. Today our lives can go on perfectly fine if others gossip about our differences, traits, or vulnerabilities—yet it still seems to bother us.

Our psychosocial vestigial traits promote the unnecessary release of stress hormones and "feel bad" neurochemicals when we perceive (or misperceive) that our social standing is threatened in the group. The more primitive parts of our brain want us to heed the social information and make us somatically experience distress in order to sound the threat alarm. Misperception and misinterpretation occur in this archaic brain region that survival is at risk. We deeply personalize and feel these experiences as they reverberate throughout our bodies. These are our "kick in the stomach" or "strike to the heart" kind of experiences. They no longer serve us as they did our ancestors. We really will be okay if someone happens not to favor us or if we do not get that social invitation.

The less we personalize, the better (unless as always, it is truly a threat to our livelihood). The quicker we can call "false alarm," the sooner we can return to preserving precious biochemical resources. The more we conserve unnecessary biochemical output, the more energy we have to put toward thriving in our lives.

A valuable aspect of crucial thinking is being flexible and open to exploring alternative strategies for assistance with issues. Role models and mentors often can offer new ways of dealing with these types of work issues. We have travelled internationally to observe different work cultures and speak directly to the people who are performing different types of work. There are striking divides between work customs and practices, from how people are treated, how they perceive work, and how satisfied they are in their work. In many cultures, the notion of thriving at work is non-existent; the goal is just to survive. In other cultures, thriving is key. Workers in Denmark are reported to be among the "happiest" in the world, reporting their jobs as interesting, meaningful, and satisfying (Ennova,

2018). Danish citizens, in general, have also been identified as some of the happiest people in the world (World Happiness Report, 2019). We study their work model to try and understand how they thrive. A number of interesting words have emerged from their culture. Words sometimes can have therapeutic value. Certainly, there are many complex factors that go into the Danish work culture, but we highlight one three-letter word here. The word is "pyt" (pronounced "pid") which describes the Danish cultural attitude about creating the healthiest thoughts to manage stress (Helweg-Larsen, 2019). Dr. Helweg-Larson reports that this untranslatable word comes closest to our notions of "stuff happens," "don't worry about it," and "oh, well." Danish workers use this word when they are faced with stressful or frustrating experiences that are out of their control. They utter "pyt" in order to move on without having their mood be negatively affected by various daily hassles.

Later in this chapter (Figure 7.6) we share a gauge assigning values of distress to different workplace events. What if we could collectively decide that with any event lower than "50," we were going to try to dismiss, let go of, depersonalize, breathe away, and utter "pyt?" We would eventually most likely scan less for their occurrences and our sympathetic nervous system would receive a well-deserved break. We share "pyt" here because we have not found a similar English word that promotes or describes a similar collective and cultural movement in the US. Whatever strategies we use (that come without adverse consequences themselves) to lower our stress loads are steps toward moving beyond surviving to thriving at work.

Post-Traumatic Growth: The Better News

Some of the most inspiring of individuals are those with significant adversity in their life story. They have gone beyond recovering to being more enriched human beings than before their bad experiences. This is not because they have erased their experiences—rather, they have integrated them and are motivated to tell their stories and to help others. Support groups are valuable in this way because they often have members in varying places on their paths of recovering. Group members who have moved to the place of championing relevant causes and narrating their resilience and strength serve as positive role models. They provide a possibility. We have lost some wonderful individuals in this world who have taken their own lives, in part, because they did not envision that they could ever move through the pain. They could not yet see that a place of resilience and growth in their futures was possible. Intense emotions and sensations that emerge with trauma disallow perspective, and often people feel as if the overwhelming pain will never end. Experiences can take on different forms when safety is restored and integration underway. A narrator can take the same story and make it into anything from a horror story to an inspiring tale of triumph.

The concept of post-traumatic growth (PTG) was developed by psychologists in the 1990s who were working with individuals who had suffered traumatic life events. They observed that some individuals eventually learned to cope with the negative aspects of their adversities and even went on to gain positive benefit from them. Some of these people discovered inner strengths and other aspects of themselves that they had never known prior (Tedeschi & Calhoun, 2004). Though the term "post-traumatic growth" is relatively new, this concept is as old as human suffering itself. An ancient Chinese proverb captures the modern neuroscientific concept of neuroplasticity and the brain's capacity to adapt: "A wise man adapts himself to circumstances as water shapes itself to the vessel that contains it." The concepts of fluidity and adaptability emerge again as important life possessions. Recovering is a winding path onward. We never go back to how we were before adverse events. No "reverse" gear exists in this lifetime. We only have a "forward," unless we freeze and stop altogether. Each moment brings a new normal.

Like most other aspects of human existence, there is a spectrum of responses to adverse events. And these responses are so fluid that someone can be diagnosed with PTSD and later identified with PTG. Someone can have aspects and traits of both at the same time. Someone may initially be shut down and numb and later become emotionally reactive and act out. We place PTSD and PTG at opposite ends of the response spectrum for the sake of simplicity. We have emphasized the negative post-trauma symptoms in previous chapters. The brain is also wired for resilience and to carry on after adversity. This has been documented for both primary and secondary trauma. Occupational trauma can be a catalyst to making positive changes in both the workplace and personal arena. Resilience is an active process that someone must participate in; it is not a passive process that just happens to someone. We must take active steps to search for that "silver lining," and these steps are not expected to occur before some amount of grieving has occurred. The goal of immediately "shaking off" adverse life events is unrealistic. However, the adversity can launch someone on a path of personal development that might not have occurred if the event(s) had not taken place in their lives.

The first step in an action plan toward PTG is becoming aware that it is possible. Countless others have experienced adversity and grown from it. Those who have suffered remarkable adversity have also triumphed and gone on to be great leaders and models of PTG. Meaning and purpose in life have followed for these individuals from their tragedies suffered and adversities endured. Humans love stories about personal triumph, and there are many of them. Some of the elements associated with PTG are increases in life appreciation, sense of meaning, personal trust in self and resilience, coping strategies, and social connectedness. What is also great news is that about half to two-thirds of people who experience adversities go on to achieve PTG (Tedeschi & Calhoun, 2004). These are encouraging and hopeful odds. We know that genetics, epigenetics, and previous history influence whether an individual will develop PTSD and PTG. We also know there are actions that can facilitate PTG, as described below:

- Awareness of the possibility
- Intention to move toward
- Seeking role models with PTG
- Acceptance of the non-linear process
- TDM facilitating time stamp and historical context of trauma
- Gratitude practices for self and others
- Philosophical/spiritual/religious/scientific reconciliations of life meaning
- Political and social activism
- Self-compassion and nurturance
- Personal narration of strength, resilience, and triumph
- De-identification with trauma identity and re-identification with full self
- Commitment and effort to grow despite and because of adversity

PTG affirms we can integrate the issues and offer ourselves soothing narratives for our minds and calming practices for our bodies. Those who have been hurt often go on to help. There is an altruistic component to this, and sometimes there is a self-healing component as well. Assisting in the lives of others can help move us from a state of helplessness to helpfulness. Helping ourselves first is essential though.

One of the best PTG examples to witness is that of a harassed and micromanaged employee who goes on to move up the hierarchy to become a compassionate and wise leader. Earlier, we described how the brain could learn from observing another do something. We can also learn how not to be. For some leaders, earlier traumatic experience positively informs their leadership style and contributes to their success. This type of individual has learned and evolved because of their earlier experiences. They have not repeated the experience and acted it out on others. They have learned and evolved and used the trauma to contribute positively to others in the workplace. Figure 7.5 depicts examples of PTG in the personal realm.

ADVERSITY HISTORY AND PTG POTENTIAL GROWTH

TRAUMA. WORKACHE. STRESSOR.	EVENTUAL GROWTH
Early Attachment Insecurity	▪ Intentionally bonded parent who ends intergenerational transmission of pathology ▪ Secure attachments in relationships to others
Workforce Annihilation	▪ Beloved mentor of new hires
Loss of Loved One to Road Hazard	▪ Runs for City Council seat to forge responsible city maintenance
Refugee History / Status	▪ Sociopolitical change agent
Workplace Harassment	▪ Advocate for fair and protected work environments
Near Death Experience	▪ Greater appreciation and engagement in life ▪ Second career as life coach or counselor

Figure 7.5

In Chapter 5, we discussed the workache of secondary or vicarious trauma. We learned that trauma could be infectious. Here, we learn that resilience too can be infectious. The concept of vicarious resilience reveals the power of witnessing the triumph of an individual who has dealt with adversity (Hernandez et al., 2007). When HHS professionals witness traumatized individuals manage their trauma and emerge enriched with strength and wisdom, they can grow too. Resilience can be shared and spread. Many of our clients and customers become our teachers when they offer us lessons in resilience. We have borne witness to the powerful and inspiring spirit of human resilience.

Scientists across the globe are searching to identify self-regulatory mechanisms that can help people better manage maladaptive impulses. Those who commit crimes or harm others are not all psychopathic individuals or inherently evil individuals. We know that certain genes predispose individuals to commit violence against others. However, we have also learned that in a fraction of a second when the neocortex goes off-line, and the lower parts of the brain react, bad stuff can happen. Blind rage trumps crucial thinking and rationally directed actions and can result in awful acts of aggression. All are vulnerable to workplace threats and triggers—as victims and as perpetrators.

We have dedicated our focus to the victims, receivers, or survivors of relational violence and workaches. Post-traumatic growth, however, is also possible for the perpetrators of workaches. Unless someone has significant levels of personality issues and traits such as narcissism, psychopathic deviance, or various other anti-social traits, most do experience some level of regret and shame after instigating and engaging in interpersonal violence. Perpetrators who have a capacity for self-reflection and cognitive dissonance have the potential to evolve too as individuals. Here we offer the case of Victor to illustrate:

Victor was a 33-year-old male who worked as an office assistant in a county agency. He had left a gift basket of erotica on the desk of a coworker (Anne) for whom he professed his love. Anne notified her supervisor, a Title IX complaint was filed, and appropriate steps were taken. Victor utilized his three in-house EAP sessions and was referred into the community for further psychological treatment. He had the possibility of transferring his position to another location if treatment was successful based on the assessment of the treating provider.

The treatment plan consisted of impulse management skills, insight development, empathy training, and retribution and responsibility taking. Victor had misinterpreted Anne's attention and kindness toward him. In the development of his personal narrative, it became clear that Victor perceived himself as unattractive and inadequate. He felt he needed to gain a competitive edge over the others in the office and make a clear sexual move toward Anne. Victor's history, feelings, impulse-control issues, and misperceptions led to his maladaptive behavior.

The most challenging part of empathy training with Victor was his difficulty understanding that he did not really know Anne. He struggled with the concept that she even might have been the object of past sexual harm and the basket could have served to retraumatize her. He eventually did acknowledge the possibility that Anne could have been harmed and came to understand her fear about what he thought was a gift. Victor independently wrote a letter of apology to Anne. She chose not to receive it, and this became part of his insight development. Victor was attempting to take responsibility for scaring Anne. He had to eventually integrate his feelings of helplessness over Anne's choosing not to accept his apology, explanation, or remorse. A primary goal of treatment was learning about the process of sexual harm and gaining insight and empathy.

Treatment for individuals who perpetrate the harm is important too. We can reduce workplace threats and triggers by helping those who are inclined to commit them. Promising research is being conducted in training people to maximize the attributes, abilities, and wisdom of the prefrontal cortex to minimize acting on impulses or to maintain TDM (Chiu et al., 2013).

Well-Being: Caring and Compassion for the Self

Self-care does not begin after work. It must start on the ride in and keep going for the ride back home, and then it must also extend into personal life. Our threat response systems are on 24/7, so why shouldn't our self-care systems be on 24/7? We know that the threat response originates from the deeper, out-of-awareness center of the brain that is always on standby. Survival and physical self-preservation are a priority here. As discussed previously, making a conscious decision to pursue thriving is our responsibility. Self-care originates from the rational centers. One must make a conscious and ongoing commitment to self-care, or it can easily fall off our psychological radar. HHS professionals frequently find their self-care going to the "back of the line" while they more naturally place others in front. When we arrive in the workforce, we are typically better trained in how to perform our jobs than in how to take care of ourselves. We are more likely to have received training in activities of daily living, such as how to do laundry (surviving skills), but not necessarily in how to rejuvenate and self-actualize (thriving skills). A common question in childhood is "what do you want to do when you grow up?" We typically do not get asked, "how do you want to take care of yourself when you grow up?" Few ask about our intended future leisure and creative pursuits. We get primed and socialized to do (survive) rather than to be (thrive). A significant difference exists between doing and being. Self-care takes motivation and effort. You are not expected just to "know" how to do it, especially if it was not modeled for you in your prior groups. Most importantly, if survival was threatened and questionable early on, it is even that much more difficult to convince the brain to relax and pursue thriving.

Self-sacrifice is not necessarily altruism. To be in service of another does not have to mean being in disservice to the self.

Humans are naturally wired to survive yet can sometimes be manipulated to surrender self-concern and self-care. Altruism is a natural and beautiful human quality when balanced with self-care. Caring for the other is most commonly on auto-pilot for HHS professionals. Caring for oneself is not. Taking care of oneself is an essential ingredient of self-preservation and enhancement and therefore of being able to serve others fully and consistently—a win-win for both the self and the group. Recent research has helped revise notions about self-care, which is now seen as a skill (Davidson, 2015). The good news about this is that skills can be learned.

A nice feature of modern cars is the feedback offered about needs. Fuel gauges indicate the miles driven, and if it is time to refuel. Temperature gauges warn that the vehicle is too hot and that we need to stop. We can even calculate the costs of a journey to decide if it is worth taking or not. Many indicators and warning signs exist to call our attention and they are difficult to ignore for too long. We do not have these as humans, at least until it is too late, and physical and emotional symptoms appear. Unfortunately, symptoms and disease processes become the wakeup call or gauge for some. Assessing needs before a system breaks down due to lack of care is vital. Those who serve others are typically adept at doing a needs assessment of clients. One of the first steps in the care of the self is determining needs. We invite you to do a needs assessment for yourself.

Needs Assessment for: _your name here_ (You)

If you step back and pause, think about how you would assess your needs. Sometimes it is helpful to complete the following sentences to help you discover what your needs are:

- If I were my own parent, I would see that I need ______ ______________________________.
- If I were my own teacher, I would see that I want to learn ______________________________.
- If I were my own social worker, I would see that I need intervention with ______________________________.
- If I were my own boss, I would notice that I need to be ______________________________.
- If I were my own friend, I would see that I need ______ ______________________________.
- If I were my own spouse, I would understand that I need ______________________________.
- If I were my own eligibility assessor, I would be eligible for ______________________________.
- If I were my own health care provider, I would see that I need assistance with ______________________________.
- If I were my own playmate, I would see that I want to ______________________________.
- If I were my own psychotherapist, I would offer myself ______________________________.

Recalibrating Your Psychosocial Gauge

An essential part of healing is restoring or establishing healthy coping strategies and safeguards. Most people possess a physical "gauge" that alerts them when another is stepping on their toes or invading physical boundaries. Another type of gauge alerts when another person is invading or assaulting psychological territory. A history of personal or professional adversity often "breaks" this gauge of self-awareness. When one is used to being physically punched, for example, a tap no longer registers. This gauge often then requires repair or recalibration. When physical wounds are repetitively poked, the body begins to employ a process called habituation or going numb to the sensation in the offended area. A very similar process occurs with psychological wounds—we often stop feeling the full sensations of the unfairness, invasion, or poke. But we need these types of gauges to inform us when someone is, for instance, taking advantage, or being abusive or offensive. Individuals who have experienced adverse events often have their experiential "gauges" overwhelmed and broken. People who have been used as objects in childhood are at increased risk of being used as objects in adulthood. A higher risk of revictimization exists (Widom et al., 2008).

In the workplace, this gauge is needed to assess and measure workaches during the workday. When someone defensively goes numb to psychosocial aggressions, they do not even register on the gauge. This is dangerous because, as outlined earlier, we need this input to most adaptively protect ourselves. If an individual, for example, does not experience the full sensations of anger, they have difficulty perceiving when someone is invading their space or threatening them. On the other end of the spectrum are those individuals with a history of adversity who have amplified sensations and feelings that create the opposite experience—workaches are experienced profoundly and are exaggerated by the brain. Here we can see over-reactions that are maladaptive. Assessment of one's own gauge is valuable, so it can be restored if needed as an adaptive tool of awareness and protection in the workplace.

In organizational training, we give participants a piece of paper with the gauge depicted in Figure 7.6 to come to an agreement and reach consensus about what number on a scale of 1-100 corresponds with a psychosocial event. We invite participants to take a top-down brain management approach to be guided about what is truly worthy (or not) of being placed higher or lower on the scale. We start out by practicing getting agreement about the current temperature in the room in which we are meeting. People typically find this a relatively easy task, though temperature perceptions do vary a few degrees. A more difficult task is when we ask participants to agree on psychosocial perceptions and impacts. We always start with labeling 100 with death because this sets an anchor of comparison when considering how bad an event is. Most people agree that loss of life should be at the highest point of distress on the gauge. We then together label and set our 0 point at complete stillness. Below is an example of an agreed-upon gauge built at a 2016 conference with the consensus of 72 participants. For brevity, we have only included 10 points on the scale. There were wide differences and many disagreements before consensus was reached with these assigned gauge numbers.

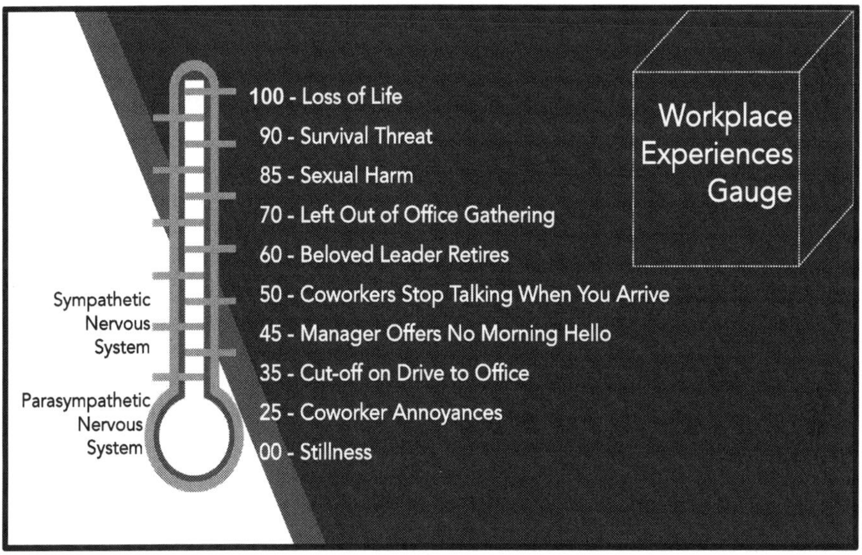

Figure 7.6

REFLECTION

Please think about how you would rate the above incidents before collaborating and re-calibrating with a group of peers. Do you think you would have a tendency to amplify ratings or to minimize?

No right or wrong scaling is implied in this exercise. This calibration may be congruent with your sense of things or not, because we all have different sensitivities and vulnerabilities. We often get about a 5- to 20-

point variability between groups. Participants do find it useful to have others to compare their responses and reactions to. It is sometimes striking to hear the initial range of numbers applied to the different events. This exercise is most useful to the outliers—those people who assign a very low or very high number to experiences. We examine how their history may have affected their ratings and whether it might be beneficial to recalibrate in their own lives. A goal is to move most experiences to as low as possible on the gauge (unless they are real threats) so we minimize activation of the threat response and its biochemical costs.

Stress Management: Disengaging the Sympathetic Nervous System

In order to engage the parasympathetic nervous system, we must disengage the sympathetic nervous system. This system is not binary in the sense of one being "off" while the other is "on." Both are always on, but it is a matter of relative degree or balance. The goal is to have the sympathetic system revved up only if we really need it. We need to consciously "convince" our brain that we have addressed the threats and are safe. Or we must convince the brain of a false alarm. A stressor is basically any person, event, or situation that is perceived as a threat and triggers a cascade of biochemical responses. Stressors are different for different people. Past stress compounds with new stress and makes us even more vulnerable to the adverse effects. We have learned that the presence of stress and the presence of helplessness or powerlessness is that much more tormenting. So, even if we cannot avoid the stressor, doing something about it to mitigate the stress is important. Even a small step can move the brain away from an experience of helplessness. The military has long employed the command "soldier at ease" to help individuals begin the process of disengagement of the sympathetic division of the nervous system.

We encourage people to decide what number on the gauge in Figure 7.6 qualifies as a legitimate point to trigger and engage the sympathetic nervous system. We want to train our brains to alarm only when necessary. The aim is to build neuropathways from our conscious prefrontal region to our limbic region where the threats are first perceived and assessed. The consensus in the group in the above example was that a point of 80 or above was a legitimate threat and required sympathetic engagement. We agreed because if the set point for the alarm to trigger is too low, it will continuously be alarming in any modern workplace and wasting precious resources. As soon as we are back in TDM, we can work to dismiss threats as false alarms if they fall below 80. This does not mean that there is not a problem to solve if we assign a score of less than 80; it just means it is not a threat that requires sympathetic activation and stress. The stress response can be likened to a gas-heater pilot light. We want the flame to be on, but at the lowest setting possible to be able to ignite when we need heat. We want it at its lowest setting to be ready, but not wasteful. The same holds true for our threat response. We want it lying in wait with the least amount of cost. Otherwise, we waste biochemical resources and adversely impact our bodies and minds.

Calming Practices: Engaging the Parasympathetic Nervous System

The relaxation response is at the other of the spectrum from the stress response. The relaxation response was first described by Herbert Benson, MD, the founder of the Harvard Mind and Body Institute (Benson, 1975). Dr. Benson introduced the idea of using different techniques such as meditation and progressive relaxation to counteract the body's fight-or-flight stress system. Although some of the currently in-vogue relaxation strategies have been practiced for millennia, Dr. Benson scientifically condoned them, and in that way legitimized their use.

One tried-and-true, cost-free, and straightforward manner by which to engage the parasympathetic nervous system exists—breathing.

All we have to do is remember to breathe, and our bodies will take care of the rest. This system has an impact on every cell of our bodies. Breathing is the only physiological function that is both consciously and nonconsciously controlled. The brainstem (reptilian part) is responsible for the nonconscious, automatic nature of breathing. We also have conscious control of our breath. We can hold it, slow it down, or speed it up. We cannot do this, for example, with our digestive system because it is only under nonconscious, automatic control. Because breathing is both consciously and nonconsciously controlled, we can use it to hack or fool the brain. An interesting feedback loop exists in the brain. By consciously breathing deeply, such as with diaphragmatic breathing, the increased oxygen levels in the body are detected. This informs the brain that you must be safe, or you would not be breathing so deeply. We breathe much more shallowly when we are stressed by a threat to conserve energy for the fight or flight reactions. Slow breathing activates the vagus nerve, which has connections to the heart, lungs, and digestive tract and creates relaxation.

Coherent Breathing is a method of breathing that has been researched and shown to significantly reduce stress and enhance relaxation (Brown & Gerbarg, 2012). These researchers suggest gently slowing down breathing to about five breath cycles (inhalation + exhalation) per minute to achieve maximum benefits. Inhalations and exhalations should be of equal duration. As always, even with breathing, it is important to consult your healthcare provider just in case there is a respiratory or another issue that might contraindicate this type of practice. Otherwise, what a simple and easy gift for all to enjoy and employ.

Discovery of what works to calm and relax is a highly personalized pursuit for each person. What is wonderful about a lot of areas for engaging the relaxation response is that they often come free of charge or are of minimal expense. No mandatory monetary cost is associated with breathing, revising thoughts, pursuing soothing beliefs and feelings, learning, creating loving and supportive relationships, reducing negative self-talk, listening to music, dancing, walking, exploring nature, or just being. There is no cost to self-compassion and discovery. There is no cost to self-love, acknowledgment, and commendation for struggling through human existence and all it entails. There are no costs to affirmations such as: "I have survived, so, soldier at ease." "I can now move toward thriving in my life." "I am awake, and I take care of myself." "I trust myself to be present and show up in the best ways possible to deal with issues on my work path." "I passionately and mindfully work." "I passionately and mindfully exist." "Work is a meaningful part of my identity." So, whether it is packaged as stress reduction, relaxation, meditation, biofeedback, progressive muscle relaxation, massage, yoga, prayer, guided imagery, hypnosis, emotional freedom technique, or somatic intervention—the underlying aim is to seek that relaxation response and some inner peace.

Mindfulness has emerged as a valuable concept and practice in our contemporary society. Mindfulness practice is a form of mental training that emphasizes a non-judgmental awareness of sensations, thoughts, and feelings in the present moment. Mindfulness has ancient roots and has traveled from East to West and from a religious practice to a secular one here. Jon Kabat-Zinn is credited with spreading the idea and practice of mindfulness in America. He developed a stress-reduction program in the 1970s that incorporated mindfulness practices and founded the Center for

Mindfulness, in Massachusetts. Similar to Dr. Benson, with the relaxation response, Dr. Kabat-Zinn has skillfully and successfully integrated the religious history and underpinnings of mindfulness with Western science. He and others have scientifically shown the benefits of this practice. Mindfulness is often associated with meditation and the positive psychology movement, which emphasizes human strength and thriving (Seligman, 2002).

Both work and leisure have taken on some unfortunate connotations in our society. Work for some has become perceived as drudgery and leisure as escaping the drudgery with permission to be unproductive. Work began to gain this reputation following the Industrial Revolution. Recall the nonconscious driver of survival underlying human behavior. Work is seen as necessary in the competition for survival. In some cultures, taking time for leisure is viewed as losing the competitive edge. In the primitive realm, this translates to losing in the competition to produce, succeed, and gain wealth and status. The concepts of work and leisure in modern society are elegantly elucidated by Alex Soojung-Kim Pang in his book, *Rest: Why You Get More Done When You Work Less.* Ideally, both work and leisure may be perceived as meaningful and productive existential pursuits. Both are expressions of identity and creativity that contribute to life satisfaction.

Appendix C lists some resources to address stress and other aspects of trauma. We highlight the Provider Resilience (PR) app here because we have found it to be of particular assistance to HHS staff (Figure 7.7).

THERE'S AN APP FOR THAT

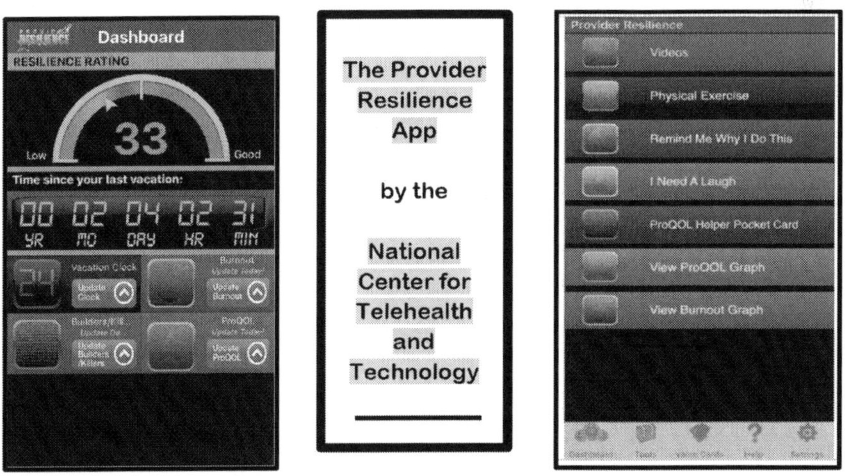

Figure 7.7

The app (which is available at no cost for both Android and Apple mobile devices) was designed for healthcare providers who serve military members and offers tools to guard against the occupational hazards of serving those experiencing adversity and suffering. It features tools for resilience and stress reduction. Users can periodically take the Professional Quality of Life (ProQOL) inventory that measures compassion fatigue and satisfaction, burnout, secondary traumatic stress, and vicarious traumatization and vicarious transformation (proqol.org). The PR app has been shown to be effective for reducing burnout and compassion fatigue in different disciplines such as oncology nursing and mental health care (Wood et al., 2017).

We Are Wired to Survive—the Thrive Is on Us

Beyond surviving, recovering, and healing is thriving. To thrive in this existence generally implies growing, flourishing, gaining existential perspective, and achieving a sense of fulfillment and inner peace. Once again, seeking to thrive is an effortful, non-linear, and ongoing process. Thriving is not a static and rigid end-state that someone gets to and remains at. Thriving is the desired state to return to as much as possible in a lifetime. Our primitive ancestors bequeathed us nonconscious survival mechanisms, but they were not as generous in leaving us with automatic thriving mechanisms. Survival was not as sure for them, so they adapted more to surviving than thriving, and their (our) brains developed accordingly.

Anthropologists and archaeologists have shared no evidence with us of cavemen on vacations (interestingly, historians tell us that vacations were first noted in the ancient Roman Empire only about 2,000 years ago). Our early human ancestors achieved their goal—they survived. We know this or else we would not be here to discuss it. We now certainly must preserve our human survival but have also been afforded the opportunity to go beyond survival and thrive. Early adverse experiences such as poverty, abuse, prejudice, or family unrest and loss place thriving pursuits at the back of the line. Survival (and even misperceived threats to it) will always supersede thriving in the brain. Survive is on automatic pilot. Thrive must be self-piloted.

Seeking and Creating Meaning and Inspiration

We end this chapter on recovering from workaches with a note on inspiration. We are sensitive and vulnerable beings who require ongoing inspirations, attachments, ideas, and wisdom to motivate and soothe us along our way. Philosophical perspectives on life and work are valuable. Money is a significant reward for work in capitalistic societies. When one works in certain fields, such as HHS, money is not necessarily abundant, but there is another "M" that may be more valuable than money—meaning. Interestingly, even in capitalistic economies, people report higher satisfaction from meaningful rewards than from financial compensation (Chamorro-Premuzic, 2013).

As has been evident throughout *Workaches*, we emphasize action. When we refer to resilience, we view this not as a static or passive state that can be reached but as an active, fluid process. We introduced the notion of trauma in this same manner. Even a single episode of trauma at one point in time cannot be perceived as "over and done with" due to the manner it is experienced and stored in the brain. The human brain is too complex, and learning is too fluid for experiences (positive and negative) not to be active ongoing processes. We view inspiration in this manner too. It is important to actively seek inspiration and renewal via other people, experiences, activities, senses, and thoughts.

So, lastly, we offer some grist for the mill—inspiration via a nice notion and scientific calculation:

ODDS OF YOU EXISTING

Recovering from adversity is difficult. But another event that is also hard is getting born. Actually, it is next to impossible (Spector, 2012). You have already beat the odds of all odds! You have already won the most important competition of them all. The chance of coming into existence in this universe is minuscule. Scientists, statisticians, and others have done the calculations, and the chance is about:

$$1 \text{ in } 10^{2,685,000}$$

The odds of you having come into this existence are actually close to ZERO.

Just for comparison, so you can further appreciate how small that number really is, the number of atoms in the known universe is 10^{80}.

Chapter 7: Key Concepts

1) Healing and hurting are timeless and ongoing.
2) Recovering entails restoring safety, building new neuropathways, and integrating the trauma in different brain regions.
3) Post-traumatic growth (PTG) can be an outcome of adversity.

8

POST-SURVIVAL: ORGANIZATIONAL THRIVING

The power of people joining together to fulfill a mission is a mighty force.

We typically consider the ideal home to be a place where individuals within are safe to develop, learn, and thrive. If we think of work environments as professional homes where we also spend a great deal of our lives, they too, ideally, are a place where individuals within are safe to develop, learn, and thrive. The workplace can be a home for professional contributions, purpose, and existential meaning. In previous chapters, we discussed how our primitive ancestors worked together without division between work, life, and family. We also described the regions within our brains that remain from those early days and how socially connected we are. Identifying workaches illustrated how we react to one another, sometimes harm, and activate threat triggers in each other. All this creates stress and reduces learning, creativity, and productivity. These findings have significant implications for organizations. We discover that behind all the complex organizational theories and scientific data are some pretty simple emergent concepts and practices. We now put all these puzzle pieces together to form and look at a bigger picture inside the contemporary organization, especially as it relates to relationships at work. This chapter is for you—whether you are an individual in a management position or a staff member in the organization. All are in service of the collective mission of the organization and thereby need to become invested in all aspects of its functioning.

YOU ARE HERE

Human History Anthropology → Human Brain Basics → Social Brain Interpersonal Dynamics → Organizational Thriving

Facilitating Working at Work

A core goal of the workplace is to enable the workforce to work. So, we want to examine what facilitates and what disables some individuals from working at their full potential. We traversed the social neuroscientific, anthropological, psychological, and organizational realms to examine what work is and what impacts it. In Chapter 5, we listed and described workaches that become obstacles and interrupt productivity for some individuals by triggering the threat response and stress. Because the nervous system gives priority to survival, these factors absorb tremendous biochemical resources. They are costly to the human body because they enlist internal resources needed for battle. Preparation for interpersonal battle is prioritized over cooperating, learning, creating, or working. Figure 8.1 simply illustrates the piece of the pie that detracts from the simple goal of working in the workplace.

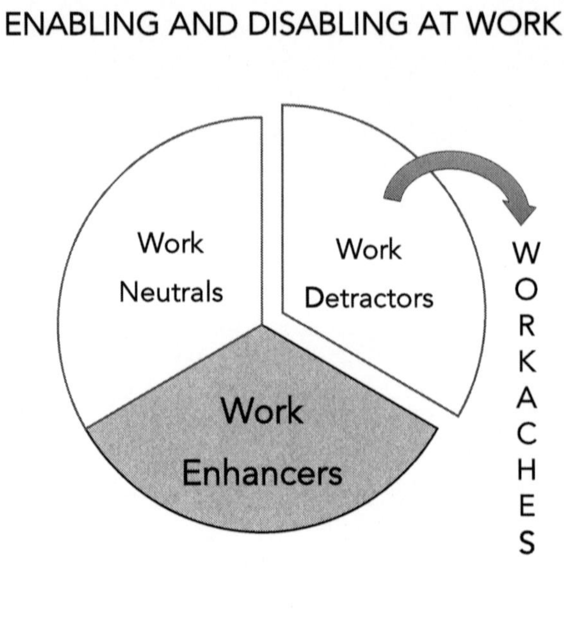

Figure 8.1

Two fundamental prerequisites for enabling thriving at work are: 1) eliminate or decrease as many workaches as possible; and 2) increase and add as many work enhancers as possible. To move toward thriving in the workplace, we must eliminate enough stress to reduce chronic activation of the threat system. Once stressors are reduced, we can focus attention on those factors that make employees feel good—about themselves, their work, and their organizations. We can attend to those factors that induce activation of the reward system. Rewards engage the parasympathetic nervous system and enhance motivation, learning, productivity, and creativity. They are biochemically, and therefore experientially, enhancing.

Figure 8.2 illustrates two different management mindsets we commonly find in the workplace.

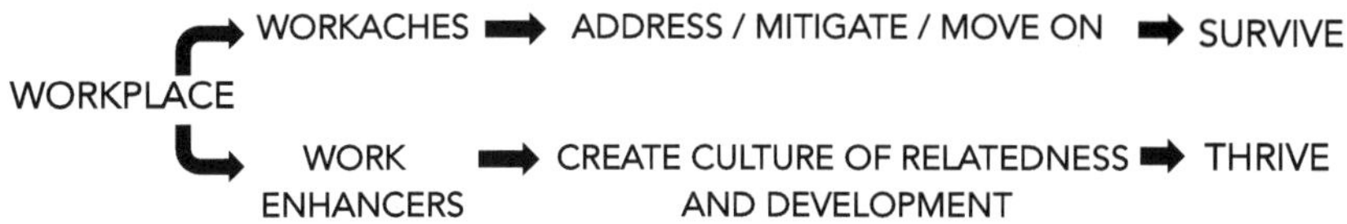

Figure 8.2

The first deals with workaches as they emerge, in a style similar to the carnival game "whack-a-mole." This mindset is based in beliefs about mitigating negative outcomes after adversity. After-the-fact interventions include post-incident stress management, often employed as a strategy for risk management and liability mitigation. The second or growth mindset addresses workaches before they even emerge. This type of proactive mindset promotes prevention and resilience in response to emergent issues in an organization. This growth mindset promotes the belief that the workplace is an environment in which to thrive, and it reflects the strong relationship between work satisfaction and life satisfaction. This latter type of organizational ethos certainly includes identifying and addressing workaches but goes beyond just problem-solving hazards and promotes growth and development. For example, we certainly want children to survive within their family of origin. However, we do not want to stop there—we want the family home to be an environment where each member can develop specific talents and strengths to work toward maximal fulfillment and contribution. This serves the family, its members, and society. This type of growth mindset in organizations also serves the organization, its individual members, and those served. A growth mindset facilitates learning (Dweck, 2015).

Relationship Building and Enhancement

Employees and organizations are in a relationship—ideally, a long-term, satisfying, and mutually beneficial one. We can borrow the steps of a human-to-human partnership to illustrate the phases of most relationships. Both individuals have an identity; if each one's identity is attractive to the other, they move toward the next step. They check out their compatibility by getting to know one another beyond initial attraction. If that is a go, they advance to further building the relationship. They invest in each other, satisfy each other's needs, and achieve mutuality. The relationship evolves and both individuals ideally grow together. Each party has the option of exiting the relationship at any stage if they discover the relationship is abusive, or if needs are unfulfilled and they no longer find the relationship rewarding. Each party has the option of identifying, communicating, and working through any of the issues and obstacles that emerge at any given stage of relationship development.

Identity → Attraction → Compatibility → Relationship → Mutuality → Growth

Building the foundation for a long-term, mutually beneficial relationship is essential from the start. All relationships have a beginning, middle, and end—and each phase deserves attention and address. Four important phases are part of establishing, maintaining, and ending relationships with staff members (Figure 8.3).

ATTRACT	WELCOME	STAY	GOODBYE
▪ Community Reputation ▪ Employer of Choice ▪ Relationship	▪ Hiring ▪ Onboarding ▪ Position Description ▪ Openness ▪ Communication ▪ Relationship	▪ Relationship ▪ Engagement ▪ Safety ▪ Stimulation ▪ Communication ▪ Development	▪ Closure ▪ Exit Interview ▪ Relationship ▪ Succession Planning

Figure 8.3

The goal is to make each phase the best it can be. If you think about a personal relationship, you can detect these phases too. First, one must attract another to initiate contact and create interest. Then they must get to know one another. Communication becomes important in the third phase to further develop the relationship and be aware of inevitable conflicts to address them. Though every relationship ends in one way or another, some relationships, unnecessarily, end prematurely. Many individuals avoid this phase and do not see it as worthy of attention. However, if we view all four phases as significant, the ending is a legitimate and meaningful phase that deserves our attention, especially in the workplace. An employee who is leaving or has left can potentially offer valuable insight about the reasons for their departure. We gain an opportunity to recognize and to possibly address a needed issue with the goal of retention. So, this phase is important to facilitate a positive goodbye, allow for closure on both sides of the relationship, and collect valuable data.

Attracting Employees

Engaging individuals in the mission and purpose (identity) of an organization is crucial. The identity of an organization is also known as its personality or culture. Organizational culture refers to aspects of the workplace environment, such as psychosocial atmosphere, habits, vision, and underlying values and beliefs (Tsai, 2011). The culture of an organization was ranked the second most important factor that job seekers consider when applying for a job (first was compensation and benefits) (Global Brand Health Report, 2018). Engagement factors are critical to attract individuals to an organization and then to have them stay. The quality of management and intra-organizational relationships have remarkable impact on retention (Garcea, 2009). Before even onboarding new employees, organizations can begin the process of engagement. Developing a positive reputation in the community is valuable to attracting talent. Knowing who you are as a person or organization establishes an identity. If we look at private industry, we can easily identify Google and Nike, for example, by their clear and strong identities from visual symbols that represent them to clearly defined goals, products, and services. Certainly, public organizations are different than private and for-profit corporations that have large marketing budgets and can pour tremendous profits into image promotion. However, HHS organizations offer unmatched humanitarian services to communities.

Media shaming of HHS organizations can focus on the one possibly mishandled case to tarnish its reputation. Counteracting such bad press is important. Spreading the word to the community about daily efforts and successes reveals the truer service of HHS organizations. In addition, the community-at-large must be continually educated and informed about what joining the HHS workforce can offer. Building a reputation as having a workplace culture that supports the well-being and needs of its employees is vital. Joining the HHS workplace can offer unmatched meaning and value to professionals and contribute to their personal development. Ang (2014) described five traits that can make an organization an "employer of choice": 1) show your employees they matter; 2) value your employees' personal time; 3) make your organization's success your employees' success; 4) empower and advance your employees; and 5) care for your employees' well-being. All this establishes the identity of an organization. When organizations have positive reputations, they become more attractive to talent.

Most of us can rattle off a list of employers of choice in the private sector. A term even exists for it— "sector envy." Vying to be an employer of choice in the public sector can create healthy competition in order to grow programs and enhance reputations. Becoming known as a dedicated service organization that also cares for the well-being of its employees seems mutually beneficial and optimal. Figure 8.4 offers a list of some of the factors currently identified as attractive to potential work candidates. These offerings reveal to potential and existing staff that the organization as a whole acknowledges them and their needs and does what it can to build mutually rewarding relationships.

ATTRACTIVE EMPLOYER OFFERINGS
authentic relations
professional training & development
flexible work schedules / telecommuting
work-life integration
attuned awareness of HHS challenges
childcare & dependent care provisions
safety planning & updated facilities
mentoring
self-care & well-being offerings
gym / nutritional snacks
individualized and team recognition
positive community image

Figure 8.4

Supporting individuals in working well and living well is crucial in the contemporary workplace. Increasingly, work encroaches on personal life, and personal life encroaches on work. People no longer need to cross the physical threshold of their offices to know of needs, task demands, and communications. The same typically holds true in knowing what is going on in one's personal life while at work. It is becoming harder to know where personal life ends, and work life begins and vice versa. As people are connected 24/7 to it all, we must find ways to better integrate life and work with less resentment and threat. More "personal" life may need to be facilitated at work.

Once an attractive identity is built, it is important to have clearly delineated position descriptions to determine compatibility. Position descriptions are often more important than employers realize. We have found that often they are outdated and do not truly reflect what the role encompasses. We have spoken to countless employees who feel that the position they find themselves in did not match what was advertised or promised. Similar to romantic relationships, individuals become resentful when they believe they were "sold a bill of goods" after the fact. People want and deserve to know what they are getting into, in any relationship. Being blindsided breeds discontent and frustration for many. We encourage organizations to offer employees clear statements of mission and purpose. Position descriptions ideally are scheduled for review and updated as staff take on different roles and responsibilities. Today's HHS organizations must address their rapidly changing nature and resultant demands on staff.

Welcoming: Selecting, Hiring, and Onboarding Employees

Resumes are limited in how they mirror or reveal a candidate's fitness for a position. The goal is to have as many lenses into each candidate as feasible in a hiring strategy. We are seeing high-tech innovations attempting to go beyond what humans can detect in the recruitment and hiring processes. HireVue is an artificially intelligent application that helps employers select employees for open positions (Bell, 2019). HireVue screens resumes and electronically recorded interviews for approximately 25,000 key data points including specific words used in response to specific questions it crafts with the employer, scans facial expressions, and monitors voice tones as part of its selection process. The goal is to choose the best fit between candidate and job, and to find those with empathy and social adeptness, for example, if those are desired attributes for the position. Potential candidates record their answers to questions collaboratively crafted by the employer and HireVue. The application then analyzes responses and records, for example, how many times the candidate smiles. An additional goal of HireVue is to remove the biases that humans bring nonconsciously to the recruitment process.

Another method in which to attract and get to know potential candidates is to develop internship and co-op programs in the workplace. There are a number of college campuses across the country that continuously seek placements for their students in their areas of study. Affording this opportunity to students offers them needed exposure and experience. Additionally, it offers the organization the ability to get to know potential and competent future candidates. This type of relationship is often mutually beneficial. Both parties can collect data to see if there is a fit between them.

Social and emotional intelligence is an important ingredient in working with other humans. These factors are important aspects of team players and potential emerging leaders in organizations. Managers, however, do not necessarily get to see this in candidates' resumes. We promote staying aware of the qualities and traits required for the position in which recruitment is taking place. Some positions, for example, require a stronger EI than even IQ. We share an elucidating example from television media of an employer attempting to assess SI and EI here.

The Rebel Billionaire: Branson's Quest for the Best

The successful entrepreneur, Richard Branson, was part of a reality television show from 2004 through 2005 that was conducting a search for an acting president of one of his Virgin companies. In Episode 1, Sir Branson used quite a clever strategy to screen the candidates upon meeting them for the first time. Branson disguised himself as a London cab driver and picked up each candidate at the airport and drove them to their hotel. He utilized the time in the cab to assess how each treated him (disguised as a taxi driver). The first two contestants eliminated from the contest were those who treated him with the least respect and acknowledgment. The criteria he used to eliminate these contenders were based on a measure of the candidate's emotional and social intelligence.

Indeed, the above example is an implausible recruitment strategy in real life. Nonetheless, we can appreciate the value that Sir Branson placed on equal respect and fairness for all in his organization. Resumes and interviews have traditionally assessed fit for the content of a position versus assessed for emotional or other forms of intelligence that, as we have discussed, are vital for a diverse workforce.

Research has suggested that the typical interview process that includes standard questions about a candidate's content expertise alone does not correlate with their future success in work positions (Bock, 2016). For example, asking candidates about their strengths and weaknesses or how they envision themselves in five years yields minimal authentic information. A comprehensive meta-analysis published in 1998 found that questions about a candidate's historical work performance predicted success at work only about "12 percent better than a coin flip" (Schmidt & Hunter, 1998). An example of a more predictive question of ultimate success on the job is having a candidate offer problem-solving steps that they would take to address current issues in the organization (Sullivan, 2016).

There are additional and unique traits that deserve assessment when hiring for HHS organizations. Issues such as staff retention, burnout, and, secondary trauma must be kept in mind. As we discussed previously, emotional intelligence (EI), social intelligence (SI), resiliency quotient (RQ), and adversity quotient (AQ) are desirable characteristics of potential candidates for HHS positions. Building an interview process to include these traits, as well as cognitive style, is vitally important.

Some research has indicated that an assessment and impression of a candidate during an interview may be fixed within the first 15 seconds of an interview (Prickett, 2000). We know that first impressions are important, especially to the limbic system or fast-processing aspect or our brains. Speed dating operates in this manner, though individuals are typically given 15 minutes rather than seconds. Unfortunately, we sometimes get it wrong when we rely on our "gut" or first impression. Remember that a "gut" response is not necessarily some intuitive or quick rational analysis—it is often nonconscious bias or our drive to like people who are more similar to us. Potentially well-suited candidates can be lost to this human trait, so it is wise to remain aware of it in oneself and in hiring committees, and to non-judgmentally challenge and manage it. In his book, *Blink: The Power of Thinking Without Thinking*, Malcolm Gladwell describes this human phenomenon of how our brains make instant ("in-a-blink") impressions from brief observations of someone. This phenomenon has also been developed and further explored in the concept of "thin-slicing" introduced into the literature by social psychologist Frank Bernieri. Thin-slicing is the process of making assessments of another person from just observing a few seconds of their behaviors. These initial impressions can range from highly accurate to highly inaccurate. First impressions are considered the initial conditions in assessing, analyzing, and forming impressions about the different layers of another person. They are part of our interpersonal sensitivity systems (Bernieri, 2001).

REFLECTION

Reflect back on an interview process that you participated in or imagine one where you just interviewed diverse candidates for the position you currently hold. Which candidate stood out for you? What attributes or traits made you immediately like this person? How soon did you know you favored them? Did you see yourself in this candidate? For example, did you like someone who shared similar personality or other traits as you? If you did, this is possibly a bias that you want to step back and reflect on. This candidate may potentially not bring diverse perspective and skill into the collective intelligence of the organization if they are a duplicate of you. Now reassess the candidates with your second perspective in mind. Any changes in your evaluation, preference, or decision?

Next, comprehensive onboarding and integration into the entire organization are vital. Assisting new or prospective hires to understand the totality of the organization from its geography to its policies will be beneficial for the organization as well as for employees, because gaining perspective on one's context in any system larger than the self can often yield a better sense of meaning and purpose. Below, we offer a case that, though not in the HHS realm, illustrates the importance of employee engagement, awareness of value, and knowledge of the organizational mission.

Maria worked on an assembly line at an aircraft facility that built planes. She was responsible for inspecting a small component of the plane engine after it had been assembled. Maria was struggling with her mental health and was referred for evaluation. Although there were other remarkable issues contributing to her psychiatric symptoms, there was one relevant work factor that was contributing to her depressed mood. Maria felt unimportant and marginalized at work. She had become demoralized there. We discovered that Maria had no idea what she was assembling beyond a vague notion that the workplace was building planes. Nobody had ever described the part she was inspecting and the crucial importance that it, and therefore *she*, played in ultimately keeping passengers safe to travel the globe. Maria was unaware that her component was a part of the engine. She had never been offered a tour of the full facility to gain the big picture of which she was an important part. Maria was an essential and crucial part of aircraft construction, and she sadly had no clue. She viewed her work as meaningless, insignificant, and of little value. Maria's work identity negatively impacted her self-identity and self-esteem.

Once a candidate comes on board, other active and ongoing processes of engagement and protection of the new employee become relevant. A great example of an innovative program and assessment of employees used from the "welcome" stage through the "stay" stage is one used by the United States military. The program is called the Global Assessment Tool (GAT) and is used extensively by the Army (Vergun, 2014). The assessment emerged from a long-term and global initiative the Army constructed under a program called "Comprehensive Soldier Fitness." We cite it here because we feel it is applicable to HHS professionals who often face adversity and social battles, and it has been shown to be a valid and reliable assessment tool. The GAT 2.0 is an online assessment tool (taking about 23-minutes to complete) that measures five dimensions of health, including emotional, social, spiritual, familial, and physical. The physical dimension measures sleep, nutrition, and activity. Because military soldiers experience and witness intense human adversity, assessing dimensions such as psychological health and resilience is vital. The aspect of the GAT that is most impressive is that once an individual receives their confidential scores, self-awareness and self-care are promoted. Individuals are directed for further feedback and training in identified areas of risk and need. Recruits and soldiers at all levels have ongoing access to the GAT to continue to develop self-awareness and self-care.

We are currently working toward orchestrating the collaboration and sharing of this incredible resource for HHS. There are many parallels to public service (military or social), and the GAT would require minimal adaptation to cross-over for civilian use. The Army has already allowed civilian use of the GAT by recognizing that work stress also infects individuals outside the professional realm. The GAT is now available for military spouses. Workache contagions can spread and infect family and friends, too. Psychosocial infections, like viral infections, do not only remain inside an office.

One workache that we did not previously identify (because it occurs before an employee comes on board) deserves mention here. This stressor has been labeled employer "ghosting" (Lucas, 2018). Ghosting refers to an employer going silent and having no communication with a candidate after a job interview. This includes the employer not returning voicemails and emails from interviewees. We increasingly hear concerns and complaints regarding the time between the interview and the job offer or denial. This time interval creates stress for candidates who are eagerly awaiting word of their fate and not knowing, for example, if they should accept an alternative job offer or submit a resignation to their current employer. We promote clear timelines and intermittent communications with all candidates. Ghosting stresses candidates and harms an organization's reputation. A 2018 survey conducted by *Hired* revealed that 50 percent of respondents reported that they would engage with an organization that sent a personalized message after an interview (hired.com). This type of personalized practice reflects a thoughtful work culture to the prospective employee.

Retaining Employees

HHS organizations are currently experiencing problems with staff retention (Wareing Evans, 2018). Figure 8.5 offers a non-exhaustive list of factors that contribute to motivation, productivity, and engagement at work. These factors help individuals work to their full potential and they have been identified as increasing employees' desires to remain in an organization. As is evident in this list, many of the factors that attract potential employees are the same as those that retain employees.

FACTORS CONTRIBUTING TO WORK ENHANCEMENT

acknowledgment
recognition
fairness
compassion
perceived support
equity
predictability
affiliation / connectedness
fair compensation
relationships
team bonding
resiliency training
work-life integration support
organizational mission / values
purpose / meaning
health and well-being advocacy
communication

Figure 8.5

Stay interviews are considered a vital part of engaging and retaining employees. These types of interviews are important conversations with employees in order for management to understand and earnestly problem-solve staff experiences and needs. Examples of effective stay interview questions include:

- What do you predict about your day on your ride to work?
- How do you feel at the end of most workdays?
- What is the top aspect of your job that needs to change?
- Which area of self-improvement would you like to work on?
- How can we help you develop toward a professional goal?

Stay interviews can be viewed as part of prevention of staff departures or minimizing exit interviews with valued employees. Identified problems may be able to be solved or mitigated before it is too late. Finnegan (2015) emphasizes the importance of direct supervisors conducting these interviews and shifting the focus off of job performance to how the organization can improve employees' work lives. A 2017 Gallup poll on employees who voluntarily left their jobs revealed...

> **Over half of the employees who voluntarily left their organizations reported that in the three months prior to their exits, "neither their manager nor any other leader spoke with them about their job satisfaction or future with the organization."**

The report goes on to chronicle the financial costs of employee exits. Gallup analytics calculated a loss of a trillion dollars per year to organizations (McFeely & Wigert, 2019). We cannot calculate the psychosocial costs in the same manner, but we estimate that they too are substantial. Effective communication is essential to reducing both the financial and psychosocial impacts of voluntary exits.

Miscommunications, Misperceptions, and Misinterpretations

There are going to be miscommunications, misperceptions, and misinterpretations in human exchanges. We have spent the preceding chapters setting the stage for how utterly complex human relations are and how they become even more complicated inside organizations. Language (both verbal and nonverbal) adds significantly to the complexities of human relations. Psychosocial dynamics surrounding both verbal and nonverbal exchanges are intense and the potential for conflict and confusion is great. We have learned that with each interpersonal exchange between individuals, there are both above- and below-ground (conscious and nonconscious) messages given and received.

The below-ground or nonconscious is scanning for any and all potential threats in the metacommunications. These brain regions are actively looking for signs of being devalued, excluded, and shamed because they signal a risk to survival. We encourage leaders to remain aware of this in their interpersonal exchanges with staff. The goal is to counterbalance the anxiety that goes on beneath the surface with as much assurance of value, respect, and inclusion as possible. Just being called by one's name can make a remarkable difference in an interpersonal exchange. In

Chapter 2, we reviewed the harm of any hint of annihilation or abandonment in interpersonal relations. These early attachment issues remain relevant through all stages of adulthood and extend even into professional relationships. The safer an organization is psychologically, the more employees are able to both offer and receive communications (Edmondson, 2018).

Some individuals unfortunately arrive in the workplace with histories that render them unable to receive most communications and feedback in an emotionally "neutral" zone. Their defenses (which arise for self-protection) disallow or deflect communications even before they are fully processed by the brain. The fast processing of incoming information does not involve higher regions. When someone has a history of trauma, as we have learned, the brain is on high alert and most incoming information is primarily processed as threat detection. Misperceptions and misinterpretations occur with all and in even some of the most benign communications.

We communicated with a supervisor who was anxious because each time her manager came into her office, he remarked about how cold it was in there. The employee took this as criticism that she was wasting money on air conditioning. Interestingly, we had previously had coaching sessions with this same manager who struggled with social anxiety and perceiving himself to be socially awkward. He was examining his work relationships and wanted some strategies for "small talk" with staff and was trying not to communicate only about job-related issues. We had suggested to him some simple strategies such as sharing a song he had just heard or even commenting on the weather!

The measure of the quality of an adaptive communication is sometimes how one assesses the message was communicated versus how the receiver took it in. Unless someone has requested that the communications stop, it is ideal to restate the message in as many ways as possible in an attempt for the receiver to take it in.

Communication is about speaking *and* listening. Sometimes the listening is the most important aspect of the communication. Just as speaking contains both verbal and nonverbal messages, so does listening. Some crucial questions to ask yourself when listening include: Am I distracted? Am I checking my email or text during this conversation? Am

I offering eye contact? Am I giving the nonverbal signals of interest or disinterest? When you want to convey a message to somebody, here are some crucial questions to ask yourself when speaking: Am I in TDM? Is my listener in TDM? Is anything interfering with the person listening to me? Does my body language appear to be intimidating my listener? Is our conversation private? Would this individual better listen or receive information via written communication? Are there nonverbal signs that I have lost my audience? As psychologists, we often may communicate a message in different ways until it is received by a client. Communication—both speaking and listening—is key to all phases of a relationship, even at the end.

Saying Goodbye/Leaving the Organization

Any relationship, however long it lasts, will have an end. Ending the relationship between the organization and an employee should be done with as much attention to psychosocial factors as any other phase of the relationship. Significant cost ranging from the financial to the emotional accompanies high turnover of HHS employees. Calculating the financial costs is easier than calculating the psychological costs to individuals, teams, and communities served. The external community's loss of a beloved staff member that cared for them can impact generations. The internal system has to reorganize itself with each former member's exit and new member's entrance. Long-term staff members sometimes leave with a wealth of organizational information that no remaining employees possess. Short-term staff members who prematurely leave often exit before sharing their unique talents and information. Often, workloads have to be shifted to existing employees until a new hire comes aboard. This just adds extra work to already over-burdened staff. Unless the individual is a significant problem for the organization and just really needs to go, the goal is retention. Exits also stir the ambivalence of remaining employees, who may begin questioning, "Did my coworker know something I don't?" "Should I leave too?" This can spread an emotional contagion. The full costs are unmeasurable and often unnecessary.

There are ways to mitigate these potential costs. Succession planning for each key member of a workforce is essential. Often it is difficult to plan for the departure of a key organizational leader. Anxiety facilitates our avoiding loss of beloved and stabilizing leaders. However, because continuity is so important to the functioning of any organization, there must be practices built to facilitate succession planning. Having what we call "organizational bridging" in place before gaps occur is important. Bridging standardizes the process and structure that will occur during transitions. It is separate and apart from the identification of specific individuals for positions. Identifying suitable "understudies" that are already a part of the organization that can be mentored and trained to succeed is an adaptive process.

When an employee does leave an organization for whatever reason, an exit interview can yield insights that may help the organization deal with the loss of this employee and continue the forward movement toward becoming a thriving organization. Exit interviews, like stay interviews, are essential conversations from which valuable data can emerge.

Some endings are due to the retirement of an employee. Over the years we have learned that many employees fear retaliation or fear becoming irrelevant in their positions if they inform their employer of their intended departure date. They often just give the agreed upon notice even when they have known for significantly longer when they intended to leave. This can result in organizations being less prepared for the turnover with little opportunity for transition planning. We recommend that organizations certainly work on employee retention, but also acknowledge and communicate to staff that relationships inevitably end. Leaders must create a culture in which endings are a natural part of any workplace. Welcoming the opportunity of building transitions with the employee who is departing can greatly benefit the organization. It can also allow for that individual to leave with a sense of value and meaning.

Some public service agencies rehire retirees, which can offer great benefit to both the retiree (who can slowly transition into retirement by working fewer hours) and the employer (retirees can provide valuable knowledge about their work content, process, and other organizational information). If we apply some crucial thinking, we may be able to move away from the binary notion of stop and start. There can be value to having overlap (whenever possible and indicated) between one individual starting in a position that another is leaving. Let us extend this notion to the United States Presidency. Would it be beneficial to the country if a sitting president stayed for, let's say six months, as the newly-elected president was transitioning into office? Even if this is a bad idea, we want our minds to be free enough to rethink all positions and explore all possibilities and updates that might be advantageous. As we reviewed earlier, it is very difficult for our brains to do this. Our brains prefer certainty and prediction and drive us to do things the way we did them yesterday.

Multidimensional Nature of Leadership

Though an HHS organization may have a singular name, it is composed of different individuals, units, departments, stakeholders, elected officials, community leaders and partners, constituencies, and alliances; many individuals, both inside and outside the organization, are essential to its thriving. Individuals who may never have the titles or acknowledgment as leaders, exist within organizations and have an incredible impact by modeling and mentoring inside. They are typically the unsung heroes who model resilience, support, and comradery. They are dedicated to the evolution of the organization and to the support of other staff. When one of these individuals retires or leaves, many feel the impact of their loss and reverberations throughout the work environment.

We place quite a tall (sometimes impossible) order on contemporary leaders to be aware of triggers, issues, personalities, preferences, and interpersonal dynamics in staff. Historically, leaders did not have to deal with all the protections and rights of workers. Recall that our primitive ancestors would kill off the non-producers of the group. We have evolved, which is positive, but nonetheless, sociopolitical rights and protections are yet another weight on the shoulders of our leaders today. We ask them to be mindful and compassionate, when they themselves may have never received and experienced this. They may have no role models from any of their own former groups. Self-awareness and other-awareness take remarkable effort and study, especially if they have not been modelled and developed early on. Leadership involves being aware of and attempting to adaptively manage all those deep, nonconscious, timeless brain regions of each individual, along with all the interacting relational dynamics between individuals in each group. In addition to managing relations, leaders are also responsible for policy, vision, oversight, laws, and implementation. We have learned that you can take the human out of ancient times, but you cannot take the ancient primitive out of the human. Leadership today is an onerous responsibility. We seem to be asking our leaders to be a little bit parent, friend, and counselor.

Relationships that leaders form with staff are fundamental and a crucial aspect of leadership. A resume and interview provide little compared to what leaders used to know about group members who grew up among them. Our cultural evolution is occurring at a rapid pace and changing individuals and organizations. However, one consistent aspect of the workplace has been the relationship. Fast-paced changes are threatening to many in the workgroup, which makes stable relationships that much more rewarding. Cognitive challenges of these tasks are intense and complex. However, if we focus on the relational aspects of leadership and management, we can simplify things. Humans need relationships that have basic ingredients including recognition, kindness, and respect. Contemporary and emerging leaders can begin to understand their staff by understanding the basic fundamentals of evolutionary psychology, family systems, and neuroscience. The more we know about ourselves and others, the better equipped we become to manage our teams. Once we understand human nature in general, it is time to understand each member of the team. If we return to and borrow the words we assigned to ideal parenting, we can now address the fundamentals of attuned and attached leadership. Ideally, parents know (have some coherent story) about themselves before they develop, guide, and get to know their own children. Ideally, leaders know themselves before they have staff that look to them for guidance. Knowing oneself facilitates knowing the other.

The scientific literature informs us that staff bring their unique histories with authority figures and others with them to work. These neural shadows cast distortions over those in leadership positions. We also know that power can distort perceptions. We encourage leaders to appreciate (and honor) their own power and to stay aware that their staff have unconsciously perceived them in this way. Leaders who stay mindful of this to maximize employee guidance and enrichment often report having more satisfying leadership experiences. The work organization is now in the neuronal shadow of the family. We are still working with some of those primitive brain regions.

Inevitable Challenges for Organizations

As we have seen, despite all the updates in working conditions and technology, relationships remain most important to people. A great deal of workplace stress comes from the relational underground. The organizational system is the sum of the parts—all its collective individual units and their interactions impacted by more global systems and missions. Though an organization typically has a singular name, it is a multilayered, multidimensional, very "plural" entity. Once again, quite similar to that brain of ours. The "sweet spot" of the organization is at the point where all constituent parts are in harmony with one another, with its fluidity and creativity fulfilling its mission and purpose. This is a transient state due to all the impacts and disruptions on a system, but one to which we can always attempt to return.

So, what is it that keeps an organization from staying in that "sweet spot"? Figure 8.6 is a simple schematic of two individuals working together that illustrates the basic differences in how our ancestors worked as a whole unit to get the job done, how it changed over time, and what it seems to be struggling to return back to today. Once agriculture was cultivated in one place and goods manufactured for many, circumstances changed, and we began to see modern versions of "employer" versus "employee," and "competitive coworker" versus "competitive coworker." These are some artifacts of civilization that are getting reexamined and reconsidered today.

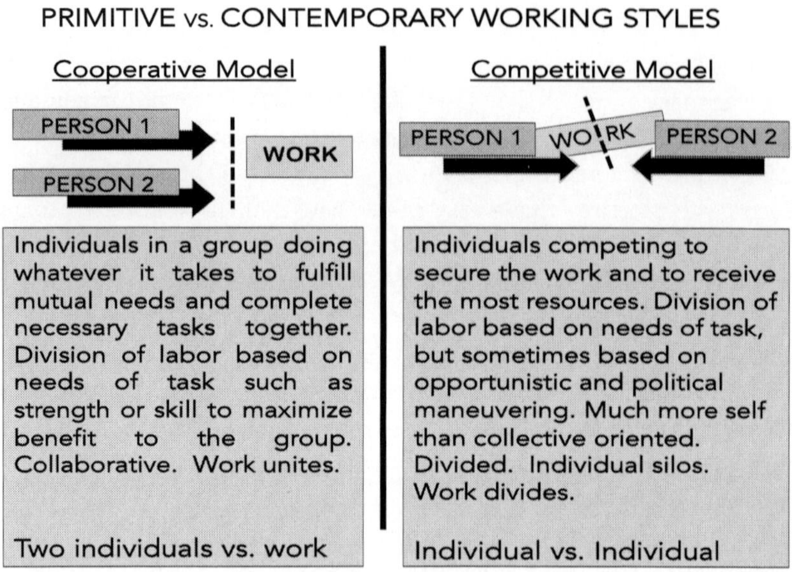

Figure 8.6

This is a simplistic diagram to illustrate a simple system—our primitive threat system. Once someone is perceived to be on the "other side of the line," they are a potential threat to the nonconscious. Work has, unfortunately, become that in some respects. Many employees feel taken advantage of on the job. Many employers too feel resentful and unappreciated. Most feel a level of antagonism. Many things "come back around" in human society. With all the progress and technology that has flooded workplaces, we may be seeing the return of the very basic human relationship as an essential and vital tool.

Systems and organizations have grown exponentially from the times of our primitive ancestors—in terms of the sheer number of members and complexity of goals. Our brains have some difficulty with this newer style of big organization (versus small clan). We like to be able to name the whole organism—to understand it, predict it, know how it operates, and be aware of a potential threat to us. When a system gets "too" large for us to identify it simply, things get complicated. It becomes impossible, in a binary manner, to claim the organization as good or bad, this or that. Yet, we try. It becomes difficult to identify the enemy and the one to blame when the other is this big, amorphous, conglomerate of different identities. The threat system wants to be able to detect and to identify the enemy or perpetrator; otherwise, the threat is too ambiguous, and this primitive system is rendered helpless if there is an unidentifiable lurking threat. This ambiguity sometimes leads to labeling the entire organization as bad or the enemy. Going to work each day to an organization that you perceive in this manner leads to chronic stress and feelings of helplessness. Productivity suffers as well. Leaders need to be aware of how their staff are perceiving them. With good communication, an organization can communicate itself as an imperfect but evolving system made up of each individual. Otherwise, it is a binary "us" (staff) versus "them" (leadership) system. So, ideally leaders encourage feedback and suggestions and ensure that staff feel a part of the system at large.

The understanding that there is no one person that is the organization itself is relevant when we are upset with our workplace. We are as much of a representative of the organization as any other member. The organization does not exist without its members. So, who is to blame? If a Ford Corporation staff member is upset at the company, they can no longer point to Henry Ford. Is the CEO to blame? Is it the stockholder? Is it the customer? Is it the direct supervisor? Is it the Board of Directors? Who is responsible? The answer to this question varies based on who is doing the blaming and what their agenda is. However, more often than not, staff will point the finger at the next person up in the hierarchy with whom they do not have a positive relationship. This individual is most likely the one we cast a negative parental shadow on. The brain needs a target on which to direct anger so it can somewhat relieve itself of the threat. Leaders who do not develop relationships with their staff and remain as "blank screens" are more at risk for being projected upon.

Being able to trust at least some of the individuals that make up the group or at least to trust the coherency and operating principles of the group is important. Otherwise, we remain vigilant and in survival mode.

We need to feel that we are cared about by specific individuals or the organization as a whole. A core aspect of caring for another is attending to their vulnerabilities or harm. Organizations are evolving to create systems that acknowledge and care for the vulnerabilities of clients and customers, as well as staff. Awareness of the potential of trauma in individuals interacting with the organization, at any level, is one of those evolving arenas.

On Becoming a Trauma-Informed Organization

In the course of any relationship, including organizational ones, we must acknowledge, expect, and prepare for challenging times. A key objective during these times is to manage them in the most adaptive and supportive manner for all involved. Employers that actively monitor and address workaches communicate their dedication to the well-being of employees. Predicting and preparing for secondary trauma is an important aspect of this. Installing programs for unpredicted traumas and other adverse events is crucial. Organizations can be sensitive to trauma by taking the necessary steps to install protocols and practices that protect, prevent, or mitigate harm, reduce triggers, and reflect caring. Trauma-informed organizations are those that acknowledge human vulnerability and adversity and are sensitive to trauma. Trauma-informed care has historically focused on clients and customers of organizations, but the research data on secondary trauma is supporting and highlighting the need for staff to be considered and protected too. In *Workaches*, we focus on those aspects of a trauma-informed practice that pertain to all employees of an HHS organization. Policy makers and governing bodies are at the helm of implementing and advancing HHS organizations. The goal is to have policies in place that are in alignment with best practices that promote psychosocial well-being in the workforce. This is not an easy task. However, it is essential to provide care for each and every human being in the workforce, so they can take the best care of clients served. The healthier our staff, the healthier our communities. One of the quality markers of an organization or agency is the experiences of staff "on the ground." Updating organizations to being trauma-informed is one of those adaptive changes for all—staff included. We want "no employee left behind."

According to the Substance Abuse and Mental Health Services Administration (SAMHSA): "a program, organization, or system that is trauma-informed realizes the widespread impact of trauma and understands potential paths for healing; recognizes the signs and symptoms of trauma in staff, clients, and others involved with the system; and responds by fully integrating knowledge about trauma into policies, procedures, practices, and settings" (SAMHSA 2014). SAMHSA has identified core principles with trauma-informed care: 1) safety; 2) trustworthiness and transparency; 3) peer support; 4) collaboration and mutuality; 5) empowerment, voice, and choice; and 6) cultural, historical, and gender issues. Further guidelines for building an organization that cares about trauma in those served and staff can be found on the SAMHSA website (samhsa.gov).

Awareness and education are the first steps in creating a trauma-informed organization. A number of mindful leaders have told us over the years, for example, that they just never realized the importance of having lockable restrooms. They had not connected a history of sexual trauma to vulnerability inherent in unsecured restrooms. But we have never experienced management that, once they are informed, have not moved forward to enhancing privacy and safety in restrooms. We are all moving from not knowing to knowing more and more about trauma and its ongoing effects.

We can divide any type of experience in three—before, during, and after—or, pre, peri, and post (Figure 8.7).

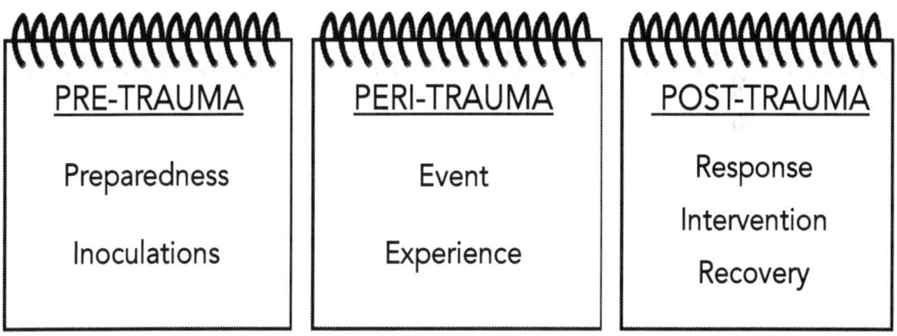

Figure 8.7

We can assume that in the HHS field there is going to be trauma witnessed and resultant secondary trauma issues. There are also going to be the internal stressors such as organizational challenges and obstacles. Predicting stress and trauma leads to prevention and intervention efforts before the fact. This approach is similar to managing other natural disasters. We design disaster preparedness programs for before, during, and after a disaster to maximize assistance.

Pre-Trauma / Inoculation Training (Psychological Immunity)

Part of evolving a system is updating it. This occasionally means returning to something that worked better in the past. We have brilliant new technology to assist with the evolution of HHS organizations. We no longer send our military soldiers directly into battle before extensive preparation and training. This would neither be good for the soldier nor the goals of the military. Yet, we often send new HHS staff into social battlefields without adequate preparation and training. There are relatively few "boot camps" for HHS across the globe. Unfortunately, unless a new employee has a good mentor or has been in a relevant internship, they most likely will be deployed to the field with mostly theoretical knowledge. We propose inoculation training (pre-incident versus post-incident debriefings) that is essential for preparation. If we can lay down as many neural pathways as possible prior to facing some of the adverse events to be encountered on the job, why not? HHS professionals often must complete job tasks under stressful conditions. Virtual reality (VR) training prior to entering the field, used extensively by the military now, is growing (Cosic et al., 2010). Stress inoculation trainings through the use of VR aim to improve stress resistance. Through virtual exposures, the goal is to add learning and skills that provide immunity to stressors encountered on the job in the real world. We need policies and training that anticipate and employ necessary action steps for the reality of psychosocial stressors in HHS positions.

Resiliency Training and Raising AQ

Social scientists have long studied the question of why some individuals emerge from adversities and tragedies differently than others. Answers to this question emerge from the study of resilience. Some people fall to the deepest depths of psychological and existential despair after adversity. Others can triumph and attain higher levels of functioning than prior to the trauma. Individuals can also change in response to traumas over time. We have learned that resiliency is a fluid and trainable trait. The American Psychological Association has described resilience as, "the process of adapting well in the face of adversity, trauma, tragedy, threats or significant sources of stress—such as family and relationship problems, serious health problems or workplace and financial stressors. It means 'bouncing back' from difficult experiences" (APA, 2018).

Paul Stoltz (1997) introduced a valuable concept to the resiliency literature called the Adversity Quotient (AQ). Dr. Stoltz describes AQ as a measure of how an individual responds to adversity. The higher one's AQ score, the more adaptively they respond to adverse events, and the less they are ultimately impacted. AQ can be measured and strengthened, which is important in HHS. The Positive Psychology Center at the University of Pennsylvania has a program in building a resilience skill set. Some of the essentials of the resiliency program include self-awareness, self-regulation, mental agility, optimism, human relations, and thought restructuring.

We know that any organization that is involved with health and human services is inevitably going to be exposed to adversities and stressors. Tremendous costs are involved in continued exposure to and confrontation with adversity. HHS staff require compensatory strategies. Resiliency training in preparation for the inevitable in HHS ideally begins at onboarding and continues thereafter. HHS staff are facing remarkable and significant events and experiences that take their toll.

A sometimes overlooked aspect of resiliency training in HHS is that of recalibrating role expectations. Earlier, we addressed disillusionment with leaders as a workache. We also experience disillusionment with our own selves, especially if we hold ourselves to high, even impossible expectations. An aspect of resiliency training is revising thoughts and beliefs to be more realistic and humane about ourselves and others. It is difficult enough to have to attend to a tragedy. Adding an unrealistic expectation to our response to that tragedy is an additional and unnecessary threat and energy drain. New physicians, for example, report significant stress over not being able to "do their job" and save a life, so teaching them to reframe their role of "healer" or "savior" to that of "comforter" or "supporter" becomes valuable. The goal is to assist them with defining their job roles with much more realistic terms. Otherwise, we see them chronically disappointed with themselves, occasionally even blaming themselves for illness and loss of life. The physician who can update their professional mission, in this case, is no longer saving the patient but performing the meaningful task of allowing them to transition to their death in the most comfortable and supportive manner. A crucial aspect of any resiliency program in HHS should include exercises in building realistic expectations.

Peri-Trauma Awareness and Intervention

Nobody in an organization wants to experience a tragic event and at the same time discover that their safety plan is significantly flawed—

sometimes so flawed, that it increases or causes further harm. We have witnessed widespread confusion inside organizations after a tragic event.

Staff had just arrived at their offices when they heard screaming outside. Some staff immediately ran to windows and witnessed a law enforcement officer shooting a young man who was pointing a firearm. One individual who had already sustained injury was on the ground.

Once the crime scene was stabilized and secured, there was remarkable confusion on how to proceed inside the building. Most managers released their staff to go home. One manager, significantly shocked by the shooting, demanded that her staff return to their desks and complete their work. Some staff members expressed their safety concerns and emotional needs. This manager informed them that she would "write them up" for insubordination if they left. After ten minutes, one employee left and went directly to the director's office. The director informed her that all was safe, but staff were dismissed for the day. The employee informed the director of her manager's behavior and left. The director went directly to the office to release the employees and speak to the manager.

It became clear that the manager was in her threat response and attempting to regain control in a reactive and maladaptive manner. HR later weighed in and explained that the manager had no right to take away free will by demanding her employees stay and work. The manager was sent to an EAP for counseling and supervisor training. The director realized the need for updated safety planning and sought collaboration with the safety committee to address necessary protocol changes.

We expect unexpected adverse events to create immediate fear and chaos. Building a critical incident plan that management can understand and refer to is vital. Periodic rehearsal of the plan decreases risk. Assessment of how well the safety or critical incident plan worked during the incident informs necessary updates, and communication with staff about what worked and what did not during the incident is an important part of this process. This also assists with staff reintegrating a sense of safety at work. Additionally, it is assuring for staff to be aware that there are dedicated individuals within the organization assigned to safety roles should an unexpected incident occur. Organizing chaos brings some level of relief during adverse events.

Post-Trauma Awareness and Intervention (Debriefing): Essential Programming Elements

Individuals vary widely in their responses, both internally and externally, in the aftermath of trauma. A fair assumption, however, is that all are impacted in some way. Sometimes we can interpret someone in shock as their being unaffected. Some core strategies to address trauma are briefly outlined in Figure 8.8.

TRAUMA RESPONSE STAGED INTERVENTIONS

INTERVENTION	EXAMPLES
PSYCHOLOGICAL FIRST AID	practical assistance / contact and engagement / safety and comfort / information gathering
DEBRIEFING	facilitated conversation / recounting experiences and responses / reviewing facts / expressing emotions / education about varied responses and potential post-trauma effects
ONGOING ASSESSMENT	immediate and then periodic assessments of post-trauma responses
REFERRALS	EAP / counseling, medical list of community providers available if no EAP / pre-check if mental health benefits bundled medical insurance are adequate
WELL-BEING CHECKS	"how are you doing" "anything I can assist you with?"
RELATIONSHIP FORTIFICATION	peer support / leadership engagement / group meetings / uniting group
RESILIENCE BUILDING	ongoing education / group facilitation / well-being practices
MEMORIALS / RITUALS	meaning seeking / post-incident events / anniversary planning

Figure 8.8

A key goal after adverse events is to provide ongoing interventions that minimize the risk of diagnoses such as PTSD or depression. An increasing number of HHS organizations are moving toward building trauma-informed policy, protocol, and practices. They are also moving toward an emphasis on health and well-being.

Workplace Well-Being: Policy, Protocol, and Practice

Ensuring the well-being of all employees of an organization is essential. Organization-specific protocols and practices help define each work culture. Practices are established procedures and behaviors. For example, a practice in an organization might be to offer a nutrition course or mindfulness training. Protocols establish these practices as part of the culture. The protocols and practices of a work culture inform the workforce of their status and value. See Figure 8.9. As organizations move toward an emphasis on well-being, it is optimal to update or write policy to reflect this. Policy provides a more fixed understanding of a work culture.

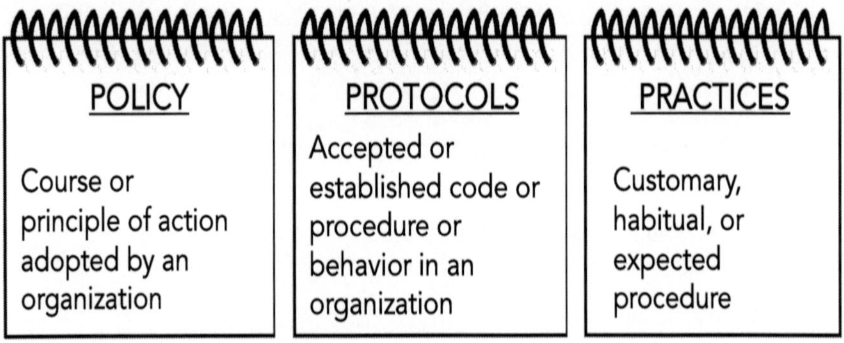

Figure 8.9

HHS staff are invaluable and necessary resources for the well-being of our communities. If we do not take care of them, who will take care of our communities? HHS professionals impact our communities in ways many constituents do not fully understand. They provide "survival" services to those in need. Most individuals crossing an HHS organization's threshold have needs that exceed their own personal capabilities to meet them. They need public assistance. Many are in crisis and have trauma histories. Despite HHS staff desire to meet their customers' or clients' needs, often resources are limited. Many discuss organizational challenges as frustrating and exhausting. We cannot afford to have our communities move into crisis by being unable to fill those public services vacancies with competent and motivated employees.

HHS organizations are at a crossroads. Across the nation, many organizations are reporting increasing difficulty in hiring and retaining staff. Staff report high levels of burnout, fatigue, hypervigilance, and secondary trauma, as well as other physical and psychological symptoms. These conditions greatly affect productivity, job satisfaction, and engagement, and talented staff members are leaving HHS organizations (APHSA, 2017). Organizations that have already implemented protocols, practices, and policy for workforce well-being are reporting positive results (Wareing Evans, 2018); preliminary observations show improvements in retention, job satisfaction, and engagement. Leaders who have been the drivers of these updated protocols and practices have in this way communicated their concern, care, and appreciation for staff.

Authentic Leadership: Adaptive, Mindful, and Engaged

Leaders have unique responsibilities and roles in the creation and maintenance of relationships in the workforce. Authentic leadership is defined by several core traits, including self-awareness, relational openness, humility, internalized moral perspective, and balanced processing (Walumbwa et al., 2008). These researchers found that authentic leadership had a positive correlation with employees' job satisfaction and productivity (Figure 8.10).

LEADERSHIP STYLES AND STAFF RESPONSES				
Authoritarian	Power Control Dictates	▪ I am higher than you and I will tell you what to do, how to do it, and when. ▪ Punitive ▪ Shaming	Threat Response ON	Stressed Working Fear of Errors Rigidity Stymied
Mindful	Influence Inspiration Guidance	▪ I have a different role than you. We all work together for the same goal and mutual benefit ▪ Instructive ▪ Empowering	Threat Response OFF	Rewarded Working Fluidity Creativity Autonomy Dopamine Stimulated

Figure 8.10

The style of authentic leaders tends to turn off the threat response and turn on engagement and seeking of rewards. Authentic leaders seek and appreciate the diversity of their staff. They possess emotional intelligence and know their own personal stories and those of their staff. These leaders are aware of the collective intelligence of their staff. They personalize assignments and focus development toward individual strengths and desires.

Authenticity gets communicated in both verbal and nonverbal ways. Authentic communications are honest, transparent, and genuine in nature and are consistent with one's stated values, ethics, and actions—what we mean by "walking one's talk." Authentic communication facilitates feelings of safety and flourishing relationships (Campbell, 2005). Because so much communication occurs below the surface, or in the nonconscious realm, between people, communication in the conscious realm is needed to correct and counteract misperceptions and misunderstandings. Here, we share an illustration of the importance of authentic communication—and what can happen when a manager may not be operating from a conscious realm—from a consultation we conducted a few years ago.

Sam was a mid-level manager at a county facility where a tremendous amount of the resources had been redirected to an emergent methamphetamine crisis in the community. The economy was slumping, and the county already had significant budget constraints, so caseloads were large and stress rampant in the organization. Sam had been informed by leadership that layoffs were imminent. Sam was concerned for his own viability at the agency but was mostly worried about his staff who would almost certainly be slated for layoffs. Sam's threat system was triggered. He was told by leadership not to discuss the situation with anyone, especially with his staff. Sam's typical defense against anxiety was avoidance. Sam began to avoid his staff as much as possible. Staff picked up their manager's anxiety and avoidance and sensed something was wrong. Employees' threat responses were now activated due to triggers of uncertainty and the unknown. They did not really know what was going on, but they all had their own stories and vulnerabilities. Fear and anxiety spread like wildfire through the department. Increased stress led to decreased productivity and increased absenteeism and sick days. Sam was emotionally tortured by anticipating the upcoming days when he would have to be the one to lay off his hard-working and dedicated employees. He knew of their personal stories, and the effects layoffs would have on their lives. All were deeply affected by the harsh reality of organizational politics and the larger effects of a changing economy, budgets, and social priorities.

The above case study is an unfortunate yet all too frequent reality. Employees can pick up nonverbal signs and signals and, in the absence of direct information, make their own interpretations. Nonverbal and nonconscious communications that are in contrast to what is verbalized can be confusing and stressful. Typically, authentic leaders communicate ethically and consistently across situations, which leads to the building of trust with their staff.

Sam was a compassionate leader and cared deeply about his staff. However, his communication style during the devastating time in the organization was lacking in authenticity and directness and therefore was misunderstood. Sam's relations with staff remarkably changed and his staff were confused. They ultimately blamed Sam for their situations once the layoffs arrived, and he bore the brunt of misplaced anger. His lack of communication made him appear disengaged and uncaring, though he was neither. Sam's dilemma can also be examined from a lens of the human need to blame or find a responsible party, which we do when we seek to reduce the anxiety of a threatening event. When we target an enemy in order to remove the threat, we may firmly believe that we have assigned guilt to the guilty, but sometimes it is our emotional region needing to restore safety too soon. Misidentification feels better than nonidentification—where uncertainty and unsafety can lurk. The situation may have been different had Sam known of his maladaptive reaction—the avoidance—and instead maintained his typical relationship and communication style. Our brains are designed to find the threat so we can restore safety and predictability. Those with more authoritarian management styles or with poor communication are ripe targets for blame.

Creating a context for the disclosure of an upcoming organizational crisis is important. Sam was in a bind. However, Sam could have expressed some of his own distress about work issues and acknowledged that they were interfering with his typical leadership style. Instead, he uncharacteristically withdrew, which created more uncertainty and anxiety. Adaptive leaders who practice authentic communication acknowledge and even predict future times of uncertainty and stress. Even if a bad event occurs without warning, the group is able to trust that relevant details will be shared when appropriate and as they become available. Otherwise, in addition to the environment feeling unsettled, employees may be concerned they are being lied to. Trust is compromised. The goal is to communicate with as much authenticity as reasonable at the point it becomes clear that staff perceives there is unrest in the organization. A group has a better chance of remaining cohesive and facing the crisis as a united team.

Leaders who have more authoritarian styles often do not practice authentic communication because they believe that it is not "staff's business" to share or be involved in the exclusive leadership realm of knowledge and strategy. Sometimes this can create suspicion and induce anxiety in staff. We usually do not need scientific research studies to inform us that we tend to like and feel most comfortable with warm, compassionate, and empathic leaders. However, we also need organizations to appreciate and compensate these types of leaders fully. An interesting study was conducted a few years ago which showed that though being nice lends itself to being liked at work, it does the opposite when it comes to wages, especially for males (Silverman, 2011)— "nice" or agreeable men earned an average of 18 percent less and same-traits females about 5 percent less. This is one of those nonconscious workaches that affects males more than females. Especially when threatened, our nonconscious bias for survival may favor aggression and incivility. Another factor may be that more aggressive males are more likely to intimidate during salary negotiations. Females have consistently been and continue to be paid less in wages than males for the same work (Pew Research Center, 2018). We must stay aware of biases and inequities toward all. As we have seen, the nonconscious can be manipulated greatly if survival is even misperceived as being threatened. Organizations must remain aware of this and consciously avoid rewarding aggression and authoritarianism in the workplace. Clear evidence shows the importance of civility and compassion.

We now have learned that the brain can change significantly once an individual has gained and sustained power over others. Science is neutral and assigns no blame. This is just how things happen up there. However, we do have responsibility. The human brain is capable of stepping back and gaining perspective on itself and others. Figure 8.11 suggests the brain process underlying an exchange between an authoritarian boss and vulnerable employee.

BRAIN TRIGGERS WITH AUTHORITARIAN BOSS

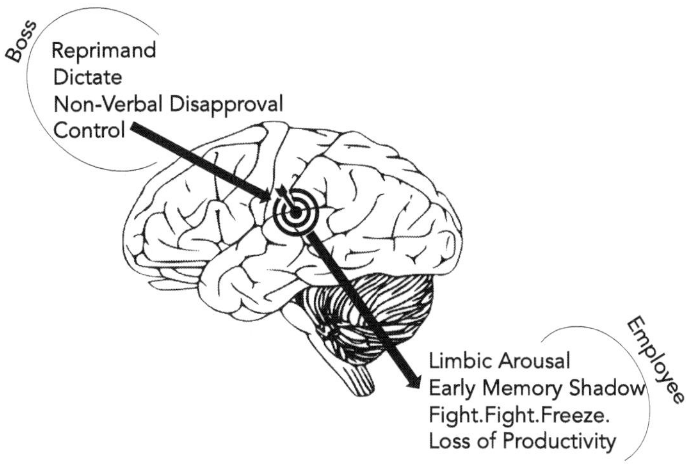

Figure 8.11

Leaders are responsible for staying aware of the possibility of these changes in themselves, such as diminished empathy and decreased collaboration.

Self-monitoring for any signs and symptoms of the hubris syndrome or other issues is essential. Self-reflection is a strength in a leader, and self-awareness is a characteristic of authentic leadership. The ability to hold oneself in ambivalence—occasionally questioning and not always knowing if one's decisions are sound, or if all relationships are in order—is considered a healthy trait. Certainly, at times leaders need to project images of invulnerability and empowerment. At others, modeling vulnerability and humility is more adaptive. Leaders with more adaptive leadership styles can often sense what aspect of their leadership style is needed given the situation at hand.

Occasionally, leaders forget what it was like to be line staff, the longer and higher they climb in the hierarchy. A great deal of space lies between the different layers of leadership and those working on the ground of an organization. Whereas the top layer of an organization can approach organizational missions from a more theoretical perspective, there is often a gap with those on the ground attempting to translate theory into practice. The television show, *Undercover Boss*, reveals the value of having those on the top of the hierarchy of an organization visit the ground where day-to-day work gets done. In most episodes, we witness the boss being deeply struck by situations that he or she is seeing and how hard staff work. Directly talking to staff who are on the ground level of an organization can yield highly useful data that often helps in identifying needs, barriers to service, blockades to accessing resources, and unreasonable expectations. When this type of learning extends beyond a reality television show, positive results emerge.

We encourage both leaders and individuals to remain in or return to TDM whenever the situation or experience is best served by wisdom leading emotions leading actions. The collective intelligence of our own brains (e.g., emotional and cognitive) and the collective intelligence of the diverse individuals within an organization can best be maximized within a context of compassion, encouragement, and engagement. Figure 8.12 illustrates the parallel process in both the organization of the mind and larger workplace system.

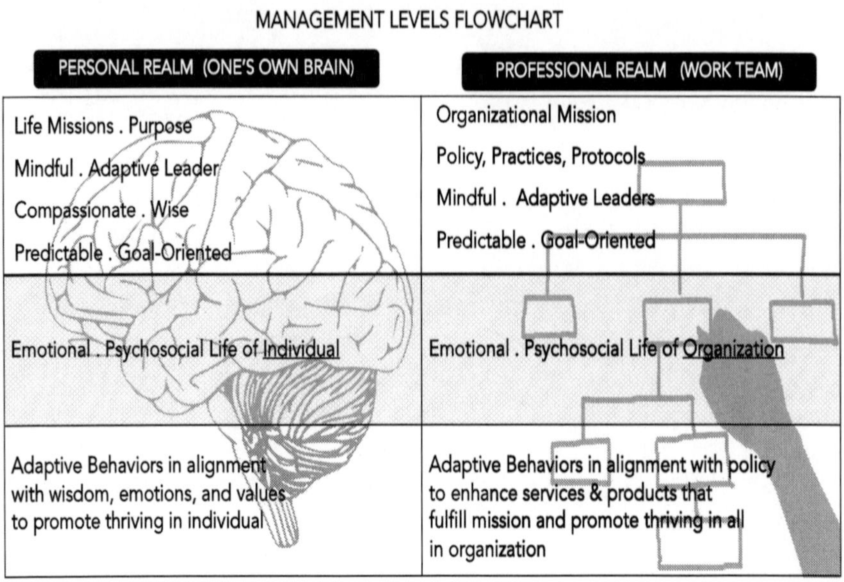

Figure 8.12

The same principles apply whether one is leading oneself or others. Optimal management includes recognizing: 1) each part of the system is needed and valuable; 2) hierarchy is based in the need for top-down management when there is disharmony, in order to coordinate different parts to fulfill a mission; 3) harmony in a system is facilitated by integration and communication; 4) healthy relationships between all parts of the system are crucial; and 5) beyond survival, the goal of the entire system (i.e., individual or organization) is to thrive.

Cooperation is typically better than competition when there is really no real threat to livelihood when completing work tasks. Figure 8.13 depicts the two paths when you do have a choice (remembering that the threat response turns on automatically when necessary). The goal is to return to the cooperative mode as soon as possible and to engage others in their cooperative mode as well.

WISDOM OF CHOOSING COOPERATION OVER COMPETITION

Figure 8.13

REFLECTION

Think about the times in your workday when you assess that you are in your cooperative mode (parasympathetic) versus competitive mode (sympathetic) system? Are there specific individuals who trigger different modes? What situations trigger different responses? If you drive to work, are you in your cooperative or competitive mode while driving? Fantasize about the difference of being in the driver's seat in the two different modes. Which feels better? Which feels safer? How about at work? Do you believe it is necessary to be in one mode over another? Are you able to bring yourself from a stress response to a relaxed response when you choose? Are you able to bring yourself from a relaxed state to a stressed state when you choose? Imagine yourself giving or receiving a performance evaluation in your relaxed state.

The Fine Line between Feedback and Humiliation

Learning about yourself through receiving the thoughts and reflections from another with whom you have a relationship is ideally part of cooperation and growth. Seeking constructive feedback and listening to concerns from staff is also an adaptive leadership trait. To learn from others, we must first create or restore relational safety. Feedback that is given while someone is in their threat mode is typically more aggressive. This type of feedback triggers the receiver's defenses and minimal learning or growth occurs.

> If someone is going to be a lifelong student of oneself, learning about one's identity in adulthood will often come from other people, not books. Healthy and cooperative relationships provide tremendous potential for growth. The nervous system, though, must be in its social-engagement versus threat mode in order to effectively learn.

We know that it takes brave subordinates to offer their leaders honest feedback. Most staff are unwilling to risk such ventures with their management. Perceived criticism triggers the threat response and leads to defensiveness, which shuts down openness and learning. Staying aware, even as a leader, that it is a strength to be a student of yourself and grow from feedback can counterbalance this defense. The delicate nature of feedback is evident in all directions in any hierarchy. Leaders too are vulnerable to defensive strategies that guard against feelings of inadequacy that sometimes disallow necessary growth and learning. Leaders can evolve from constructive feedback and the open expression of organizational concerns. Because of the intimidating nature of offering feedback to management, alternative methods of delivery have been developed and tested, such as conducting organizational culture surveys or ongoing 360 evaluations, which allow subordinates and colleagues an opportunity to provide an assessment of supervisors and managers (Forbes Human Resources Council, 2018). Management must assure anonymity to facilitate genuine responses and allow for editing to remove shaming aspects of responses. Both the receiving and offering of feedback is a sensitive endeavor for most. The goal of any feedback is to learn and thereby grow. We have seen, however, that once the brain perceives shame, learning is shut down and the feedback fails to be constructive, and at worst becomes destructive to the receiver as well as to the relationship between the giver and the receiver of feedback.

Feedback is fuel for learning and growth, and leaders can foster this by fulfilling the educator part of their leadership role. In order to stimulate growth and development in a team, leaders must offer feedback to staff on their performance, and more broadly, they must lead and organize the types and delivery methods of feedback in the workplace. There is an art to the offering (and receiving) of feedback without offending or triggering threat. Once the primitive brain takes it as a warning signal of disapproval from the group, the nonconscious fear of being cast off and perishing takes center stage. Defense processes take precedence. Most individuals become threatened and defensive in the face of perceived criticism, so how to provide useful feedback that staff will take in non-defensively should be an ongoing study for managers.

Constructive feedback can be misconstrued as criticism. Communication with each other in the workplace must be attuned to the individual and respectfully constructed so that the feedback may be thoughtfully considered, learned, and integrated. Otherwise, the communication triggers defensiveness. It can further backfire for the organization because the employee is now wounded and angry. Having employees give themselves evaluations, feedback, and professional development goals can sometimes minimize these reactions.

Robert Kegan has been a pioneering researcher in the field of professional development and has written extensively about the value and art of delivering feedback to others in a most adaptive manner. Dr. Kegan promotes a practice of instilling as early as the recruitment phase the belief that the organization wants to develop each employee's "best self" and will continually offer feedback toward that aim (Walsh, 2016). Holding this mindset from the beginning may initiate learning in people, since they will know the feedback is part of their relationship with management and is for the purpose of their own growth, professional development, and work enhancement (versus for punitive and shaming purposes) as below:

FEEDBACK → PART OF COMMUNICATIVE RELATIONSHIP FOR LEARNING, GROWING, AND PROFESSIONAL DEVELOPMENT → SOCIAL ENGAGEMENT SYSTEM (PARASYMPATHETIC) → LEARNING

FEEDBACK → PUNITIVE, EVALUATIVE, COMPARATIVE WITH COWORKERS, WHAT YOU NEED TO CHANGE, SHAMING → THREAT SYSTEM (SYMPATHETIC) → DEFENSE, NO LEARNING

When people know that they are being evaluating, it is natural to want to seek praise (reward chemicals) and to avoid criticism (threat chemicals). Learning is typically not the goal. "Performance learning" may have been a much better label than "performance evaluation" at work. Shifting the fundamental perception of a performance evaluation—from the boss either criticizing or complimenting to the boss attempting to share and teach about potential arenas for learning and growth—resets expectations. The mindset of the boss becomes: "I am neither here to shame you nor to praise you, I am here to help you learn and guide you toward agreed-upon work goals."

When shame floods learning environments, our brains defend against the anxiety of being inadequate. Future learning can be dampened when it is met with such a defense. Embarrassment, despair, and demoralization shut down learning, because protecting one's pride can become more important than openness to new ideas. Historical issues can also make it difficult to receive feedback, even if it is delivered constructively. When a work culture is set up to provide growth opportunities, managers ideally assess the optimal manner in which to offer feedback to each individual staff member.

Being open to learning and receiving feedback may be especially difficult for employees who experienced shame around their performance in Group 1 or 2. For instance, many brilliant employees, who also became brilliant leaders have childhood histories of what have been labeled learning disabilities. These labels have changed over the years, however, and many different forms of intelligence are now considered learning differences, rather than disabilities. However, often the shame associated with the label "disabled" may linger. An individual is not traditionally considered disabled if they are unable to build an engine. They merely do not possess the requisite spatial capabilities to perform this task. Building an engine (which requires nonverbal spatial reasoning) is not typically an academic measure. But if an individual is unable to perform basic math equations or read at a certain grade level, they are traditionally considered disabled. Academic performance measures are typically specific to what is valued in a society at any given time. A lack of success in school does not necessarily reflect deficient intellect; academic achievement does not necessarily correlate with intelligence. Often in counseling, those who have not done well in school, or have been labeled as academically disabled, struggle with unfounded beliefs about being "dumb." These feelings of inadequacy often follow individuals into the workgroup.

Dawn was a 48-year-old female who had worked her way up in information technology and computer programming in a public agency from entry-level to mid-level management. She aspired to continue advancing in her professional course but was terrified. Dawn had a secret. She was dyslexic and had severe difficulty with reading. Dawn had been terrorized in school. She had come from a small town where in third grade she was placed in special education due to poor academic performance. She was made to believe that she would be unable to complete college let alone become an expert in computer technology. Dawn's manager provided her with a referral to EAP for executive coaching as part of her individualized development plan (IDP). For the first time, Dawn shared her secret with her coach. Coaching sessions helped Dawn: 1) identify misunderstanding and lack of information about learning differences in her early school environment; 2) gain better understanding of the many different aspects of intelligence; and 3) own her intellectual strengths and talents. Dawn was eventually hired as the county's chief administrative officer.

Optimizing Work Environments: NeuroLeadership Model

We have seen that human affiliation and social connectedness are natural aspects of any human group. The workplace is rich in psychosocial experiences, needs, communications, perceptions, misperceptions, threats, rewards, and the full spectrum of emotions and feelings. This realm is much more than just a place to get work tasks completed. The workplace is a social system. And we have learned that the human brain treats social needs as necessary for survival. Social experiences translate into deep neural experiences within us. We may not be consciously aware of this, but our social brains are always operating based in our perceptions of ourselves with others. A prime assessment that we make is that of our relative status within the group.

Status and shame have a strong relationship. We know status is nonconsciously perceived as connected to survival by our primitive brain regions. Status is perceived as relative to another's status. Even someone with a socially high status is going to be triggered (threatened) by someone with a "higher" status. Status is on a never-ending hierarchy. The "totem-pole" never ends in this most primitive of contests. There can always be someone stronger, smarter, younger, richer, taller, faster, more powerful, more attractive, and more famous. The alpha always has a challenger just waiting to command that position. Humans are quite sensitive to their relative status in a group because of its prehistorical ties to survival, and shame is the response to a lowered status in a group.

Awareness of these aspects of status is the first step to managing it. Status is so important to us that the identical circuitry is activated whether we are competing with a computer, video games, ourselves (e.g., solitaire) or another human (Chiao, 2009). Because shame underlies many workaches and triggers the threat response, awareness of shame and status issues is a major step in leadership training and updating work culture. Devaluing a person does not motivate—it demoralizes and threatens, and sets up an unfortunate and defeating dynamic in the workforce.

Leaders who understand this very sensitive dynamic use their power, role, and afforded status to trigger reward versus threat. If an employee perceives that the leader's power will be used to promote and protect them, that is rewarding. If it is used to shame or overpower them, that is a threat. Leaders are faced with the incredibly difficult task of organizing the structure of an organization. Organizing individuals and functions in any system is essential and differentiation of roles inevitable. However, we must remain mindful of assigning different "status values" to the individuals who occupy these roles. In our society, each role comes with a different amount of pay, office location, and other perks. These inequalities trigger different feelings between people at work. We must strive to counterbalance the inherent inequities that come with hierarchical positions. The timepiece used earlier was used as an analogy for this same issue. The ideal goal is to have all valued as essential components of the same system.

Leaders who create fluid organizational structures that change based on the needs and missions at any given time are ideal. A parent in Group 1 may have to "pull rank" near a busy road and control the child. The parent may be able to flatten the hierarchy when the child is creatively exploring with crayons on paper. Rank or status can be irrelevant when all are cooperating and in harmony with the group. The concepts of attunement and fluidity are relevant again here. What we have seen in organizations that we have evaluated and reorganized is that staff are less triggered by role hierarchy than status hierarchy. Bottom line: there is no perfect organizational system that is going to fit every organization and member at every given time. A surfer recognizes this pattern in the ocean and fluidly adapts to the waves and never assumes the ocean will be the one to adapt. Organizational systems are always changing, and therefore styles of management and leadership that are fluid are most adaptive.

Understanding and managing our complex social arena can be facilitated by a simplified model. The research and strategies that have emerged from the NeuroLeadership Institute align well with concepts we have discussed in preceding chapters. Dr. David Rock, the founder of the Institute, has forged worldwide research and interest in the neuroscience behind human behavior at work and leadership development (Rock, 2009). He introduced the SCARF model of leadership in 2008, which integrates neuroscience research on human social behavior and leadership styles. SCARF is an acronym for the five domains identified as having remarkable impact on whether someone feels safe or unsafe at work (Figure 8.14). An online SCARF self-assessment can be taken at no cost. The SCARF model of leadership has been employed successfully in organizations across the globe.

We know that when people feel safe, their creative energies and talents are maximized. If they feel threatened, their energies go into defense or into protecting themselves. Rock and his associates have conducted many brain-imaging experiments that have confirmed that when subjects are treated poorly by others, they have the same neurobiological response that they would have if a predator were threatening their physical survival. When subjects are valued and feel socially connected, they have the same neurobiological response as if they were being offered food or nurturance. The SCARF domains identify arenas that influence behavior in the workplace that can set off our threat or reward systems. Increased employee motivation, engagement, and productivity have been shown in organizations sensitive to these domains.

SCARF MODEL FOR ORGANIZATIONS

Status is an employee's perceived importance as compared to others

Certainty involves the ability to predict the future

Autonomy is a sense of control by being offered choices at work

Relatedness involves perceptions of psychosocial safety in the group

Fairness is the perception of how equitable exchanges are in the group

Figure 8.14

When we examine the SCARF Model what becomes evident is that the above five factors are related to things that human beings create for one another in their relationships and groups. We do not have to rely on technology or natural events to create these qualities. We only have to rely on ourselves to promote and enhance these qualities at work. We have to build systems that are structured to do their best at creating a sense of importance for all who are a part, a level of predictability, a sense of self-control, and a perception of equality and equity for all.

A major goal in the development of the SCARF model was to assist leadership and management to structure psychosocial aspects of workplaces in a manner that helps employees feel safe. In Figure 8.15, we provide some examples of what leaders can do to enhance each domain. Awareness of these domains and associated behaviors can assist leaders and managers with minimizing perceived threats and maximizing the positive feelings associated with rewards.

STATUS
Offer public and private acknowledgment and praise
Provide opportunities for professional development
Be both a teacher (educate) and a student (ask questions, learn from) employee
Acknowledge and utilize specialized skills and expertise
Encourage participation in special events and outside opportunities

CERTAINTY
Create clear job roles and responsibilities
Share as much as possible about upcoming (good or bad) events
Break complicated projects into smaller discrete steps
Predict hypothetical future events and their potential address and outcomes
Communicate clear expectations for projects, meetings, and group events
Share what will remain the same during organizational changes and transitions

AUTONOMY
Allow employees some flexibility around work stations and areas
Offer expectations but provide flexibility around work tasks whenever possible
Provide employees options around work schedule
Allow staff to choose from professional training options
Provide latitude around work choices whenever possible

RELATEDNESS
Promote mentorship and sharing of talents in groups
Encourage relationship building across organization
Respect individual differences in relating (e.g., introverted vs. extroverted styles)
Connect employees with the organization's mission, values, and purpose
Reveal the relationship that each employee has to the organization and community at large
Connect in person or personalize electronic communications whenever possible

FAIRNESS
Communicate the unique value of each member of the organizational team
Allocate rewards with clear criteria and equitable distribution
Share your rationale behind difficult and impactful decisions
Provide equal room for each individual's responses and feelings
Ensure equal access to organizational information when possible
Equally protect and promote each individual's place and voice within the organization

Figure 8.15

Employee Assistance Program as an Organizational Essential

Even adaptive organizations with authentic management and well-written policies and practices are not expected to be able to predict and address all that emerges in staff and the organization as a whole. Workaches that emerge along with issues that employees bring with them are beyond the scope and wheelhouse of most employers. This is where Employee Assistance Programs (EAPs) come in. As we described in Chapter 2, EAPs are confidential on- or off-site counseling programs for employees that provide a range of benefits from mental health counseling to organizational consultation and executive coaching. People-centered organizations are discovering that it is cost effective to promote and care for employee well-being. Many benefits of EAPs have been documented to date, (Richmond, 2017), including those listed in Figure 8.16:

EMPLOYEE ASSISTANCE PROGRAM BENEFITS

Increased productivity
Decreased absenteeism and presenteeism
Reduction in disability claims
Reduction in healthcare costs
Reduction in workers compensation claims
Improvement in organizational morale
Increased engagement in employees & supervisors
Increased preparedness for critical events
Improvement in employee retention
Increased attraction for new employees
Attractive return on investment (ROI) for employers
Improvement in organizational wellness
Improvement in conflict resolutions

Figure 8.16

There are three basic types of EAP models—external, internal, and hybrid. The internal model has EAP staff on site that are employees of the organization. The external model is when an organization contracts with an outside vendor to deliver EAP services utilizing community counselors and crisis support specialists. The hybrid model is a customized blend of both internal and external resources. Each of these models is based on promoting the social and emotional health of employees and organizations, but one may be a better fit for an organization than another (Pompe et al., 2017). Here, we focus on internal and external EAP models.

Both types of EAPs typically offer both prevention and intervention services. Depending on a particular EAP's mission, it can house varied programs that are designed to attend to the concerns and needs of all employees that may not be addressed anywhere else in the organization. One such program is organizational well-being. These programs exponentially increased after the Affordable Care Act provided economic incentives for employers to offer such programs. Programs and services can be offered to individuals as well as larger groups such as whole units or departments.

INTERNAL EAP

ADVANTAGES	DISADVANTAGES
Ease of onsite private offices and timely access	Confidentiality concerns / visibility in seeking services
EAP staff direct awareness of on-site agency, culture, morale, trends, changes, stressors	Administrative and staffing concerns
Breadth of customized services and programs adapted to current needs and management consultations	Conflict of interest concerns / questions and perceptions of who EAP serves—employee or employer
Immediate response for threat assessments, violence prevention, crisis and critical incident interventions, post-trauma response	Difficulty with securing private and protected on-site EAP physical locations

Figure 8.17

In his article, "An Internal EAP Might Still Be Right for Your Organization," Pompe states that an internal EAP core service model includes a breadth of services that are customized to the needs of the HHS culture. This model provides a timelier response to employee needs, and clinicians typically possess greater insight into the organizational culture. Because the EAP staff are HHS employees, their mission is also to adapt services to the ever-changing organizational climate and culture. Although internal EAPs also offer counseling services, their staffing typically includes both clinical and organizational specialists. Therefore, they are able to offer many more services than external EAPs. Most internal EAPs also provide emergency response, violence prevention, threat assessments, sexual harassment interventions, trauma-informed practice education, mediation, group facilitation, and resiliency and well-being programming.

EXTERNAL EAP

ADVANTAGES	DISADVANTAGES
Potential cost containment	Decreased familiarity with organizational culture and needs
Larger pool and diversity of counselors from which to choose and increased availability for family members	Reduced accessibility to timely services or employees having opportunities to drop in during breaks
Increased perceptions of confidentiality and fewer privacy concerns	More depersonalized sense of access and connection to caring relationship
Fewer conflict of interest potentials	Less internal organizational support

Figure 8.18

The internal EAP is unfortunately no longer the dominant model in most organizations (Frey et al., 2018). As we outlined above, each model comes with its unique advantages and disadvantages, and one size does not fit all. However, a major loss that we have witnessed with the decline of internal EAPs is the loss of identifiable individuals within the organization who consistently staff the EAP. These individuals are available to the workforce (Group 3) to consistently and reliably assist with diverse issues and offer varied services such as stress reduction, education, and counseling. EAP professionals that are on site can offer caring, familiar, trusted, and reliable relationships.

We have also installed what we have labelled Manager Assistance Programs (MAP) in HHS organizations which exclusively serve management. We started this practice after managers reported to us that they felt uncomfortable seeking and receiving services from their EAP. Manager assistance includes organizational consultations to leadership, management, and supervisors. Issues can range from departmental team issues to problem employees. All organizational roles are occupied by humans and all roles come with their unique psychosocial challenges. No human or role is immune.

Working Out Workaches at Work

We need not judge workaches, we just need to address them. We consider it essential that there are individuals within an organization dedicated to the identification and mitigation of workaches. If employing such individuals is unfeasible, seeking outside resources is important. As an example, for workaches fueled by unconscious bias, there is a powerful educational resource called the "Check Your Blindspots." This is a mobile program touring the nation which offers participants the use of multimedia technology to see their unconscious biases in action. Participants use virtual reality to explore being in the "shoes" of different others and have opportunities to pledge actions for change. This tour is sponsored by the CEO Action for Diversity & Inclusion which is an organization working for diversity and inclusion in the workforce (ceoaction.com, 2019). These types of resources facilitate organizations staying current and active in employee engagement and the address of all types of workaches.

Questioning oneself (without judgment) facilitates self-exploration and understanding. With our conscious minds we "fish" in the sea of our nonconscious for possibilities. Questioning or being a student of oneself can lead to adaptive and enriching change and growth which contribute to thriving in this existence.

REFLECTION

Think privately about human traits that might annoy or scare you. How do you handle these feelings? Do you avoid these people? Do you think they can tell how you feel about them? What are some of your thoughts or bodily sensations when you are near people who have these traits? What are your conscious biases—the ones you are aware of? What might be your unconscious biases? How have they emerged (overtly or covertly) with people you work with? Do you think your family of origin had these same biases? Do you possess any of the traits for which you yourself have bias?

The Power Is in the Relationship

The value of relationships in the workplace, unfortunately, is not easy to calculate or quantify. Many employers are just now gaining awareness of the financial value in allotting time, money, and other resources to facilitating healthy interpersonal relations in their workforce. Supervisors and managers are not typically coached to develop relationships with their staff. Sometimes management is tentative and apprehensive about forming these relationships. A warm alliance with appropriate boundaries as a professional relationship with all staff members does not imply an inappropriate personal relationship. In previous chapters, we learned about the importance of relationships for optimal brain functioning. Time is allotted to many different tasks in the workplace. Time is carved out to complete performance evaluations (which are often experienced as threatening to people), but not necessarily for relationship building (which is often rewarding to people). In Chapter 2, we described the value of attunement as one of the four "A's" in the development of humans and relationships. The relevant translational aspect of attunement is paying attention to the other and inquiring about relevant aspects of being and doing. Examples in the different developmental groups include a parent who inquired about your interests to discover how to promote your unique identity; a teacher who inquired about how you learned best to teach you best; and, a boss who asks how you are doing or what you need. These types of attuned inquiries promote an individual's thriving in a group, and they are part of relationship building.

Here, we offer an example in healthcare of the difficult issue of getting employers to recognize the value of human relations in patient care and even in relation to their bottom line. The quality versus quantity issue is illuminated here. Patient-doctor relationships are not billable procedures and, perhaps partially due to this, relationships are not recognized as essential to care. However, there is a new movement in the medical field with physicians. With the advent of the computer and electronic medical records, we began to observe doctors addressing their patients while looking at their computer screen. Furthermore, with managed care reducing the time allotted to each patient and the need to document visits, we witnessed the diminishing of the relationship with the patient, evidenced for example, in a loss of eye contact and undivided attention. Contact with the computer in the visit appeared to some patients to be more important than contact with them. Yet we know that the physician-patient relationship is vital to patient care (Tingley, 2018). The Comprehensive Care Program at the University of Chicago, launched in 2012 and built on the ongoing research of a physician at the forefront of evolving medical care, has yielded data that are already pointing to the value of the doctor-patient relationship (Easton, 2018). The researchers wanted to know if having the same physician through medical visits and hospitalizations was better than seeing multiple, random physicians during these visits and stays. The study data has already revealed that the personal relationship model, in which one patient receives care from one physician consistently, lowers hospitalization rates and improves care. Depersonalization of the physician, while it may help hospitals serve more patients and increase profits, does not appear to be the best solution for care. Adults fare better if they see the physician with whom they have a relationship rather than any available provider. One remedy has been to free up physicians from having to chart. Some medical organizations are hiring medical scribes (people who chart for physicians) so physicians can have more face-to-face time with patients to promote the relationship.

Adults need healthy relationships too. This intervention correlates with the neuroscientific findings regarding the importance of relationships and attachments. Our human brain has evolved to be quite social and connected to others. The foundation of this connection is the human-to-human relationship.

Reinventing the Wheel: Resisting Resistance

As creative as humans are, we are also resistant to change and fear the unknown and unpredictable. We now know the different brain regions that come into conflict with each other when it comes to the "known versus unknown," "exploration versus staying safe," and "change versus no change." Below, we explore changes in design and policy that resulted in positive and adaptive evolution in two different systems. These examples highlight our points about continually assessing and updating policies and procedures.

The old saying, "don't reinvent the wheel," may have emerged from the less creative, resource-conserving, and more frightened region of the human brain. In fact, the wheel has been reinvented recently. Due to this change, many soldiers on the ground are now safer because they can maneuver their vehicles out of places that traditional wheeled vehicles could not. The Defense Advanced Research Projects Agency (DARPA) of the United States military redesigned the wheel on some combat vehicles. The teams that did this had to dismiss the cognitive force of not even believing it should or could be reinvented. This cognitive readjustment may have been the more difficult feat than actually creating the specific mechanics of the new wheel itself. They had to get beyond a belief system or a mindset, which we know is very difficult to do. When systems have been in place and operating the same way for a long time, it becomes difficult to envision them differently and to execute change (Diaz, 2018).

DON'T REINVENT THE WHEEL

PLEASE DO REINVENT THE WHEEL

The Las Vegas police department (LVMPD) is another example of reinventing the wheel based in need and in updated research findings. After remarkable numbers of officer-involved shootings, the department instituted a massive investigation which ultimately resulted in the "Collaborative Reform Model" in 2014. The recommendations in this report emerged from research studies, multiple and varied conversations across disciplines, and in-depth assessments of policing tactics and strategies (Fachner & Carter, 2014).

The LVMPD is a great model of an organization that reexamined their policies and procedures. Some of the pilot programs and policy changes they have employed illustrate a number of translations of the concepts we have reviewed in *Workaches*. We have discussed the importance of TDM in the management of our own brains and those of others. TDM is of utmost importance to individuals who work in fields such as law enforcement. When someone spits in your face, commits a crime, or threatens your survival in some other way, a temporary loss of TDM is predictable. Some will lose it longer than others, but all will lose it for at least a few milliseconds. If you are chasing the suspect, by the time you apprehend them, your brain will have changed. During this time, the suspect has likely been categorized by your primitive brain regions as dangerous—of the out-group—and potentially has been dehumanized as a threatening object. This reactive time period, however long or short, is full of risks. In both the fleeing subject and the pursuing officer, we can predict the threat response will be active, with full limbic engagement. The risks from bias, stress, and emotional reactivity will be at their highest during this period.

One of the critical policy revisions in the LVMPD that was implemented as a pilot program in 2011, even before the Collaborative Reform Model, was a change in foot pursuit policy. An investigation revealed that a high percentage of use-of-force incidents happened immediately after foot pursuits. The investigators concluded that "adjusting the situation so that the officers experiencing an adrenaline-pumping chase were not the ones to go 'hands-on' with a possible criminal should help police from succumbing to identity traps." So, LVMPD required that, whenever possible, the pursuing officer would not be the arresting officer. The LVMPD saw a 23-percent reduction in the use of force the following year. The LVMPD went from being one of the deadliest police forces in America to a role model as a law enforcement agency.

This story vividly exemplifies the importance of clear policy and procedures. It also points to the importance of training that anticipates difficult situations. High-stress interactions with clients and customers is an arena where VR can be useful. Virtual trainings for predicted interactions that have formulaic behavioral procedures to follow can help to build and strengthen neuropathways before unfortunate reactive behaviors occur in human interactions.

The Road Forward: Organizational Evolution

Humans have difficulty not following already laid footprints, as we are often suspicious of the unprecedented and unexplored. We can see and thereby better predict a path that someone else has taken—or that we ourselves have taken many times, such as with a habit. Both individuals and organizations can become threatened by the unknown and thereby favor the familiar. However, we know that if we choose to pursue creativity and thriving, we must forge some new paths and take a different journey. We must continue to examine and reexamine work and all it entails in order to move it from being a place to just survive to one in which to thrive. Australia has emerged as a leader in innovating and evolving its work culture and in creating cutting-edge programs for not only the physical health, but also the psychosocial health of its workforce (Safe Work Australia, 2016). Studies there have shown that prioritizing employees' psychosocial well-being and emotional health have resulted in significant economic gains for organizations (Zadow et al., 2017).

Organizational cultures can progress and evolve. But they can also devolve. The system must be continually assessed for mobility and fluidity. An evolving organization grows and progresses, and growth can become the norm that members look forward to. However, like any system, if there is a threat that enters and spreads through the organization, cultural evolution stops: organizations can "go backwards." Any system can go from thriving to not even surviving. We have even seen this in cultures that have been thriving for long periods of time. If, for example, a new leader enters who makes immediate and unannounced changes, this is perceived as a threat, and we can see ripple effects throughout the system. The organization is thrown out of balance, and we can see a very different work environment where trust, feelings of control, and cohesion can quickly break down.

Ongoing assessment of employee perceptions and satisfaction is therefore recommended, given the transient nature of the threat system that can be turned on at any point and change everything. Organizational coherency and harmony are never static—in the sense that once it is present, it stays, because one change (e.g., new rule or manager) can shift the system out of balance and cause it to become quite a different system.

The system must be committed to continually achieving and re-achieving a balanced and evolving level of growth.

PROMOTING ORGANIZATIONAL GROWTH

ENGAGING GROWTH MINDSET AT ONBOARDING
LISTENING SESSIONS TO PROMOTE STAYING
QUICK SURVEYING
FORMALIZED ASSESSMENTS
SUBGROUP DISCUSSIONS
MIXED DEPARTMENT COLLABORATIONS
EDUCATION ON MISSION & CULTURE
CREATION OF ENVIRONMENT SAFE FOR SHARING
EXIT INTERVIEWS

Figure 8.19

We end this section by revisiting the concept of growth mindset. A growth mindset captures a key message of *Workaches*, which is to utilize cutting-edge information and concepts from science to continue to evolve adaptively, both as individuals and as organizations. Carol Dweck (2006) introduced the concept, based on her research, that people differ in how they think about themselves in terms of successes and failures. Those who have a growth mindset believe that they can learn from so-called failures, grow, and develop. They do not fear failure or feedback because they see it as part of the path of learning. Other individuals, who have what Dweck labels as fixed mindsets, hold more rigid beliefs and see their abilities and intelligence as fixed quantities; this belief holds them back from developing further. Dweck has extended these ideas to groups and organizations. Grant, Cox, and Rock (2016) of the NeuroLeadership Institute have furthered Dweck's ideas as they apply to the workplace. They highlight the impact of a growth mindset on learning, performance, self-regulation or TDM, resilience, and leadership. Organizations are encouraged to stimulate growth mindsets in their employees. All of these processes are becoming part of evolving organizations that have a commitment in their workplace culture to continually improve, adapt, and remain current. Remaining current means keeping up not only with the latest technology, but also with cutting-edge research suggesting organizational values such as compassion, authenticity, integrity, equality, and fairness are best practices for organizations.

In Chapter 2, we briefly described cultural evolution and its rapid pace in our technological society. Just as with other evolutionary changes, some individuals go first in adapting to the new. We certainly need these highly adaptable individuals to execute all the technology. On the other hand, some people are slower to adapt or cannot adapt. We need diversity in the workplace, and cultural evolutionary diversity offers this. A great and growing divide exists between those who are digital natives, digital immigrants, and those that are neither. The great variability among staff in digital and technical savvy can be based in age or areas of interests and strengths. We listed technology as a workache because it threatens many individuals in terms of pace, ability, and their chances to be competitive. However, we can also view this issue from a lens of growth. Figure 8.20 displays the ages of individuals we find in a typical workplace.

WHO IS AT WORK?

GENERATION	BIRTH YEARS (approximate)
Generation Z / Nexters	2000s–today
Millennials	1980s–2000s
Generation X	Late 1960s–1980s
Baby Boomers	1946–1964
Silent Generation/Traditionalists	1928–1945
Greatest Generation	Before 1928

Figure 8.20

Generational diversity brings challenges and therefore growth opportunities to the workplace. Organizational evolution requires updates in what is attractive to all generations in the workplace. A core element of evolving is being able to continually look at things anew—and to consider the benefits of both the new and old, because different generations add to the collective intelligence of a workplace. So, we do want to be able to reinvent the wheel, but also to put back the old one when it is most adaptive. In other words, we ultimately benefit from diversity in the workplace.

The Simple Beneath the Complex

At this point in *Workaches*, we have offered many words in our attempt to understand and improve human relationships at work. A major aspect of our mission was to identify those aspects of work relations that detract from our work and create obstacles to deriving the deepest satisfaction and thriving from what we do for so much of our day and lives. We called these detractions and obstacles workaches. We have searched back in time, inside the depths of the brain, and into the work organization. We even looked inside our first two developmental groups—family and school. We have uncovered wonderful knowledge and advances in our understanding of how humans operate.

Nonetheless, we return to realize that we know less than we thought. Together, we must continue to wonder, guess, think, reflect, communicate, and stimulate ideas to keeping working on further discovery of who we are and how we operate most optimally. We need to know one another. We need to know ourselves. Much depends on our relationships to others and ourselves. And as we continue to gain the technologies that facilitate incredible advances, we must remember that much is "personal," because, as we have learned, the dominant nonconscious areas of our brains are relationship oriented and emotionally driven. Our brains are sculpted by the personal relationships we have with one another. We are not machines, yet. We need to treat ourselves and be treated as vulnerable and sensitive beings who need other people for our self-esteem and fulfillment. We need to discriminate between when and where our wondrous technology is helping us and where it is hurting us. We must step from behind our machines to engage each other as people, not objects.

Human relationships and conflicts are a natural part of human relating. Conflicts in the family, classroom, and at work will exist. As we have seen, some of the dynamics of our conflicts will be in our conscious awareness, but most will be out of our awareness. Some of these conflicts will have nothing really to do with the person we are fighting with, others will. Some of our competitive dynamics will have more to do with a primitive ancestor than our coworker.

The complexity of the dynamics of human relations is a natural wonder. We can annoy those we like and charm those we dislike. We can marry someone we once hated. We can divorce someone we once loved. What an odyssey!

With emergent technology, some arenas for human conflict may come to an end, such as on highways. We are likely to witness the end of road rage as humans give up the wheel and move to the back seat with driving. The nonconscious and more primitive behaviors that emerge on highways, especially crowded ones, are where people have no relationships with one another. This lack of relationship further facilitates an environment ripe for projections, misperceptions, and acts of interpersonal aggression. But the new self-driving vehicles are not being programmed to engage in primitive struggles for survival that elicit shame and rage. They are being constructed without a threat system. Their fuel will wisely be used just to get us safely from point A to B. When we have relationships—rather than the anonymity of the road—like in the workplace, we may have the same dynamics triggered as we do while on the road. However, when these same dynamics are held within a relationship, they are typically managed quite differently. Relationships matter. Optimizing work organizations and enhancing employee experiences and engagement translate into improving relationships.

Forward-looking employers are creating better relationships with their employees. They are blazing trails toward updated and evolved ways of working in contemporary society. Both individuals and organizations stand to benefit from these innovations and updates. Workaches of all kinds are being measured and examined with the intention of increasingly and more adaptively addressing them in the workplace. With threats minimized and rewards maximized, employee engagement, creativity, and productivity, along with work satisfaction, can only increase. Communication (verbal and nonverbal) is vital in relationships. Wise and compassionate communications are key to establishing and maintaining thriving relations. Additionally, wise and compassionate self-talk is essential to internally "talk us through" what we have to externally "walk us through" in our work environment.

The secret is in the relationship—the one you have with yourself and others.

We must seek social rewards versus threats in order to enjoy work and thrive. Otherwise, our energies are going into surviving and competing and stressing which do not feel good. Work can be recovered as a meaningful, enhancing, and mutually rewarding experience. Younger generations are actually seeking to work more similarly to our primitive ancestors rather than how older generations have been working. For example, Gen Z individuals in general want more flexibility in hours and work spaces. They want a better sense of meaning or purpose in what they are doing. Gen Z individuals want friendlier or more social work environments, but prefer to work more independently than collaboratively. And although they are digital natives, they prefer in-person dialogues over those conducted over electronic devices (Patel, 2017). Younger generations want, and more and more will require, better work-life integration or less division between working and living. We envision this too.

Work is a major vehicle for participating in and creating the world at large. Each work task, whatever it may be, impacts the group in ways that are untraceable into the future. Work contributions are timeless. If we step back in time, just once more, and look at the builders of the pyramids in Egypt we see their wondrous creations, yet very tragic stories as workers. Most were treated poorly, and many died during construction in work accidents. X-rays of their skeletal remains have revealed arthritis, dislocated bones, and lower vertebrae compressions that document the perils of their labor. We wish that those who built these amazing structures could have somehow had perspective on what they were doing and been enriched by their own work. They were not afforded this possibility—many did not survive, let alone thrive. The relationship their leader or employer (pharaoh) had with them was one of "I and It" versus "I and Thou," in the words of philosopher Martin Buber (Buber, 1923). Buber described the "I and Thou" relationship as one of mutual bonding in which the other person is viewed and experienced as valuable and unique. He described the "I and It" relationship as one in which the other person is perceived and used like an object and is not viewed as a valuable, unique, and worthy human being. Valuing work contributions implies valuing the individuals doing the work.

We offer our work to others and receive theirs. We benefit from the tangibles produced and services provided that we share with one another through what we do. I may not remember the name of the social worker who intervened in my family's dysfunction, but she gave me a gift for my lifetime. These mutual gifts are often given between mere strangers in order to create, help, heal, preserve, rescue, entertain, save, amuse, enhance, and fulfill each other's lives. We are intertwined by work into one connected system, albeit a human and therefore complicated and convoluted one! We collectively work to eliminate more and more of the pain and adversity. We work for and with each other to just make things better in this existence, for all. The secret is in the relationship. Here's to thriving at work.

"Work is love made visible."

—Kahlil Gibran

APPENDIX A

Workaches Resources: Trauma and Healing Sites

The American Academy of Experts in Traumatic Stress	aaets.org
American Red Cross Disaster Services	redcross.org
Association of Traumatic Stress Specialists	atss.info
Center for the Study of Traumatic Stress	cstsonline.gov
Center for Culture, Trauma and Mental Health Disparities	semel.ucla.edu/cctmhd
Greater Good Science Center	greatergood.berkeley.edu
The International Critical Incident Stress Foundation, Inc.	icisf.org
International Society for the Study of Trauma and Dissociation	issd.org
The International Society for Traumatic Stress Studies	istss.org
International Trauma Training Institute	traumaonline.net
Vicarious Trauma Toolkit	vtt.ovc.ojp.gov/tools-for-victim-services

APPENDIX B

National Resources for Protections at Work

U.S. Commission on Civil Rights	usccr.gov
U.S. Department of Justice Civil Rights Division	usdoj.gov/crt
U.S. Department of Labor	dol.gov
Occupational Safety and Health Administration	osha.gov
Employee Benefits Security Administration (EBSA)	dol.gov/ebsa
U.S. Equal Employment Opportunity Commission (EEOC) National Headquarters	eeoc.gov
U.S. Merit Systems Protection Board	mspb.gov
The National Institute for Occupational Safety and Health (NIOSH)	cdc.gov

APPENDIX C

Resources for Stress Reduction and Thriving

Provider Resilience app	hprc-online.org
Breathe2Relax app	breathe2relax.soft112.com
Center for Healthy Minds	centerhealthyminds.org
Jon Kabat-Zinn	Wherever You Go, There You Are: Mindfulness Meditation in Everyday Life
Greater Good Science Center	ggsc.berkeley.edu
University of Pennsylvania Positive Psychology Center	authentichappiness.sas.upenn.edu
UCLA Mindful Awareness Research Center	uclahealth.org
Insight Timer app	insighttimer.com
The American Institute of Stress	stress.org

APPENDIX D

Workaches Screening Inventory (WSI)

Using the scale below please check a number (from 1-5) for each statement below that best reflects your experience at your current job:

Strongly Disagree	Disagree	Neutral	Agree	Strongly Agree
1	2	3	4	5

	1	2	3	4	5
1 I feel part of a team or group at my workplace					
2 I generally feel physically safe at work					
3 I generally feel psychologically safe at work					
4 There are people that I can trust at work					
5 My job gives me meaning and satisfaction					
6 People gossip about me at work					
7 My work stress comes from supervising others					
8 I worry about my physical appearance at work					
9 I feel stressed traveling to work					
10 My organization promotes my professional advancement					
11 My work defines a large part of my identity					
12 My physical health suffers due to my job					
13 Stress reduction options are available at my workplace					
14 I have been sexually harassed at work					

	1	2	3	4	5
15 I feel most stressed at the end of my workday					
16 I feel humiliated or shamed by my bosses					
17 My work stress comes from relating to management					
18 My organization takes bias and discrimination seriously					
19 I have someone at work that I can seek guidance from					
20 Leadership cares about my well-being					
21 My work stress comes from relating to clients / customers					
22 I feel out of place or different than others at work					
23 My personal life suffers due to my work					
24 I am not given opportunities for growth and development					
25 If had to pick again, I would re-choose this workplace					
26 I feel as competent as my coworkers					
27 I cover up a great deal of who I really am at work					
28 My coworkers and I are treated equally					
29 I am compensated fairly for the work I do					
30 I feel valued and respected at work					
31 My feelings often get hurt at work					

	1	2	3	4	5
32 At times work reminds me of how I felt in my family growing up					
33 I have been bullied at work					
34 Sometimes I feel frustrated and angry at work					
35 I worry about losing my job					
36 Relating to others at work makes me anxious					
37 Witnessing the suffering in those I serve brings me down					
38 I feel burned out at work					
39 Sometimes I feel out of control at work					
40 Most days I feel overwhelmed by my job duties or workload					
41 My work is valuable and meaningful to the community					
42 Feedback and evaluations make me anxious					
43 I cannot wait to leave this organization					
44 My coworkers make hurtful comments about others					

Please tell us about yourself by writing in or circling the most appropriate group with whom you currently identify. Please feel free to leave blank any questions you prefer not answer.

GENDER IDENTIFICATION: ______________________________

BIRTH YEAR: Before 1928 1928-1945 1946-1964 1965-1985 1986-1999 2000 or after

WORK ROLE: Line-staff Supervisor Manager Leader

TOTAL HOURS WORKED PER WEEK: ____ (include time spent working at home)

Thank you for your participation. *Preliminary Version WSI ©2019

REFERENCES

American Psychiatric Association. (2013). *Diagnostic and statistical manual of mental disorders (5th ed).* Arlington, VA: American Psychiatric Publishing.

American Time Use Survey (ATUS). (2017). *Bureau of Labor Statistics.* Retrieved from https://www.bls.gov/news.release/pdf/atus.pdf.

Anda, R. F., Felitti, V. J., Bremner, J. D., Walker, J. D., Whitfield, C. H., Perry, B. D., Dube, S. R. & Giles, W. H. (2005). The enduring effects of abuse and related adverse experiences in childhood. *European Archives of Psychiatry and Clinical Neuroscience, 256*(3), 174-186. doi:10.1007/s00406-005-0624-4

Anderson, C., & Brion, S. (2014). Perspectives on power in organizations. *Annual review of organizational psychology and organizational behavior, vol. 1,* 67-97. https://doi.org/10.1146/annurev-orgpsych-031413-091259

Anderson, C., & Kilduff, G. J. (2009). The pursuit of status in social groups. *Current Directions in psychological science, 18*(5), 295-298. doi:10.1111/j.1467-8721.2009.016 55.x

Anderson, C., & Kilduff, G. J. (2009). Why do dominant personalities attain influence in face-to-face groups? The competence-signaling effects of trait dominance. *Journal of Personality and Social Psychology, 96*(2), 491-503. doi:10. 1037/a0014201

Aquino, K., & Thau, S. (2009). Workplace victimization: Aggression from the target's perspective. *Annual Review of Psychology, 60*(1), 717-741. doi:10.1146/annurev.psych.60.110707.163703

Aron, E. (1997). *The highly sensitive person: How to thrive when the world overwhelms you.* New York, NY: Broadway Books.

Ballard, J. (2015). *Decoding the workplace: 50 keys to understanding people in organizations.* Santa Barbara, CA: Praeger Publishing.

Banaji, M. R., & Greenwald, A. G. (2016). *Blindspot: Hidden biases of good people.* New York, NY: Delacorte Press.

Bandura, A. (1997). *Self-efficacy: The exercise of control.* New York: WH, Freeman.

Bandura, A. (2012). On the functional properties of perceived self-efficacy revisited. *Journal of Management, 38*(1), 9-44. doi:10.1177/0149206311

Baron-Cohen, S. (2012). *The Science of evil: On empathy and the origins of cruelty.* New York, NY: Basic Books.

Bateson, G. (2000). *Steps to an ecology of mind.* Chicago, IL: The University of Chicago Press.

Baumeister, R. F., Bratslavsky, E., Finkenauer, C., & Vohs, K. D. (2001). Bad is stronger than good. *Review of General Psychology, 5*(4), 323-370. doi:10.1037//1089-2680.5.4.323

Beauchamp, G. (2014). *Social predation: How group living benefits predators and prey.* Elsevier: Academic Press.

Beck, J. (2014). *New research says there are only four emotions.* Retrieved from https://www.theatlantic.com/health/ archive/2014/02/new-research-says-there-are-only-four-emotions/283560/

Becher, H., Dollard, M. F., Smith, P., & Li, J. (2018). Predicting circulatory diseases from psychosocial safety climate: A prospective cohort study from Australia. *Int J Environ Res Public Health, 15*(3), 415. doi:10.3390/ijerph15 030415

Bell, T. (2019). This bot judges how much you smile during your job interview. Retrieved from https://www.fastcomp any.com/

Bender, J. (2013). *What are the differences between PTS and PTSD?* Retrieved from brainline.org.

Benson, H., Greenwood, M. M., & Klemchuk, H. (1975). The relaxation response: Psychophysiologic aspects and clinical applications. *The International Journal of Psychiatry in Medicine, 6*(1-2): 87-98. doi:10.2190/376w-e4mt-qm6q-houm.

Berlin, H. A., & Koch, C. (2009). Neuroscience meets psychoanalysis. *Scientific American Mind, 20*(2), 16-19.

Bernieri, F. (2000). *The importance of first impressions in a job interview.* Chicago, IL: Conference: Midwestern Psychological Association.

Bachelard, G. (1999). Water and dreams: An essay on the imagination of matter (Blachelard translation series). Dallas Instit Humanities & Culture.

BLS. (2019). *United States Bureau of Labor Statistics.* Retrieved from https://www.bls.gov/

Bock, L. (2016). *Work Rules! Insights from inside Google that will transform how you live and lead.* New York, NY: Twelve.

Bonanno, G. A., & Mancini, A. D. (2011). Toward a lifespan approach to resilience and potential trauma. *Resilience and Mental Health: Challenge Across the Lifespan.* New York, NY: Cambridge University Press.

Books, E. (2015). *Mindset by Carol S. Dweck, Ph. D. key takeaways, analysis & review: The new psychology of success.* Scotts Valley, CA: CreateSpace.

Bremner, J. D. (Ed.). (2016). *Posttraumatic stress disorder: From neurobiology to treatment.* San Francisco, CA: Wiley-Blackwell.

Brockhouse, R., Msetfi, R. M., Cohen, K., & Joseph, S. (2011). Vicarious exposure to trauma and growth in therapists: The moderating effects of sense of coherence, organizational support, and empathy. *Journal of Traumatic Stress, 24*(6), 735-742. doi:10.1002/jts.20704

Brooks-Gunn, J., Han, W., & Waldfogel, J. (2010). *Monographs of the Society for Research in Child Development, 75*(2), 7-9. doi:10.1111/j.1540-5834.2010. 00562.x

Brosnan, S. F., & Waal, F. B. (2003). Monkeys reject unequal pay. *Nature, 425*(6955), 297-299. doi:10.1038/nature01963

Brown, R. P., & Gerbarg, P. L. (2012). *The healing power of the breath: Simple techniques to reduce stress and anxiety, enhance concentration, and balance your emotions.* Boston, MA: Shambhala.

Buber, M. (1933). *Die Tröstung Israels, aus Jeschajahu, Kapitel 40 bis 55; mit der Verdeutschung von Martin Buber und Franz Rosenzweig.* Berlin: Schocken-Verlag.

Buchanan, T. (2007). Retrieval of emotional memories. *Psychological Bulletin, 133*(5), 761-779. doi:10.1037/0033-2909.133 .5.761

Campbell, S. (2011). *Saying what's real: Seven keys to authentic communication and relationship success.* Novato, CA: New World Library.

Centers for Disease Control and Prevention. (2016). *Adverse childhood experiences (ACE).* Retrieved from https://www.cdc. gov/index.htm

Chamorro-Premuzic, T. (2013). *Seven rules for managing creative-but difficult people*. Retrieved from http://blogs.hbr.org/cs/2013/04/seven_rules_for_managing_creat.html

Chan, T. (2018). *China is monitoring employees' brain waves and emotions -- and the technology boosted one company's profits by $315 million*. Retrieved from https://www.businessinsider.com/

Check Your Blindspots (2019). *CEO Action for Diversity & Inclusion*. Retrieved from ceoaction.com

Chen, Z., & Williams, K. D. (2012). Imagined future social pain hurts more now than imagined future physical pain. *European Journal of Social Psychology, 42*(3), 314-317. doi:10.1002/ejsp.1861

Chiao, J. Y., Harada, T., Oby, E. R., Li, Z., Parrish, T., & Bridge, D. J. (2009). Neural representations of social status hierarchy in human inferior parietal cortex. *Neuropsychologia, 47*(2), 354-363. doi: 10.1016/j.neuropsychologia.20 08.09.023

Chiao, J. Y. (2010). Neural basis of social status hierarchy across species. *Current Opinion in Neurobiology, 20*(6), 803-809. doi: 10.1016/j.conb.2010.08.006

Cohen, B. (2018). The making of a health and human services workforce advocate. *APHSA Policy & Practice*. Retrieved from https://aphsa.org/APHSA/PolicyandResources/policy practice.aspx

Cohen, K., & Collens, P. (2013). The impact of trauma work on trauma workers: A metasynthesis on vicarious trauma and vicarious posttraumatic growth. Psychological Trauma: Theory, Research, Practice, and Policy, 5(6), 570-580. doi:10 .1037/a0030388

Collier, L. (2016). Growth after trauma. Retrieved from http://www.apa.org /monitor /2016/16 growth-trauma.aspx

Comas-Diaz, L., & Luthar, S. (2017). The road to resilience. Retrieved from https://www.apa.org/helpcenter/roadresilience.

Comprehensive Care Program. (2012). Would your health care be better if you had the same doctor in clinic and in the hospital: Join the University of Chicago medicine comprehensive care program study and help us find out. Retrieved from https://ccpstudy.uchicago.edu/

Cosic, K. (2010). Physiology-driven adaptive virtual reality stimulation for prevention and treatment of stress related disorders. Retrieved from https://www.Liebertpub.com/doi /abs/10.1089/cyber.2009.0260

Cozolino, L. J. (2002). The neuroscience of psychotherapy: Building and rebuilding the human brain. New York, NY: Norton & Company.

Cozolino, L. J. (2017). The neuroscience of psychotherapy: Healing the social brain. New York: NY: Norton & Company.

Dardis, C. M., Strauss, C. V., & Gidycz, C. A. (2019). The psychological toll of unwanted pursuit behaviors and intimate partner violence on undergraduate women: A dominance analysis. Psychology of Violence, 9(2), 209-220. doi:10.1 037/vio0000189

Davidson, R. J., & Begley, S. (2013). The emotional life of your brain: How its unique patterns affect the way you think, feel, and live - and how you can change them. New York, NY: Penguin Group.

Davis, J. (2015). Two awesome hours: Science-based strategies to harness your best time and get your most important work done. Los Angeles, CA: Harper One, Harper Collins Publishers.

DeWall, C.N., MacDonald, G., Webster, G.D., Masten, C.L., Baumeister, R.F., Powell, C., Combs, D., Schurtz, D.R., Stillman, T.F., Tice, D.M. &

Eisenberger, N. I. (2010). Acetaminophen reduces social pain. Psychological Science, 21(7), 931-937. doi:10.1177/0956797610374741
Dewall, C. N., & Bushman, B. J. (2011). Social acceptance and rejection. *Current Directions in Psychological Science, 20*(4), 256-260. doi:10.1177/0963721411417545
Dhabhar, F., & Richter, R. (2012). *5 questions: Dhabhar on the good and bad aspects of stress.* Retrieved from http://med.Stanford.edu/
Dias, B., & Ressler, K. (2014). Parental olfactory experience influences behavior and neural structure in subsequent generations. Nature Neuroscience (17) 89-96.
Diaz, J. (2018). *DARPA is literally reinventing the wheel.* Retrieved from fastcompany.com
Doidge, N. (2017). The brain that changes itself: Stories of personal triumph from the frontiers of brain science. New York, NY: Penguin Books.
Dollard, M. F., Winefield, H. R., Winefield, A. H., & Jonge, J. (2000). Psychosocial job strain and productivity in human service workers: A test of the demand-control-support model. Journal of Occupational and Organizational Psychology, 73(4), 501-510. doi:10.1348/096317900167182
Dollard, M., Winefield, H. R., & Winefield, A. (2001). Occupational strain and efficacy in human service workers: When the rescuer becomes the victim. London, UK: Kluwer Academic Publishers.
Dollard, M., Dormann, C., Boyd, C., Winefield, H., & Winefield, A. (2003). Unique aspects of stress in human service work. Australian Psychologist, 38(2), 84-91. doi:10.1080/00050 060310001707087
Donnachie, I. L. (2005). Robert Owen: Owen of New Lanark and New Harmony. Edinburgh: Tuckwell Press, Ltd.
Duckworth, M. P., & Follette, V. M. (2012). Retraumatization: Assessment, treatment, and prevention. New York, NY: Routledge, Taylor & Francis Group.
Dutt, A. J., Wahl, H. W., & Rupprecht, F. S. (2018). Mindful vs. mind full: Processing strategies moderate the association between subjective aging experiences and depressive symptoms. Psychology and Aging, 33(4), 630-642. doi:10.10 37/pag0000245
Dweck, C. (2015). Mindsets and skills that promote long-term learning. Retrieved from ed.Stanford.edu
Dweck, C. S. (2016). Mindset: The new psychology of success. New York, NY: Ballantine Books.
Easton, J. (2018). Comprehensive care physician model improves care, lowers hospitalization. Retrieved from news.uchicago.edu
Edmondson, A. C. (2013). Teaming: How organizations learn, innovate, and compete in the knowledge economy. Josey-Bass Pfeiffer.
Edmondson, A.C. (2018). The fearless organization: Creating psychological safety in the workplace for learning, innovation, and, growth. Hoboken, NJ: Wiley
Ehlers, A., & Clark, D. M. (2000). A cognitive model of posttraumatic stress disorder. Behaviour Research and Therapy, 38(4), 319-345. doi:10.1016/s0005-7967(99)00123-0.
Einarsen, S. (2003). The nature causes and consequences of bullying at work: The Norwegian experience. Norway: University of Bergen, Norway.
Einarsen, S. (2005). The nature causes and consequences of bullying at work: The Norwegian experience. Perspectives Interdisciplinaires sur le Travail et la Santé, (7-3). doi:10.40 00/pistes.3156

Eisenberger, R., Huntington, R., Hutchison, S., & Sowa, D. (1986). Perceived organizational support. *Journal of Applied Psychology, 71*(3), 500-507. doi:10.1037/0021-9010.71.3.5 00

Eisenberger, N. I., Lieberman, M. D., & Williams, K. D. (2003). Does rejection hurt? An fMRI study of social exclusion. *Science, 302*(5643), 290-292. doi:10.1126/science.1089134

Eisenberger, N. I., Jarcho, J. M., Lieberman, M. D., & Naliboff, B. D. (2006). An experimental study of shared sensitivity to physical pain and social rejection. *Pain, 126*(1-3), 132-138. doi: 10.1016/j.pain.2006.06.024

Eisenberger, N. I. (2012). The pain of social disconnection: Examining the shared neural underpinnings of physical and social pain. *Nature Reviews Neuroscience, 13*(6), 421-434. doi:10.1038/nrn3231

Ekman, P. (2014). *Moving toward global compassion.* Lexington, KY: Paul Ekman Group.

Enam, S. (2006). Factors influencing the development of self-concept in pre-adolescent boys and girls. *Journal of Life and Earth Science, 1*(2), 55-59. doi:10.25255/jss.2019.8.1.90.105

Fachner, G., & Carter, S. (2014). *Collaborative reform model: Final assessment report of the Las Vegas Metropolitan Police Department.* Retrieved from Community Oriented Policing Services Office website: https://ric-zai-inc.com/Publications/ cops-p287-pub.pdf.

Felitti, V. J., Anda, R. F., Nordenberg, D., Williamson, D. F., Spitz, A. M., Edwards, V., & Marks, J. S. (1998). Relationship of childhood abuse and household dysfunction to many of the leading causes of death in adults: The Adverse Childhood Experiences (ACE) Study. *American Journal of Preventive Medicine, 14*(4), 245-258. doi:10. 1016/s0749-3797(98)00017-8

Fernald, R., & Maruska, K. (2012). Social information changes the brain. *Proceedings of the National Academy of Sciences of the United States of America.* Retrieved from https://doi.org/10.1073/pnas.1202552109

Fields, D. (2016). *Why we snap: Understanding the rage circuit in your brain.* New York, NY: Dutton.

Figley, C., Huggard, P., & Rees, C. (Eds.) (2013). *First do no self-harm: Understanding and promoting physician stress resilience.* Oxford, UK: Oxford University Press.

Figley, C. R., & Figley, K. R. (2017). Compassion fatigue resilience. *The Oxford handbook of compassion science.* Oxford, UK: Oxford University Press.

Finnegan, R. P. (2015). *The stay interview: A manager's guide to keeping the best and brightest.* New York: AMACOM American Management Association.

Finnegan, R.P. (2018). *The power of stay interviews for engagement and retention. (2nd ed).* Society for Human Resource Management.

Fleming, P. (2018). *The Guardian: Do you work more than 39 hours a week? Your job could be killing you* Retrieved from http:/ /newsintweets.com/the-guardian-do-you-work-more-than-39-hours-a-week-your-job-could-be-killing-you-https-t-co-vkxmfepm6r-2/

Forbes Human Resource Council. (2018). *12 signs your employee is disengaged (and how to respond).* Retrieved from https://www.forbes.com/sites/forbeshumanresourcescouncil/2018/11/30/12-signs-your-employee-is-disengaging-and-how-to-respond/

Forbes Human Resources Council. (2018). *Eight ways companies can transform their employee review system.* Retrieved from Forbes.com.

Fox, S. E., Levitt, P., & Nelson, C. (2010). How the timing and quality of early experiences influence the development of brain architecture. *Child Development, 81*(1), 28-40. doi:10.1111/j.1467-8624.2009.01380.x
Franco, G., & Franco, F. (2001). Bernardino Ramazzini: The father of occupational medicine. *American Journal of Public Health, 91*(9), 1382-1382. doi:10.2105/ajph.91.9.1382
Frey, J. J., Pompe, J., Sharar, D., Imboden, R., & Bloom, L. (2018). Experiences of internal and hybrid employee assistance program managers: Factors associated with successful, at-risk, and eliminated programs. *Journal of Workplace Behavioral Health, 33*(1), 1-23. doi:10.1080/15555240.2017.1416293
Friedman, S., & Laurison, D. (2019). *The class ceiling: Why it pays to be privileged.* Bristol, UK: Policy Press.
Gardner, H. (1993). *Multiple intelligences.* New York, NY: Basic Books.
Gazzaniga, M. S., & Pak, I. (2016). *Who's in charge? Free will and the science of the brain.* Seúl, Korea: Chungrim.
Genetics Home Reference - NIH. (2018). Retrieved from https://ghr.nlm.nih.gov/
George, B. (2007). *Discover your true north: Becoming an authentic leader.* San Francisco, CA: Wiley.
Gladwell, M. (2013). *Blink: The power of thinking without thinking.* New York, NY: Back Bay Books.
Goh, J., Pfeffer, J., & Zenios, S. (2015). Exposure to harmful workplace practices could account for inequality in life spans across different demographic groups. *Health Affairs, 34*(10), 1761-1768. doi:10.1377/hlthaff.2015.0022
Goldman, B. (2017). *Study shows how slow breathing induces tranquility.* Retrieved from https://med.stanford.edu/news/all-news/2017/03/study-discovers-how-slow-breathing-induces-tranquility.html
Goldman, R. (2018). *The 'nuclear button' explained: For starters, there's no button.* New York: The New York Times.
Goldstein, K. (1939). *The organism: A holistic approach to biology derived from pathological data in man.* New York, NY: American Book.
Goleman, D. (2011). The brain and emotional intelligence: New insights. Florence, MA: More Than Sound, LLC.
Goleman, D. (2012). Social intelligence: The new science of human relationships. Journal of Psychological Issues In Organizational Culture, 3(2), 75-78. doi.10.1177/2319510X1 6650058
Goleman, D. (2014). Emotional intelligence. London, UK: Bloomsbury Publishing.
Goleman, D., & Davidson, R. (2018). Science of meditation: How to change your brain, mind and body. London, UK: Penguin Life.
Gračanin, A., Bylsma, L. M., & Vingerhoets, A. J. (2014). Is crying a self-soothing behavior? Frontiers in Psychology, 5, 502. doi:10.3389/fpsyg.2014.00502
Greenfield, S. (2017). A day in the life of the brain: The neuroscience of consciousness from dawn till dusk. UK: Penguin Book Publishers.
Harari, Y. N. (2016). Sapiens: A brief history of humankind. Toronto, Ontario: Signal, McClelland & Stewart.
Harmon-Jones, E., & Inzlicht, M. (2016). Social neuroscience: biological approaches to social psychology. UK: Routledge.
Harter, J. K., Schmidt, F. L., & Keyes, C. L. (2003). Well-being in the workplace and its relationship to business outcomes: A review of the Gallup studies.

Flourishing: Positive psychology and the life well-lived, 2, 205-224. doi:10.10 37/10594-009
Harter, S. (2012). The construction of the self: Developmental and sociocultural foundations. New York, NY: Guilford Press.
Helliwell, J. F., & Aknin, L. B. (2018). Expanding the social science of happiness. Nature Human Behaviour, 2(4), 248-252. doi:10.1038/s41562-018-0308-5
Helliwell, J., Layard, R. and Sachs, J. (2019). World Happiness Report 2018. Retrieved from https://s3.Amazonaws.com/ happiness-report/2018/WHR_web.pdf
Helweg-Larsen, M. (2019). A Danish word the world needs to combat stress: Pyt. Retrieved from http://theconversation.com/a-danish-word-the-world-needs-to-combat-stress-pyt-112216
Henderson, M. (2016). *Millennials suffer from 'vacation shame': Here's what it is and why it happens*. Retrieved from https://www.forbes.com/millennials-suffer-from-vacation-shame-heres-what-it-is-and-why-it-happens/
Henderson, L. (2018). *Why our brains see the world as "us" versus "them"*. Retrieved from https://neurosciencenews.com/
Hernández, P., Gangsei, D., & Engstrom, D. (2007). Vicarious resilience: A new concept in work with those who survive trauma. *Family Process, 46*(2), 229-241. doi:10.1111/j.1545-5300.2007. 00206.x
Hired. (2018). *2018 Global Brand Health Report*. Retrieved from https://hired.com/
HireVue.com. (2018). *HireVue - hiring intelligence assessment & video interview software*. Retrieved from https://www.Hirevue. com/
Hirth, F. (2010). On the origin and evolution of the tripartite brain. *Brain, Behavior and Evolution, 76*(1), 3-10. doi:10.1159 /000320218
Hvistendahl, M. (2018). *In China, a three-digit score could dictate your place in society*. Retrieved from https://www.wired.com /story/age-of-social-credit/
Iacoboni, M. (2008). *Mirroring people: The science of empathy and how we connect with others*. New York, NY: Farrar, Straus and Giroux.
Jastrow, J. (1900). *Fact and fable in psychology*. Boston and New York: Houghton, Mifflin and Company.
Jha, A., Iliff, A., Chaoui, A., Defossez, S., Bombaugh, M., & Miller, Y. (2018). *A crisis in health care: A call to action on physician burnout*. Harvard: Global Health Institute, Massachusetts.
John, G. (2001). Judging Rapport: Employing Brunswik's lens model to study interpersonal sensitivity. In J. A. Hall & F. J. Bernieri (Eds), *Interpersonal sensitivity: Theory and measurement*. Mahwah, NJ: L. Erlbaum Associates.
Kabat-Zinn, J. (2005). *Wherever you go, there you are: Mindfulness meditation in everyday life*. New York, NY: Hachette Books.
Kabat-Zinn, J. (2017). Loving kindness meditation. *Mindfulness, 8*(4), 1117-1121. doi:10.1007/s 12671-017-0757-3
Kalma, A. P., Visser, L., & Peeters, A. (1993). Sociable and aggressive dominance: Personality differences in leadership style. *The Leadership Quarterly, 4*(1), 45-64. doi:10.1016/10 48-9843(93)90003-c
Kearney, M., & Weininger, R. (2011). Whole person self-care: Self-care from the inside out. In *Whole person care*. New York, NY: Springer.
Kegan, R. L. (2002). *How the way we talk can change the way we work: Seven languages for transformation*. San Francisco, CA: Jossey-Bass.
Keltner, D. (2017). *The power paradox: How we gain and lose influence*. UK: Penguin Books.

Kendler, K. S., Hettema, J. M., Butera, F., Gardner, C. O., & Prescott, C. A. (2003). Life event dimensions of loss, humiliation, entrapment, and danger in the prediction of onsets of major depression and generalized anxiety. *Archives of General Psychiatry, 60*(8), 789-796. doi:10.1001/archpsyc.60.8.789

Kohll, A. (2018). *5 reasons social connections can enhance your employee wellness program.* Retrieved from: https://www.forbes.com/sites/alankohll/2018/01/31/5-ways-social-connections-can-enhance-your-employee-wellness-program/#320f9bc5527c

Koski, J. E., Xie, H., & Olson, I. R. (2015). Understanding social hierarchies: The neural and psychological foundations of status perception. *Social Neuroscience, 10*(5), 527-550. doi:10.1080/17470919.2015.1013223

Krakow, B., Hollifield, M., Johnston, L., Koss, M., Schrader, R., Warner, T.D., Tandberg, D., Lauriello, J., McBride, L., Cutchen, L. & Cheng, D. (2001). Imagery rehearsal therapy for chronic nightmares in sexual assault survivors with posttraumatic stress disorder: A randomized controlled trial. *Jama, 286*(5), 537-545. doi:10.1001/jama.286. 5.537

Kurland, N. B., & Pelled, L. H. (2000). Passing the word: Toward a model of gossip and power in the workplace. *Academy of Management Review, 25*(2), 428-438. doi.10.5465/ amr. 2 000.3312928

LaMarca-Ghaemmaghami, P., Dainese, S., Stalla, G., Haller, M., Zimmermann, R., & Ehlert, U. (2017). *Mothers stress affects baby through amniotic fluid.* Retrieved from https://neurosciencenews.com/

Lambert, S., & Holzman, E. (2010). *Undercover boss: Inside the tv phenomenon that is changing bosses and employees everywhere.* San Francisco, CA: Jossey Bass.

Leets, L., & Sunwolf. (2005). Adolescent rules for social exclusion: When is it fair to exclude someone else? *Journal of Moral Education, 34*(3), 343-362. doi:10.1080/0305 72405 00211618

Levari, D., Gilbert, D., & Wilson, T. (2018). Prevalence-induced concept change in human judgment. *Science, 360*(6396), 1465-1467. doi: 10.1126/science.aap873.1

Levine, P. A. (1997). *Waking the tiger: Healing trauma.* Berkeley, CA: North Atlantic Books.

Levine, P. A. (2008). *Healing trauma: A pioneering program for restoring the wisdom of your body.* Boulder, CO: Sounds True.

Lewis, M., Haviland-Jones, J. M., & Barrett, L. F. (2010). *Handbook of emotions.* New York, NY: Guilford Press.

Lewis, D. M., Al-Shawaf, L., Conroy-Beam, D., Asao, K., & Buss, D. M. (2017). Evolutionary psychology: A how-to guide. *American Psychologist, 72*(4), 353-373. doi:10.1037/a00 40409

Liu, Y., Wang, Y., & Jiang, C. (2017). Inflammation: The common pathway of stress-related diseases. *Frontiers in Human Neuroscience, 11*, 316. doi:10.3389/fnhum.2017.00316

Lucas, S. (2018). *Job candidates, sick of recruiters going dark, have started ghosting as well.* Retrieved from inc.com

Lynch, S. (2015). *Why your workplace might be killing you.* Retrieved from https://www.gsb. stanford.edu/insights/why-your-workplace-might-be-killing-you

Mackey, J. D., Perrewé, P. L., & Mcallister, C. P. (2016). Do I fit in? Perceptions of organizational fit as a resource in the workplace stress process. *Group & Organization Management, 42*(4), 455-486. doi:10.1177/1059601115625155

MacLean, P. D. (1990). *The triune brain in evolution: Role in paleocerebral functions*. New York, NY: Plenum Press.
Maestas, N., Mullen, K. J., Powell, D., Wachter, T. V., & Wenger, J. B. (2017). *U.S. workplace is physically and emotionally taxing*. Retrieved from http://www.rand.org/pubs /research _reports/RR2014.html
Majolo, B., & Maréchal, L. (2017). Between-group competition elicits within-group cooperation in children. *Scientific Reports, 7*, 43277. Retrieved from https://www.nature.com /articles/srep43277
Marca-Ghaemmaghami, P. L., Dainese, S. M., Stalla, G., Haller, M., Zimmermann, R., & Ehlert, U. (2017). Second-trimester amniotic fluid corticotropin-releasing hormone and urocortin in relation to maternal stress and fetal growth in human pregnancy. *Stress, 20*(3), 231-240. doi:10.1080/10253890.2017.1312336
Maslow, A. H. (1943). A theory of human motivation. *Psychological Review, 50*(4), 370-396. doi:10.1037/h0054346
Max, D. (2017). *How humans are shaping our own evolution*. Retrieved from https://www.Nationalgeogra phic.com/magazine/2017/04/evolution-genetics-medicine-brain-technology-cyborg/
Mccauley, C. (2017). Toward a psychology of humiliation in asymmetric conflict. *American Psychologist, 72*(3), 255-265. doi:10.1037/amp0000063
McFarlane, A. C., Weisaeth, L., & Bessel, V. D. (2007). *Traumatic stress: The effects of overwhelming experience on mind, body, and society*. New York, London: The Guilford Press.
McFeely, & Wigert, B. (2019). *This fixable problem costs U.S. businesses $1 trillion*. Retrieved from gallup.com
Meeks, T. W., & Jeste, D. V. (2009). Neurobiology of wisdom: A literature overview. *Archives of General Psychiatry, 66*(4), 355-365. doi:10.1001/archgenpsychiatry.2009.8
Mercier, H., & Sperber, D. (2017). *The enigma of reason*. Cambridge, MA: Harvard University Press.
Meyer, M. L., Williams, K. D., & Eisenberger, N. I. (2015). Why social pain can live on: Different neural mechanisms are associated with reliving social and physical pain. *PloS One, 10*(6), e0128294. doi: 10.1371/journal.pone.0128294
Miller, A. (1994). *The drama of the gifted child: The search for the true self*. New York, NY: Basic Books.
Molnar, B., Sprang, G., Killian, K., Gottfried, R., Emery, V., & Bride, B. (2017). Advancing science and practice for vicarious/secondary traumatic stress: A research agenda. *Traumatology, 23*(2), 129-142.doi:10.1037/trm0000122
Moshagen, M., Hilbig, B.E., & Zetler, I. (2018) The dark core of personality. *Psychological Review*, 125, 656-688. doi: 10.1037/rev0000111
Muhlhausen, D. (2017). *Blueprint for reorganization: An analysis of federal departments and agencies*. Retrieved from https:// www.heritage.org/sites/default/files/2017-06/BlueprintforReorganization-DepartmentsandAgencies _1.pdf.
Murray, J. (2004). *The Rebel Billionaire: Branson's Quest for the Best*. Fox Broadcasting Company. Retrieved from https://www.imdb.com/title/tt0412106/
Murray, R. (2012). The crucial role of recess in school. *Pediatrics, 131*(1), 183-188. doi:10.154 2/peds.2012-2993
Music, G. (2017). *Nurturing natures: Attachment and children's emotional, sociocultural and brain development*. UK: Routledge.

Neubert, F., Mars, R., Thomas, A., Sallet, J., & Rushworth, M. (2014). Comparison of human ventral frontal cortex areas for cognitive control and language with areas in monkey frontal cortex. *Neuron, 81*(3), 700-713. doi:10.1016/j. neuron.2013.11.012
Neuroskeptic. (2019). Retrieved from blogs.discovermagazine.com/neuroskeptic/
Obhi, S. (2019). *Obhi lab*. Social Brain Body and Action Lab, McMaster University. Retrieved from https://www.obhilab.com/
Ochsner, K., & Gross, J. (2005). The cognitive control of emotion. *Trends in Cognitive Sciences, 9*(5), 242-249. doi:10.10 16/j.tics.2005.03.010
Oconnor, M., & Elklit, A. (2008). Attachment styles, traumatic events, and PTSD: A cross-sectional investigation of adult attachment and trauma. *Attachment & Human Development, 10*(1), 59-71. doi:10.1080/14616730701868597
Oertelt-Prigione, S. (2013). *Sexual Harassment* (Rep.). Nijmegen: Radboud University Medical Center.
Oishi, S., & Graham, J. (2010). *Social ecology: Lost and found in psychological science*. Retrieved from https://www.science daily.com/releases/2010/08/100805111231.htm
Orloff, J. (2018). The empath's survival guide. Sounds True Publishing.
Osório, C., Probert, T., Jones, E., Young, A. H., & Robbins, I. (2017). Adapting to stress: understanding the neurobiology of resilience. *Behavioral Medicine, 43*(4), 307-322. doi:10.1080/08964289.2016.1170661
Otten, M., & Jonas, K. J. (2014). Humiliation as an intense emotional experience: evidence from the electro-encephalogram. *Social Neuroscience, 9*(1), 23-35.
Owen, D., & Davidson, J. (2009). Hubris syndrome: An acquired personality disorder? A study of US Presidents and UK prime ministers over the last 100 years. *Brain, 132*(5), 1396-1406. doi:10.1093/brain/awp008
Paltoine, B. (2018). *The abused brain: Neural adaptation, resilience, and compensation for childhood maltreatment*. Retrieved from dana.org
Pang, A. S. (2018). *Rest: Why you get more done when you work less*. New York, NY: Basic Books.
Parkinson, C., Kleinbaum, A. M., & Wheatley, T. (2018). Similar neural responses predict friendship. *Nature Communications, 9*(1), 332. doi:10.1038/s41467-017-02722-7
Patel, D. (2017). *8 ways generation Z will differ from millennials in the workplace*. Retrieved from forbes.com
Payne, P., Levine, P. A., & Crane-Godreau, M. A. (2015). Somatic experiencing: using interoception and proprioception as core elements of trauma therapy. *Frontiers in Psychology, 6*(4), 423. doi:10.3389/fpsyg.2015.00093
Pellegrino, G. D., Fadiga, L., Fogassi, L., Gallese, V., & Rizzolatti, G. (1992). Understanding motor events: A neurophysiologic study. *Experimental Brain Research, 91*(1), 176-180. doi:10.1007/bf00230027
Peri, T., & Gofman, M. (2014). Narrative reconstruction: An integrative intervention module for intrusive symptoms in PTSD patients. *Psychological Trauma: Theory, Research, Practice, Policy, 6*(2), 176-183. doi:10. 1037/a0031965
Perrottet, T. (2008). *Napoleon's privates: 2,500 years of history unzipped*. New York, NY: Harper Collins Publishers.
Perry, B. D. (2006). *Boy who was raised as a dog*. New York, NY: Basic Books.
Peterson, C. K., Gravens, L. C., & Harmon-Jones, E. (2010). Asymmetric frontal cortical activity and negative affective responses to ostracism. *Social Cognitive and Affective Neuroscience, 6*(3), 277-285. doi: 10.1093/scan/nsq027

Pfeffer, J. (2010). *Power: Why some people have it and others don't.* New York, NY: Harper Business.

Pfeffer, J. (2018). *Dying for a paycheck: How modern management harms employee health and company performance and what we can do about it.* New York, NY: Harper Business.

Pfeffer, J., & Zenios, S. (2015). *Why your workplace might be killing you.* Retrieved from https://www.gsb.stanford.edu /insights/why-your-workplace-might-be-killing-you.

Phelps, E. A. (2004). Human emotion and memory: Interactions of the amygdala and hippocampal complex. *Current Opinion in Neurobiology, 14*(2), 198-202. doi:10.1016/j. conb.2004.03.015

Pindek, S., Krajcevska, A., & Spector, P. E. (2018). Cyberloafing as a coping mechanism: Dealing with workplace boredom. *Computers in Human Behavior, 86,* 147-152. *doi:10.1016/j.chb.2018.04.040*

Pinsker, J. (2019). *The 'hidden mechanisms' that help those born rich to excel in elite jobs.* The Atlantic. Retrieved From https://www.theatlantic.com/entertainment/archive/2019/02/class-ceiling-laurison-friedman-elite-jobs/582 1 75/

Platt, M. (2018). *What monkeys can teach us about advertising.* Retrieved from https://blogs.scientificamerican.com/observations/what-monkeys-can-teach-us-about-advertising/

Platt, M., Barton, J.M., & Freyd, J. (2009). A betrayal trauma perspective on domestic violence (E. Stark & E. Buzawa, Eds.). In *Violence against women in families and relationships.* Westport, CT: Greenwood Press.

Pompe, J., Sharar, D., & Frey, J. J. (2017). *EAP options for today's workforce: Maximizing value by design.* Retrieved from Benefitspro.com.

Porges, S. (2011). *The polyvagal theory: Neurophysiological foundations of emotions, attachment, communication, and self-regulation.* New York, NY: W.W. Norton & Company

Poushter, J., & Castillo, A. (2018). *Females paid less.* Retrieved from http://www.pewresearch .org/

Prickett, T., Gada-Jain, N., & Bernieri, F. J. (2000). *The importance of first impressions in a job interview.* University of Toledo

Prinstein, M. J. (2017). *Popular: The power of likability in a status-obsessed world.* UK: Penguin Books.

Radford, T. (2011). *The untold story of evolution.* The Guardian. Retrieved from https://www.theguardian. com/science /2011/apr/25/evolution-human-history-apes

Rains, M., & McClinn, K. (2006/13). *Resilience questionnaire.* Augusta, Maine: Southern Kennebec Healthy Start.

Ramachandran, V. S. (2012). *The tell-tale brain: A neuroscientist's quest for what makes us human.* New York, NY: W. W. Norton.

Reardon, J. (1998). The history and impact of worksite wellness. *Nurs Econ, 16*(3), 117-121.

Richmond, M. K., Pampel, F. C., Wood, R. C., & Nunes, A. P. (2017). The impact of employee assistance services on workplace outcomes: Results of a prospective, quasi-experimental study. *Journal of Occupational Health Psychology, 22*(2), 170-179. doi:10.1037/ocp00 00018

Riggle, R. J., Edmondson, D. R., & Hansen, J. D. (2009). A meta-analysis of the relationship between perceived organizational support and job outcomes: 20 years of research. *Journal of Business Research, 62*(10), 1027-1030. doi: 10.1016/j.jbusres.2008.05.003

Robson, D. (2011). *A brief history of the brain.* Retrieved from https://www.newscientist.com/article/mg21128311.800-a-brief-history-of-the-brain/
Rock, D. (2008). SCARF: A brain-based model for collaborating with and influencing others. *NeuroLeadership Journal, 1*(1), 44-52. doi:10.1107/s0108768107031758/bs5044 sup1.cif
Rock, D. (2009). *Your brain at work: Strategies for overcoming distraction, regaining focus, and achieving all day long.* UK: Harper Business.
Rock, D. (2009). *Managing with the Brain in Mind.* Retrieved from strategy-business.com/article/09306
Rock, D., & Ringleb, A. H. (2013). *Handbook of NeuroLeadership. NeuroLeadership Institute.* Marlborough, MA: Albella Publishing.
Roediger, H. L., & Mcdermott, K. B. (2000). Tricks of memory. *Current Directions in Psychological Science, 9*(4), 123-127.
Ross, D. A., Arbuckle, M. R., Travis, M. J., Dwyer, J. B., van Schalkwyk, G. I., & Ressler, K. J. (2017). An integrated neuroscience perspective on formulation and treatment planning for posttraumatic stress disorder: an educational review. *JAMA psychiatry, 74*(4), 407-415. doi:10.1001/jamapsychiatry.2016.3325
Salovey, P., Sluyter, D. J., & Goleman, D. (1997). *Emotional development and emotional intelligence: Educational implications.* New York, NY: Basic Books.
Sauter, S., & Murphy, L. (2014). *Stress at work.* Retrieved from https://www.cdc.gov/niosh/docs/99-101/default.html
Saval, N. (2015). *Cubed: A secret history of the workplace.* New York, NY: Anchor Books.
Sayin, A., & Ceylan, M. (2013). The neurobiology of transference. *Mind Behav, 34*(3), 233-258. doi:10.1007/s12124-012-9197-8
Seligman, M. E. (2004). *Authentic happiness: Using the new positive psychology to realize your potential for lasting fulfillment.* New York, NY: Free Press.
Seligman, M. E. (2012). *Flourish: A visionary new understanding of happiness and well-being.* New York, NY: Atria Books.
Selye, H. (1936). A syndrome produced by diverse nocuous agents. *Nature, 138*(3479), 32-32. doi:10.1038/138032a0
Seppala, E., & Cameron, K. (2015). *Proof that positive work cultures are more productive.* Retrieved from hbr.org
Shanafelt, T., West, C., Sinsky, C., Trockel, M., Tutty, M., Satele, D., Carlasare, L., & Dyrbye, L. (2019). *Changes in burnout and satisfaction with work-life integration in physicians and the general US working population between 2011 and 2017.* Retrieved from mayoclinicproceedings.org. doi.org/10.1016/j.mayocp.2018.10.23
Sher, L., & Stanley, B. (2008). The role of endogenous opioids in the pathophysiology of self-injurious and suicidal behavior. *Arch Suicide Res, 12*(4), 299-308. doi.org/10.10 80/138111108 02324748
Sieff, D. F. (2015). *Understanding and healing emotional trauma: Conversations with pioneering clinicians and researchers.* London: Routledge.
Siegel, D. J. (2010). *The mindful therapist: A clinician's guide to mindsight and neural integration.* New York, NY: W.W. Norton
Siegel, D. J. (2011). *Mindsight: The new science of personal transformation.* New York, NY: Bantam Books Trade Paperbacks.
Siegel, D. J. (2012). *Mindsight: Change your brain and your life.* Brunswick, Vic.: Scribe Publications.

Siegel, D. J. (2012). *Pocket guide to interpersonal neurobiology: An integrative handbook of the mind.* New York, NY: W.W. Norton.

Siegel, D. J. (2015). *The developing mind: How relationships and the brain interact to shape who we are.* New York, NY: Guilford Press.

Silverman, R. (2011). *Hey, you! Mean people earn more, study finds.* The Wall Street Journal (WSJ). Retrieved from https://www.wsj.com/articles/SB10001424053111904823804 5 76502763895892974

Singh, A. A., & Dickey, L. M. (2017). *Affirmative counseling and psychological practice with transgender and gender nonconforming clients.* American Psychological Association. doi.org/10.1037/14957-000

Slepian, M. L., Chun, J. S., & Mason, M. F. (2017). The experience of secrecy. *Journal of Personality and Social Psychology, 113*(1), 1-33. doi:10.1037/pspa0000085

Smith, C. P., & Freyd, J. J. (2013). Dangerous safe havens: Institutional betrayal exacerbates sexual trauma. *Journal of Traumatic Stress, 26*(1), 119-124. doi:10.1002/jts.21778

Smith, C. P., & Freyd, J. J. (2014). Institutional Betrayal. *American Psychologist, 69*(6), 575-587. doi:10.1037/a0037564

Solomon, M. F., & Siegel, D. J. (2003). *Healing trauma: Attachment, mind, body, and brain.* New York: W.W. Norton.

Sonnenstuhl, W. J., & Trice, H. M. (2018). *Strategies for Employee Assistance Programs: The crucial balance.* Ithaca, NY: Cornell University Press.

Southwick, S. M., & Charney, D. S. (2012). *Resilience: The science of mastering life's greatest challenges.* Cambridge, MA: Cambridge University Press.

Spector, D. (2011). *The odds of you being alive are incredibly small.* Business Insider. Retrieved from https://www.businessinsider.com/infographic-the-odds-of-being-alive-2012-6

Stoia, R. (2016). *Care of the self.* Proceedings of the 4th Global Virtual Conference. Retrieved from http://www.gv-conference.com/

Stoltz, P. (1999). *Adversity quotient: turning obstacles into opportunities.* New York, NY: Wiley.

Substance Abuse and Mental Health Services Administration, U. (Ed.). (2014). *TIP 57: Trauma-Informed Care in Behavioral Health Services.* Retrieved from https://store.samhsa.gov/product/TIP-57-Trauma-Informed-Care-in-Behavior al-Health-Services/SMA14-4816

Sukel, K. (2017). *When is the brain "mature?" Dana Foundation - Home.* Retrieved From http://dana.org/

Sullivan, J. (2016). *7 Rules for job interview questions that result in great hires.* Harvard Business Review. Retrieved from https://hbr.org/2016/02/7-rules-for-job-interview-questions-that-result-in-great-hires.

Sullivan, R., Sullivan-Wilson, T. and Raineki, C. (2017). Neurobiology of infant attachment: Nurturing and abusive relationships. *Reference Module in Neuroscience and Biobehavioral Psychology*, 17, 1-6.

Sykes, B. (2002). *The seven daughters of Eve.* New York, NY: W.W. Norton.

Tawakol, A. (2017). *Uncovering the link between emotional stress and heart disease.* Retrieved from https://www.Health. harvard.edu/heart-disease-overview/uncovering-the-link between-emotional-stress-and-heart-disease

Tedeschi, R. and Calhoun, L. (1996). Posttraumatic Growth Inventory. *PsycTESTS Dataset*, 9(3), 455-71. doi:10. 1037/t03776-000

Tedeschi, R., & Calhoun, L. (2004). Commentaries on "posttraumatic growth: Conceptual foundations and empirical evidence." *Psychological Inquiry,*

15(1), 19-92. doi:10.1207/s 15327965pli1501_02
Tedeschi, R. G., & Calhoun, L. G. (2004). A clinical approach to posttraumatic growth. *Positive Psychology in Practice.* Hoboken, NJ: Wiley.
Terburg, D., & Honk, J. V. (2013). Approach–avoidance versus dominance–submissiveness: A multilevel neural framework on how testosterone promotes social status. *Emotion Review, 5*(3), 296-302. doi:10.1177/17540 73913477510
The Conversation (2018, June 25). Why our brains see the world as "us" versus "them." *Neuroscience News.* Retrieved from http://neurosciencenews.com/neuroscience-bias-9431/
The state of play: Gallup survey of principals at school recess. (2009). The Robert Wood Foundation. Retrieved from ERIC Number: ED540730 at eric.ed.gov.
Thomas, L. (1978). *The lives of a cell: Notes of a biology watcher.* New York, NY: Penguin Books.
Tiedens, L. Z., & Fragale, A. R. (2003). Power moves: Complementarity in dominant and submissive nonverbal behavior. *Journal of Personality & Social Psychology, 84*(3), 558-568. doi:10.1037//0022-3514.84.3.558
Tingley, K. (2018). *Trying to put a value on the doctor-patient relationship.* New York, NY: New York Times.
Todorov, A. (2017). *Face value: The irresistible influence of first impressions.* Princeton and Oxford: Princeton University Press.
Trauma-informed care in behavioral health services. (2014). *U.S. Department of Health and Human Services, Substance Abuse and Mental Health Services Administration, Center for Substance Abuse Treatment.* Retrieved from https://www.ncbi. nlm.nih.gov/ books /NBK207201/
Tsai, Y. (2011). Relationship between organizational culture, leadership behavior and job satisfaction. *BMC Health Services Research, 11*(1), 98.
Tulving, E., & Craik, F. I. (2005). *The Oxford handbook of memory.* New York, NY: Oxford University Press.
Underwood, E. (2018). *Your gut is directly connected to your brain, by a newly discovered neuron circuit.* Science AAAS. Retrieved from https://www.sciencemag.org/news/2018/09/your-gut-directly-connected-your-brain-newly-discovered-neuron-circuit
Van der Kolk, B. (2006). Clinical implications of neuroscience research in PTSD. Annals of the New York Academy of Sciences, 1071(1), 277-293.
Van der Kolk, B. (2014). *The body keeps the score: Brain, mind, and body in the healing of trauma.* New York, NY: Penguin Books.
Vergun, D. (2014). *Thousands using new ArmyFit for self-improvements.* Retrieved from https://www.army.mil/
Vestergaard, T., CEO. (2018). *Danish employees among the happiest in the world.* Retrieved from ennova.org
Vingerhoets, A. J., Ven, N. V., & Velden, Y. V. (2016). The social impact of emotional tears. *Motivation and Emotion, 40*(3), 455-463. doi:10.1007/s11031-016-9543-0
Violence Prevention. (2016). Retrieved from https://www.cdc.gov/violenceprevention/acestudy /about_ace.html
Viorst, J. (2010). *Necessary losses.* New York, NY: Simon and Schuster.
Wallace, B. H., Roth, E. G., Zimmerman, S., & Eckert, J. K. (2016). Microaggressions: An approach to understanding the health of workers in long term care settings. *Journal of the American Geriatrics Society, 64*(12), e309. doi:10. 1111/jgs.14664
Walsh, B. (2016). *Feedback that works.* Retrieved from gse.harvard.edu

Walumbwa, F. O., Avolio, B. J., Gardner, W. L., Wernsing, T. S., & Peterson, S. J. (2007). Authentic leadership: Development and validation of a theory-based measure. *Journal of Management, 34*(1), 89-126. doi:10.1177/0149 206307308913

Wang, M., Zhou, L., & Liu, S. (2014). *Multilevel issues in leadership research.* Oxford: Oxford Handbooks Online.

Wareing Evans, T. (2018). *Igniting the Potential Part 1.* Retrieved from aphsa.org

Waytz, A. (2009). *The psychology of social status.* Scientific American. Retrieved from https://www.scientificamerican.com /article/the-psychology-of-social/

What is the average human walking rate? (2017). Retrieved from www.answers.com

What other people think about us matters here's why (2012, June 4). Retrieved from blogs.scientificamerican.com

Widom, C. S., Czaja, S. J., & Dutton, M. A. (2008). Childhood victimization and lifetime revictimization. *Child Abuse & Neglect, 32*(8), 785-796. doi: 10.1016/j.chiabu.2007.12.0 06

Wilcock, K. D. (2004). *Hunting and gathering in the corporate tribe: Archetypes of the corporate culture.* New York, NY: Algora.

Williams, K. D., & Carter-Sowell, A. R. (2009). Ostracism: Effects of being ignored and excluded. *Advances in Experimental Social Psychology, 41*, 279-314. doi.org/10.1017CBO97 80511804465.006

Wilson, E. O. (2013). *The social conquest of Earth.* New York, NY: Liveright.

Wismeijer, A. A., Van Assen, M., & Bekker, M. H. (2014). The relations between secrecy, rejection sensitivity and autonomy-connectedness. *The Journal of General Psychology, 141*(2), 65-79. doi:10.1080/00221309.2013.862200

Wolf, C. (2018). *Post-traumatic stress disorder can be contagious.* Scientific American. Retrieved from https://www.scientific american.com/article/post-traumatic-stress-disorder -can-be-contagious/

Wood, A. E., Prins, A., Bush, N. E., Hsia, J. F., Bourn, L. E., Earley, M. D., Walser, R. D & Ruzek, J. (2017). Reduction of burnout in mental health care providers using the provider resilience Mobile Application. *Community Mental Health Journal, 53*(4), 452-459. doi:10.1007/s10597-016-0076-5

Woodyatt L., (2015). *The power of public shaming, for good and for ill.* Retrieved from http://theconversation.com/the-power of-public-shaming-for-good-and-for-ill-38920

Woolley, A. W., Chabris, C. F., Pentland, A., Hashmi, N., & Malone, T. W. (2010). Evidence for a collective intelligence factor in the performance of human groups. *Science, 330*(6004), 686-688. doi:10.1126/science.1193147 Work-related psychological health and safety. (2019). Retrieved from www.SafeworkAustralia.gov.au

Yau, N. (2015). *A day in the life of Americans: this is how America runs.* Retrieved from http://flowingdata.com /2015/12/ 15/a-day-in-the-life-of-americans/

Yuan, J., Liberman, M., & Cieri, C. (2006). *Towards an integrated understanding of speaking rate in conversation.* Retrieved from www.idc.upenn.edu/myl/llog/icslp06_final.pdf

Zadow, A. J., Dollard, M. F., Mclinton, S. S., Lawrence, P., & Tuckey, M. R. (2017). Psychosocial safety climate, emotional exhaustion, and work injuries in healthcare workplaces. *Stress and Health, 33*(5), 558-569. doi:10.1002/smi.2740

INDEX

ABOUT THE AUTHORS

Deborah Robin Winograd

Deborah Winograd received her undergraduate degree (BS) in Psychobiology with Departmental Honors from the University of California, Los Angeles (UCLA) and her graduate degree (PhD) in Counseling Psychology from the University of Southern California (USC) where she studied existential psychology. Her research and clinical interests include interpersonal neurobiology, cognitive theory, and identity development. Dr. Winograd is a psychologist, consultant, curricula developer, and writer in the social neurosciences. She is the clinical director of the Organizational Mind Group, A Psychological Corporation.

Beth Amy Cohen

Beth Cohen received her undergraduate degree (BA) in Psychology from Ithaca College, attended law school at Weidner University Law School, and received her doctorate degree (PhD) from Alliant International University, Los Angeles with an emphasis in clinical and organizational psychology. Dr. Cohen is a psychologist, national speaker, certified meditation instructor, and organizational consultant. Her expertise includes trauma, threat assessment, organizational and individual well-being, and disaster/critical incidents response. Dr. Cohen has built and directed programs for the University of California and across the nation in both the private and public sectors. She has an extensive background in human resources, employee assistance, occupational health, and risk management. Dr. Cohen serves as a thought leader for diverse organizations across the country. She is founder and administrator of the Organizational Mind Group, A Psychological Corporation

Printed in Great Britain
by Amazon

50169684R00194